Counting Islam

Religion, Class, and Elections in Egypt

Why does Islam seem to dominate electoral politics in the countries of the so-called Arab Spring, especially when endemic poverty and deep economic inequality would seem to render new Arab democracies promising terrain for a politics of radical redistribution rather than one of religious conservativism? This book argues that the answer lies not in the political unsophistication of voters, the subordination of economic interests to spiritual ones, or the ineptitude of secular and leftist politicians, but in structural factors that shape parties' opportunities for reaching potential voters. Tracing the performance of Islamists and their rivals in Egyptian elections over the course of almost forty years, this book not only explains why Islamists win elections but also illuminates the possibilities for the emergence in Egypt and the Arab world of the kind of political pluralism that is at the heart of what we expect from democracy.

Tarek Masoud is an associate professor of public policy at Harvard University's John F. Kennedy School of Government. His writings on political Islam, Egyptian politics, and U.S. foreign policy have appeared in the *Journal of Democracy*, the *Washington Quarterly*, *Foreign Policy*, the *New York Times*, and the *Wall Street Journal*, among others. He is the co-editor of *Problems and Methods in the Study of Politics* (Cambridge University Press, 2004) and *Order, Conflict, and Violence* (Cambridge University Press, 2008). He was named a Carnegie Scholar by the Carnegie Corporation of New York and received the 2009 Aaron Wildavsky Prize for best dissertation in religion and politics from the American Political Science Association. He is a recipient of grants and fellowships from the National Science Foundation, the Paul and Daisy Soros Foundation, and the Harvard Medical School and is a term member of the Council on Foreign Relations. He holds a Ph.D. from Yale and an A.B. from Brown, both in political science.

Problems of International Politics

Series Editors:
Keith Darden, American University
Ian Shapiro, Yale University

The series seeks manuscripts central to the understanding of international politics that will be empirically rich and conceptually innovative. It is interested in works that illuminate the evolving character of nation-states within the international system. It sets out three broad areas for investigation: (1) identity, security, and conflict; (2) democracy; and (3) justice and distribution.

Titles in the Series:

Şener Aktürk, *Regimes of Ethnicity and Nationhood in Germany, Russia, and Turkey*
Donald Horowitz, *Constitutional Change and Democracy in Indonesia*
Adria Lawrence, *Imperial Rule and the Politics of Nationalism: Anti-Colonial Protest in the French Empire*
Steven Levitsky and Lucan A. Way, *Competitive Authoritarianism: Hybrid Regimes after the Cold War*
Harris Mylonas, *The Politics of Nation-Building: Making Co-Nationals, Refugees, and Minorities*

Counting Islam

Religion, Class, and Elections in Egypt

TAREK MASOUD

John F. Kennedy School of Government, Harvard University

CAMBRIDGE
UNIVERSITY PRESS

CAMBRIDGE
UNIVERSITY PRESS

32 Avenue of the Americas, New York NY 10013-2473, USA

Cambridge University Press is part of the University of Cambridge.

It furthers the University's mission by disseminating knowledge in the pursuit of education, learning and research at the highest international levels of excellence.

www.cambridge.org
Information on this title: www.cambridge.org/9780521279116

First published 2014

A catalogue record for this publication is available from the British Library

Library of Congress Cataloguing in Publication data
Masoud, Tarek E.
Counting Islam : religion, class, and elections in Egypt / Tarek Masoud.
pages cm. – (Problems of international politics)
Includes bibliographical references and index.
ISBN 978-1-107-00987-5 (hardback) – ISBN 978-0-521-27911-6 (paperback)
1. Islam and politics–Egypt. 2. Jam'iyat al-Ikhwan al-Muslimin (Egypt)
3. Arab Spring, 2010– 4. Elections–Corrupt practices–Egypt.
5. Authoritarianism–Egypt. 6. Muslims–Egypt–Social conditions.
7. Egypt–Politics and government. I. Title.
BP64.E3.M37 2014
324.962'05–dc23 2013040413

ISBN 978-1-107-00987-5 Hardback
ISBN 978-0-521-27911-6 Paperback

Contents

Figures

Tables

Preface

This is a book about how religious parties come to dominate the political life of a nascent democracy – in this case, Egypt, a country that in February 2011 overthrew its long-reigning dictator, Hosni Mubarak. Meet any Egyptian, and though he or she will more often than not be religious, he or she will almost certainly be many other things besides. She may be a farmer, a parent, a worker, an inhabitant of the Ṣaʿīd, a doctor, a member of the Ḥuwayṭāt clan, an Alexandrian, or one of any number of combinations of these things. And yet, a survey of elections conducted in the two years following Mubarak's ouster would seem to give the impression that in matters political, all those identities were trumped by one: Islam. In the country's first postauthoritarian parliamentary election, held in the winter of 2011, Islamists – led by the Muslim Brotherhood – won two-thirds of the seats in parliament. Six months later, they captured the country's presidency (before being ejected from it by the military scarcely a year later).

To many observers used to being surprised by events during the so-called Arab Spring, the dominance of Islamists in postauthoritarian elections was the one thing that was expected. After all, during the Mubarak era, the Muslim Brotherhood amassed an impressive string of electoral victories that had, by the waning years of Mubarak's term, rendered it practically the sole opposition voice in Egypt's legislature. Why did Islam seem to reign in Egyptian politics, especially when the country's endemic poverty and deep economic inequality would seem to render it promising terrain for a politics of radical redistribution rather than one of religious conservativism?

The conventional wisdom has long held that the answer lies somewhere in the Egyptian mind – that Egyptian citizens display both a desire for God's law and a strong antipathy to nonreligious, leftist ideologies that are thought to have failed around the world. This book argues that such ideological factors matter little. Instead, Islamist victories and leftist defeats can be chalked up to the institutional and social landscapes in which those parties must operate. Under Mubarak, the left lost because it couldn't compete with the regime for the suffrages of the poor. Islamists avoided this fate by appealing to middle-class voters that the left could not reach. After Mubarak, though the votes of the poor were up for grabs, Islamists were more able to capture them as well, by virtue of their embeddedness in a religious social infrastructure that dwarfed the kinds of social institutions on which leftist parties rely – such as labor unions and occupational associations.

Tracing the Muslim Brotherhood's electoral victories and the secular left's losses over the course of nearly forty years, this book argues that the party system that emerged in transitional Egypt reflected not the structure of basic conflict in that society, but the structure of political opportunities that allowed Islamists to better convince voters of their superiority not in matters of faith, but rather in their ability and willingness to use their power to deliver more worldly benefits. They would eventually prove unable to deliver on this promise, with disastrous results.

This book is about more than why Islamists triumphed in elections, however. In the course of explaining Islam's (fleeting) victories, it explores the possibilities for the kind of political pluralism that is at the heart of what we expect from democracy. And although the majority of the empirical terrain covered by this book is located in Egypt, the answers this study generates are ones that will have resonances far beyond the banks of the Nile.

Acknowledgments

Eight years ago, I stood outside a police station in the Nile Delta town of al-Zaqāzīq, awaiting the results of a just-concluded parliamentary election. Around me were hundreds of Muslim Brothers, eager to know if their candidate – an incumbent whose fiery speeches against the regime had earned him a national reputation – would be returned to office for five more years. Inside the police station, the incumbent and his opponent – a former traffic officer who had been backed by the ruling party – watched as judges counted the ballots. Throughout the evening, we received reports on the tally from a Brother who was in cell-phone contact with the incumbent or one of his aides. Increasingly, his reports seemed to indicate that a Brotherhood victory was in the offing. This made sense – though the incumbent had angered the regime, the passion of his supporters was palpable, and the Brotherhood had been performing well in other districts throughout the country. Word of this particular Brother's impending success rippled through the crowd, which took on a cautiously celebratory atmosphere. It was not to last. After what seemed like several hours, word came that the judge overseeing the vote counting was huddled in fevered telephone consultations, presumably with superiors in Cairo. The mood turned darker. It seemed that although the Brother had come out on top, the judge had been commanded to swap the two candidates' tallies. The Brotherhood candidate, we heard, was arguing with him, pleading with him to fear God and do the right thing. The judge, who likely had plenty of more worldly things to fear if he actually took the candidate's advice, was reportedly apologetic. As he put pen to paper to complete the foul deed, he allegedly turned to the Brother and said, "All I ask is that if you want to curse someone, please just curse me and not my children."

I do not know if the Brother complied with the judge's request, but I often like to think of that judge and to imagine what must have gone through his mind when, seven years after that day, he watched (along with millions of other Egyptians) as the man to whom he had denied a seat in parliament – an engineering professor by the name of Mohamed Morsi – was elected to his country's presidency. And in these dog days of the summer of 2013, I increasingly find myself thinking of Mr. Morsi and what must have gone through *his* mind when, just a year after winning office, he was deprived of yet another electoral victory, this time by his own minister of defense.

For this author, those three episodes – Morsi's loss in a rigged election, his victory seven years later in a relatively fair one, and the eventual abrogation of that result – represent the signposts of an intellectual journey that began during the final years of the Mubarak regime and that now comes to fruition as what seemed like the opening of a hopeful democratic experiment has given way to what some fear is the beginning of a long dark period in that country's politics. Along the way, I accumulated many debts. And while some of my creditors may have at times felt like cursing me *and* my children, I hope that these modest words of thanks will begin to repay friends and relations without whose generosity and love this project would have foundered.

This book began its life as my doctoral dissertation at Yale University, completed in 2009. My dissertation chair, Frances Rosenbluth, is that rare breed of scholar who combines analytical precision with a fondness for bold arguments. The other members of my committee – Ian Shapiro, James Scott, and Ellen Lust – offered support, counsel, and criticism at key junctures in this project's development, long after it outgrew its roots as a dissertation about a narrow period in Egypt's political life. I am particularly grateful to Ellen for becoming a partner and collaborator after I left Yale, most notably in a series of surveys conducted in Egypt after the revolution, the first of which is analyzed in this book. I am also grateful to Ian and to Keith Darden for selecting this book for their series on problems in international politics and for allowing me the time to broaden its temporal aperture to encompass the dramatic changes – and depressing continuities – of the so-called Arab Spring. Thanks are especially due to the two anonymous reviewers who offered invaluable comments on the initial manuscript, and to Lew Bateman of Cambridge University Press for his faith and patience. I'm also grateful to Shaun Vigil and Abidha Sulaiman for steering this book through the shoals of the production process. I am proud as well to record my gratitude to the Carnegie Corporation of New York (and particularly to Patricia Rosenfeld of that institution) and to the Dubai Initiative of the Kennedy School of Government (in particular Ashraf Hegazy) for their support of this work.

For their helpful comments and suggestions on various parts of this project at various stages of its development, I record my gratitude to Amel Ahmed, Matthew Baum, Eva Bellin, Jason Brownlee, Melani Cammet, Dara Cohen, Candelaria Garay, Greg Gause, Mona El-Ghobashy, Josip Glaurdic, Ellis Goldberg, Jill Goldenpine, Steve Heydemann, Stathis Kalyvas, Jytte Klaussen, Stephen Kosack, Ahmet Kuru, Pierre Landry, Vickie Langohr, Marc Lynch, Quinton Mayne, Jeff Miley, Tamir Moustafa, Rich Nielsen, Elizabeth Nugent, David Patel, Thomas Pepinsky, Danilo Petranovich, Marsha Pripstein Posusney, Ahmed al-Rahim, Nassos Roussias, Bruce Russett, Bruce Rutherford, Kenneth Scheve, Jonah Schulhofer-Wohl, Ryan Sheeley, Samer Shehata, Joshua Stacher,

Mark Tessler, Lisa Wedeen, Elisabeth Wood, and Sean Yom. Nathan Brown and Jillian Schwedler read the entire manuscript at a critical earlier phase in its existence, and both made comments and suggestions that practically sent me back to the drawing board. Amaney Jamal, my collaborator on a new project on Islamism, was a source of valuable counsel and encouragement, particularly as I neared the finish line. In Egypt, I benefited from conversations with Muḥammad ʿAbd al-Ghanī, Moheb Zaki, Gamal ʿAbd al-Gawād, Ezzat Ibrahim, Maggie Michael, Karim Haggag, Amānī Qandīl, Saadeddin Ibrahim, Gehad Auda, Ṣubḥī ʿIsīla, Yusrī al-ʿIzbāwī, al-Sayyid al-Badawī, Zakī Shaḥāta, Muḥammad Kamāl, Amīr Bassām, al-Saʿdani Aḥmad,ʿAli al-Dīn Hilāl, Muḥammad Kamāl, Aḥmad Sarḥān, Ḥamdī Ḥassan, Wafīq al-Ghīṭānī, and ʿAmr Hāshim Rabīʿ. Finally, Emad Shahin and John Esposito were kind enough to invite me to contribute to their excellent *Oxford Handbook on Islam and Politics*. I am grateful to them and to Oxford University Press for allowing me to adapt some of that material for this volume.

I would also like to thank my colleagues at the Harvard Kennedy School, one of the greatest places for a political scientist interested in politics to work. It would not be an exaggeration to record the names of the school's entire faculty and staff – so indebted am I to almost everyone there – but a few deserve special mention: Graham Allison, Arthur Applbaum, Mary-Jo Bane, Gretchen Bartlett, Matthew Baum, Mary Anne Baumgartner, Iris Bohnet, Nicholas Burns, Ash Carter, Julian Chang, Suzanne Cooper, Pepper Culpepper, Mayumi Cutler, David Dapice, Jessica Eykholt, Archon Fung, Marshall Ganz, Krysten Hartman, Arn Howitt, Noelle Janka, Steven Kelman, Alex Keyssar, Asim Khwaja, David Lazer, Jenny Mansbridge, Marty Mauzy, Quinton Mayne, Richard Parker, Hilary Rantisi, Jay Rosengard, Tony Saich, Kathleen Schnaidt, Moshik Temkin, Thomas Vallely, Steven Walt, Barbara Whalen, Julie Wilson, Kenneth Winston, and Richard Zeckhauser. The Kennedy School also provided me with a stellar group of students: Paul Much, Ahmed Kouchouk, Jake Stefanik, Hummy Song, Ozge Guzelsu, Aaron Miller, Todd Mostak (now a brilliant researcher and inventor), and Kash Patel asked me probing questions about my work, offered me new ways of thinking about things, and reminded me of my responsibility to say something of real-world importance. I also had spectacular research assistants: Daniel Masterson (who now is pursuing his own scholarly career at Yale), Safia Trabelsi, Julia Groeblacher, Duncan Pickard, Ibrahim Ouf, and Rania Elhattab all contributed to this project in essential ways. I am grateful to them all. Also at Harvard, Leila Ahmed, Bill Granara, Roger Owen, and Malika Zeghal have been extraordinary engaged colleagues from whom I have learned much about the region we all study. Finally, Martha Stewart has been a friendly face at numerous events on campus, who generously gave of her time and photographic expertise to help me with this book's cover design.

I wish also to thank people close to me who have offered me aid and comfort throughout my academic career: Brian, Jeffrey, and Nancy Alcorn are the best in-laws a boy from Sandanhūr, Egypt, via Oshkosh, Wisconsin, and al-Khobar, Saudi Arabia, could have. Mohamed Badr has been my friend for most of my life, a fact that makes me smile as I type it. My favorite Irishmen, William J. Dobson and Frank Gavin, knew just when to buck me up or cut me down to size. Drew Erdmann, Stanley Hegginbotham, Warren Ilchman, Aftab Karim, Andrew Loewenstein, Neysun Mahboubi, Douglas McGray, Jonathan Rosenberg, Joshua Rosenblum, Daniel Sagalyn, Peter Scoblic, and Nicholas Thompson all offered pleasant diversions and sage counsel at numerous points during the writing of this project and in some ways contributed directly to it. Finally, Fareed Zakaria has been a generous mentor and loyal friend ever since I first interned for him almost twenty years ago.

I dedicate this book to my parents, El-Miselhy Abdel Hamid Masoud and Nadia Hamid al-Banna. When my father was nine years old, my grandmother sent him from his tiny Nile Delta village to begin his formal schooling ten miles away in al-Zaqāzīq, the city that Mohamed Morsi would represent in parliament fifty years later. My father died shortly before I began graduate school, but I think he would have been surprised, and gratified, to learn that, sixty years after his own sojourn there, his American-born son would also trek to Zagāzīg (as it is pronounced locally) in search of knowledge. A Freudian might conclude that this was no accident, that a subconscious desire to remain close to my father dictated the course of my research. This is almost certainly true, as much for the subject matter as for the geography. Some of my earliest memories of life are of swimming in the pool at our local YMCA while my dad read from black leatherbound volumes by the Brotherhood's founder, Ḥasan al-Bannā, and Sayyid Quṭb, one of its leading ideologues. I like to think he would have found much in this book to disagree with, and debate, but ultimately, to be proud of.

The great Egyptian poet Ahmad Shawqī (1868–1932) wrote, "The mother is a school. If you prepare her, you prepare a nation of noble character." If this is true, then my own mother is a university unto herself. It was my mother – a schoolteacher – who taught me to read and write, who encouraged me to bury myself in books, who helped me with my homework, and who later gave me the nudge I needed to pursue an academic career over one as a journalist. She is my first telephone call whenever I'm feeling low or in need of advice on the parenting of energetic young children, but also whenever I'm having trouble putting a survey question into elegant Arabic or need to think through the latest developments in Egypt's ever-changing and always-entertaining political landscape. I like to joke that I am the least favorite of my mother's five sons (on account of the fact that I alone eschewed medicine and engineering), but she knows that I have never felt anything other than incredibly loved and nurtured by her. To her, and to my late father, I offer my deepest thanks and love.

My brothers, Nader, Wesam, Amir, and Hesham, were throughout this academic journey what they have been to me my entire life – my best friends, my right-hand men, my collective Rock of Gibraltar. Nader, the eldest, reminds me more of our late father every day. His pep talks keep me going and help me to ward off the demons of self-doubt. My younger brother, Wesam, lifts my spirits with his warmth and sense of humor and is never without biting insight into the political sentiments of Cairo's glitterati (of which he is a fast-rising member). Amir offered such invaluable commentary and suggestions on practically every aspect of this work that I am convinced that his decision to become a physician was a crippling loss for the social sciences. And Hesham, my youngest brother (and also a physician), has enriched our lives in Boston immeasurably. Most important, he has been there for my two sons – taking them to movies, watching their soccer games, and generally hanging out – when I've been traveling, teaching, or holed up writing.

Finally, there is so much to thank my beloved wife Kristin for that to do the job properly would take a book of its own. To her and to my boys, Hamza and Ali, I can only offer my gratitude for their patience and my most profuse apologies for being too wrapped up in the politics and history of Egypt to take them to the beach. I can't promise life will be terribly different now that this book is done, but I promise to always do my best to make my time away from them worth it.

A Note on Transliteration

Transliterating Arabic is difficult and time-consuming. It's little wonder, then, that many books on the Arab world begin with disclaimers noting that "correct" transliteration of Arabic's many unique vowels and consonants has been foregone in the interests of simplification, ease of communication, and so on. That has not been done here. The heavy reliance of this text on Arabic sources means that proper transliteration of those sources is essential if readers and researchers are to be able to track them down and build on the findings presented here. Therefore, Arabic terms and proper names have been transliterated according to the system established by the Middle East Studies Association, described below.

Short vowels are rendered **a**, **i**, and **u**. Long vowels are rendered **ā**, **ī**, and **ū**. Emphatic versions of the consonants *s*, *d*, and *t* are rendered **ṣ**, **ḍ**, and **ṭ**. The voiceless glottal fricative (the familiar *h* sound) is rendered **h**, whereas the voiceless pharyngeal fricative (the "hard" *h* characteristic of Arabic and other Semitic languages) is rendered **ḥ**. As is common practice, the voiced velar fricative is rendered **gh**, the voiceless velar fricative is rendered **kh**, and the voiceless uvular plosive is denoted by **q**. The voiced alveolar fricative is written **z**, the pharyngealized voiced dental fricative is rendered **ẓ**, the voiced dental fricative is written **dh**, and the voiceless dental fricative is denoted by **th**. Egyptian proper names with the letter *jīm* (the voiced postalveolar affricate in classical and modern standard Arabic, as well as in most regional dialects) are spelled with a **g**, reflecting the Egyptian practice of pronouncing the letter *jīm* with the voiced velar plosive (the familiar "hard" *g* in English). Thus an individual who shares the given name of Egypt's military ruler from 1952 to 1970 would see his moniker written Gamāl, not Jamāl. Otherwise, *jīm* is rendered **j** as it would be in standard Arabic. Geminate consonants are indicated by writing the letter twice (as in the family name of the Muslim Brotherhood's founder, al-Ba**nn**ā). Finally, the voiced pharyngeal fricative (i.e., the Arabic letter *ʿayn*) is indicated by ʿ, whereas the glottal stop (known as the *hamza*) is indicated with ʾ. Thus the Arabic word for "dominant" would be rendered *sāʾid*, whereas the imperative form of "to help" would be written *sāʿid*.

Still, there are some departures from this scheme. When place names have English variants, I use those. Thus al-Qāhira is Cairo, al-ʾIskandariyya is Alexandria, Dumyāt is Damietta, al-ʾUqsur is Luxor, al-Suways is Suez, and so on. Likewise, the names of prominent figures are rendered as they most often appear in the press. Thus Egypt's longest-serving president is written here as Hosni Mubarak (as the *New York Times* and *Washington Post* do it) instead of Husnī Mubārak. Finally, if I am aware of the way an individual spells his or her own name in English, I employ that spelling, except in cases where there is an established and well-known English rendering. Thus I write Gamal Abdel Nasser, Mohamed Morsi, Wael Ghonim, and Mohamed ElBaradei instead of Jamāl ʿAbd al-Nāṣir, Muḥammad Mursī, Wāʾil Ghunīm, and Muḥammad al-Barādʿī. Finally, until someone invents a spell-checker for Arabic romanizations, I beg the reader's forgiveness for any errors that may have crept into the text.

Introduction: An Islamist Monopoly

The years following the overthrow of Egypt's long-reigning dictator, Hosni Mubarak, have been unkind to those who hoped for a new era of liberty and pluralism in the Arab world's most populous country. Though the protests that resulted in Mubarak's departure on February 11, 2011, seemed at first to have been inspired and organized by a diverse group of liberal, progressive, and technologically savvy young people – represented, in Western minds at least, in such personalities as Wael Ghonim, a U.S.-educated Google employee, and Gihan Ibrahim, a graduate of the American University in Cairo – that heady victory gave way to a nearly unbroken string of triumphs for religiously conservative Islamist parties that had been at best reluctant participants in Egypt's revolutionary drama.[1] First, in January 2012, the Freedom and Justice Party (Ḥizb al-Ḥurriyah wa al-ʿAdālah) – the political arm of the eighty-five-year-old Society of Muslim Brothers (Jamāʿat al-Ikhwān al-Muslimūn) – captured 37 percent of the vote and 46 percent of the seats in the country's first post-authoritarian parliament (before

[1] I define Islamist parties as those that arise out of Islamic pietist movements, such as the Muslim Brotherhood (Jamāʿat al-Ikhwān al-Muslimūn) and the Salafi Call Society (Jamāʿat al-Daʿwa al-Salafiyya). These parties invariably call for the application of some version of *sharīʿa*, but I refrain from using a stated desire for *sharīʿa* as a definitional criterion because Egyptian parties generally recognized as non-Islamist often pay lip service to *sharīʿa* as well. For example, Islamic themes once figured prominently in the platform of Egypt's ruling National Democratic Party, which, according to Egyptian columnist Fahmī Huwaydī, called not only for the primacy of the *sharīʿa* but also for the strengthening of religious education and the use of state-owned media for the reinforcement of religious principles and values. See Fahmī Huwaydī, "*Misr … Al-Marjāʿiyya al-Dīniyya Bayn al-Ḥaẓr wa al-Tawẓīf* (Egypt: The Religious Frame of Reference between Prohibition and Exploitation)," *Al-Sharq al-Awsaṭ*, Issue 10347, March 28, 2007. Similarly, the platform of Egypt's Wafd Party – long referred to as "secular," "liberal," or both – declares that "Islam is the official religion of the state and therefore the Islamic *sharīʿah* must be the principal source of legislation." (See *Birnāmij Ḥizb al-Wafd: Al-Shuʾūn al-Dīniyya* (Wafd Party Platform: Religious Matters); available at http://www.alwafdparty.org/details.aspx?t=prog&id=136.) An alternative, and useful, definition of Islamism is provided by Hegghammer (2013, 1), who calls it "activism justified with primary reference to Islam," although what constitutes "primary reference" is of course subjective.

the body was dissolved by the country's highest court). In addition, an even more conservative newcomer called the Party of Light (*Ḥizb al-Nūr*) – variously described as "populist-puritans,"[2] "ultra-Orthodox," or "ultra-conservative religious monsters,"[3] – captured 28 percent of the vote and 24 percent of the seats. Six months later, in June 2012, the Muslim Brotherhood's Mohamed Morsi captured the country's presidency. Given the Brotherhood's electoral dominance, one could have been forgiven for concluding the Egypt's revolution had simply replaced one hegemonic ruling party with another. To many, the eighteen days from January 25, 2011, to Mubarak's resignation, during which U.S. President Barack Obama reportedly wished aloud for "the kids on the street to win and for the Google guy to become president" came to seem like a distant and outlandish dream.[4]

In fact, wherever the so-called Arab Spring gave rise to elections, Islamists captured pluralities, if not majorities, of voters. For example, in Tunisia, the country that touched off the current upheavals, the Renaissance Movement Party (*Ḥizb Ḥarakat al-Nahḍa*) – which promised to end the marginalization of Islam in public life and which had been brutally suppressed during the dictatorship of Zayn al-ʿĀbidin Bin ʿAlī – captured 89 of 217 parliamentary seats and 40 percent of the vote in the October 2011 constituent assembly elections. In the July 2012 elections to Libya's General National Congress (al-Muʾtamar al-Waṭanī al-ʿĀm), the Brotherhood – affiliated Justice and Construction Party appeared at first to have done relatively poorly, placing second and garnering only 17 of the 80 seats reserved for party lists. However, Brotherhood allies later picked up an additional 60 of the 120 seats reserved for individual constituencies, bringing the party to within a few seats of being the largest bloc in the country's first democratically elected legislature.

Nor were political Islam's electoral gains restricted to those polities that managed to unseat their strongmen and ruling parties. In Morocco – a country not yet free of the authoritarian yoke – the Party of Justice and Development (Ḥizb al-ʿAdālah wa al-Tanmiya), which claims an "Islamic frame of reference" (*marjaʿiyya Islāmiyya*), won more than a quarter of legislative seats in November 2011 and now leads the country's government.[5] In Kuwait, Islamists of various ideological stripes and organizational affiliations, ranging from the Muslim Brotherhood–affiliated Islamic Constitutional Movement (al-Ḥarakah

2 Robin Wright, "Don't Fear All Islamists, Fear Salafis," *New York Times*, August 20, 2012; available at: http://www.nytimes.com/2012/08/20/opinion/dont-fear-all-islamists-fear-salafis.html?_r=0.

3 Khalil al-Anani, "Egypt's 'blessed' Salafi Votes," ForeignPolicy.com, May 5, 2012; available at: http://mideast.foreignpolicy.com/posts/2012/05/02/egypts_blessed_salafi_votes.

4 Mark Landler, "Obama Seeks Reset in the Arab World," *New York Times*, May 11, 2011.

5 References to the PJD's "Islamic frame of reference" can be found on the party's website, http://www.pjd.ma. See, for example, the section entitled "The project," which states in its opening line, "The Party of Justice and Development is a nationalist political party that strives – based on its Islamic frame of reference and in the context of a constitutional monarchy based on the command of the faithful – to contribute to the building of a modern, democratic Morocco." Available at: http://www.pjd.ma/pjd/page-8; accessed March 1, 2012.

al-Dustūriya al-Islāmiyya) to the ultra-Orthodox Islamic Salafi Alliance (al-Taḥāluf al-Islāmī al-Salafī) to various ideologically congenial independents, won a majority in the February 2012 elections for the fifty-seat Chamber of Deputies. The entire region, it seemed, was voting for Islam.

For many observers, the political ascent of the partisans of political Islam was entirely expected. Though many of those who make it their business to understand the Middle East would famously prove unable to predict such events as the flight of Bin Ali, the resignation of Mubarak, the scourging of Qaddafi, and the ongoing struggle against al-Assad, they were nevertheless able to predict almost perfectly what would occur if democracy (or, rather, more-or-less free elections) were to alight on the Arab world. For example, to return the focus to Egypt, the scholar Fawaz Gerges wrote in 2006 that "if free and open elections were held today, the Brotherhood would win a comfortable majority."[6] Also in 2006, the *New York Times* informed us that the Brothers "would probably sweep any wide-open elections."[7] In 2007, an Israeli official testified that "if free elections were held in Egypt today, the Muslim Brotherhood would win by a landslide."[8] That same year, sociologists Nancy J. Davis and Robert V. Robinson (2007, 23) wrote that "if truly open elections were held in Egypt today, the Muslim Brotherhood would win in a landslide." In 2004, an Egyptian leftist activist divined that "if there were free elections tomorrow, the Brotherhood would win 60 percent of the seats" (Onians 2004). Even earlier, in the 1990s, Hishām Mubārak, the late Egyptian human rights activist (and no relation to the former dictator), confided to Miller (1996, 65) that "if the Brotherhood ever ran in a free election, it would win overwhelmingly." More restrained was the analysis of the *Jerusalem Report* more than twenty years ago, which ascribed to "many observers" the belief that if the Brotherhood "ran free elections and was given free access to the media, its supporters would take no more than ten years to become the parliamentary majority."[9] In actuality, it took less than ten months.

What explains the totality of the Islamists' victory? Why did a revolution whose principal demand was not for the rule of the *Qurʾān* but rather for "bread, freedom, and social justice [*ʿaysh, ḥurriyah, ʿadālah ijtimāʿiyya*]" yield so quickly to the dominance of religious political parties? After all, it is frequently reported that 40 percent of Egyptians subsist on less than two dollars per day (in 1993 international prices).[10] The country's per capita income of $5,349 places it in the

6 Fawaz A. Gerges, "Making Sense of the Cartoon Controversy: From Protests to Recent Elections, Islamists Hold Sway," ABC News, February 8, 2006; available at: http://abcnews.go.com/International/story?id=1595281&page=1.

7 James Glanz, "A Little Democracy or a Genie Unbottled," *New York Times*, January 29, 2006.

8 Uri Dromi, "Reverberations in Egypt: Gaza Fallout," *International Herald Tribune*, June 22, 2007; available at: http://www.iht.com/articles/2007/06/22/opinion/eddromi.php.

9 Jeffrey Phillips, "A Holy War on the Nile," *Jerusalem Report*, June 18, 1992.

10 Most invocations of the figure leave off the fact that it is denominated in 1993 dollars. See, for example, Tadros (2005), El-Khawas (2012a), and Bush (2011), as well as Amitai Etzioni, "It's the Egyptian Economy, Stupid," *The National Interest*, January 24, 2013. For journalistic uses,

lower half of nations. Ranked by its score on the United Nations Development Programme's human development index (which aggregates health, education, and national income indicators), Egypt places 112th, behind Cape Verde and Guatemala and just ahead of Nicaragua.[11] Egypt would thus seem to possess a large and ready constituency for a politics of class rather than creed, of redistribution rather than religion. And yet, in the 30 months from Mubarak's ouster to the military's overthrow of his successor, Mohamed Morsi, whenever Egyptians took to the polls, they cast ballots not for the tribunes of workers and peasants but for Islamist parties led by technocrats (such as President Morsi, a U.S.-trained engineering professor) and businessman (such as Khayrat al-Shāṭir, a multimillionaire entrepreneur and the Muslim Brotherhood's second-in-command). To echo a question asked by anthropologist Lila Abu Lughod (1995, 54), why is it that Egyptians, who are overwhelmingly poor, seem to find so appealing a "political discourse in which morality replaces class as the central social problem?" Is it a case of some false consciousness? To expropriate the title of a well-known American book, should we be asking "What's the matter with Cairo?"[12]

Scholarly attempts to answer this question have coalesced around two types of responses. The first, and most influential among the public, is that there is simply something special about Islam. It may be that Muslims are primed by their creed to desire Islamic government (leaving aside, for the moment, what exactly Islamic government might require), or that Muslims find religious rhetoric inherently comforting in hard and uncertain times, or that secular ideologies have been tried and failed, or that Islamic messages are simply more easily understood and processed by the average Egyptian than, say, Marxist ones. Though these mechanisms differ from each other in important ways, they all locate the source of Islamist parties' electoral success in the *religious* nature of their discourse and ideology. The second family of explanations for Islamist success is organizational. In these accounts, Islamists are hypothesized to be more disciplined, competent, and cohesive than their secular counterparts; to run better election campaigns; or to expend more effort to purchase the loyalties of voters with social services and other goods that the state should, but does not, provide. In short, these accounts hold that Muslims aren't necessarily voting for Islam when

see John Ydstie, "Empty Pockets Stoked Discontent in Egypt, Tunisia," National Public Radio, February 1, 2011; Jeffrey Fleishman, "Under Egypt's Political Unrest Seethes the Rising Anger of the Poor," *Los Angeles Times,* February 2, 2013; Tony Karon, "From Bad to Worse: Economic Woes May Compound Egypt's Pain," *Time*, January 29, 2013; Yolanda Kell, "The Complicated Legacy of Egypt's Hosni Mubarak," *BBC News*, January 25, 2013. Given inflation, $2 per day in 1993 prices is equivalent to approximately $3 in current (2012) prices. The actual number of Egyptians subsisting on less than two (current) dollars a day is closer to 15.4 percent. See *2006 World Development Indicators*; available at: http://data.worldbank.org/sites/default/files/wdi06.pdf.

11 *Human Development Report 2009*, United Nations Development Programme. See http://hdrstats.undp.org/en/countries/country_fact_sheets/cty_fs_EGY.html.

12 Thomas Frank, *What's the Matter with Kansas? How Conservatives Won the Heart of America*, Henry Holt and Co., New York, 2004.

they mark their ballots for groups such as the Muslim Brotherhood but rather are responding to Islamist effectiveness or expressing gratitude for free healthcare or writing off secular parties for being so feckless and divided.

All these arguments undoubtedly capture important reasons for political Islam's electoral prowess. Anyone who has witnessed a Muslim Brotherhood rally firsthand cannot help but be struck by the totemic power of religious rhetoric, by the ways in which invocations of the will of Allah and the way of Muhammad can imbue voters with a sense of righteous duty. Anyone who has witnessed the well-oiled machine of a Muslim Brotherhood election campaign, with its disciplined cadres and unified messaging, would be hard-pressed to find greater displays of political competence in Egypt. And finally, anyone who observed the decay of that country's institutions and infrastructure, the increasing immiseration of its poor, and the seeming nonchalance of its former authoritarian rulers to both would have had little difficulty believing that any movement that stepped into the breach and took it on itself to provide sustenance and care would reap rewards at the ballot box.

And yet these explanations for Islamism's remarkable rise are partial at best. If Islam is sufficient to explain why Islamists win, then we would observe little variation in Islamist success over time and space. Instead, in reality, we see that not all Arabs vote Islamist, and those who voted Islamist in one election may not do so in another. Indeed, as we saw in July of 2013, when the Muslim Brotherhood's Mohamed Morsi was overthrown in a military coup, a country that once elected Islamists to office in vast numbers could scarcely a year later celebrate its army as it escorted those same individuals from the halls of power to the country's prisons. And if Islamist victories were purely the function of efforts to fill empty stomachs, or of slick and well-run electoral campaigns, we would have to wonder why it never occurred to their opponents to do these things. Why should Islamists have a monopoly on organizational discipline or machine politics?

This book argues that the secret of political Islam's stunning electoral successes – both under authoritarianism and during Egypt's founding elections – is not to be found purely in the minds of voters or in the tactics of political parties, but in broader, structural factors that shape both citizens' choices and parties' strategies. Specifically, this book argues that Egypt's relative economic underdevelopment generates two primary dynamics that advantage Islamists and disadvantage parties of the left. The first is by limiting the ability of voters to choose. For although Egypt's economic backwardness may generate large numbers of voters with a theoretical hospitality to parties of the left, with their programs of wealth redistribution and state provision of welfare, poverty robs citizens of the ability to vote based on their long-term economic interests – not because they are unable to perceive those interests, but because disadvantage renders them susceptible to vote buying, offers of patronage, and other forms of clientelism (Lust 2006; Blaydes 2010). This was particularly true during the Mubarak era, when the ruling National Democratic Party was able to capture impoverished voters through its command over state resources. A leftist party that wanted to reap the suffrages of Egyptians during that grim period had to either try to compete with the ruling party's patronage machine (largely impossible) or to redirect its attentions to more affluent voters (who were less likely to be receptive to the party's radically redistributive aims). The Muslim Brotherhood, on the other hand – which began its life as a movement of the educated middle classes and which espoused a vague economic platform that could appeal across class lines – faced little difficulty in attracting affluent voters. As a result, the Brotherhood racked up a string of victories during the Mubarak years while its secular counterparts built only a reputation for failure.

The second way in which underdevelopment advantages Islamist and inhibits the growth of leftist parties is by stunting the organizational basis on which left parties are typically erected. Scholars have long recognized that forms of social organization, such as labor unions and mutual-benefit associations for workers and farmers, constitute the principal channels through which leftist parties link themselves to potential voters (Radcliff and Davis 2000, Levitsky 2001, Roberts 2003). However, such forms of collective life are weak in most of the Middle East, and in Egypt in particular. The most often cited reason for this weakness is that the authoritarian state severely curtailed the ability of workers and farmers to organize themselves independently and press for their rights (Bianchi 1986, Posusney 1997). But as important, I argue, are developmental factors external to the policies of the military-backed regime that dominated Egypt for most of the last sixty years. The country's vast agrarian workforce – dominated by small landholders – and its sizable informal sector are simply inconducive to large-scale, class-based mobilization. To the extent that such forms of collective action exist, they are limited to the country's small industrial enclaves and do not constitute the basis for a national political movement capable of claiming a share of power. In contrast, the country is replete with religious institutions, from mosques to religious societies to charitable associations that, though forced to be apolitical during Mubarak's reign, embed both ordinary citizens and Islamist political activists in common "networks of social action" (Desai 2002), making it easy for the latter to build trust with the former when an opening in the political system finally presented itself.

I argue, then, that the electoral successes of Islamist parties both before and after Egypt's 2011 revolution did not mean that economic issues were somehow less salient than matters of faith, that citizens were somehow sublimating their "real" interests on the altar of religion. On the contrary, I find that when we examine the correlates of support for the Muslim Brotherhood's Freedom and Justice Party in Egypt's first parliamentary election after Mubarak's overthrow, citizens voted for that party not because of its stance on the application of Islamic law, but because they believed it would pursue economic policies on behalf of the poor. That leftist parties were unable to capture these votes has less to do with their lack of Islamic garb than with their lack of means of connecting to voters. Social scientists are accustomed to inferring from the nature of a country's party system the dominant sociopolitical "cleavages" (Lipset and Rokkan 1967) or "master narratives" (Varshney 2002) that shape its political life. This book argues that to do so in the case of the polities of the Arab world courts misunderstanding. Although, as we shall see, some people certainly do vote for Islamist parties because of their positions on religious issues, the lopsidedness of the Egyptian party system in favor of Islamist parties is less a reflection of the collective mind's thirst for God than it is of resource asymmetries that endowed Islamists with more opportunities to convince voters of their ability to serve Mammon. In short, this book argues that Islamist electoral victories are not, in the main, about Islam.

An important implication of this argument is that the electoral advantage enjoyed by Islamists is likely to be temporally bounded, limited principally to so-called founding elections (Schmitter 1986) when the party system is less a "system" than a highly fluid menagerie of organizations and personalities with little in the way of name recognition or reputation. This would not be the case, of course, if Islamists were swept into power on the basis of religious rhetoric and a popular passion for Islam (Murphy 2002). In such a universe, we would expect popular support for Islamist parties to be durable even in the face of continuing economic hardship or increasing popular immiseration. But if the Islamists' advantage is primarily organizational, and based on beliefs about their likely economic policies, it stands to reason that the Islamists' acquisition of power would provide voters with opportunities to update those beliefs. And as the post-authoritarian state opens media access to parties and politicians from across the political spectrum, the magnitude of the informational advantage that Islamists enjoyed in founding elections should diminish. As we shall see, the fundamentally economic nature of voting for the Muslim Brotherhood in the aftermath of Mubarak's overthrow helps us to understand how an organization that seemed to have won hearts and minds across classes and ideological affiliations could lose all but its most hard-core supporters scarcely a year after assuming power.

This book proceeds in two parts: Part I investigates the fortunes of Islamists in elections during Egypt's long authoritarian period, explaining how the Muslim Brotherhood was able to establish itself as the principal opposition to the authoritarian state and how the left – despite a moment of intellectual energy in the late 1970s – became by the end of the Mubarak years a virtual cipher in Egypt's electoral landscape. Part II takes up the story of the Muslim Brotherhood and its rivals after the 2011 revolution. Though that period seemed to disrupt old authoritarian dynamics and open up previously unfathomed possibilities, they were possibilities that the left – hobbled both by reputation and structural factors – was distinctly ill equipped to take advantage of. The remainder of this introduction describes each of the book's chapters.

Chaper 1 explores the state of theorizing on the rise and electoral success of Islamist movements. I argue that the two most influential answers found in the literature – those emphasizing cognitive features of Islamist discourse and those emphasizing the organizational strategies and tactics of Islamist parties – have proven unable to explain variation over time and space in the size and nature of the Islamist movement's base of supporters. I then lay out the argument of this study, which redirects our attention to the ways in which the social and institutional environment constrains parties' abilities to appeal to voters, shaping whom they can and cannot reach. Chapter 2 then takes up the story of political Islam's dominance during the Mubarak era by asking not why Islamists won but the inverse: Why is it that non-Islamist parties – particularly those of the left – were singularly unable to establish themselves as credible elected opponents of the Mubarak regime? In contrast to theories that locate the sources of leftist enfeeblement in the discrediting of their ideology, or the fall of the Soviet Union, or their co-optation by the authoritarian state, this chapter demonstrates how parties of the left were systematically disadvantaged by the very nature of an electoral game built not on policies but rather on the politics of patronage and clientelism.

Chapter 3 turns to the question of how the Muslim Brotherhood was able to overcome the dynamics that led to the electoral enervation of the Egyptian left. I argue that a regular assertion in the literature – that Islamists won by mobilizing the poor recipients of Islamic social services – actually neglects the ways in which the authoritarian state worked to prevent precisely such an outcome, both by destroying Islamists' own "bricks and mortar" institutions (Cammett and Issar 2010) and by heavily policing their links to other ones. Thus, though Islamic political activists continued to join and participate in religious social services networks during the Mubarak era, they were profoundly unable to turn these into a base for clientelistic politics that would have allowed them to challenge the state for the political loyalties of the poor.

But, if Islamists did not win through the provision of social services to the masses, how were they able to routinely defeat candidates of the ruling party and emerge with their storied reputation for electoral prowess? Chapter 4 shows that the Muslim Brotherhood won elections under Mubarak by mobilizing a small middle-class constituency that could afford to forego offers of regime patronage and instead cast their ballots as "paper stones" (Przeworski and Sprague 1986) against the regime. This middle-class basis, I argue, was reflected in everything from the makeup of the organization's leaders to the types of services the movement's parliamentarians offered to voters to the socioeconomic profiles of the districts in which they fielded candidates. Moreover, I show that the appeal to the middle classes is one that the Brotherhood was better positioned than other parties to make, given its long history of recruiting primarily among the educated.

Thus, by the end of the Mubarak era, parties of the secular left appeared to have permanently failed, whereas the Muslim Brotherhood looked increasingly set to inherit the country's future. And then came the events of January 25, 2011 and its aftermath, which demarcate Part II of this book. Though we had long been taught to expect that the greatest threat to the durability of the Mubarak regime came from the forces of political Islam, in the end it was photogenic, wired, Western-oriented young people who seemed to lead the charge. Moreover, the left appeared to be heavily represented among the forces of revolution. Protests were organized by such groups as the Revolutionary Socialists (al-Ishtirākiyūn al-Thawriyūn) and the April 6 Movement (Ḥarakat 6 Abrīl), which took its name from the date of an aborted textile workers' strike in al-Maḥalla al-Kubrā in 2008. The relative absence of Islamists from Taḥrīr Square in the revolution's early days caused many to wonder if perhaps political Islam had been overrated. Wael Ghonim – the "Google guy" who was reportedly the focus of President Obama's hopes – went so far as to dismiss concerns about a Muslim Brotherhood takeover by declaring that the movement constituted no more than 15 percent of the protesters.[13] However, as the days after Mubarak's February 11 resignation turned to weeks and weeks to months, it appeared that the youths who had sparked that revolution had done little more than trade one single-party regime for another. Where once the country's legislature had been dominated by Mubarak's satraps, it was now dominated by the Muslim Brotherhood and its ultra-Orthodox allies, who seemed every bit as illiberal as their National Democratic Party predecessors (albeit in different ways).

Chapter 5 asks what, precisely, Egyptians were doing when they fulfilled decades of social scientific and journalistic prediction and voted overwhelmingly for Islamists in the country's first free and fair parliamentary elections. Were they enacting a long-theorized desire to deepen the role of religion in public life, finally bringing to office those who promised the *sharīʿa*-based governance that they had always craved? Did the fact that the elected legislature would be charged with writing a new constitution generate popular anxiety over the place of religion in public life, causing Egyptians to vote into power Islamists who would preserve the country's Islamic heritage and make sure to encode it in the nation's new charter? Drawing on a combination of qualitative and quantitative evidence, I argue that the issue of *sharīʿa* and the legislation of morals appeared to matter little to voters in that election. Though the Salafist Nūr party may have ridden to office on the backs of the quarter of the voting population that had religion front of mind, the plurality of voters who cast ballots for the Freedom and Justice Party appeared to do so beause they believed that the party would pursue the policies of wealth redistribution and strengthening of the social safety net that the Mubarak regime appeared to have long abandoned.

The fact that so many Egyptians voted for the Muslim Brotherhood for identifiably redistributive and welfare-statist reasons again raises the question of why the left performed so poorly. Given the dissolution of Mubarak's party, and with it the diminution of the patronage politics that robbed the left of its natural constituencies, one might have expected parties of the left to finally reap the rewards of their long championing of economic policies for which Egyptian voters had

13 Usāma Khālid, "*Ghunaym li al-Miṣrī al-Yawm: Maṭālibunā lam yakun tanaḥī al-ra'īs* (Wael Ghonim to al-Miṣrī al-Yawm: Our Demands Did Not Include the President's Resignation)," al-Miṣrī al-Yawm (Cairo), February 9, 2011; available at: http://www.almasryalyoum.com/node/313710.

demonstrated a considerable and sustained appetite. However, on examining citizens' perceptions of political parties and their stances, we find that most Egyptians appeared to think that leftists stood *against* redistribution and that Islamists were *more* redistributive than the non-Islamists who had made redistribution their bread and butter for the better part of half a century. Chapter 6 explains why this was so. It argues that although the revolution temporarily disrupted the patronage structures that had previously deprived the left of access to its most likely voters, it did not magically put in place an organizational and social infrastrucure that could offer parties of the left a means of establishing sustained contact with those voters.

Instead, in the postrevolutionary scramble to establish linkages to the vast majority of previously depoliticized Egyptians, Islamists could take advantage of religious forms of collective life to make their case for why they should be entrusted with the country's economy, whereas the forms of associational life that the left could mobilize, such as labor unions and occupational associations, were not nearly so encompassing. As a result, voters (thought they) knew more about Islamists than they did about parties of the left. Drawing on aggregate and individual-level econometric evidence, I show that a voter's assessment of a party's economic positions was powerfully conditioned by the associations in which he or she was embedded. Those embedded in Islamic networks thought that Islamists were redistributive and welfare-statist. Those embedded in networks of labor organization thought leftists were. The problem for the left was simply that many more people were embedded in Islamist networks than in labor unions. And while this fact is partially attributable to a long legacy of state policies designed to co-opt and weaken independent forms of political organization among the poor, it is also a function of the fact that such forms of organization are notoriously hard to build in agrarian, nonindustrialized societies.

If the story up to this point is one of success after Islamist success, Chapter 7 explores the changing trajectory of Islamist support after Egypt's founding elections. By the time the country had moved to presidential elections in the summer of 2012, the Islamist advantage appeared to have faded. Voters who had supported the Freedom and Justice Party on the basis of their perceptions of its economic policies now turned away from it, viewing the party – and the movement behind it – more as a grasping hand that sought to replace the NDP as a new hegemonic party than as the best steward for the country's resources. The broad coalition that had delivered to the Muslim Brothers nearly 45 percent of the seats in parliament had, by the presidential election, given way to a far narrower one, made up primarily of religiously minded voters who had supported the Salafist Nūr party. And though the Brotherhood's candidate, Mohamed Morsi, eventually won office – buoyed in large part by the votes of revolutionaries who could not abide the alternative, a former minister and prime minister under the ousted Mubarak – the results of that election revealed that the Egyptian people had a far wider variety of affiliations and allegiances than the earlier, lopsided parliamentary result would have suggested. The Muslim Brotherhood's superior embeddedness in Islamic social networks may have endowed the movement with opportunities to convince voters that it would pursue their economic betterment, but it could not cover for its failures to do so once in office. The mass protests that convened in Cairo and other Egyptian cities in June 2013 to demand the resignation of President Morsi are a powerful testament to just how fragile political Islam's dominance really was.

Chapter 7 offers additional tests of the theory. If Islamists win because they are able to take advantage of more extensive social networks than their rivals, it stands to reason that Islamists should do less well in places in which their opponents are able to call upon their own local networks (particularly those rooted in tribe and clan) to communicate with voters. We find this to have been the case in Egypt's first presidential election, where the Brotherhood lost electoral districts that were distinguished from districts in it won only by the fact that a non-Islamist rival hailed from there. Similarly, in an analysis of Tunisia's 2011 constituent assembly election, we find that places that voted against the Islamist al-Nahḍa Movement did so not because their inhabitants were less religiously-inclined, but because they could give their suffrages instead to local sons (including, in one case, the man who became Tunisia's first post-revolutionary president). What all of this suggests is that it was a party's (or candidate's) connections to voters, and not its position on issues of creed, that most determined its chances of victory in the first elections of the so-called Arab Spring.

Chapter 8 explores the causes and consequences of the dramatic overthrow of Mohamed Morsi in July 2013. For some observers, what happened on that day was a new democratic revolution to unseat an increasingly heavy-handed, theocratic, and authoritarian leader. For others, it was a military coup engineered by a so-called "deep state" that had never reconciled itself to the prospect of democracy. The argument in this book, however, suggests a different interpretation. Egypt's first experiment in democracy gave way to a military coup not because Islamists were insufficiently committed to democracy or because the military was champing at the bit to assume power, but because repeated, lopsided electoral results had convinced non-Islamists that the electoral deck was perpetually stacked against them. Thus, as we shall see, when former President Morsi called for parliamentary elections to take place in 2013, his opponents, cognizant of their inability to wage district-by-district campaign battles against their Islamist rivals, called instead for a presidential election, in which they could channel diffuse, popular anger against the president into support for a single, non-Islamist candidate. In short, each side wanted elections it knew the other side would lose. The result was a rift wide enough for the men with guns to roll their tanks through.

Finally, we take up the question of the Muslim Brotherhood's future. Observers have fretted that the impact of Morsi's overthrow on the Muslim Brotherhood and political Islamist movements more broadly will be a searing one, sending them back into the violence from which they are thought to have emerged and that the scholarly wisdom says they only recently (and half-heartedly) left behind. The orgy of violence on the streets of Egypt in July and August of 2013 would appear to confirm these grim predictions, bringing to mind the decade-long Algerian civil war, which also came after an Islamist victory was reversed by the military. But I argue that it is too early to make this judgment. The Muslim Brotherhood's electoral tradition – it may be going too far to call it a democratic one – is strong. Moreover, though the Brotherhood's (and, by extension, Islamist movement's) popularity has waned, recent survey research reveals that it retains a modicum of goodwill among a small but not insignificant portion of Egyptians, which it could parlay into a modest number of parliamentary seats (if it were allowed to). As we shall see in this book, the Brotherhood is no stranger to having elections stolen from it or abrogated, and yet it continued to participate in the electoral game despite the machinations of Egypt's authoritarian rulers. For those fearful that the Brotherhood may give itself over fully to the temptations of violent resistance, the movement's long electoral tradition may be Egypt's best hope for avoiding the abyss. The bigger question is whether those who now dominate Egypt will permit the Brothers to partake of that electoral tradition.

I began this introduction by noting how the electoral sweeps of Islamists proved disheartening to those hoping that the so-called Arab Spring would lead to pluralism. This may seem a rather quaint concern today, when military coups, and not lopsided electoral results, have proven the real danger to democracy. However, these two things are linked. For it was the repeated victories of Islamists that convinced Egypt's so-called liberals that democratic elections were a mug's game, a mere delivery system for Islamist government rather than a genuine opportunity for political competition. More than seventy years ago, American political commentator Walter Lippmann wrote that the survival of democracy "depends upon a sufficiently even balance of political power to make it impracticable for the administration to be arbitrary and for the opposition to be revolutionary and irreconcilable."[14] This no more existed in the Egypt of Mohamed Morsi than it did in the Egypt of Hosni Mubarak. It was perhaps unsurprising, then, that Egypt's democratic experiment took its undemocratic turn in the summer of 2013.

It would be disingenuous of me, however, to leave readers with the impression that the only threat to democracy posed by Islamist electoral dominance lay in the antidemocratic reaction of their thwarted opponents. This study, begun during the last years of the Mubarak era, was driven in part by concern over the Brotherhood's ideological commitments and political programs, which depart in significant respects from the liberal ideals that animate much of Western political thought, and which are – in this author's view – the surest foundation for government that is respectful of and accountable to its people. The inviolability of the individual, the equality of citizens regardless of gender or belief, the toleration of different conceptions of the good life, and the necessity of pluralism in politics are all, if not entirely alien to the Islamist worldview, far from

14 Walter Lippmann, "The Indispensable Opposition," *Atlantic Monthly*, 164, 1939; reprinted in Clinton Rossiter and James Lare, eds., *The Essential Lippmann: A Political Philosophy for Liberal Democracy*, Harvard University Press, 1982, pp. 232–234

settled within it. This study began from the premise that the electoral dominance of parties uncommitted to these principles is not something that should occasion equanimity, even if it arises as the result of processes we consider legitimate. This project, then, is my own small attempt to contribute to the cause of pluralism in Egypt by identifying the factors that made Islamists strong and their rivals weak and by piercing the aura of Islamist command and inevitability (so that voters, politicians, policy makers, and pundits can envision and begin to coordinate around alternative equilibria).

At the same time, this project also embraces the premise that, while legitimate processes may not always yield good outcomes, they should nonetheless remain inviolable. The costs of violating the rules of the democratic game may prove higher than the costs of abiding by them, even to those who found Morsi and his Muslim Brotherhood uncongenial. In a society long bereft of genuine democratic procedures, in which the ballot box was a thing sometimes manipulated and often ignored, the abrogation of an election – even one that brought to power an illiberal member of the illiberal Muslim Brotherhood – cannot but be a grave setback. And though millions of Egyptians seem genuinely supportive of what the military has wrought, one wonders how durable this satisfaction will prove to be. As Egypt continues to struggle with the economic and structural problems that proved so difficult for Morsi and his Brothers to manage, and as the so-called deep state restricts the zone of hard-won liberties in the name of "fighting terrorism," those currently celebrating the ouster of a genuinely unpopular leader may soon wonder what, precisely, they won on July 3, 2013.[15]

[15] In October 2013, the military-appointed interim government of Prime Minister Ḥāzim al-Biblāwī proposed a new law to regulate political protests, which stipulated, among other things, that would-be protesters must first secure the permission of the Ministry of the Interior. See Manṣūr Kāmil, "*Maṣādir: khilāfāt bil-ḥukūma ḥawl qānūn al-taẓāhur wa wuzarāʿ yaḥdhirūn min ghaḍab al-quwā al-madaniyya*" (Sources: "Disagreements over the Protest Law; Ministers warn of the Anger of Civil Society Forces"), *al-Miṣrī al-Yawm* (Cairo), October 31, 2013; available at: http://www.almasryalyoum.com/node/2254731.

1

Explaining Islamist Dominion

Much of the current state of theorizing on the electoral successes of Islamist parties can be captured in two Egyptian newspaper items, written more than 55 years apart. The first is a cartoon that appeared in the Muslim Brotherhood's newspaper in 1945 (Figure 1.1).[1] In it, we see two candidates addressing the same constituency. In the first panel, the (presumably secular) candidate proclaims, "I'll dig irrigation canals and drainage ditches for you. I'll get you more rations. I'll get your sons government jobs. Etc. Etc." The voters, however, appear unmoved. Turning their backs on the candidate, they grumble, "We have had our fill of such promises." In the second panel, we see the Muslim Brotherhood candidate. "God is our destiny!" he declares, reciting the first item from the Muslim Brotherhood catechism. "The Prophet is our leader! The Qur'an is our constitution! And death in the path of God is our fondest wish!" The voters lean toward him intently, smiling in approval, exclaiming, "What is more beautiful than such talk?" Presumably the next panel, if there were one, would show the Brother contentedly counting votes.[2]

The second item is a December 22, 2012 story that appeared in the Cairo-based opposition newspaper *al-Dustūr* during the referendum on the 2012 Egyptian constitution. That constitution, now suspended, had been written by an Islamist-dominated constituent assembly, and was opposed by practically every non-Islamist political party in Egypt for, among other things, its insufficient attention to the rights of women and non-Muslims. Headlined, "Oil and sugar are distributed among the poor in exchange for voting 'yes' in al-Munūfiyya," the story alleged that a leader of a local branch of the Muslim Brotherhood's Freedom and Justice Party was busily delivering basic foodstuffs to poor voters in his area and then busing those voters to polling stations to cast their ballots for what the story described as "the Brotherhood's constitution." It's impossible to know whether

[1] This and all subsequent translations are mine unless otherwise noted.

[2] The irony, of course, is that the cartoon could just as easily be read as an indictment of the Brothers, painting them as cynical manipulators of the unsophisticated masses' religious sentiments.

Figure 1.1 A cartoon depiction of religion's political appeal. From *Jarīdat al-Ikhwān al-Muslimīn* (the Brotherhood's official newspaper), January 1945.

that story is true, but if it is true, it's clear that those vote-buying efforts did not work – al-Munūfiyya's citizens actually voted against the 2012 constitution by a slim majority.

Nonetheless, both of those newspaper items - the story of the Muslim Brotherhood lavishing oil and sugar upon voters, and the cartoon depicting Egyptians swooning to the Brotherhood's Islamic oratory - encapsulate much of our thinking about the sources of political Islam's success. The cartoon reflects the widely-shared view that the Brotherhood's *religious* nature gives it a powerful advantage at the ballot box. After all, if, as Ernest Gellner (1991, 2) declared, "the hold of Islam over its believers is as strong, and in some ways even stronger, now than it was 100 years ago" – it stands to reason that parties that don religion's mantle court victory. The story of the Brotherhood's disbursement of staples reflects an alternative view of Islamist success, one that understands it not as an emotional or ecstatic reaction to the provision of spiritual incentives, but as a logical response to the provision of material ones. This account may rob Islamists of their claims to purity, but it restores to voters their reason and rationality.

These two accounts – one stressing the power of Islamist ideas, the other stressing the power of material inducements – are by no means exhaustive, but they are illustrative of the twin poles in a longstanding debate about the nature of political

Islam's success. This chapter surveys the scholarly contributions to that debate. It argues that, while both types of account have enriched our understanding of the phenomenon of political Islam, each leaves important questions unanswered. Those that locate Islamist success in Islam itself are unable to explain, let alone anticipate, variation in support for Islamist parties. By telling us why Islamist victories had to happen, they blind us to the possibility that they may not always happen (despite the impressive record amassed by Islamists since the so-called Arab Spring). In contrast, if ideational accounts are unable to explain variation in the dependent variable, existing material accounts have so far left unexplored the causes of variation in the independent variable. If Islamists are better than other parties at providing material goods to voters (or more interested in doing so), what makes them so? What prevents those other parties from mimicking the strategies and tactics that made Islamists the principal elected opposition during authoritarian rule, and the inheritors of every democratic opening since the onset of the Arab Spring?

After surveying the state of theorizing, this chapter attempts to answer these questions. Building upon previous accounts of Islamist success, it outlines an explanation for Islamist victories that anticipates variation in the phenomenon over time and space, and that can account for some of the observed differences in the behavior and organizational prowess of Islamists and their rivals over more than 50 years of Egyptian political history.

1.1 Ideational Explanations

As we have seen, for many scholars, the victories of Islamist parties across the Muslim world are a testament to the ways in which political Islam is a natural outgrowth of Islam itself. For example, Huntington (1993, 307) has argued that Islam "rejects any distinction between the religious community and the political community," and "demands that in a Muslim country the political rulers should be practicing Muslims, *sharīʿa* should be the basic law, and *ulema* should have a decisive vote in articulating, or at least reviewing and ratifying, all governmental policy." In this telling, the source of the Islamist advantage is doctrinal: Muslims are taught that erecting Islamic law and Islamizing the polity are religious imperatives. "In Islam," writes Lewis (1996, 61), "there is from the beginning an interpenetration, almost an identification, of cult and power, or religion and the state: Mohammed was not only a prophet, but a ruler." Thus, whereas Muslims constantly seek to reenact the politics of seventh-century Arabia, installing in power those who promise to rule, as Muhammad did, by the Holy Book, Christians "have distinguished between throne and altar, church and state." This theory is echoed by the political scientist James Q. Wilson, who, in one of his few interventions on the politics of Islam, tells us, "Jesus asked Christians to distinguish between what belonged to God and what belonged to Caesar. Islam made no such distinction; to it, Allah prescribed the rules for all of life, encompassing what we

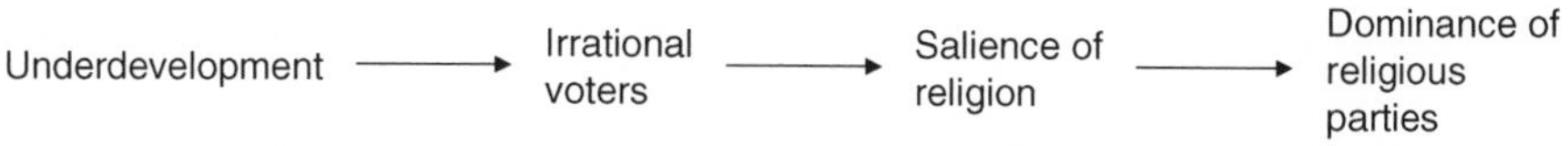

Figure 1.2 Relationship between economic development and religious politics, according to the secularization thesis.

now call the religious and secular spheres."[3] In this account, thus conditioned by their faith to demand theocracy, Muslims dutifully vote for parties that promise to impose God's will on Earth.

These kinds of arguments are often dismissed as essentializing (Said 1978), but they are also empirically problematic. Muslims can want the *sharīʿa*, or at least pay it an aggressive lip service, while voting for a variety of parties for a variety of purposes. For while it is true, for example, that 80 percent of Egyptians polled by the 2000 World Values Survey "agreed" or "strongly agreed" with the proposition that the country's laws should be based on the *sharīʿa*, 37 percent of them actually signaled a preference for the then-ruling National Democratic Party of Hosni Mubarak, while only 11.2 percent chose "independent candidates" – a category that included members of the then-banned-but-tolerated Muslim Brotherhood. Similarly, in the May 2012 contest that brought Egypt's first democratically elected president to power, only a quarter of voters cast their ballots for the Muslim Brotherhood's candidate (and eventual winner) Mohamed Morsi. Islam may or may not demand that its followers seek implementation of the *sharīʿa*, but this does not easily or automatically translate into support for political parties purporting to pursue this goal.

For other scholars, popular support for Islamist parties is less a unique outgrowth of Islamic doctrine than it is a function of economic underdevelopment and the resulting cognitive habits it engenders. The so-called secularization thesis holds that the political salience of religion is inversely related to prosperity (Norris and Inglehart 2011). Weber (1946) argued that development – the term he used was *modernity* – was instrumental in changing the way individuals think, loosing them from the shackles of superstition: "The fate of our times," he wrote, "is characterized by rationalization and intellectualization and, above all, by the disenchantment of the world." Similarly, Lipset and Rokkan (1967, 107) argued that citizens in industrialized societies "choose sides in terms of their economic interests, their shares in the increased wealth generated through the spread of the new technologies and the widening markets" rather than on the basis of faith, identity, or values. By these lights, Egypt's endemic poverty, high rate of illiteracy, and large agrarian sector mean that its citizens have not yet undergone these salutary rationalization processes and thus remain vulnerable to religion's siren song. The basic structure of this argument is outlined in Figure 1.2.

[3] James Q. Wilson, "The Reform Islam Needs," *Wall Street Journal*, November 13, 2002.

However, this narrative is at odds with much recent scholarship on Egyptian and Muslim politics. For example, ʿArafāt and Bin Nafīsa (2005), Blaydes (2006), and many others have documented the ways in which poor Egyptian voters during Mubarak-era elections sold their suffrages to the highest bidder, displaying not a lack of rationality but a surfeit of it. And, as we will see below, the cadres of the Muslim Brotherhood have long been drawn primarily from among well-educated Egyptians of the middle classes – precisely the kinds of people that Weber thought were most likely to have outgrown the type of enchanted thinking he associated with deep religious belief (see also Ibrahim 1980; al Sayyid 1993; Fahmy 1998b; Clark 2004a). We are thus unlikely to get much traction on the question of political Islam's appeal if we ascribe it solely, or even primarily, to alleged cognitive characteristics of Muslims.

Discursive Advantages

Many sensitive students of the politics of Muslim lands, drawing on theoretical literature in the study of social movements (see in particular Snow and Benford (1988); Benford and Snow (2000)), have attempted to move us beyond such declarations about the nature of Islam and toward an appraisal of the ways in which religious rhetoric may help Islamic movements to communicate with potential followers and voters. For example, Singerman (2004, 151) argues that "the vague call 'Islam is the solution' resonates on so many levels in the Muslim world and as a result it influences multiple social and political fields and encourages a collective identity." Likewise, in her learned study of Islamic mobilization in Egypt, Wickham (2003, 157) tells us that Islamists were better able than other political groups to recruit followers in part because they "adapted a respected cultural repertoire to new purposes. By framing their outreach as engaging in the *daʿwa* [proselytizing], the Islamists endowed it with a cultural legitimacy it otherwise would have lacked."[4]

Underlying all of these arguments is the notion that appeals framed in Islamic terms will be more readily understood, processed, and accepted by Muslims than those that are not. Indeed, this was clearly the theory endorsed by the government of ousted dictator Hosni Mubarak, which shortly before parliamentary elections in 2005 passed a law explicitly banning the use of religious

4 The notion that Islam has special political properties has also figured in accounts of regime durability in the Middle East. Several scholars have argued that Arab regimes deploy Islamic rhetoric and symbols to maintain the acquiescence – and quiescence – of the masses. For example, according to Eickelman and Piscatori (1996, 12), "rulers such as Sadat in Egypt and Hasan II ... in Morocco have legitimized the existing political hierarchy by referring to themselves as 'the President-Believer' (*al-raʾis al-muʾmin*) and the 'commander of the faithful' (*amir al-muʾminin*) respectively." And in the last article published on the subject of Islamic fundamentalism in *American Political Science Review*, G. Hossein Razi (1990, 75) argues that religion is a "primary source" of regime legitimacy because it "generate[s] the widest of bonds of commonly held values in the region."

slogans in campaigns.[5] When the Muslim Brotherhood's strong showing in those contests proved the new law insufficient, the regime went one step further and enshrined the prohibition on religious politicking in Article 5 of the constitution.[6]

Though arguments about the resonance of religious rhetoric have advanced our understanding of political Islam considerably, they can be faulted on two grounds. First, as Wedeen (2002, 713) has pointed out, they too risk essentialism, potentially reducing the Muslim to what the Syrian scholar Sadik J. al-Azm (1997) has called a "Homo-Islamicus," who "will always revert to type under all circumstances and regardless of the nature and depth of the historical changes he may suffer or undergo." Second, these arguments pay insufficient attention to the variation in receptivity to Islamically inflected political appeals. There is a variety of political preferences and allegiances that exist in the Muslim world. As we have seen, not all Muslims respond to the Islamist call, and even those who do now may not have in the past (and may not in the future). Moreover, in many of these countries, there are multiple "Islamic" parties, all of which deploy Islamic rhetoric and symbols, but not all of which are able to capture votes and seats. For example, in Jordan, in addition to the Muslim Brotherhood-affiliated Islamic Action Front (Jabhat al-ʿAmal al-Islāmī), we have the Islamic Centrist Party (Ḥizb al-Wasaṭ al-Islāmī) and the Arab Islamic Democratic Movement (al-Ḥarakah al-ʿArabiyah al-Islāmiyah al-Dīmuqrāṭiyah). In Egypt, in addition to the Muslim Brotherhood and a host of smaller Salafist parties, we have the Ummah Party, founded in 1983 on a pro-*sharīʿa* platform but which nonetheless has not managed to put any sort of stamp on Egyptian political life.[7] The poor fortunes of these Islamist also-rans demonstrates that however stirring Islamic rhetoric may be, it is unlikely to be the reason that some Islamist parties succeed.

Arguments about Islam's "resonance" and "cultural legitimacy" are actually specific forms of a broader class of explanations about the mobilizing power of religious appeals in general. Laitin (1986, 178) argues that political leaders "will find that their own cultural repertoires constitute a powerful mobilizing resource. The more they can demonstrate the sharing of culture with potential supporters, the more they can generate political trust." Likewise, Tarrow (1998, 112) tells us that religion is a potent tool for seducing the masses because it is "so reliable a

5 Article 11 of Law 175 of 2005 (amending Law 38 of 1972 on the People's Assembly).

6 See Ministry of Information (Wizārat al-ʿIlām), *Jadwal muqārin lil-mawād alatī taḍamanhā ṭalab al-sayyid ra'īs al-jumhūriyya li-taʿdīl 34 māda min mawād al-dustūr muqārana bil-naṣ al-qā'im fī al-dustūr wa al-naṣ kamā wāfaq alayhi majlis al-shūrā wa al-naṣ kamā wāfaqat alaihi lajnat al-shu'ūn al-dustūriyya wa al-tashrīʿiya bi majlis al-shaʿb wa al-naṣ al-nihā'ī kamā wāfaq alaihi majlis al-shaʿb* (Comparative table of the articles contained in the request of the President of the Republic for the amendment of 34 articles of the constitution compared to the current text of the constitution and the text agreed upon by the Consultative Council and the text agreed upon by the Constitutional Affairs Committee of the Peoples Assembly and the final text agreed to by the People's Assembly), 2007; available at: http://www.nilenews.tv/Files/AdminFTP/documents/1.pdf.

7 Makram Ebeid (1989, 38) wrote of the party that it "is indeed a petty opposition ... with hardly any members."

source of emotion" and offers "ready-made symbols, rituals and solidarities that can be assessed and appropriated by movement leaders." According to Perry and Aminzade (2001, 161), "Religious leaders do not have to rely only on rational persuasion since their followers can be 'moved by the spirit' rather than persuaded by rational arguments." A somewhat different argument – though similar in its attribution of special qualities to religion and culture – is Chwe's (2001) contention that religious ritual can help to grease the wheels of collective action by creating "common knowledge," letting potential participants in group endeavors know that they will not be alone in risking their necks.

But such arguments only take us so far. If religion is such a potent mobilizing resource, why don't political leaders always and at all times rush to don its mantle? Testaments to the intrinsic mobilizing power of faith bring to mind Marx's line about religion being the opiate of the masses, except that here religion is more like an amphetamine, used to whip the masses into a reliable frenzy. As noted earlier, such theories have so far left us unable to explain the variation – among countries, over time, and within countries – in the success of religious political movements. After all, Islam is a constant; the outcome we want to explain – Islamist electoral success – is a variable.

Social Changes and Psychological Strains

Of course, not all "ideational" explanations rely on such static conceptions of "Islam" or "religion" as something that always endows Islamic parties with greater potency. Many scholars argue that the force of religious appeals depends on the social context in which they are made. For example, drawing on Emile Durkheim's (1951) explanation of suicide, one influential set of accounts of political Islam's success argues that it is a function of shifts in social, economic, and political conditions (see Munson 2001, 490–4). According to Durkheim, abrupt social changes – such as sudden economic booms or busts – disrupt traditional norms, generating psychological strains that lead some individuals to kill themselves. "Every disturbance of equilibrium," he writes, "even though it achieves greater comfort and a heightening of general vitality, is an impulse to voluntary death. Whenever serious readjustments take place in the social order, whether or not due to a sudden growth or to an unexpected catastrophe, men are more inclined to self destruction" (Durkheim 1951, 246).

Neo-Durkheimian scholars of political Islam argue that social change drives people not to suicide but into the arms of the Muslim Brotherhood and the comforting certainty of its religious message. It may appear odd that a theory originally generated to explain self-immolation would be adopted by those attempting to explain the political appeal of religion, but in fact, the adaptation of Durkheim to this particular purpose is a function of just how puzzling the political power of religion has proven to be to social scientists. After all, the secularization thesis led us to believe that modernization and economic growth would consign "the political and psychological impact of religion" to the history books (Gellner 1991). So aberrant, perhaps, was the appearance of political Islam that its explanation required a theory designed for what many saw as the *ultimate* aberration: the taking of one's own life.[8]

There are multiple glosses on the Durkheimian narrative of Islamism, each identifying a different social phenomenon as the source of the strain – crushing poverty, modernization, urbanization, and authoritarianism, to name a few. For example, Monroe and Kreidie (1997, 41) tell us that "much of the attractiveness of Islamic fundamentalism lies in its ability to provide a basic identity for its adherents" at a time when such identities are in constant flux. Others argue that fundamentalism represents a backlash against modernization's assault on religious values. This is the view espoused by Appleby, Almond, and Sivan (2003, 121) who tell us that "the defining and distinctive structural cause of fundamentalist movements is secularization." As Barrington Moore (1967, 384) puts it, "In many parts of the world, when an established culture was beginning to erode, threatening some of the population, people have responded by reaffirming the traditional way of life with increasing and frantic vigor."

Others have argued that it is not necessarily modernization, but the failure of modernization, that has turned people toward religion. Berman (2003, 258) writes that Islamism thrives in societies in which "development has proceeded far enough to offer citizens a glimpse of what modernity has to offer, but not far enough to deliver it." Wickham (2003, 77–80) singles out authoritarianism, which, she says, gives rise to feelings of powerlessness and alienation. Lewis (1990) highlights Western ascendancy, telling us that Islamic fundamentalism represents "the perhaps irrational but surely historic reaction of an ancient rival against our Judeo-Christian heritage, our secular present, and the worldwide expansion of both." Barber (1995) has written of fundamentalism as a defensive response to the spread of American popular and consumer culture. Nobel laureate V. S. Naipaul (1998, 242) offers us the verdict rendered by his guide in Iran, a young man named Ali, who seems to implicate all the preceding factors in Islam's rise to political power in his country:

> This new wealth came to the cities, and the majority of the people lived in the rural areas. The younger generation of the farmers who had migrated to the cities realized that they were being cheated. More and more, from 1970 on, Islamic organizations started mushrooming. . . . And these Islamic groups also expressed the people's ideas about the Shah and his group, that they were not Islamic. The Shah and the Queen and her group started having artistic festivals. They invited musicians, poets, dancers, and all kinds of artists from abroad. There was one group that was completely nude, and they danced. There were many of those occasions. It was like putting gas on fire.

[8] It's worth noting that Durkheim's framework has been enthusiastically adapted to explain everything from the appearance of snake-handling cults in Appalachia (Flint 1980), to witch hunts in fifteenth-century Europe (Stark 2003), to political instability in developing countries (Huntington 1968).

One can be forgiven for concluding that we have not managed to move beyond Ali's exhaustive (and exhausting) litany. In large part, the proliferation of Durkheimian narratives of social strain and religious fundamentalism is a function of the difficulty of adjudicating among them. As Munson (2001, 493–4) has pointed out, this is so because such theories deal primarily with psychological states that are difficult to observe directly or test empirically. Spatial and temporal variation in support of Islamists can give us some leverage on some of the most prominent Durkheimian accounts, such as those emphasizing urbanization or other easily measurable socioeconomic variables. But every society at any given point in time is undergoing some kind of social change and the potential number of Durkheimian narratives is endless. If change underlies the success of political Islam, then the hope of observing, let alone explaining, variation in the phenomenon is likely a forlorn one.

That said, the transformations of the so-called Arab Spring give the Durkheimian paradigm new relevance. The victories of Islamists after the Arab Spring could be attributed to anxieties generated by authoritarian collapse, in which the shape of future Egyptian institutions was thrown into doubt, potentially rendering voters more receptive to those proposing to use the laws of sharīʿah to mend the country's institutional rupture. This happens to be a testable proposition. And, as we shall see, there is limited support for it. Though *sharīʿa* figured in the discourse of political elites on both sides of the religious divide, survey research conducted by the author and by independent scholars demonstrates that voters throughout Egypt's transitional period were in the main motivated by more quotidian concerns.

1.2 Material Explanations

The difficulty faced by most ideational accounts of Islamism in explaining variation in the phenomenon or in lending themselves to empirical testing has sent scholars in search of other, more tangible factors behind Islamist political success. Scholars working in this vein have generated three sets of explanations for the rise and spread of political Islam. The first focuses on the actions of the authoritarian states of the Middle East and the ways in which their repressive strategies advantaged Islamists over their secular counterparts. The second set of explanations empahsizes the actions of Islamist parties themselves, investigating how they reach out to voters, engaging in grassroots mobilization and social-service provision – such as handing out bottles of cooking oil and bags of sugar, as alleged in the newspaper report with which we opened this chapter. Finally, the third set of explanations focuses on the internal characteristics of Islamist parties, contrasting their organizational cohesion and discipline with secular parties' ostensible lack of these things.

Suppression of Secular Avenues of Protest

The first school of thought views the emergence and success of Islamism as a function of authoritarian policies designed to suppress secular forms of organization. The basic intuition behind this argument is articulated by Esposito (1999, 110), who tells us that in the Shah's Iran, "Mosques served as centers for dissent, political organization, agitation and sanctuary. The government could ban and limit political meetings and gatherings, but it could not close the mosques or ban prayer." This is echoed by Halliday (1995): "As in other societies where secular forms of protest are blocked off, religion in Iran became a symbol and an organizing center for protest that might otherwise have taken a more conventional secular form." In Egypt, Munson (2001, 502) tells us, "Mosques were the only forum in which the government would permit large congregations of people." And Kuran (1998, 122) has noted that the inability of Arab governments to "close down" mosques meant that "Islamism offer[ed] the safest forum for venting frustrations."[9]

There is much to commend this account, but, there are two ways in which it is incomplete. The first is that it neglects the ways in which regimes do suppress sacred spaces (Kurzman 1994). If mosques became focal points of dissent under authoritarianism, they did this *despite* the presence of heavy regulation by the regime. In many areas of Mubarak's Egypt (as well as Bin ʿAlī's Tunisia), mosques were locked up between prayer times. Campaigning in Egyptian mosques and churches was expressly prohibited by the electoral law, and local imams (who are employees of the Ministry of Religious Endowments) and other mosque employees actively enforced the statute.[10] During Egypt's 2005 parliamentary elections, I observed Muslim Brotherhood candidates berated on several occasions by mosque caretakers for trying to make political speeches either before or after prayers. Even sympathetic imams would urge candidates to keep their remarks brief or try to deny them the use of the microphone altogether. One imam, after failing to dissuade a Muslim Brotherhood candidate from speaking after prayer, took it on himself to rebut the man's arguments, exhorting his flock to "give our votes to him who has given us the most" – a thinly veiled reference to the candidate of the ruling National Democratic Party (NDP), who the week prior had just furnished the mosque with new carpets (the NDP candidate was a floor-coverings magnate). The totality of the regime's control of sacred space is captured in the testimony of Usāma Darra (2011, 30-1), a young Muslim Brotherhood member who broke away from the movement in 2011. The Brotherhood's antagonistic relationship with Mubarak had caused it to "lose the mosques," he lamented. Owing to the government's assiduous policing, "we [were forced to] practice our calling in the eye of a needle, and some of our youth would have killed to be able to give a brief sermon after ʿaṣr (late afternoon) prayers in a small prayer room in a remote village."

The second way in which such accounts are incomplete is that they fail to fully identify the link between mosques or religious institutions as protest spaces and

9 See also Bertus Hendriks on the political role of mosques in contemporary Iraq, "Iraq: The Complexities of an Artificial Nation," Radio Netherlands, January 27, 2005; available at: http://www.radionetherlands.nl/currentaffairs/region/middleeast/irq050127; accessed August 15, 2006

10 Article 11, Law 38 of 1972 on the People's Assembly, Arab Republic of Egypt, July 2005.

the adoption of a religious ideology by the dissidents who gather there. Though Wiktorowicz (2004) declares that the Islamist use of mosques is "analogous to the use of churches by the civil rights movement in the United States," the analogy reveals a key lacuna in the theory: the mere employment of churches as organizing centers did not cause the leaders of the civil rights movement to pursue the application of Biblical punishments for violations of God's law. Why, then, is the use of mosques thought to have had this effect in the Arab world? What is thought to take place in the mosque to transform anti-regime dissent into *Islamic* dissent? After all, the 2011 protests that brought down Hosni Mubarak made significant use of mosques, such as Masjid 'Umar Makram near the protests' epicenter in Taḥrīr Square, but this fact did not turn that uprising to some religious purpose. And after Mubarak's overthrow, mosques have even been used as staging points for protests *against* Islamists, as in February 2013, when protesters marched on the presidential palace – then occupied by the Muslim Brotherhood's Mohamed Morsi – from two mosques in the Cairo suburb of Heliopolis after the conclusion of Friday prayers.[11] What all of this demonstrates is that the link between religious forms of collective life and the dominance of Islamist political parties is more tenuous, contingent, and variable than previously thought. Greater theoretical precision about the precise role of these institutions, and the conditions under which they operate to generate Islamist victories, is necessary.

Provision of Social Services

The second materialist school of thought holds that it is the particular strategies of Islamic parties that render them more effective contestants for the suffrages of voters. Several authors have suggested that Islamists earn the loyalties of the masses through their provision of social services to those unable to afford them. An emblematic statement in this vein is Wedeen's (2003, 55): "As the state has retreated economically in the Middle East, Islamicist movements have tended to fill in the gaps, providing goods and services states do not proffer." This fundamentally clientelistic account of Islamism's appeal is echoed by Berman (2003, 260), who tells us that: "private, grass-roots, voluntary associations run by Islamists became important providers of social goods normally associated with the state." Sullivan and Abed-Kotob (1999, 23–4) suggest that "the willingness of Islamist groups, led by the Brotherhood, to step in and help local communities suffering from unemployment, poverty, inflation, and government neglect" is the major source of their "popularity" and "legitimacy." Likewise, Tessler and Nachtwey (1998, 624) attribute Islamist popularity to "the fact that many of these movements carry out an extensive array of welfare and development activities

[11] Basil El-Dabh and Ahmed Aboul Enein, "'Morsy Is Mubarak' Protesters Chant," *Daily News Egypt*, February 11, 2013; available at: http://www.dailynewsegypt.com/2013/02/11/morsy-is-mubarak-protesters-chant/.

at the grassroots level especially in poorer neighborhoods." According to Wiktorowicz (2004, 11) "Islamic NGOs [nongovernmental organizations], such as medical clinics, hospitals, charity societies, cultural centers, and schools, provide basic goods and services to demonstrate that 'Islam is the solution' to everyday problems in Muslim societies." Mahmood (2005), Rubin (2002), Kepel (1985), Ismail (1998), and Bayat (2002) all offer important contributions to this large and influential literature.

There is much to commend these explanations, which have deepened our understanding of how Islamist parties operate. However, much theoretical and empirical work remains to be done, both to measure the extent of Islamic social-service provision and to understand how it generates the electoral outcomes that are the focus of this study. The literature has generally avoided micro-level examination of the actual service-provision activities of Islamist parties. In part, this has been due to the difficulty of conducting political research in the authoritarian Middle East. As a result, the presence of Islamic – not Islamist – clinics, schools, and hospitals is simply assumed to lead directly and inexorably to popular support for Islamist parties.[12] However, without a detailed account of the link between Islamist services and Islamist electoral victories, endogenizing support for political Islam to the presence of Islamic services might be akin to attributing support for the Republican Party to the presence of the Salvation Army.[13] In fact, the pathbreaking contribution by Clark (2004b) actually found that Islamic social services in Jordan, Egypt, and Yemen were far more modest than previously believed, geared not to the poor but toward affluent individuals who could afford to pay higher prices, and, most notably, divorced from the activities of political parties.

Moreover, as noted earlier, another shortcoming of existing narratives of Islamist exchange of services for votes is that they have been insufficiently attentive to the nondemocratic, highly repressive, and extremely intrusive contexts in which Islamists have operated for much of their history. Authoritarian regulation of civil society would, at the very least, complicate any attempt by Islamists to employ the clientelistic strategy ascribed to them. Finally, and most important, we have yet to explain why competitors to Islamists are unable to provide the social services that are thought to have proven so useful to the partisans of religion. Inasmuch as social-service provision is a strategy open to all parties, why is it thought to be exclusively the province of Islamists? Is there anything to prevent nonreligious parties from distributing bottles of oil and bags of sugar?

[12] See Cammett (2013) and Cammett and Issar (2010) for important exceptions.

[13] This despite the fact that the Salvation Army (founded 1865) espouses conservative social positions. The organization's International Moral and Social Issues Council has issued positional statements on such issues as gambling, Sabbath observance, and abortion that align it with the most conservative elements of the American political landscape. See Salvation Army, International Social Justice Commission, http://www1.salvationarmy.org/IHQ/www_ihq_isjc.nsf/vw-dynamic-index/0DE8368F450505098025761B00653CEB?openDocument.

Party Organization

In recent years, scholars seeking to identify nonideological factors behind Islamist success have increasingly turned to the internal, organizational characteristics of Islamist parties. Scholars of the Muslim Brotherhood in particular have highlighted the movement's emphasis on obedience and discipline, its highly selective recruitment procedures, and a cellular structure that enabled it variously to elude the depredations of the authoritarian state, monitor and discipline its members, and generate ties of loyalty and affection among its cadres.[14] And though this literature has generally focused on the Egyptian case, similar testimonials to the superior organization of Islamists can be found in Jordan (Taraki 1995; Kamrava 1998; Wiktorowicz 2000), Tunisia (Waltz 1986; Alexander 2000), Saudi Arabia (Byman 2005), and Indonesia (Liddle and Mujani 2005), to name a few.

Such accounts raise several questions, however. First, to the extent that formal organizational structures such as clandestine-cell systems and restrictive recruitment practices are thought to have any effect on a party's electoral fortunes, the literature on parties outside the Middle Eastern context has generally suggested that this effect is negative. For example, in his study of opposition-party politics in Mexico, Greene (2007) has argued that one of the reasons opposition parties in hegemonic party systems *lose* elections is that they transform into niche parties with highly restrictive recruitment procedures designed to attract only the most committed activists, whose emphasis on ideological purity forces the party to pursue programs of limited popular appeal. In other words, precisely those characteristics that are thought to be a source of Muslim Brotherhood electoral success are identified by scholars of other regions as sources of party failure.

Second, if differences in parties' internal structures have electoral consequences, why do Middle Eastern parties not converge on the most successful model? For example, Michels (1915) famously argued that the necessities of political competition would cause all political parties to tend toward bureaucratic oligarchy. Likewise, Downs (1957) argued that parties eventually converge in their programmatic orientations on some median voter, becoming ideological ciphers like Kirchheimer's (1966) "catch-all" parties (although he recognized that the extent to which this happened depended in some part on the electoral rule). As Scarrow (1996, 13) explains, scholars have long argued that "the characteristics of parties' extra-parliamentary organizations would converge as party organizers recognized the vote-winning effectiveness of their competitors' organizational

[14] See, for example, Shadi Hamid, "How Egypt's Muslim Brotherhood Will Win," Foreignpolicy.com, November 3, 2011; available at: http://mideast.foreignpolicy.com/posts/2011/11/03/how_the_muslim_brotherhood_will_win); Eric Trager, "The Unbreakable Muslim Brotherhood," *Foreign Affairs*, July 2011; Mohamad Adam, "Brotherhood youth say tight structure is the key to its success," *Egypt Independent*, January 27, 2013; Tarek Masoud, "Why Islam Wins: Electoral Ecologies and Economies of Political Islam in Contemporary Egypt," Ph.D. thesis Yale University, Department of Political Science, December 2008, 204–14.

innovations." If this convergence has failed to occur after forty years of political competition between Islamists and their rivals, we need a theory that can account for it.

One might argue that it is the *religious* nature of Islamist parties that makes them so disciplined. This would explain both the absence of organizational isomorphism among religious and nonreligious parties in Egypt, and also why Islamist parties such as the Nūr Party are electorally potent despite not sharing the Brotherhood's formal organizational features (such as its cellular structure or restrictive recruitment practices). For example, Springborg (1989, 185) has suggested that secular parties are "vulnerable to ... fissuring because they lack the abstract appeal of membership in the community of the faithful and the organizational backbone provided by the religious structure" that, presumably, Islamists enjoy. As DiMaggio (1998) has argued, religion can provide groups with a strong "organizational culture" that allows them to remain cohesive in a fluid environment. Even policy makers have endorsed this view. In recent remarks directed at Egyptian opposition parties during the administration of Mohamed Morsi, former U.S. Secretary of State Hilary Clinton noted that "all too often people who are in the moderate, liberal world don't have the same commitment to organization and follow through" possessed by "those whose beliefs are so certain that they know exactly what they are going to try to achieve."[15] After all, the Brotherhood is not just a political organization, it is also a group of believers. As al-Bannā wrote, "We are, oh people, without boasting, the friends of God's Prophet, peace be upon him, carriers of his standard ... and God's mercy to all mankind."[16]

It is impossible to spend time with the Brothers and not observe some evidence for the proposition that religion provides a powerful resource for maintaining cohesion within groups. Those who hold positions of authority within the Brotherhood (and, by extrapolation, Salafi parties) may do so because they are seen to be effective activists or good managers, but invariably they are also thought to have reached some enhanced level of piety and understanding of the faith. Thus, vertical ties between elites and subordinates are freighted with religious and spiritual authority in a way that may not exist in other organizations. This was demonstrated to me most vividly almost seven years ago, during the parliamentary campaign of the man who from June 30, 2012, to July 3, 2013, was president of Egypt, Mohamed Morsi. I had spent an evening during the month of Ramadan making the rounds of the district's mosques with Morsi, his eldest son, and several other Brothers. In each mosque we would join the prayers – every evening during Ramadan there are long nightly prayers (*ṣalāt al-tarāwīḥ*) – and during a lull in the prayers, the candidate would get up to make a speech. We ended the

15 Speech by Secretary of State Hilary Rodham Clinton, "International Religious Freedom," Carnegie Endowment for International Peace, July 30, 2012; available at: http://www.c-spanvideo.org/program/307322-1.

16 Ḥasan al-Bannā, *Al-Ikhwān al-Muslimūn taḥt rāyat al-Qur'ān*, Dār al-Tawzīʿ wa al-Nashr al-Islāmiyya, n.d., 33

evening – by this time it was near dawn – in a mosque near Morsi's home in a part of al-Zaqāzīq called Filal al-Jāmiʿa (or University Villas).

The area was populated, as the name implies, by university faculty, and the mosque – Masjid al-Madīna al-Munawwara – was largely attended by Brotherhood members affiliated with the university and its teaching staff. The mosque had an upper floor where women and small children could attend prayers, and on this night, the mosque was nearly filled to capacity. The *fajr* (dawn) prayer was approaching, and we could hear the children upstairs running and playing and the women conversing with each other. Morsi took the microphone and began to give a version of the speech he had been giving all night – explaining how Muslim countries were in decline because they had strayed from Islam, how the West was betting on Muslims to remain neglectful of their faith, and how Muslims must confound their bet. The – admittedly mild – noise from the women's gallery continued, and I watched as Morsi's annoyance seemed to grow. Finally, he could contain himself no longer. Interrupting his speech, he thundered, "Fear God! We are not here to whoop it up, to have a nice outing with the kids! We are here to worship Allah!" It became clear that he was directing his comments squarely at the women upstairs: "Many brothers no longer come to the mosque for *laylat al-qadr* because the sisters and their children have ruined the atmosphere," he complained. The mosque grew quiet. Morsi concluded his harangue by instructing everyone to beg for forgiveness, asking them to repeat after him: "Oh Lord, you are forgiving, you love forgiveness, so forgive us." Everyone dutifully murmured their supplications.

The incident was unlike any interaction I had ever seen between a political candidate and his potential constituents. Morsi was not afraid of losing the votes of these women or their husbands or even of alienating them or hurting their feelings. Morsi's command was uncontested by that crowd. I remember thinking that Morsi's authority over his fellow Brothers and their families must clearly be religious in nature because, unlike at the other mosques, where he prayed behind the imām like the rest of us, when the time for the dawn prayer came in Masjid al-Madīna, Morsi led it. One could be forgiven for concluding, as I did then, that the Brotherhood's religiously inflected "organizational weapon" (Nasr 1994) was the source of its success. It is little wonder that one author went so far as to call the movement "unbreakable" (Trager 2011).

Even if religion constitutes a powerful resource for groups such as the Brotherhood, the question for us is whether it is somehow superior to other ideologies in generating the discipline, cohesion, and capacity for concerted action that is so often attributed to the Muslim Brotherhood. Though the results of recent Egyptian elections would seem to support this proposition, widening our empirical aperture undermines it. In order to ascertain whether religion endows religious parties with unique organizational advantages, I conducted a survey of the English-language scholarly and journalistic literature (using the Google Scholar and Google News databases) to identify all works that identify political parties with reference to their organizational qualities. My aim was to determine whether religious parties are disproportionately represented among the ranks of the most organized. Specifically, I collected all works that identified a particular political party as the "best" or "most" "organized," "disciplined," "cohesive," or "unified" party in its country. I emerged with 228 news articles and 96 scholarly articles. The earliest reference is a *New York Times* report on the victory of the Social Democratic Party in Germany, which quotes a local analyst's assessment that "the Socialists have to-day the best organized party in Germany."[17]

In all, the 324 news and scholarly articles collected refer to 108 political parties, which were then coded with respect to their ideological orientation. For example, thirteen were communist parties (as identified by their names), twenty-five were socialist (determined by whether they had the word *socialist* in their names or were listed in the member database of the Socialist International), and twelve were religious (including such parties as India's Hindu Bharatiya Janata Party, the Social Christian Party of Ecuador, the Lebanese Shīʿī party Hezbollah, and perhaps unsurprisingly, Egypt's Muslim Brotherhood). The majority of parties defied straightforward categorization, and I assigned them to a residual category of "other." This includes parties that might reasonably be identified as leftist, such as the Iraqi Baʿth, the Action Group of 1950s and 1960s Nigeria, and the Scotch Nationalists. I justify this on the grounds that their most salient ideological characteristic was something other than their position on economic and distributional issues. The breakdown of party types is presented in Figure 1.3. What these data suggest is that, when we look at parties around the world and across different time periods, there is little reason to think religious parties have an inborn organizational advantage.

Indeed, from among the parties we were able to identify, the modal party in the list of most organized, disciplined, unified, and cohesive parties was leftist. This should not surprise us: There is no a priori reason to expect leftist ideologies such as Marxism or Communism to be less capable than religious ones of generating the deep commitment necessary to cement and empower political parties. Both are organized systems of belief, with their own comprehensive conceptions of the good, and equally encompassing metaphysical assumptions. Indeed, according to Zeldin (1969, 100) scholars have long argued that "Communism is itself a religion," that Marxism "is 'like a religion,' 'a spiritual phenomenon,' [and] 'a new faith.'" As Bertrand Russell (1954, 209) put it, "Christians have faith in the Resurrection, communists have faith in Marx's Theory of Value." This is evident in the way people often talk about ideologies – as things they believe in. For example, Lee (2006, 62) recounts a conversation with a Soviet citizen in the 1970s, in which her interlocutor declared, "I *believe* in Marx and Lenin. ... You Americans are more decadent and spiritually bankrupt than we are, and that's going to destroy you in the end, mark

17 "The Royalists Rejoice: A Great Party Gain and also a Protest against Militarism," *New York Times*, June 17, 1893; available at: http://select.nytimes.com/gst/abstract.html?res=F50715F83F5515738DDDAE0994DE405B8385F0D3.

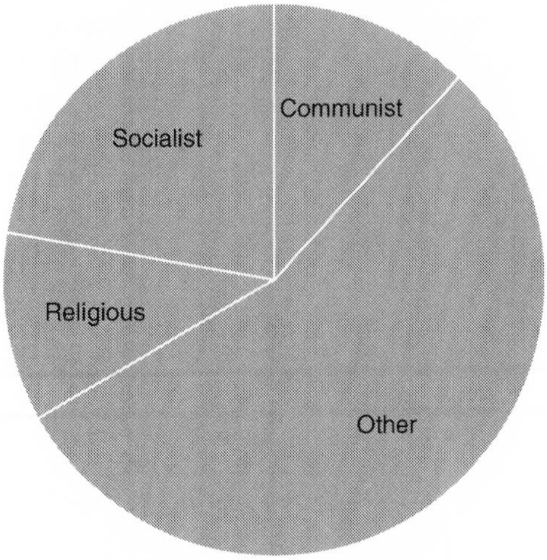

Figure 1.3 Types of parties labeled best/most "organized," "disciplined," "unified," or "cohesive" in English-language scholarly and journalistic literature, 1893–2011 ($N = 108$).

my words." Similarly, Kerr (1962, 132) describes the (no doubt opportunistic) reaction of an Egyptian journalist to Nasser's nationalization of the press, "I shouted with joy into the telephone, 'Wonderful! Wonderful!' … I had known that this law would be issued some day, not because anyone in the government had told me, but because I *believe* in socialism." (Italics are mine.) Thus, if left parties have deficits when compared with Islamist ones, a lack of "religion" is not one of them.[18]

1.3 Social and Political Institutions and Islamist Success

All the preceding accounts no doubt shed light on important aspects of Islamism, and adjudicating among them may be a mug's game. After all, as Shapiro (2002) has noted, a particular social phenomenon may admit of multiple explanations. A voter casting a ballot for the Muslim Brotherhood may be defending the *sharīʿa*, expressing gratitude for social services, choosing a trustworthy steward of the

[18] One might respond that the familiarity of Islam to Muslims renders it more capable of generating commitment than the unfamiliar ideologies of the left, which Muslims are unlikely to have grown up with in the way that they have with Islam. This is almost certainly true, and yet it is irrelevant to the hypothesis tested here – which is that Islamist parties are organizationally advantaged as a result of their ideology. Given that the number of active members of any party is small (and, as we saw in the case of the Muslim Brotherhood, deliberately kept so by restrictive recruitment practices), the question is whether members of the Brotherhood are, as a result of that group's religious ideology, more committed to their cause than members of leftist movements are to their own. There is little reason to believe this is the case.

economy, responding to a particularly well-run parliamentary campaign, or – if he or she was voting before February 11, 2011 – striking a blow against an authoritarian regime. Or he or she may be doing some subset of these things simultaneously. What this study aims to do, then, is not so much clear the decks of alternative explanations as to subject them to careful empirical testing, explore the conditions under which they apply, determine how much of the observed variation each explains, and ultimately to enrich our understanding of the phenomenon of political Islam.

However, to put it plainly, in the debate between ideational and material explanations of Islamist electoral success, this book comes down primarily on the side of the materialists. As we shall see, explanations that emphasize the emotional power and attractiveness of Islamic ideology are simply insufficient to explain the variation we observe in the support for Islamists over time and space. Instead, we are more likely to gain purchase on the question of Islamist success by attending to the Islamists and their rivals primarily as political parties (El-Ghobashy 2005), whose primary business is the courting of votes. Thus, this book stands with Przeworski and Sprague (1988, 9), who declare that "the voting behavior of individuals is an effect of the activities of political parties." What it attempts to do, then, is to identify the factors that determine what activities different parties can pursue, to whom they can appeal, and their likelihood of reaping votes in return.

I argue that the key to understanding Islamist victories lies not in ideas or party tactics, but in the different political opportunities facing Islamists and their rivals. Key in this account are the social networks that voters inhabit and the ability of political parties in new, underdeveloped party systems to access these networks and communicate with voters. In an agrarian society such as Egypt, where 32 percent of the workforce is employed in agriculture, traditional patriarchal networks, dominated by landed elites, clan leaders, and local "notables," are enduring features of the rural social order (ʿArafāt and Bin Nafīsa 2005).[19] Citizens in more urban, industrialized quarters inhabit different sets of networks, including labor unions, workers' cooperatives, and civic associations based on occupation, but also including clientelistic networks dominated by employers, businessmen, and "powerful, honored" leaders (zuʿamāʾ) of poor "popular" (shaʿbī) communities (Singerman 1995, 170). And throughout the country, people participate in "everyday networks" (Varshney 2002) of religious activity, such as mosques and Islamic charities. The relative density of these types of networks, the relative number of voters encompassed by them, and the relative embeddedness of party elites and militants within them, are important determinants of party success – especially as the disruption of authoritarianism creates moments of genuine electoral competition.

The account offered here builds on and validates much of the materialist perspective, and in particular the "resource mobilization" school, that points to Islamist parties' superior command of "societal and institutional" resources

[19] Source: *CIA World Factbook, 2012*; available at: https://www.cia.gov/library/publications/the-world-factbook/geos/eg.html.

(Wiktorowicz 2004, 34). But this study differs from those earlier contributions in three important respects. First, it attempts to explain the source of political Islam's hypothesized resource advantage. As noted earlier, the scholarly literature has either assumed that Islamists' enjoy greater resources because they work harder to establish grassroots ties to citizens, or because the authoritarian state is less able (or less willing) to repress them than their secular counterparts. This study tests those explanations and offers an alternative argument, rooted in the role of development processes in shaping the social institutions in which voters and parties are embedded. Second, it explores how Islamists use their resource advantage. Scholars have assumed that Islamists are able to employ mosques and religious institutions to mold the preferences and values of voters, transforming vague grievances into a belief in the necessity of the religious reformation of society. This study offers a much more limited view of the role of religious institutions in generating Islamist political victories. Specifically, it argues that these institutions provide opportunities for Islamists to communicate with voters and convince them of their ability to meet preexisting, exogenous, and largely nonreligious policy demands. And finally, this study interrogates the limits of the Islamist resource advantage, showing how its effect is mediated by political institutions, and how Islamists' real world policy performance can mitigate the advantages conferred on them by their superior embeddedness in mosques and other forms of religious collective life.

In the following section I describe the broad social landscape of Egypt before outlining how it contributed – both during authoritarianism and after – to the electoral strength of Islamists and the corresponding weakness of nonreligious parties, especially those that advocate on behalf of workers and the poor.

The Associational Landscape

The civic terrain in which Egyptian political parties operate is a mixture of formal and informal institutions and networks. Among the most prominent are those based on family and locality, particularly in rural areas (al-Munūfī 1980; ʿAbd al-Majīd and Musʿad 1992; Bin-Nafīsa and ʿArafāt 2005; Lust-Okar 2006). As Brown (1990, 112) writes in his pathbreaking study of peasant collective action in early twentieth century Egypt: "The family, very broadly defined, often formed the community involved in an action. From most accounts of incidents, it is clear that individuals often received the support not only of household members and close relatives but also scores, even hundreds of relatives (close and remote), friends, and associates (generally referred to as *ansar* in the newspaper accounts)." Though many of these informal networks of kith and kin were disrupted by agrarian reforms in the 1950s that broke up large landholdings and with them much of the power of the old landed families (Ansari 1986) and by steady migration to the cities, local loyalties appear to have remained strong. Watts (1993) notes that "the importance of the lineage, the family and clientage is felt at all levels of society. ... At the provincial and local levels, local notables, as reformed in the years after the 1952 revolution, have been able to act as intermediaries between ordinary people and the state." Singerman (2000, 49) has argued that the family "is an important avenue of participation that complements or parallels the formal political sphere."

If family and clan loom large in Egypt's informal associational terrain, the formal space has long been dominated by religious institutions.[20] For example, Western chroniclers of Egypt have for centuries noted the ubiquity of mosques in that land.[21] The great Orientalist Edward William Lane wrote in his 1836 *Account of the Manners and Customs of the Modern Egyptians* that "the mosques of Cairo are so numerous, that none of them is inconveniently crowded on the Friday."[22] Though Lane's observation about the capaciousness of Cairo's mosques no longer holds true – Friday prayers in most urban mosques are routinely crowded, and worshippers often spill out onto a mosque's surrounding streets – his description of their great number remains accurate. Figure 1.4 displays the number of mosques in Egypt as of 2006, broken down by governorate and type of mosque – "Friday mosques" (*jawāmiʿ*, singular *jāmiʿ*) are those large enough to conduct congretational prayers on Friday and are administered by the Ministry of Religious Endowments; "small mosques" (*zawāyā*, singular *zawya*) are prayer rooms usually established by locals. As of 2006, there were 71,931 Friday mosques and 21,118 small mosques in Egypt, for an average of one mosque for every thousand inhabitants.

As we have seen, scholars have long hypothesized that mosques served an important political role in the authoritarian Middle East, although they have generally ignored the extent to which regime-imposed restrictions on mosque-based organizing likely limited the extent to which mosques could serve as organizing centers for Islamist electoral campaigns. With the collapse of the Mubarak regime, however, and the subsequent – if temporary – advent of genuinely competitive elections, restrictions on the political use of mosques loosened considerably. For example, press accounts of the campaigns of Muslim Brotherhood and Salafist parliamentary candidates often noted that they involved visits to local mosques, where the candidates frequently delivered formal sermons. A typical example is the Freedom and Justice Party's report of the activities of two of its newly elected parliamentarians from al-Fayyūm – Ḥamdī Ṭaha and

20 This is in contrast to predominantly tribal societies such as Jordan, where formal tribal or family associations (*jamʿiyyāt ʿā'iliyya*), registered as private voluntary organizations, exist in significant number. See Baylouny (2010).

21 See, for example, James Menzies, *History of the Late Expedition to Egypt, under the Command of Lieutenant General Sir Ralph Abercrombie*, E. Miller, Glasgow, 1803, 85; Josiah Conder, *The Modern Traveller: A Popular Description, Geographical, Historical, and Topographical, of the various countries of the Globe*, Vol. 1: *Egypt, Nubia, and Abyssinia*, James Duncan, London, 1827, 271–2; Stanley Lane-Poole, *The Art of the Saracens in Egypt*, Librairie Byblos, Beirut, 1886, 7.

22 Edward William Lane, *An Account of the Manners and Customs of the Modern Egyptians: Written in Egypt during the Years 1833, 34, and 35 Partly from Notes Made during a Former Visit to that Country in the Years 1825, 26, 27, and 28*, Vol. 1, John Murray, London, 1871, 100.

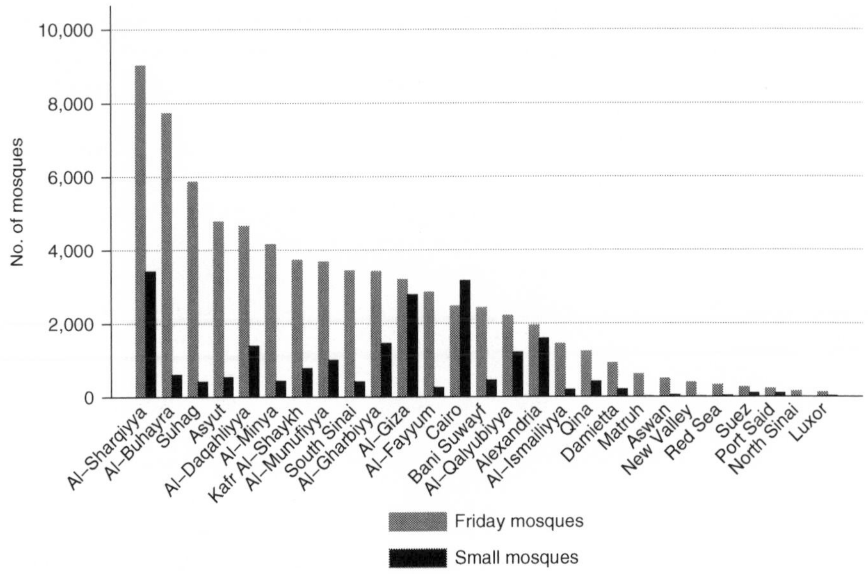

Figure 1.4 Mosques by governorate.

Aḥmad Ibrāhīm ʿUḍwī: "The tour of the two deputies began with Friday prayers, in which Aḥmad Ibrāhīm gave the sermon in the mosque of *Masākin Birnis* while Ḥamdī Ṭaha spoke in the mosque of the village of ʿAnk.[23]" Though it is likely that non-Islamist candidates also visited mosques, it was difficult for me to find reports of this. A search of the Wafd Party's newspaper revealed one story on the use of mosques in campaigning, and this was a 2010 account that criticized a Brotherhood candidate in North Sinai in 2010 for "contenting himself with offering each prayer in a different mosque and meeting the voters after each prayer."[24]

Egypt's mosques may seem like timeless features of the natural environment, but a large proportion are the product of efforts of private donors, volunteers, and Islamic charitable associations (*jamʿiyyāt khayriyya islāmiyya*).[25] The latter

[23] Manṣūr Saʿdawī and Maḥmūd Ṣalāḥ al-Dīn, "*Nuwwāb al-Ḥuriyya wa al-ʿAdālah bil-Fayyūm yuʾakkadūn* (The Deputies of the Freedom and Justice Party in al-Fayyum Affirm Their Responsibility toward the Voters)," www.hurryh.com (Freedom and Justice Party official website), December 17, 2011; available at: http://www.hurryh.com/Provinces/PartyActive_Details.aspx?News_ID=6771&ID=26.

[24] Khālid al-Sharif, "*Ihbāṭ wa ʿuzūf ʿan al-intikhābāt fī al-ʿArīsh* (Depression and Abstention from Elections in al-Arish)," al-Wafd (Cairo), November 25, 2010.

[25] Mosques are regulated by the Ministry of Religious Affairs, which places strict conditions on the building of new ones. See Aḥmad ʿAbd Allāh, "*Wazir al-ʿAwqaf al-Misri: Dawabit bina' al-masajid al-jadida hadafuha waqf iqamat al-zawāyā wa bina' masajid hadariyya* (Egyptian Minister of Religious Endowments: The Goal of the Guidelines for Building New Mosques Is to Halt the Establishment of Zawāyās and Promote Building Modern Mosques),"

make up the lion's share of private voluntary associations in Egypt, constituting what Wickham (2002) has referred to as a "parallel Islamic sector." According to Qandīl (2004), these associations have a long history in Egypt and are a natural outgrowth of Islamic traditions of almsgiving through *zakāt* (an obligatory 2.5 percent tax on savings) and *ṣadaqa* (voluntary acts of charity). The first such association, appropriately named al-Jamʿiyya al-Khayriyya al-Islāmiyya (The Islamic Charitable Society), was established in 1878 and, in addition to maintaining branches throughout the country, continues to operate a large hospital in the al-ʿAgūza section of greater Cairo. Perhaps the most well-known Islamic charity is al-Jamʿiyya al-sharʿiyya li-taʿāwun al-ʿāmilīn bil-kitāb wa al-sunna al-Muḥammadiyya (The Legitimate Society for the Cooperation of Those Who Work by the Book and Muḥammadan Traditions, henceforth abbreviated JS). This association was established in 1912, currently has almost 5,000 local units ranging from clinics to Qurʿanic study centers to preacher training institutes to day-care centers, and provides yearly support for almost half a million orphans.

There are also a large number of smaller, local associations such as al-Jamʿiyya al-Islāmiyya lil-khadamāt al-shāmila wa al-saʿāda wa al-taʿāwun (The Islamic Association for Complete Services, Happiness, and Cooperation) located in the town of Shubrā al-Khayma just north of Cairo, which offers a medical clinic, kindergarten, support for orphans, Qur'anic lessons, and a mosque. Another such association is the Islamic Beneficence Society (Jamʿiyyat al-Khayr al-Islāmiyya) in the Nile Delta governorate of al-Sharqiyya, which specializes in offering funereal services to indigent families. Figure 1.5 shows the share of private voluntary organizations, as of 2007, that are Islamic, broken down by governorate. The data are drawn from a comprehensive database of more than 17,000 private voluntary organizations maintained by the Ministry of Social Affairs in twenty-two governorates.[26] I code an association as "Islamic" if it has the words *Islām*, *Sunna*, *Qur'ān*, *Muḥammad*, *Allāh*, *Muslim*, or *Masjid* in its name; or if its official description on file with the Ministry indicates that it is Islamic, involved in teaching the Qur'an, or in building mosques; or if its postal address indicates that it is housed at a mosque. In more rural governorates, such as al-Munufiyya and al-Sharqiyya in the Nile Delta, the percentage of private voluntary organizations with Islamic characteristics approaches 50 percent. Overall, Islamic organizations account for 20 percent of the nationwide total.

Islamic charitable associations are often thought of as constituent parts of an Islamist clientelistic machine. For example, Berman (2003) has argued that the Muslim Brotherhood responded to state repression during the authoritarian period by establishing private voluntary organizations that would enable it to

al-Sharq al-Awsat, March 9, 2002; available at: http://www.aawsat.com/details.asp?article=92180&issueno=8502#.UT1AJtF4grg.

26 No data for Fayyūm, Daqahliyya, Red Sea, and South Sinai (total population 8.3 million).

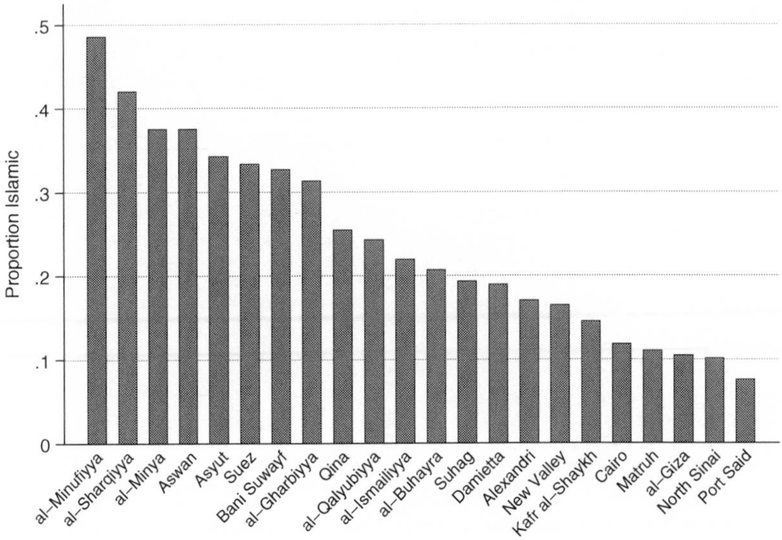

Figure 1.5 Proportion of private voluntary organizations that are Islamic, by governorate, 2007.

incubate Islamic revolution, much as Germany's National Socialists did in the early twentieth century. However, as we will see in Chapter 3, there is limited empirical support for this account. We can no more endogenize the Islamic charitable sector to the Muslim Brotherhood than we can attribute Christian charities in the West to conservative political parties. It is instead more accurate to think of religious associations as preexisting forms of social life that political parties attempt to tap into but whose existence is largely independent of those parties (Wickham 2003; Clark 2004b; Thachil 2011).

If Islamic associations only make up approximately 20 percent of the formal associational landscape in Egypt, the vast majority of associations are not religious in nature. For example, approximately 18 percent of the total number of private voluntary organizations registered with the Ministry of Social Affairs in the 2007 database are community development associations (*Jamʿiyyāt Tanmiyat al-Mujtamaʿ al-Maḥalī*). These associations (henceforth abbreviated CDAs) exist in nearly every village and community in Egypt and offer a variety of services from literacy classes to micro-credit loans to aid for the poor.

However, Egypt's CDAs are far less vital than their impressive numbers would suggest, and encompass few voters. As one writer put it, "In every village and town in Egypt there are associations bearing the name 'Community Development Association,' but they are completely divorced from what we understand as development, as corruption has nestled within them throughout the years of the old regime." Though these associations were ostensibly responsible for "encouraging small projects, developing trade and craft skills among youth and girls, innovating creative social activities," instead they functioned as "family concerns whose members were limited to relatives" of CDA chairmen.[27] The feeble nature of CDAs is in part attributable to the fact that they were more auxiliaries of the state bureaucracy than genuinely independent organizations. ʿAlī al-Muṣaylḥī, former Minister of Social Affairs, in 2010 declared that CDAs "come under the scope of the general policy of the state and the strategy of the ministry to develop local communities and increase popular participation, alongside governental efforts to determine the needs of local communities and provide the necessary resources for the implementation of development projects."[28]

The parastatal nature of CDAs is unsurprising when one considers that they actually emerged out of a government program initiated in the late 1940s to establish rural social centers to combat illiteracy and disease and "raise the standard of living in the Egyptian village in general."[29] According to Sullivan (1994, 36), the government's role in the genesis of the CDAs has given them a decidedly semiofficial character – they are often administered by public officials, receive funding from the Ministry of Social Affairs, and are generally perceived as "more of a public institution" than their religious counterparts. CDAs are often staffed by government employees paid directly by the Ministry of Social Affairs (whom they have petitioned in recent years for higher wages and permanent contracts).[30]

Other forms of nonreligious-association life are agricultural cooperatives and labor unions. Though there are more than 7,000 agricultural cooperatives in Egypt, like the CDAs, these were integrated into the state bureaucracy following the 1952 "free officers" coup (Pripstein-Posusney 1997; Bianchi 1986). Thus they are little more than "government controlled entities whose main function was to transmit government instructions about planting, marketing, and credit" (Brinkerhoff et al. 2002, 30). The same can be said of the country's formal labor unions, which are similarly quasi-state institutions. Though the Ministry of Manpower in 2009 and 2010 took the unprecedented step of recognizing independent unions for real estate tax workers, teachers, and healthcare technicians (Beinin 2012, 5), these unions remain in violation of law 35 of 1976, which stipulates that all unions must be part of the General Federation of Egyptian Trade Unions (al-Ittiḥād al-ʿām li niqābāt ʿummāl Miṣr, abbreviated GFETU). Figure 1.6 shows membership in the trade union federation, broken down by governorate, toward

27 Saʿīd al-Shaḥḥāt, "*Jamʿiyyāt tanmiya al-mujtamaʿ al-maḥalī fi ʿaṣr al-thawra* (Community Development Associations in the Age of Revolution)," al-Yawm al-Sabiʿ, April 4, 2011.

28 "*Al-Muṣaylḥī: 6898 jamʿiyya li-tanmiyat al-mujtamaʿ al-maḥali fī miṣr* (Al-Musailhy: [There Are] 6898 Community Development Associations in Egypt)," al-Misri al-Yawm (Cairo), November 15, 2010.

29 *Social Welfare in Egypt*, Ministry of Social Affairs, Royal Government of Egypt, 1950, 11.

30 Ashraf Kamāl, "*Ihtijaj muwazafi tanmiyat al-mujtamaʿ lil-mutalaba bil-tathbit Iḥtijāj muwwaẓafī tanmiyat al-mujtamaʿ lil-muṭalaba bil-tathbīt* (Protest of Community Development Employees Asking for Permanent Contracts)," al-Wafd (Cairo), July 22, 2012.

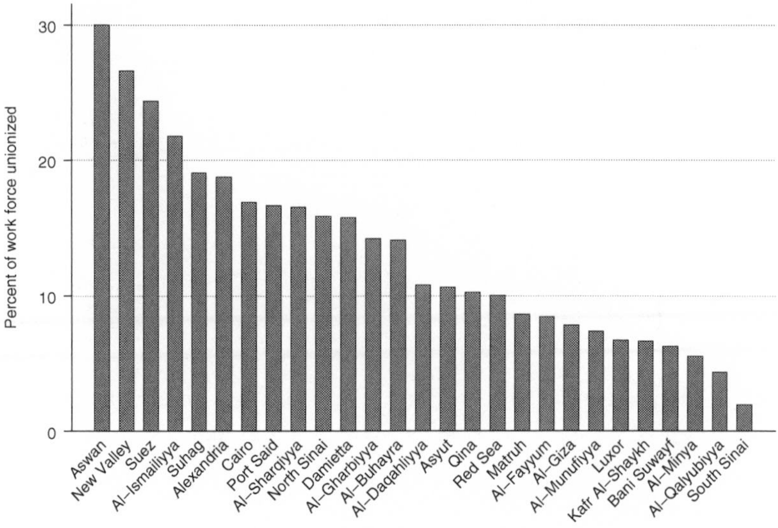

Figure 1.6 Labor union density, by governorate, 2006.

the end of the Mubarak era. Though membership in the union is mandatory, only around 12 percent of the Egyptian labor force was unionized, reflecting not only the effects of regime control but also the country's relatively small industrial base and the large informal sector, variously pegged between 40 and 60 percent of the labor force (Beinin 2012; El-Fattah 2012).

The role of Egypt's underdevelopment in limiting the size of its union sector is not well explored, as scholars have instead preferred to highlight authoritarian regulations and restrictions. However, even in the absence of such regime interventions, there would be little reason for us to expect organized labor to encompass large numbers of citizens or constitute a major component of Egyptian civic life. The mechanisms by which labor unions emerge – mass migrations to distant cities, the rending of the "institutional safety nets that had sustained [workers] in the countryside," and the development of mutual-benefit associations to pick up the slack (Hechter 2004, 422–4) – are relatively attenuated in Egypt. Thus Marx and Engels' (2012 (1848), 78) arguments about the "idiocy of rural life" aside, in the absence of massive industrialization and the attendant politics of the shop floor, class-based collective action is subordinated to traditional forms of social organization.

In order to generate a picture of the broad contours of Egyptian associational life, Figure 1.7 compares the share of private voluntary organizations made up of mutual-aid societies based on employment or occupation (such as retiree's associations or mutual-benefit societies for tradesmen) with both religious associations and CDAs. As we can see, employment-based forms of collective action are dwarfed by those based on religion and by the state-affiliated CDAs. The picture

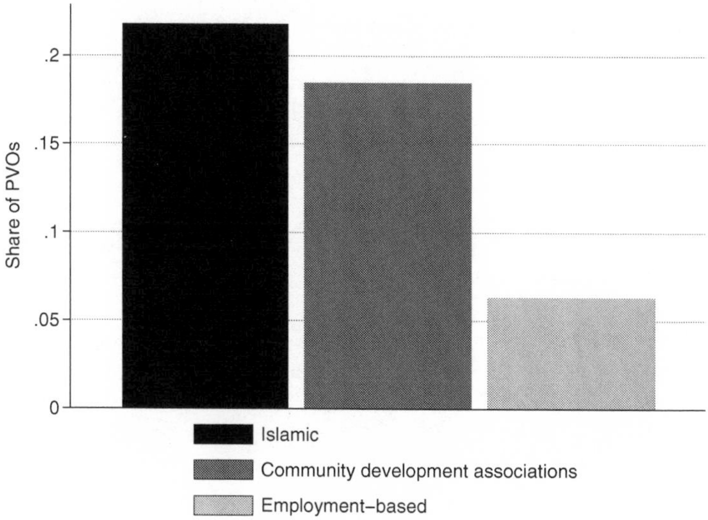

Figure 1.7 Religious vs. nonreligious associations in Egypt (based on data for 22 governorates).

we emerge with is of a formal civic landscape dominated by faith on the one hand and the state on the other, with little in the way of organizations bringing people together on the basis of class or occupation. And though one might argue that the formal sphere is deformed by the state, there is reason to believe that the informal sphere is broadly similar. Though workers and government employees have self-organized in ways that are genuinely independent of the state (Rutherford. 2008, 227–9), these primarily firm-level activities are largely concentrated in the country's industrial and urban centers (Beinin and el Hamalawy 2007).

Parties, Elections, and Communities

We now turn to the question of how the relative density of social networks of clientelism, class, and creed impact political outcomes. During the Mubarak era, in which legislative institutions were not meaningful producers of broad, national policy, electoral politics were instead about who could promise to deliver particularistic benefits to voters (ʿArafāt and Bin Nafīsa 2005; Blaydes 2010; Lust-Okar and Masoud 2010). Since the ruling party controlled the distribution of state patronage, and co-opted most clientelistic networks based on local notability, opposition party success rested on the ability to build strong programmatic linkages to their core supporters. Parties of the left, whose main constituents were precisely those poor and rural dwellers most likely to be swayed by the regime's promises of patronage or by the demands of local clientelistic relationships, were thus at a particular disavdantage. In contrast, parties that could appeal to middle class and more affluent voters – who did not need to trade their suffrages for benefits and who could instead vote based on ideological factors (such as opposition to corruption and dictatorship) – were most likely to be successful. Though the regime prevented Islamist political activists from putting their involvement in Islamic charitable and social service projects to political purposes, Brotherhood activists' embeddedness in religious institutions helped them to market their party to middle class voters who were most receptive to opponents of the ruling party.

To the extent that the advent of greater political competition after the fall of the Mubarak regime changed these dynamics, it did not do much to change the fortunes of pro-poor parties. Though the dissolution of the ruling party, and the disruption of its co-opted networks of patronage and clientelism meant that poor and rural constituencies were more available for mobilization by parties of the left, these parties – both due to decades of authoritarian control, and to patterns of underdevelopment that undermine class- and occupation-based collective action – found themselves without organic links to these constituencies. Thus, although Egyptians emerged from the Mubarak era with a strong distaste for the regime's neoliberal economic policies and an equally strong desire for redistribution and the strengthening of the welfare state, they were unable to attach these policy preferences to leftists. Instead, voters attributed these policies primarily to Islamists, who were now finally able to put their superior embeddedness in religious institutions to full political use, communicating with voters through a combination of programmatic and clientelistic appeals that few other parties could match. Thus, it was Islamists who were able to convince voters that they would correct the inegalitarian policies of the Mubarak era (even as they told other constituencies that they would continue them).

The general logic of the argument is laid out in figure 1.8. As noted earlier, in contrast to accounts that locate the superior political opportunities of Islamists, and the inferior ones of leftists, in the repressive policies of the authoritarian state, I locate them in developmental processes that limit the widespread emergence of nonkin and nonreligious social organizations. Thus, the theory presented here anticipates the same relationship between the level of development and the performance of religious parties that is posited by the secularization thesis – except where the secularization thesis holds that development's effect on the salience of religion is mediated through cognitive changes, I argue that it is mediated through social structures that affect parties' opportunities to make their case to voters. As we shall see in the following chapter, Islamists did not win – and leftists did not lose – because hordes of irrational poor people went to the polls to vote for the faith. On the contrary. The dominance of political Islam, and the tragedy of the left, is marked not by an absence of rationality, but an abundance of it.

Readers may conclude at this point that this is a book about religious parties that has precious little to say about religion. This is a charge to which I must plead guilty. By way of explanation, I offer an account of an exchange that took place almost forty years ago, between Muḥammad Ḥassanayn Haykal, former editor of

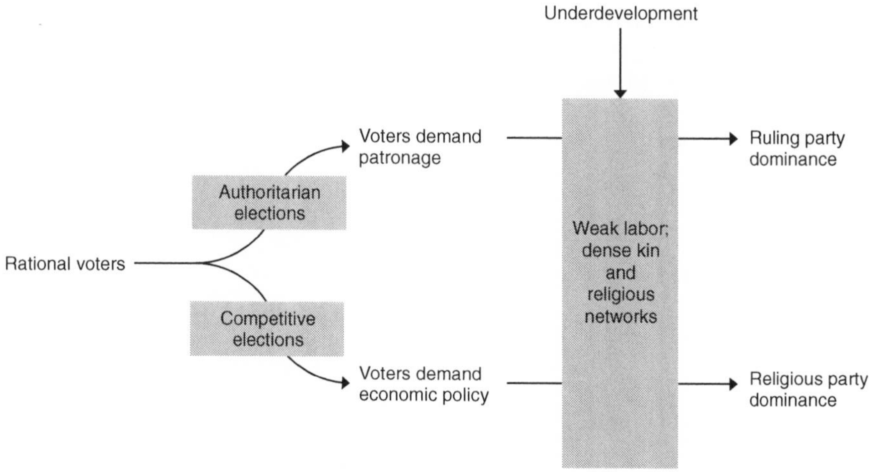

Figure 1.8 Relationship between development, political opportunity structures, and religious party dominance.

the Egyptian daily *al-Ahrām* and a top adviser to Egyptian Presidents Nasser and Sadat, and American Secretary of State Henry Kissinger amid the latter's famous "shuttle diplomacy." Haykal took it on himself to educate Kissinger as to the exact nature of the entity with which he was dealing. Egypt, he said, was far more than simply a country:

> I said to him: "You are dealing here with a force that transcends the frontiers of one country; you are dealing with an idea, a tide, a historical movement."
>
> Kissinger replied: "I don't hold with that way of thinking. I want to deal with visible forces, not with latent forces. I want to deal with states whose negotiating positions I can appraise accurately. Tell me how I am to negotiate with an idea, a tide, a historical movement?"[31]

Although Haykal probably saw Kissinger's retort as evidence of the materialistic, scheming nature of the latter's mind, this author can sympathize (if only in this) with the American Secretary of State. This book aims to treat Islamist parties not as "ideas or tides" or as elements of a diffuse social movement seen only obliquely in patterns of headscarf wearing, beard growing, or mosque attendance but as *political organizations* with strategies and resources that can be observed directly and measured with precision. Undoubtedly, something will be lost through this single-minded focus on the "visible" through this relative neglect of the power

[31] From an April 15, 1978, essay by Haykal in *al-Anwar*, a Lebanese newspaper, quoted in "Reason is Not the Key," *Journal of Palestine Studies*, Vol. 7, No. 4, (Summer 1978), pp. 156–157. The story is also recounted in Ajami (1978, 356).

of ideas and the motive force of faith. Of course, religion, faith, ideas, ideology, emotions, and passions matter, and we ignore them at our peril. Nonetheless, it is my hope that the approach outlined here will gain us more purchase on the phenomenon of interest than has hitherto been the case. In disenchanting political Islam, this study hopes to demystify it, to expose its internal clockwork, and to render it less awesome to its opponents and adherents alike.

PART I

ISLAMISTS AND THEIR RIVALS IN AUTHORITARIAN ELECTIONS

2

Clientelism and Class: The Tragedy of Leftist Opposition in Mubarak's Egypt

The mass protest that rocked Egypt on January 25, 2011, was an epoch-making event. For many, the dramatic rising up of hundreds of thousands of ordinary people to shake off the yoke of an authoritarian regime constitutes a bright line that demarcates a long, grim, dark era of stasis from a bright new one of dynamism and change. One could be forgiven, then, for thinking that there was likely to be little continuity between the politics of the old era and the new, for thinking that the Egypt of before the January 25, 2011, revolution – that country known as "Mubarak's Egypt" in much of the scholarly literature (see, e.g., Springborg 1989; Bianchi 1990; Starrett 1991; Brownlee 2002 and Blaydes 2010) – was a different place altogether from the Egypt we experience and examine today.

But, for everything that has changed in the land by the Nile, one thing has remained the same: its inhabitants continue to turn their backs on parties of the left. Though the revolution that unseated Mubarak began with the slogan "*ʿaysh, ḥurriya, ʿadāla ijtimaʿiyya* [bread, freedom, and social justice]," it ended with Islamist electoral victories that brought both the legislative and executive under the sway of religious conservatives. Likewise, during the Mubarak years, that sliver of the legislature that was captured by the opposition never featured more than a handful of leftists. Islamists – or, more specifically, the Muslim Brotherhood – dominated the space allowed to the regime's opponents (Table 2.1).

Thus, in the first parliamentary elections of the Mubarak era, in 1984, opposition parties took up fifty-eight seats (13 percent of the total), but neither of the country's main left-leaning parties, Ḥizb al-Tajammuʿ al-Waṭanī al-Taqaddumī al-Waḥdawī (National Progressive Unionist Rally, or NPUR) or the Ḥizb al-ʿAmal al-Ishtirākī (Socialist Labor Party, or SLP), managed to earn a spot, each having polled below the 8 percent threshold needed to enter parliament. In the following election, in 1987, opposition parties increased their share of the legislature to 20 percent, and yet again, the NPUR was unrepresented, having earned just 2.2 percent of the

Table 2.1 *The Muslim Brotherhood and Its Rivals in Mubarak-Era Elections*

Party	**1984**	**1987**	**1990**	**1995**	**2000**	**2005**	**2010**
National Democratic Party (al-Hizb al-Waṭanī al-Dimūqrāṭī)	390	348	360	417	388	311	420
Liberal Party (Ḥizb al-Aḥrār)	0	6	[c]	1	1	0	0
National Progressive Unionist Rally (al-Tajammuʿ al-Waṭanī al-Taqaddumī al-Waḥdawī)	0	0	5	5	6	2	5
Socialist Labor Party (Ḥizb al-ʿAmal al-Ishtirākī)	0	16	[c]	0	—	—	—
New Wafd Party (Ḥizb al-Wafd al-Jadīd)	49	36	[c]	6	7	6	6
Nasserist Party (al-Ḥizb al-Nāṣirī)	—	—	—	1	3	0	0
Muslim Brotherhood (al-Ikhwān al-Muslimūn)	9[a]	38[b]	[c]	1	17	88	1
Tomorrow Party (Ḥizb al-Ghad)	—	—	—	—	—	1	1
Democratic Peace Party (Ḥizb al-Salām al-Dimūqrāṭī)	—	—	—	—	—	0	1
Social Justice Party (Ḥizb al-ʿAdāla al-Ijtimāʿiyya)	—	—	—	0	0	0	1
Democratic Generation Party (Ḥizb al-Jīl al-Dimūqrāṭī)	—	—	—	—	—	0	1
Independents	—	4	79	13	16	24	67
TOTAL	448	448	444	444	442	432[d]	504[e]

(*Sources:* ʿAbd al-Gawwād 2005; ʿAwaḍ and Tawfīq 1996, 346; and author's calculations).

[a] In alliance with Wafd.

[b] In alliance with SLP.

[c] Election boycott.

[d] Twelve contests undecided.

[e] Four contests undecided.

nationwide vote. Though the left was represented, after a fashion, in the 1987 parliament by the Socialist Labor Party – an Islamist-cum-leftist party that emerged from the fascist Miṣr al-Fatāh (Young Egypt) Party of the monarchic period – that party earned its small handful of seats only through an alliance with the Muslim Brotherhood and the right-wing Liberal Party (Ḥizb al-Aḥrār). The peak of opposition performance came in 2005, when parties other than the National Democratic Party (NDP) captured ninety-seven (or 22 percent) of the seats in parliament. However, of these, only two went to the NPUR. The Muslim Brotherhood snared eighty-eight.

Though there is, as one might expect, some volatility in the Islamist seat share throughout the authoritarian period – because electoral successes in one round (as in 2005) were followed up by regime manipulations in subsequent ones (as in 2010, when the Muslim Brotherhood lost all but one of its seats) – the electoral transcript of the left is marked by a distressingly constant modesty. This moribund track record is particularly striking when one considers the fact that voter turnout in Egyptian elections prior to the 2011 revolution was generally skewed toward the poor. Blaydes (2010, 117) has argued that illiterate Egyptians were between two and three times more likely to vote than their literate counterparts – who perhaps could see the autocrat's electoral game for what it was. The left's chronic inability to earn votes in an electoral environment dominated by its natural constituency has been taken by many as evidence of some deep dysfunction – a pervasive organizational shortcoming, an ideology noxious to vast number of people, or some other systematic impairment that can explain not just why the left lost under Mubarak but also why it loses today and will continue to lose in the future.

This chapter offers a reexamination of the long history of leftist underperformance in the authoritarian elections of the Mubarak period. It assesses and ultimately dismisses arguments that locate the poor performance of the left in ideological factors or in leftist parties' diminished competence or insufficient desire to win votes and seats. Instead, it argues that the story of the left in Mubarak's Egypt is one of a party of committed activists being forced to play a game they could not win. The no-win nature of the game was not strictly a function of repression – after all, Islamists were able to win elections despite repeated visitation by the brutalities of the regime – but of the incentives facing voters in elections where the patronage of the regime was the mother's milk of politics. The tragedy of the left, I argue, was that poor voters, who might ordinarily constitute a natural vote bank for parties of the left, could not pass up promises of patronage from the regime and its satraps to hazard their votes on an opposition party, no matter how ideologically congenial that party might have been. After all, rational voters need not have had high discount rates in order to choose the regime's immediate beneficence over the leftist opposition's rather more distant promise of redistribution conditional on democratic transition. The choice for a party of the left under those distinctly unpromising circumstances was either to abandon the poor or to keep losing elections. The SLP, never a firm party of the left, chose the former option, allying with the Muslim Brotherhood. The NPUR chose the latter option, staying with the poor even though the poor could not stay with it. The result was a string of electoral losses that severely damaged the party's reputation and from which it has yet to – and may never – recover.

2.1 Explanations for Leftist Weakness

The weakness of the Egyptian and, more broadly, Arab left has long consumed scholars of and activists in the region. Some – usually those on the left themselves – have argued that the near absence of left parties from the legislatures and chancellories of Arab power was a function of targeted repression and electoral fraud as authoritarian governments connived to prevent the emergence of dangerous leftist alternatives. Others have argued that the left's electoral lassitude was not a function of exclusion but of its opposite. In this telling, parties of the left were co-opted by autocrats, content to feed off the occasional benifences of the ruling party rather than do the hard work of building and representing constituencies. Finally, still others have argued that the fault lies in global, world-historical developments that reduced the attractiveness of leftist ideology, sending people in search of alternatives (often found in the faith) unmarred by the left's association with the failed socialist projects of Soviet-dominated Eastern Europe. All these arguments are important and influential, and each constitutes a facet of the conventional wisdom regarding the Arab left. And not one of them stands up to empirical scrutiny.

Repression and Co-Optation

If one were to ask a leftist politician why the left won so few seats in Mubarak's elections, the response would invariably be to blame the machinations of the regime. Rifʿat al-Saʿīd, chairman of the NPUR, told one interviewer in 2010 that

> The main problem is that the whole electoral scene is rigged systematically. The security forces are intervening in favor of the ruling National Democratic Party candidates. Members of the local administration affiliated with municipal councils were heavily involved – a practice they think would secure their positions as officials since they are all members of the NDP. All that combined ruins the electoral process.[1]

Saʿīd was of course right. Egyptian elections prior to the January 25 revolution were nowhere near free and fair, despite the regime's assurances.[2] Legitimate

[1] Ahmed Zaki Osman, "Interview with Tagammu Party Chairman," *Egypt Independent*, December 22, 2010; available at: http://www.egyptindependent.com/news/interview-tagammu-party-chairman.

[2] Prior to the November 2010 elections, widely recognized to be the least free of the Mubarak era, the president had earnestly declared his and his party's "aspiration to conduct free and clean elections,

voters were frequently barred from casting ballots, whereas nonresidents and even the deceased found healthy representation on the voter rolls (al-Buraʿī 1996, 146–7). Regime-backed candidates, such as former Minister of Military Production Sayyid Mishʿal, former Finance Minister Youssef Boutros Ghali, and former Housing Minister Muḥammad Ibrāhīm Sulayān, were often accused of abusing their authority and busing in public-sector workers to vote on their behalf.[3] When this was not enough, the police would intervene to prevent the supporters of ruling-party opponents from casting their ballots. For example, during the 2005 parliamentary elections in the town of al-Zaqāzīq, supporters of the man who would go on to become Egypt's first democratically elected president, Mohamed Morsi, were prevented from voting when the Central Security Forces shut down a polling station in a Brotherhood stronghold.[4] Finally, vote tallies were often massaged to produce results favorable to the regime, often by judicial officials charged with ensuring the integrity of the balloting. Shortly after the 2005 elections, the Lawyers Syndicate released a list of twenty-two judges whom it accused of participating in vote fraud.[5]

The general impression of Mubarak-era elections as occasions of regime malfeasance is neatly summed up in a cartoon that ran in the December 1, 2005, issue of the newspaper *ʾĀfāq ʿArabiyya* (Figure 2.1). Entitled "Parliament and the ascent to the future," the cartoon depicts the NDP as a thief scaling the walls of parliament, a sack of purloined votes slung over his shoulder. A police officer, ostensibly there to ensure the integrity of the electoral process, instead abets the crime by resolutely ignoring it, declaring into his radio (presumably to some superior), "All is well, sir. We are completely nonpartisan." But, as true as such critiques of Mubarak-era elections might be, it is probably unfair to blame the entirety of the left's failures on the machinations of a grasping authoritarian regime. After all, electoral abuses hurt all opposition parties – in fact, the (now-defunct) newspaper that printed the cartoon in Figure 2.1 was actually

under the supervision of high council for elections, and the supervision of Egyptian civil society, that provide the broadest opportunity for voter participation." No one had expected him to live up to the promise, of course, and he was overthrown a few short months later.

3 See *Taqrīr markaz Sawāsīa li huqūq al-insān wa munāhaḍa al-tamyīz ʿan al-intikhābāt al-barlamāniyya 2005* (The Report of the Sawasya Center for Human Rights and Anti-Discrimination about the 2005 Parliamentary Elections), Sawasya Center for Human Rights and Anti-Discrimination, Cairo, 2005, 178; and Aḥmad Thābit, "*Idārat tanzīm wa tahdīd al-dawāʾir al-intikhābiyya* (Management of the Organization and Drawing of Electoral Districts)," Ahram Center for Political and Strategic Studies, Cairo, 2006; available at http://acpss.ahram.org.eg/ahram/2001/1/1/CONF38.HTM.

4 Ḥussayn al-ʿAdwī, "*Quwwāt al-amn taqtal 10 muwāṭinīn wa tuṣīb al-miʾāt wa tamnaʿ al-nākhibīn min al-taṣwīt* (Security Forces Kill 10 Citizens and Injure Hundreds and Prevent Voters from Voting)," *al-Shaʿb* (Cairo), December 9, 2005; available at http://alarabnews.com/alshaab/2005/09-12-2005/aa.htm.

5 Ḥusām Maḥmūd, "*Niqābat al-Muḥāmīn tuṣaddar qāʾimat al-quḍā al-muzawwarīn* (The Lawyers Syndicate Issues the List of Vote-Rigging Judges)," *Ikhwān Online*, December 18, 2005; available at: http://www.ikhwanonline.com/Article.asp?ArtID=16774&SecID=0.

Figure 2.1 An illustrated critique of Mubarak-era elections. (*Source*: *ʾĀfāq ʿArabiyya*, 1, December 2005, Vol. 1, No. 737, p. 1).

affiliated with the Muslim Brotherhood. And yet, despite also having to contend with regime trickery, the Brotherhood still managed to win seats in parliament.

In response, some on the left have argued that leftist parties were singled out for attack by the agents of the state. It is hard to credit these claims. By all accounts, it was the Islamists, and not the left, who were targeted during election times. Even Blaydes (2010, 53), who has insisted that Mubarak's elections were "genuinely competitive," has admitted that the "limited number of cases" of electoral manipulation were "usually aimed at the … Muslim Brotherhood." For example, during the 1987 parliamentary elections, Hendriks (1987, 23) reported that "a country-wide wave of arrests of Muslim Brothers, particularly prospective poll watchers, started a few days before the elections." And though the police "also arrested small numbers of leftist militants," according to Hendriks, "unlike Islamist detainees, they were usually released after a few hours." Thus, while the leftist intellectual and activist Muhammad Sid Ahmed (1982, 20) complained that "we were harassed, while all doors were open to the religious opposition," the reality is closer to the opposite.

Perhaps in recognition of this fact, still, others have argued that the left's poor electoral representation came not because it was harassed by the regime but because it was sponsored by it. In this telling, secular parties such as the NPUR were handmaidens of the dominant authoritarian order, content to play the role of loyal opposition in exchange for the state's forbearance and occasional generosity. And playing the part of the loyal opposition means not competing too avidly against the ruling party. As Lust-Okar (2005, 171) put it, parties such as the NPUR "committed themselves to the maintenance of the regime. In return, they are allowed to express their demands and enjoy the benefits of participation." During the Mubarak years, these (admittedly meager) benefits included a small annual stipend (approximately $18,000, plus $1,000 for every member of the party serving in parliament), permission to publish party newspapers, and the right to print two of those newspapers at reduced rates on government-owned printing presses.[6] Thus Zartman (1990, 236) labeled the NPUR and its counterparts among the official Mubarak-era opposition as "tame" parties that "disagreed only a little with the government, criticized only a bit, and [were] easily co-opted." Or, in the words of Azmi Ashour, "Their existence and scope of operations were contingent on a relationship of dependency on the dominant NDP that would bestow or withhold its favours at whim."[7]

This proposition was not without evidence. After all, Rifʿat al-Saʿīd, the NPUR chairman, was often criticized by activists within his own party for being insufficiently militant toward the Mubarak regime. In 1995, he was even appointed by the president to a seat in the upper house of parliament (Majlis al-Shūra), widely viewed as a sign of his accomodation with his ostensible oppressors. In an interview with *al-Ahrām* in 2005, the party leader further cemented his reputation as Mubarak's ally by criticizing his compatriots in the Egyptian pro-democracy movement Kifāya[8] for attacking the president and his family. "They insist on raising slogans like 'no to succession, no to the extension of President Mubarak's rule,' " he complained. "Why this insistence on the question of inheritance?" he asked.[9] Later that year, after his party's stunning defeat in the parliamentary elections that saw the Muslim Brothers capture a fifth of the legislature – and which saw the NPUR's founder, Khālid Muḥyī al-Dīn, lose a seat he had held for fifteen

6 Prior to the amendment of the political parties law (Law 40 of 1977) in 2005, the cash subsidy was only 50,000 pounds (which was a sum of some worth prior to the pound float in 2004), no payment per member of parliament was included, and the number of press licenses that could be enjoyed by a political party was theoretically unlimited. Prior to 1995, parties were allocated a ration of visas for the *Hajj* (the annual Muslim pilgrimage to Mecca), which a party could sell to would-be pilgrims at a tidy profit or distribute as patronage.

7 Azmi Ashour, "From Kifaya to Tamarrod," *Al-Ahram Weekly* (Cairo), June 12, 2013; available at: http://weekly.ahram.org.eg/News/2959/21/From-Kifaya–to–Tamarod.aspx.

8 Officially known as the Egyptian Movement for Change (al-Ḥaraka al-Miṣriyya min ajl al-Taghyīr. Kifāya, its informal moniker, means "enough."

9 Aziza Sami, "Rifaat El-Said: Which Way Will He Bend Next?" *Al-Ahram Weekly*, (Cairo), July 7–13, 2005; available at: http://weekly.ahram.org.eg/2005/750/profile.htm. It is important to note that Saʿīd was not indicating his assent to the succession of Mubarak's younger son, Gamal. Instead, he resisted the focus on hereditary succession because he thought, as of 2005, that it was highly unlikely: "Is it not now obvious," he said in the same interview, "that there is no longer the remotest chance of the president's son acceding?"

years – Saʿīd gave an interview to a Western reporter in which he seemed less like an opposition activist and more like someone who had "slipped into a confortable convalescence" (Dobson 2012, 134). "I am not disappointed," Saʿīd allegedly told his interlocutor. "We know how to suffer." It was not lost on his interviewer that as Saʿīd said this, bodyguards provided to him by the regime – presumably to protect against bloodthirsty Islamists – stood watch outside his office.

But Saʿīd's apparent cosiness with the regime of Mubarak is not enough to indict his party and is unlikely to help explain why the NPUR did so poorly at the ballot box. Other political parties, including the Muslim Brotherhood, also curried the favor of the regime when it suited them, and it does not take much effort to cherry-pick quotes from senior Muslim Brotherhood leaders that give them, too, the appearance of accommodation with Mubarak's dictatorship. For example, in June 2004, when Mubarak traveled to Germany for medical treatment, Muḥammad Mahdī ʿĀkif, the Brotherhood's seventh general guide, issued a press release wishing the president well and asking "almighty God to bless him with health and vigor, and to return him to Egypt as soon as possible healthy and happy, and to protect him and our beloved Egypt from all evil."[10] And in a July 2005 interview, ʿĀkif declared his willingness to "sit down" with Mubarak to solve Egypt's problems.[11] Moreover, Rifʿat al-Saʿīd's distaste for attacks on President Mubarak's person was evidently shared by ʿĀkif's successor, Muḥammad Badīʿ, who in an April 2010 interview called Mubarak "the father of all Egyptians."[12] Former member of parliament and leading anti-Mubarak dissident ʿAlāʾ ʿAbd al-Munʿim has testified to the extent of the Brotherhood's reluctance to offend the regime. He tells of a meeting of opposition figures – including two members of the Muslim Brotherhood, Muḥammad al-Biltāgī and Muḥsin Rāḍī – in his office on January 23, 2011, to craft a statement that the group would issue during demonstrations in front of the high court on January 25:

> The first line in that statement was to prohibit Muhammad Hosni Mubarak or his son from running, because the demand for the fall of the regime had not yet appeared, and the ceiling of our ambitions is that he would not run again. And the only ones who objected to these words among all of us were [Brotherhood representatives] Muḥammad al-Biltāgī and Muḥsin Rāḍī. ... They said, "We should not even mention Mubarak."[13]

[10] Muḥammad al-Sharīf, "*Ākif: Natamanā lil-raʾīs Mubārak al-shifāʾ al-ʿājil* (ʿĀkif: We Wish President Mubarak a Speedy Recovery)," Ikhwanonline.com, June 6, 2004; available at: http://www.ikhwanonline.com/new/Article.aspx?ArtID=7277&SecID=0.

[11] Ḥassan ʿAllām, "*Al-Murshid al-ʿām li-jamāʿat al-Ikhwān al-Muslimīn: Nuʾayyid tarshīḥ Mubārak wa atmanā al-julūs maʿhu* (The General Guide of the Society of Muslim Brothers: We Support the Nomination of Mubarak and I Hope to Sit with Him)," *Ākhir Sāʿa*, Issue 3691, July 20, 2005. It is important to note that though ʿĀkif takes a nonconfrontational tone toward the president, nowhere in the actual interview does he say what is attributed to him in the title of the article – that the Muslim Brotherhood supported Mubarak's candidacy for the presidency.

[12] Munā al-Shādhlī, Interview with Muḥammad Badīʿ, *al-ʿĀshira Masāʾan*, April 15, 2010.

[13] ʿAmr Adīb and Ḍiyāʾ Rashwān, Interview with ʿAlāʾ ʿAbd al-Munʿim, *al-Qāhira al-Yawm*, June 19, 2013.

Finally, there is evidence that the Brotherhood's engagement with the regime went beyond idle flattery and the avoidance of personal attacks. According to documents leaked in 2011 from State Security Investigations (Mabāḥith amn al-dawla), the arm of the Ministry of the Interior responsible for policing political opposition, leaders from the Muslim Brotherhood – including future-President Mohamed Morsi – allegedly conferred with state security officials in 2005 to coordinate its nominees in that year's parliamentary elections and agreed to reduce the number of candidates the Brotherhood would field against the ruling party.[14]

None of this – the warm words of Brotherhood leaders for President Mubarak, the reluctance to stoke the regime's ire by addressing highly sensitive topics, or even the alleged electoral cooperation between the Brotherhood and the regime – should be taken as evidence of the Brotherhood's co-optation by the regime and neither should equivalent behaviors by leaders of the NPUR. Political life under Mubarak had a particular language and grammar – both the left and the Islamists partook of it and observed its red lines. Besides, for every instance of comity between the regime and the leader of the NPUR, we have instances of genuine opposition. The party's newspaper, *al-Ahālī*, was a vociferous critic of the Mubarak regime and of its foreign and economic policies in particular. Nor was the party's criticism restricted to the medium of print: Table 2.2 is a list of street demonstrations led by the party from 2003 to 2005 and the issues they covered – the lack of political freedom was a recurring theme. This was not a quiescent handmaiden of the regime.

Finally, even if one clings to the image of the NPUR as a co-opted party, close attention to the history of the party suggests that this co-optation (to the extent that it existed) was probably less a cause of the party's electoral weakness than a consequence of it. Though the NPUR was, like other opposition parties during Mubarak's latter years, routinely derided as being the regime's plaything, it began its life as the foremost opponent of the regime of Anwar Sadat and his attempts to liberalize the country's economy and reorient its foreign policy away from Moscow and toward Washington. In fact, if one were to have tried to identify a co-opted group in Sadat's Egypt, it would not have been the left, but rather the Muslim Brotherhood, whom Sadat released from Nasser's prisons in 1971. According to Rutherford (2008, 82), Sadat "encouraged the MB to organize on university campuses in order to offset the growing influence of leftist and Nasserist groups." While the leftists were demonstrating against the president and

14 Aḥmad ʿAbd al-Fattāḥ, "*Wathāʾiq amn al-dawla: Itifāq maʿ al-Shāṭir wa Mursī ʿala ikhlāʾ dawāʾir fi intikhābāt 2005* (Documents of State Security: Agreement with al-Shāṭir and Mursī to Abstain from Some Districts in the 2005 Elections), *al-Miṣrī al-Yawm* (Cairo), March 6, 2012; and Hānī al-Wazīrī and Muḥammad Ṭāriq, "*Al-Ikhwān taʿtarif rasmiyan: Ijtamaʿnā maʿ amn al-dawla fi 2005 liltansīq lilintikhābāt* (The Brotherhood Confesses Officially: We Met with State Security in 2005 to Coordinate for the Elections)," *al-Waṭan* (Cairo), June 13, 2012; available at: http://www.elwatannews.com/news/details/15328.

Table 2.2 *NPUR Demonstrations, 2003–2005*

Date	Location	Issue
March 10, 2003	People's Assembly	Prices
December 24, 2003	Tahrīr Square, downtown Cairo	Political reform
February 23, 2004	Tahrīr Square, downtown Cairo	Palestine
March 2, 2004	Tahrīr Sqare, downtown Cairo	Iraq, Palestine
August 30, 2004	Red Cross, Cairo	Palestine
November 25, 2004	Downtown Cairo	Palestine, Iraq
December 17, 2004	People's Assembly	Prices, unemployment
December 25, 2004	NPUR headquarters, Cairo	Prices
March 9, 2005	People's Assembly	Constitutional amendments
May 23, 2005	Council of State	Referendum
July 6, 2005	Imbaba, Giza	Emergency law
July 21, 2005	Cairo	Political reform
July 31, 2005	Cairo	[Government] terrorism
August 13, 2005	Cairo/al-Gīza	Agricultural policy/corruption
September 10, 2005	Cairo	Presidential election

Source: Al-Tajammuʿ fī al-Shāriʿ (The NPUR in the Streets), n.d.

his policies, the Brotherhood's third general guide ʿUmar al-Tilmissānī was telling agitated university students to "mind their own business, stay out of trouble, and worship God" (Rutherford 2008, 83).

The NPUR was established in 1977, spun off from the former ruling party, the Arab Socialist Union (al-Ittiḥād al-Ishtirākī al-ʿArabī) during Sadat's slow reintroduction of multiparty politics after two decades of one-party rule. The NPUR's founder, Khālid Muḥyi al-Dīn, had been a member of the group of "Free Officers" that overthrew King Farouk in 1952, but had split with Nasser over the latter's anti-Communism (Sadat had dubbed Muḥyī al-Dīn "the Red Major") and abrogation of parliamentary democracy.[15] If Sadat was hoping that his old comrade would prove loyal, he was to be disappointed. Instead, the NPUR quickly established itself as a thorn in the regime's side. When Sadat announced in January 1977 the lifting of subsidies for basic foodstuffs, the NPUR threw itself into organizing protests, and the resulting demonstrations posed the most serious challenge to the regime until Mubarak's overthrow thirty-four years later. When the president made a dramatic peace overture to Israel with a trip to Jerusalem in November of that year, the party condemned him for betraying the Arab cause (Sid-Ahmed 1987, 26). The president for his part slammed the NPUR's newspaper as "full of anti-government hate and bitterness" and took steps to silence

[15] Khaled Dawoud, "The Red Major," *Al-Ahram Weekly*, No. 595, July 18–24, 2002; available at: http://weekly.ahram.org.eg/2002/595/sc81.htm.

it along with his Islamist and secular opposition (Keinle 2001, 19).[16] In fact, so frustrated was Sadat with the NPUR that he attempted to sideline it by allowing the creation of an alternative leftist party, the Socialist Labor Party (SLP), and encouraging members of the ruling party (including his brother-in-law) to join it (although eventually that party turned against him, too).[17]

The NPUR's record of spirited opposition did not end with Sadat's assassination at the hands of Islamist militants on October 6, 1981. Just days after the president's murder, the party issued a highly charged statement opposing the ascension of his vice president, Hosni Mubarak, to the presidency on the grounds that the would-be president had not repudiated his predecessor's deeply unpopular policies:

> The candidate Muhammad Hosni Mubarak has hastened to issue press statements and has given a speech to the People's Assembly in which he adopted all of the past positions of the department president Muhammad Anwar al-Sadat. These positions were opposed by our party, and we consider our opposition to them part of our patriotic political work in the past period, and these are our positions toward the Camp David Accords and the policy of a separate peace with Israel, the policy of linking Egypt to the American designs on the region, and the economic policy that has led to the immiseration and suffering of the masses.[18]

In 1987, on the eve of a referendum that would give Mubarak the second of his five terms in office, the party once again urged voters to reject the president's bid. Thus, even if the party subsequently muted its opposition to the president (and this is by no means as clear-cut as some would make it out to be), the shift was precisely that – a shift – and not a function of the party's status as an "official" opposition party.

The upshot of this discussion is that the left was neither uniquely repressed nor uniquely co-opted under the regime that dominated Egypt prior to January 25, 2011. And yet whereas Islamists were able to surmount the various difficulties thrown up by the autocrat and his agents, the left suffered defeat after defeat. What this suggests is that as despicable and devious as the authoritarian state was, its actions were probably not to blame for the chronic weakness of the Egyptian left.

16 See Christopher Wren, "Sadat Steps Up Offensive to Silence His Critics," *New York Times*, May 19, 1978; and "Sadat Plans Drive on Political Critics," *New York Times*, May 23, 1978.

17 See Zartman (1990, 236). The extent to which the SLP represented a genuine leftist alternative is debatable – its founder, Ibrahim Shukri, explicitly identified it as the reincarnation of the Young Egypt party, a fascist organization that had operated in Egypt from 1933 to 1952 under different names – including the Islamic Nationalist Party (Al-Ḥizb al-Waṭanī al-Islāmī), the Socialist Democratic Party of Egypt (Ḥizb Miṣr al-Ishtirākī al-Dimūqrāṭī), and the Socialist Party of Egypt (Ḥizb Miṣr al-Ishtirākī) – and whose ideology was a mixture of Arab nationalism, socialism, and Islamism (Jankowski 1975).

18 "*Bayān al-Tajammu' bisha'n intikhāb Mubārak lifatra al-ri'āsa al-'ūlā* (Statement of the NPUR Regarding the Election of Mubarak to the First Term)," October 11, 1981; reprinted in Khālid Muḥyī al-Dīn (ed.), *Li Hadhā Nu'āriḍ Mubārak* (For This We Oppose Mubarak), al-Ahali Publishing House, Cairo, October 1987, 497–8.

The Taint of Socialism?

If neither repression nor co-optation was the cause of the left's inability to earn a significant place in the (admittedly stunted) legislature of the Mubarak era, then perhaps the fault lies with the left itself. Several scholars have argued that left's weakness was the result of historical developments that decreased the attractiveness of statist, redistributive political projects around the world. For example, some have pointed to the dissolution of the Soviet Union as a blow from which left parties in the Arab world have never recovered. As Said (2005, 69) tells us, "Progressive forces [in the Arab world] were shattered by the collapse of the Soviet Union and the socialist bloc." Kamrava (1998, 145) remarks that the "collapse of the Soviet Union" reinforced "the general perception in the Arab world ... that leftist ideologies have largely failed." Ehteshami and Murphy (1996, 765) write that "Communist and leftist parties ... have little ideological credibility in the aftermath of the Soviet Union and the submission of communist economies around the world to the capitalist wave." And in her discussion of the decline of leftist parties in Jordan, Lust-Okar (2001, 557) speaks of the "discrediting of the ideological bases" of leftist parties as a result of "the fall of the USSR and the democracy movement in Eastern Europe." Such arguments have never been put to any substantive test, but it is difficult to credit them. After all, the experience of Latin America, which saw a resurgence of left parties more than a decade ago, beginning with the ascent of Hugo Chavez in Venezuela in 1998 (Levitsky and Roberts 2011; Cleary 2006), suggests that it is domestic dynamics and not the rise or fall of distant superpowers that determines the fortunes of leftist parties. More important, the weakness of secular leftist parties in Egypt far predates the collapse of the Soviet Union. As we saw in Table 2.1, the left's record of electoral disappointment precedes the disintegration of the Soviet empire by a number of years.

Others go back further, arguing that it is not *Perestroika* and *Glasnost* that did in the Arab left but rather the Arabs' long and bitter experience with left-leaning Arab nationalist governments that delivered only underperforming economies and military defeats. Nazih Ayubi (1980, 485) argues that Socialism had been irrevocably tainted in the Arab imagination by past experiments that did not live up to their promise: "The Arab world in particular has flirted with socialistic ideas and practices. ... Most people believe that socialism has been given a try and has failed." In the 1970s, Egyptian scholar Ali al-Din Hilal al-Dessouki (1973) – who would later go on to infamy as a spokesman of Mubarak's ruling party – traced the left's decline to the Arab defeat at Israeli hands in 1967's Six-Day War: "The 1967 *nakba* symbolized the defeat of Arab socialism." To many Arab intellectuals, Dessouki writes, it was "not a defeat of the Arab nation or the Arab armies, but a symptom of the failure of imported Western ideological trends such as secularism, liberalism, socialism, nationalism, because all of them are in contradiction with the basic principles of Islam."[19] Fuller (2004, 15) writes of how Nasser's

[19] This turn from left ideologies to Islam is confirmed by Tibi (2009), who writes that, "one-time Ba'thists, Nasserists, nationalists, and liberals ... are now rediscovering Islam as a framework for

ideology of Arab socialism "became linked with failure through its ineffective statist economics, its inability to meet social needs, its military failure against Israel, and its authoritarianism." Similarly, Brooks (2002, 612) writes of "the failure of secular ideologies – nationalism, socialism, and capitalism – to meet the spiritual and material needs of Arab populations," and Pappé (2006, 508) notes "the failure of secular nationalism to deliver any of its promises for social welfare and economic prosperity."

But such accounts actually *assume* that which they are trying to *explain*, for only voters who had already adopted an Islamist mind-set would frame their government's shortcomings as failings of *secularism*. The Middle East is full of secular, liberal opposition parties who were as innocent as any Islamist party of the derelictions of the regimes that have dominated over the last fifty years. It's unlikely that voters don't realize this, that they lump all nonreligious parties together, whether they are of the regime or opposed to it. As a more general matter, it is not obvious that the lessons voters learned from the failures of Arab leaders was that their ideologies were somehow deficient. If Nasser was deemed by citizens to have failed (and this is by no means certain), it does not necessarily follow that citizens would ascribe this to his ideology rather than to his personal qualities or, more likely, the machinations of outside powers. Moreover, such arguments assume that the Egyptian peasant or the Yemeni tribesman (or the American political science professor) decide whom to vote for by weighing the historical records of alternative world views. More likely, their vote choices are the result of persuasion, cajoling, and lobbying by real parties and real candidates operating in the real world.

In any case, there is little evidence for the proposition that voters equate the left with failure. In 2005, Egyptian participants in the fifth wave of the World Values Survey were asked to place themselves along a ten-point scale from left (*al-yasār*) to right (*al-yamīn*).[20] Though the modal Egyptian, predictably, placed himself or herself in the middle, more than 50 percent identified themselves as being on the left (see Figure 2.2), which at least suggests that being labeled a leftist carries little of the stigma one would expect it to if it were considered a synonym for failure. Similarly, a May 2012 survey conducted by the Ahram Center for Political and Strategic Studies asked Egyptians to place themselves on a nine-point continuum depending on whether they preferred a socialist presidential candidate (*murashaḥ ishtirāki*) or a capitalist one (*murashaḥ ra's mālī*) in the upcoming presidential election.[21] Given the supposed popular assessment of

a new political ideology." In the case of Egypt, the most dramatic illustration of this phenomenon was provided by the ideological transformation of the Egyptian leftist ʿĀdil Ḥussayn, of the SLP, into an Islamist who orchestrated the alliance of his party with the Muslim Brotherhood and its transformation into the Islamist Labour Party. It is worth noting that the famed slogan of the Muslim Brotherhood, "Islam is the solution," was generated not by Hassan al-Banna or any of his ideological heirs but by Hussayn.

20 Available at: http://www.wvsevsdb.com/wvs/WVSData.jsp.

21 See Tarek Masoud, Ellen Lust-Okar, and Jacob Wichman, "*Al-Intikhabāt al-Riʾāsiyya fi Miṣr: Man ʾaʿṭā ṣawtahu li man, wa limāthā?* (Presidential Elections in Egypt: Who Voted for Whom, and

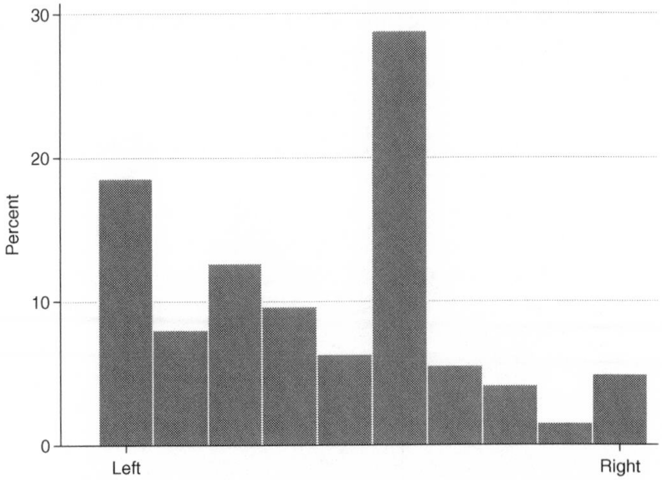

Figure 2.2 Ideological self-placement of Egyptians on "left-right" spectrum (World Values Survey, 2005).

socialism (*al-ishtirākiyya*) as a failed ideology, one might have expected even fewer Egyptians to self-describe as socialist than had identified as leftist, but in fact the opposite is true. Egyptians skewed heavily toward the "socialist" end of the spectrum with approximately 20 percent self-identifying as socialists, and only 5 percent calling themselves capitalists.

Yet further reason to doubt the claim that Egyptians equate secular, leftist, socialist government with failure is provided by the results of a May 2012 Brookings Institution survey. In it, respondents were asked an open-ended question: What leader would they most like Egypt's next president to emulate? More than a quarter (26 percent) volunteered Gamal Abdel Nasser – whom Fuller (2004) identified as a symbol of failure – and another 36 percent named Anwar al-Sadat. Only 15 percent named that global avatar of Islamist success, Turkey's Prime Minister Recep Tayyip Erdogan.[22] This should not be surprising. The policies Nasser enacted – including land reform and guaranteed employment for all high school graduates – were and remain deeply popular (despite the fact that they may also be responsible for many of Egypt's current economic ills). Goldberg (1992, 154) tells us that the average real weekly wage for industrial workers increased 45 percent between 1952 (when Nasser's "free officers" seized power) and 1958

Why?" in *Kayf yufakir al-Miṣriyūn? Istiṭlā'āt al-ra'y al-'ām* (How Do Egyptians Think? Public Opinion Surveys), *al-Ahrām* (Cairo), June 14, 2012 (insert).

22 Shilbley Telhami, "What Do Egyptians Want? Key Findings from the Egyptian Public Opinion Poll," Brookings Institution, May 21, 2012; Available at: http://www.brookings.edu/research/reports/2012/05/21-egyptian-election-poll-telhami. Full report can be downloaded at: http://www.brookings.edu/~/media/research/files/reports/2012/5/21-egyptian-elections-poll-telhami/egypt_poll_results.

and another 24 percent between 1958 and 1970 (the year of Nasser's death). In fact, so beloved is Nasser in Egypt that Mohamed Morsi was forced, shortly after being elected to the presidency, to pay homage to his predecessor, despite the fact that Nasser did more than anyone to try to crush the Muslim Brotherhood. Labeling Nasser's 1952 coup "a turning point in the history of modern Egypt," Morsi declared it "a model for other liberation movements throughout the Arab and Muslim worlds."[23] It's unlikely that the (deposed) president would have made such an overture to Nasser and his legacy had both been viewed as the unalloyed failures that the scholarly literature makes them out to be.

In short, the available data belie the claim that the left is or ever was "discredited" in Egyptian life. Decades after Egypt's defeat in the 1967 war, the death of Nasser, or the collapse of the Soviet Union, Egyptians continue to identify themselves as leftists, Nasserists, or socialists in significant number – all of which makes the left's political languor even more of a puzzle.

2.2 Dynamics of Prerevolutionary Elections

If the left was neither uniquely repressed, nor co-opted, nor discredited, why did it fail to establish itself as an electoral force in authoritarian Egypt? In this section I argue that the left's record of failure is attributable to the dynamics of elections under authoritarianism, which disadvantaged pro-poor parties in undesigned but systematic and definitive ways. Though other parties – most notably, the Muslim Brotherhood – were able to transcend these difficulties and secure a measure of representation in the People's Assembly (the subject of Chapter 4), those parties possessed options that the left did not.

Given the discussion of electoral fraud in Section 2.1, one may wonder whether anything systematic can be said about the "dynamics" of elections under authoritarianism. After all, elections in the Arab world were long thought to be sham affairs in which the maximum leader wins with 99.9 percent (or, in the case of Mubarak's 2005 reelection, 88.6 percent) of the vote (Miller 1996, 309; Rugh 2004, 34). But scholars have argued that legislative elections in the Arab world were different. Blaydes (2010) has argued that the Mubarak regime used electoral contests as a way of identifying which elites had the most support (and thus were the most useful to have in the ruling party's tent). Blatant election rigging would limit the usefulness of elections for this purpose. This hypothesis receives some support by the sheer fact that large numbers of candidates found it rational to run in Mubarak's elections – in the last contest of the Mubarak era, more than 5,100 candidates ran for 508 seats.[24] Thus, though I would not go all the

[23] "President Morsi Pays Tribute to Egypt's 1952 Revolution," *Ahram Online* (Cairo), July 23, 2012; available at: http://english.ahram.org.eg/NewsContent/1/140/48451/Egypt/First–days/President-Morsi-pays-tribute-to-Egypts–Revolution.aspx.

[24] Gamal Essam El-Din, "Brotherhood Faces Day of Reckoning," *al-Ahram Online* (Cairo), November 28, 2010; available at: http://english.ahram.org.eg/NewsContent/1/64/679/Egypt/Politics-/Brotherhood-faces-day-of-reckoning-.aspx.

way with Lust-Okar (2006, 457) and declare that authoritarian elections were "not generally manipulated," there is reason to think that they were nonetheless sites of occasionally meaningful contestation.[25] This was especially true of parliamenary elections in 2000 and 2005, in which the presence of judges in each polling station was credited with curbing (but not eliminating) election irregularities (Hawthorne 2001; El-Ghobashy 2006; Brown and Dunne 2007).[26] In short, elections under Mubarak were *just* competitive enough and resulted in opposition victories *just* often enough that we cannot simply write them off as farces. The question for us, then, is why, whenever the opposition *did* win, the left was almost nowhere to be found.

The Rubber Stamp

To understand why leftist parties lost parliamentary elections, it's essential to understand what precisely those elections were about. The scholarly consensus is that those elections were not about who gets to make policy, because that was monopolized by the president and the ruling party. According to Springborg (1989, 192), in order to keep the parliament tame, the ruling party's majority was routinely used to "terminate debate, pass legislation virtually without comment, reject opposition demands for investigation of alleged improprieties and illegal activities, and so on." The toothlessness of the legislature was also encoded in its rules of procedure, which were designed to give the executive the ability to "contain and control" (Kassem 2004, 29) members of parliament. In particular, the rules arrogated broad powers to the president of the assembly – always a member of the ruling party – allowing him to determine, single-handedly, who served on what committees, whether or not an erring member would be referred to the ethics committee, whether a member would be allowed to participate in international conferences, and whether or not a given legislative proposal from a committee was worthy of discussion. The assembly president also set the parliamentary

25 In fact, Lust-Okar (2006, 457) goes further than to suggest that elections under so-called semiauthoritarian (Olcott and Ottaway 1999) regimes were more genuine than we realize – she argues that even Bashar al-Assad's Syria and Saddam Hussein's Iraq featured competitive elections. She writes that "even in the most seemingly repressive regimes, such as Syria and Saddam Hussein's Iraq, candidates spend large amounts of time and money on everything from lavish banquets and gifts to campaign materials and votes. It is hard to imagine that . . . candidates would invest so heavily in elections if the outcomes were predetermined." Alas, as Wedeen (1998, 1999) has argued, totalitarian regimes such as Syria's pour resources into spectacles intended to signal their power and inevitability. Thus it is not at all hard to imagine why "candidates" in "elections" in totalitarian states would invest in elections whose outcomes were predetermined.

26 In March 2007, parliament passed thirty four amendments to the constitution, including an amendment to Article 88 removing the requirement of direct judicial oversight over the ballotting (Brown and Dunne 2007). The parliament followed this up in May 2007 with changes to Law 73 of 1956 (on political rights) establishing a High Elections Commission that would be provide a measure of judicial oversight at the national but not polling-station level. See Human Rights Watch, "Elections in Egypt: State of Emergency Incompatible with Free and Fair Vote," November 2010, 14.

agenda and appointed the parliament's general secretary, a powerful functionary responsible for the day-to-day workings of the assembly's bureaucracy (Al-Sāwī 2001, 18).

The broad powers of the assembly's president were accompanied by tight constraints on the ability of members to hold the government to account. For example, Article 198 of the rules of procedure allow any member to interrogate a member of the government "to hold them accountable for matters that fall under their purview."[27] However, as al-Sāwī (2001, 15) points out, there were several exacting conditions that attached to the lodging of an interpellation – including that it must be delivered orally, without the aid of written notes – and the assembly president could simply allow an interpellation to expire without ever bringing it to the floor.[28] But even without such byzantine rules of procedure, parliamentarians had an incentive to exercise a fair measure of self-discipline in challenging the government. This is so because parliamentarians who stepped out of line could expect to find themselves out of a job in relatively short order. For example, the speaker could – with the connivance of the majority – lift a parliamentarian's immunity and begin expulsion proceedings (Kassem 2004, 32–3). In fact, according to al-Sāwī, more Mubarak-era parliamentarians were disciplined for acts of *lèse majesté* than ministers were fired for violations of the public trust (al-Sawi 2001, 15, n. 12). On top of all this was the fact that the president could dissolve parliament (following a hastily convened public referendum), which, in Kassem's (2004, 24) words, "had enormous implications for the Assembly's conduct and ultimately for the balance of power within the decisionmaking process."

All these factors – the tilted rules of procedure and the abundant technologies for deterring and disciplining independent-minded legislators – suggest that the People's Assembly under Mubarak was more than deserving of the "rubber stamp" sobriquet conferred on it by scholars such as Brownlee (2002, 9) and Shehata and Stacher (2006). According to Blaydes (2010, 127), "with the ability to influence policy so circumscribed, many candidates seek office to achieve personal benefit, either professionally, financially, or both." As in other such systems, for a large segment of voters, elections tended to be less about weighing candidates' policy visions than about ascertaining which of them could most credibly commit to provide particularistic, material benefits back to the voter and the district. As Lust-Okar (2006, 460) puts it, "Voters tend to cast their ballots for candidates whom they think will afford them *wasta* [intercession with government authorities], and not for reasons of ideology or policy preferences" (see also Blaydes 2010). Thus, a 2000 survey conducted by the Ahram Center for Political and Strategic Studies found that more than 60 percent of 1,600 respondents said that a "helpful candidate" was most deserving of their votes. Only five res-

27 Article 198, *al-Lā'iha al-dākhiliyya* (Rules of Procedure), People's Assembly of the Arab Republic of Egypt, 2005, 90.

28 Rules of procedure, Article 206, 94.

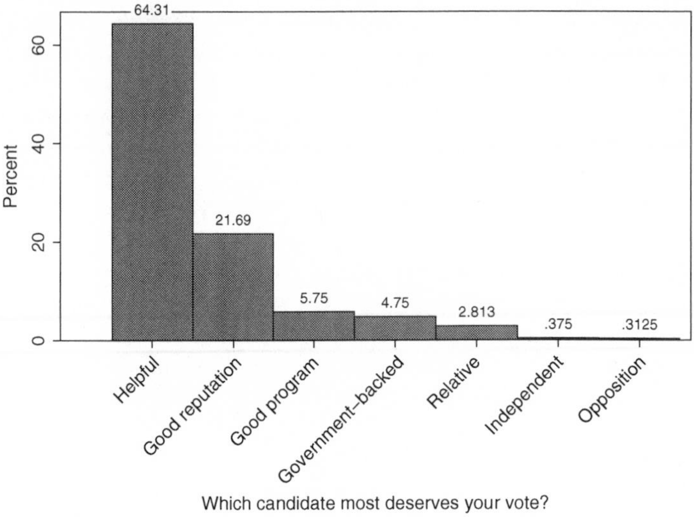

Figure 2.3 What Egyptians want in their political candidates. (*Source*: al-Ahram general survey, 2000).

pondents (or 0.3 percent) said that a candidate's membership in the opposition rendered him worthy of their suffrages (see Figure 2.3). The types of candidates poised to do well in such environments are those that have access to resources they can channel back to the voters. In the following sections I describe the principal dynamics of authoritarian elections in Mubarak's Egypt and how these worked to the particular detriment of parties of the left.

Party Lists and Ruling Party Dominance, 1984–1987

If any parliamentary elections during Mubarak's thirty years in office seemed likely to generate significant representation for the left, they were the ones held in 1984. Those elections were unique in Egypt's authoritarian history in that they were run on a system of closed party lists.[29] The system was set forth in Law 114 of 1984 (amending Law 38 of 1972), which divided the country into forty-eight electoral districts, with an average of approximately nine seats per district.[30] Article 17 of the law stated that "members of the People's Assembly are elected according to the system of party lists such that each list is given a number of

[29] The 1987 elections were also held using a proportional representation (PR) system, but with the addition of forty eight majoritarian seats that were opened up to independent candidates as well as to party members.

[30] The law reserved 31 of the 448 seats for women. Additionally, each party was required to reserve every other space on its list for candidates certified either as "workers" or "farmers" (see Article 5).

seats per district according to the proportion of votes earned by the party."[31] This system was a departure from the one that had governed elections to the People's Assembly under Anwar Sadat in 1976 and 1979, in which the country was divided into many smaller, majoritarian districts with open nomination rules. The shift to proportional representation was part of a strategy by Sadat's successor, Hosni Mubarak, to co-opt the country's nascent opposition parties at a time when he was still solidifying his rule.

Under the new system, each of the country's five official political parties – the ruling NDP, the NPUR, the SLP (Socialist Liberals Party), and the New Wafd Party – controlled who could get on the ballot and how they would be ranked. Minister of the Interior Hasan Abū Bāshā declared that the new system would benefit parties by focusing the voters' attention on their platforms as opposed to personalistic appeals:

> Elections on the system of proportional lists frees the candidate from the constant pressure of the voters, and likewise ensures a kind of political guidance on the basis of the fact that the voter chooses a party program and plan, and political competition becomes built on distinctive party programs.[32]

The opinion was seconded by Nagīb Mahfūẓ, the late Egyptian novelist and Nobel laureate, who wrote: "I am among the supporters of proportional lists, because it causes elections to turn around principles and parties instead of individuals and solidarities. It offers to the citizen a better political education."[33] As a noted professor of political science at Cairo University wrote in *al-Ahrām* at the time, "based on this system, the voter will judge and choose between parties based on their programs and not on the basis of the candidates' personalities."[34]

Though the former interior minister, Egypt's leading man of letters, and the professor were certainly on to something, the picture is more complicated than they made it out to be. After all, in a system such as Egypt's, where parliament is not the locus of policy-making authority, it is difficult to imagine policy platforms taking precedence in the minds of voters over, say, a party's ability to provide patronage. Thus, whereas closed-list electoral rules shifted the focus of elections from candidates to parties, voters still had incentives to compare those parties based on their ability to provide services rather than on their national-level programs.

31 The system included some guarantees for the ruling party. First, regardless of how well a party performed in a particular district, the law stipulated that "no party can be represented in the assembly whose lists do not earn at least 8 percent of total votes cast across the republic." This 8 percent threshold, as well as a stipulation that "left over seats are accorded to the party that received the most votes to begin with," ensured that the ruling party maintained a comfortable majority (see Jamal and Lust-Okar 2002).

32 "*Abū Bāshā Ya'lan: Intikhābāt bi al-qā'ima al-nisbiyya yastahdaf al-munāfassa al-siyāsiyya 'alā barāmij mutamayazza* (Elections by Proportional Lists Are Aimed at Political Competition over Distinctive Programs), *al-Ahrām*, May 16, 1984, 4.

33 Nagīb Mahfūz, "*Wijhat Nazẓar: 'Awda ilā qānūn al-Intikhābāt*," *al-Ahrām*, January 3, 1985.

34 Akram Badr al-Dīn, "Al-intikhābāt wa mustaqbal al-dīmūqrātiyya," *al-Ahrām*, April 28, 1984.

This, of course, was a comparison the ruling NDP was destined to win, given that the party had at its disposal the vast resources of the Egyptian state (Wickham 2002, 89). A ruling-party member was more likely than his opponents to be able to get a constituent a government job, access to subsidized medicines, or – through connections with the security services – help in extricating himself or herself from trouble with the law. They could also get things done for the district – from gettting a village wired for electricity to improving garbage collection (Blaydes 2010, 71–72). Thus, Egypt's main newspaper, *al-Ahrām*, reported in 1984 that "Candidates of the NDP contest elections on the stock of the Five Year Plan and the achievements of the government to solve the problems of the people."[35] Another preelection report brought us the testimony of several humble denizens of the Shubrā district in Cairo, who declared that they would vote for the NDP list because of "the government's palpable achievements, [such as] establishing 12 classrooms ... for 1,440 students, a clinic for heart and lung diseases, ..., a burn center, ...," as well as "improvements to local hospitals costing 82,500 L.E., twenty-eight day-care centers serving 3,000 children, and four stores selling subsidized meat."[36]

The demand for services, and thus the likelihood of voting for the ruling party, appeared to be highest in poor and rural areas. As one rural informant told Bin-Nafīsa and ʿArafāt (2005, 65), elections were taken more seriously in the countryside than in the city because "politics has a greater impact on the people here. ... In the city, everything comes to you naturally, but in the villages, the role of the member of parliament is essential, because he's like a postman for the village, relaying requests to the authorities and returning with agreements and licenses." This is bad news for opposition parties, which cannot hope to have access to the ruling party's resources (Magaloni 2006; Greene 2007; Cox 2007), but it is particularly bad news for parties of the left, whose core constituencies – the poor and rurual – are those most likely to be swayed by the regime's offers of patronage.

Figure 2.4 provides a sense of just how receptive the poor were to the ruling party's ministrations. In it, the ruling party's vote share in each of the country's forty-eight electoral districts in 1984 is plotted against the adult illiteracy rate (which here is employed as a rough proxy for socioeconomic status). A positive and statistically significant relationship is observed (Pearson's coefficient = 0.37), which is what we'd expect if the poor were more likely to cast ballots for the ruling party. Figure 2.5 shows the vote shares of the two leftist parties, the NPUR and SLP, respectively, also plotted against the adult illiteracy rate. In both we observe a negative but statistically insignificant relationship between adult illiteracy and

[35] Ahmad Nasr al-Dīn, "*Al-ahzāb al-khamsa wa laʿbat al-karāsī al-mūsīqiyya fī al-Gharbiyya* (Five Parties and a Game of Musical Chairs in al-Gharbiyya) ," *al-Ahrām*, May 13, 1984, 3.

[36] Muḥammad Bāshā, Ḥasan ʿĀshūr, Nihāl Shukrī, and ʿAbd al-ʿAẓīm Darwīsh, "*Muwājaha sākhina bayn al-nākhibīn wa al-murashaḥīn* (Heated Confrontation between Voters and Candidates)," *al-Ahrām*, May 8, 1984, 3.

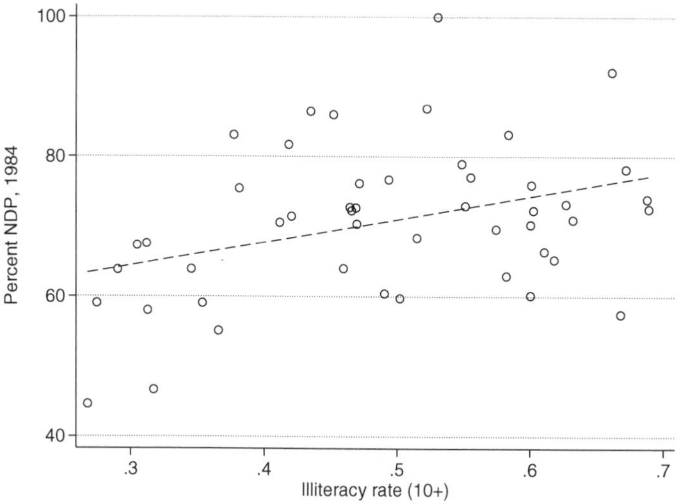

Figure 2.4 Illiteracy rate and ruling-party vote share, 1984.

the party's vote share, suggesting that whereas both parties performed poorly among all socioeconomic groups, they performed particularly poorly among the poor constituencies they ostensibly sought to serve. Careful readers of Figure 2.5 will note that the NPUR did particularly well (in relative terms) in one district – earning 18.3 percent of the vote in Banhā in the governorate of al-Qalyūbiyya. This, it turns out, was the home district of the party's founder, Khālid Muḥyī al-Dīn. The ruling party's showing in this NPUR stronghold was 72.3 percent.

Not all opposition parties did poorly under this system, however. The relatively liberal, free-market-oriented Wafd Party in particular captured 15 percent of the vote in 1984 and 11 percent in 1987. Part of the reason for the party's impressive performance in 1984 is that it had allied with the then-outlawed Muslim Brotherhood in that contest (although the alliance fell apart shortly after the elections, and the Brotherhood allied in the next election with the SLP, which transformed itself into an Islamist party). Another reason for the Wafd's success seems to have been the party's ability to pack its lists with old Wafdist notables who retained family vote banks. For example, we read in the account of the Wafd's campaign in al-Daqahliyya, "The Wafd party focused on holding rallies in Markaz Sanbalawīn where there are families with Wafdist roots, and in Markaz Bilqās because of the existence of family ties there to the president of the Wafd party."[37] During the 1987 elections in Upper Egypt, *al-Ahrām* reported that "every [party] tries to attract to its ranks the greatest degree of support from the clans, and the

[37] Mahmūd Ma'awad, "*Al-Intikhābāt fī al-Daqahliyya: Ma'raka intikhābiyya sākhina wa lākin bayn 4 ahzāb faqat* (Elections in al-Daqahliyya: A Heated Electoral Battle, but between 4 Parties Only)," *al-Ahrām*, April 21, 1984, 3.

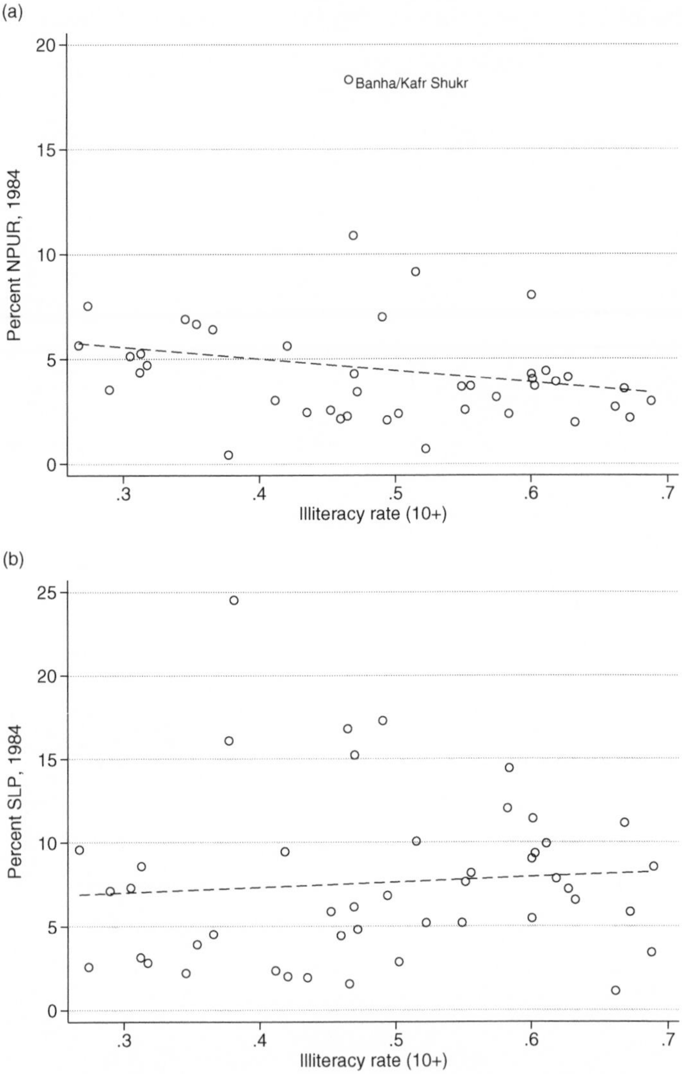

Figure 2.5 Illiteracy rate and leftist-party vote share, 1984: (*a*) NPUR; (*b*) SLP.

lists of the National Democratic Party prove this, for they include a large number of glittering names from the large families; the same goes for the Wafd party."[38] Hinnebusch (1984, 104–5) reports that the Wafd leadership at this time was made up of a disproportionate number of wealthy lawyers and landowners.

[38] ʿAbd al-Jawwād ʿAlī and Hajjāj al-Hussaynī, "*Wa fī Asyūṭ maʿraka al-ʿāʾilāt al-kabīra* (And in Asyūṭ the Battle of the Large Families)," *al-Ahrām*, March 23, 1987, 3.

Majoritarian Elections and the Politics of Personalism, 1990–2010

The proportional-representation (PR) system that governed elections in 1984 was from the outset the subject of legal challenges. Opponents of the law argued that the system of party lists violated Article 62 of the 1971 Egyptian constitution, which declared that "Citizens shall have the right to vote, nominate and express their opinions in referenda according to the provisions of the law. Their participation in public life is a national duty." The court ruled that by restrcting nominations to party members, closed-list PR denied nonpartisans the right of equal participation. In 1986, the regime – still committed to retaining the PR system – enacted Law 188, which attempted to comply with the ruling by adding to Article 5 provisions for independent candidacies: "In each constituency one member is to be elected on the basis of individual candidacies while the others are to be elected according to the system of party lists." This too was struck down by the court (on May 5, 1990), and the parliament that had been elected in 1987 was dissolved. Mubarak then issued a Presidential Decree 201 of 1990, which resulted in the abolition of the PR system and the return to the system of individual candidacies that had prevailed before 1984 (Zahran 1992, 199).

Under the new system – described by Pripstein-Posusney (2002, 43) as a "winner take all" system – the country was divided into 222 dual-member districts. Party nomination was no longer required to get on the ballot. Instead, a candidate needed only pay an entry fee (of approximately $35) and demonstrate that he was literate, held Egyptian citizenship, was over the age of thirty, and had completed his military service.[39] Because each district had two seats, voters were given two votes, which were to be cast for two different candidates. In order to win a seat, a candidate had to earn an outright majority of votes, otherwise, a runoff would be held a week later. And finally, at least one seat in each district had to go to a candidate who was registered as a "worker" or "farmer" by trade.[40] That provision – which persisted in modified form into Egypt's 2011–12 elections – attempted to ensure that at least half of the Egyptian assembly was drawn from the

[39] Article 4, Law 38 of 1972 on the People's Assembly.

[40] Article 2, Law 38 of 1972 Regarding the People's Assembly, Arab Republic of Egypt, November 2002. The text of the article follows:

> [T]he word farmer connotes a person whose only job, and whose principal source of livelihood, is agriculture, and who lives in the countryside, on the condition that he, his wife, and his dependent children may not hold, as owners or as tenants, more than 10 faddāns. [A faddān is a Middle Eastern unit of land measurement approximately equal to an acre.] One is considered a worker if he derives his income from his manual or mental labor in agriculture, industry, or services and is not a member of a professional syndicate, nor listed in the commercial register, nor is a holder of a higher degree. Excepted from this are members of professional syndicates without higher degrees, and likewise he who started his life as a worker but subsequently obtained a higher degree. In both cases, for a person to be considered a worker, he must be a member of a labor union.

laboring and peasant classes and was a holdover from Egypt's socialist-Nasserist era (1952–70). During the Mubarak era, Kassem (1999) notes, "such candidates are rarely workers or peasants, but rather wealthy landowners or merchants" who have managed, through bribes, the exploitation of loopholes, and other tricks, to become certified as "workers" or "farmers."[41]

The shift in electoral rule from closed-list PR to the winner-take-all, open-nomination system had two effects. First, it vastly increased the importance of money in elections (Carey and Shugart 1995). Under the previous system, voters could choose between a ruling party that had resources and opposition parties that did not. But once the gates of electoral participation were thrown open, the arena was flooded with local notables and businessmen who had considerable cash that they were willing to spend in the service of obtaining a lucrative berth in the legislature. Blaydes (2008, 152) thus describes the rise of a "*bīznīs*" culture during elections, in which voters sold their suffrages to the highest bidder.

For the ruling party, the appearance of new competitors with access to private resources was but a minor annoyance. Most of the new entrants into the electoral game were more interested in joining the ruling party than running against it. In the five elections held between 1990 and 2010, regime-friendly candidates who had failed to garner the ruling party's nomination ran as independents "on the principles and program of the National Democratic Party," hastening to join the ranks of the party if they were lucky enough to win a seat in parliament.[42] For opposition parties, however, the shift to an open, majoritarian electoral system was something close to a death knell. Not only did these parties still need to compete with the ruling party's promises of patronage, but they now had to deal with an influx of local notables and businessmen, all capable of wooing the poor with promises of material benefits. Moreover, no longer could a party wage a national campaign based on its platform and reputation. Instead, it would have to somehow find the cash to wage district-by-district battles. To get a sense of how unprepared a party such as the NPUR was for this, it's worth noting that in 1989, on the eve of the shift to the open-nomination, majoritarian electoral system, the party had only 244,894 Egyptian pounds (approximately $81,000 in 1990 dollars) in its coffers.[43] That said, though the shift to the open electoral system ended any possibility of the emergence of a broad pro-poor front in parliament, it did enable the NPUR to finally pick up seats in the small number of districts where its candidates could rely on local followings based on family or on the party's ties to

[41] In 1990, an investigation by the al-Wafd Party's newspaper found that among the ranks of worker/farmer deputies were holders of doctorates and high-level public-sector managers (quoted in *'Abd al-Majīd and Mus'ad*, 1992, 117).

[42] "*Mubarak: Intikhābāt al-Shūrā ikhtibār li iltizām al-sha'b bi al-ta'dīlāt al-dustūriyya* (Mubarak: The Consultative Council Elections Are a Test of the People's Commitment to the Constitutional Reforms," Egyptian State Information Service, June 8, 2007; available at: http://www.sis.gov.eg/Ar/EgyptOnline/Politics/000007/0201000000000000006426.htm.

[43] NPUR budget for 1989, available on request. Thanks to Hānī al-Ḥussainī for sharing these data with me.

limited, highly localized organized labor networks. Thus Khālid Muḥyī al-Dīn, the party's founder, represented his family's home district of Kafr Shukr in parliament from 1990 to 2005, and al-Badrī Farghalī, a labor activist and founder of the General Union of Pensioners (al-Ittiḥād al-ʿĀm li-Asḥāb al-Maʿāshāt), was voted into office for three terms from the small, industrialized governorate of Port Said.

This brings us to the second effect of the change in the electoral system – the dramatic increase in the electoral value of the networks of kinship and local notability described in Section 1.3. Moving to a candidate-centric system and eliminating the requirement of party nomination suddenly meant that many of the largest kin networks suddenly found the costs of participating in electoral politics dramatically lowered. Whereas under the old closed-list system, a large clan wishing to run one of its sons in an election would have had to cultivate a relationship with one of the handful of legalized parties, under the new, open nomination system, parties could be bypassed entirely, and every candidate with a (real or imagined) vote bank could throw his or her hat into the electoral arena.

Thus, according to ʿAbd al-Majīd and Musʿad (1992, 122–3), the 1990 elections saw the intensification of "the role of group feeling[44] as an active influence on nominations for the People's Assembly. This group feeling took the form of tribalism in the areas of the Red Sea and Marsa Matrūh and Upper Egypt (where it included Arab and Bedouin tribes) whereas it appeared in the countryside in the form of the rallying of a village behind the candidate who is a 'son of the village.' " Rabīʿ (1997, 65–8) tells us that in 1990, "there was a clear rise in the stock of the 'provincial' candidate," and that the most successful candidates were those with "with familial and tribal weight." He reports that candidates took to attacking each other not on the basis of their programs but on whether "this or that candidate was born in this district or village." For example, he describes a famous leaflet attacking Ibrāhīm Shukrī, leader of the Labor Party, who was running for a seat in Shirbīn in the governorate of al-Daqahliyya.[45] He tells us that the leaflet offered no critique of the content of Shukrī's ideological appeals or even his political alliance with the Muslim Brotherhood but rather asked a potentially more damning question: "Is Shukrī Really From Shirbīn?" According to Rabīʿ, "This represents a clear regression in the forms of political and ideological mobilization in favor of a kind of primitive struggle in which most believe that the membership indicated on a candidate's birth certificate is more important than his political message or his social activities" (Rabīʿ 1997, 67). In a discussion of the NPUR's weakness in the al-Sharqiyya governorate, Zakariyya (1990, 179) lamented that the party "could hardly benefit from the ... familism and tribalism

[44] The authors use *ʿaṣabīyya*, a term first encountered in Ibn Khaldūn's *Prolegomena*. I follow the great Yale Orientalist and translator of Ibn Khaldūn, Franz Rosenthal (1978), in rendering it "group feeling."

[45] Shukrī died in August 2008.

or the expansion of the state apparatus" that dominates the political calculus of voters.

These new dynamics were damaging to opposition parties of the right and left. For example, the New Wafd, which in 1984 and 1987 had established itself as "the greatest threat to Mubarak and the NDP" (Springborg 1989, 195), came apart at the seams. The party had been built on the old Wafd's networks of local notables (Cantori 1966; Reid 1979; Deeb 1979; Hinnebusch 1984), and their loyalty to the party was sorely tested by an electoral system that so dramatically lowered the costs of running as an independent. When the party announced its intention to boycott the 1990 elections in protest at the electoral law change, forty-two of the party's leading members – including eleven members of its twenty-eight-person parliamentary bloc and two members of the party's high council – violated the boycott, reckoning that they would run on their own steam rather than sit out an election (Raslān 1992, 178). It was a blow from which the party has not yet recovered.

If the shift from PR to an open, majoritarian system was damaging to the Wafd, it eliminated any prospect of the left becoming anything more than a marginal force in Egypt's legislature. Although the NPUR in 1990 managed to capture six seats in parliament – after defying an opposition-wide boycott – the party's leaders understood what the new dynamics meant for their chances. After all, as far back as 1987, the editor of the NPUR party newspaper had warned of the dangerous nature of clientelism for his party, arguing that familial and tribal solidarities "still play a fundamental role in the electoral process" (quoted in al-Bannā (1988, 621)). Though the party did have a handful of members with considerable followings in their home districts – foremost among them being Khālid Muḥyī al-Dīn, who would hold onto a seat in his district in al-Qalyūbiyya for three terms – it was unlikely to attract more. After all, Egypt was still an authoritarian regime. It would take a particular kind of local notable, one improbably committed to the cause of socialism, to hazard the negative attentions of the Mubarak regime and join the NPUR, especially after the post-1990 electoral system obviated the need for party membership in order to run for parliament. Moreover, it was highly unlikely that anyone with money would wish to run on the banner of a party that put forward such policy prescriptions as "preserving what remains of the public sector ..., [e]nding the policy of trade liberalization ..., revising tariffs to limit unnecessary imports and to protect domestic industry from unfair competition ..., and [e]nding the policy of unfettered reliance on the market."[46]

One of the NPUR's more arresting electoral slogans during the final years of the Mubarak era was, "We want to kill poverty; they want to kill the poor." In the end, though, it was the party that was killed by its reliance on the poor. A touching

[46] *Al-Birnāmij al-intikhābī al-ʿām: Birnāmij lī al-taghyīr al-siyāsī wa al-iqtiṣādī wa al-ijtimāʿī* (The General Electoral Program: A Program for Political, Economic, and Social Change), Ḥizb al-Tajammuʿ al-Watanī al-Taqaddumī al-Wahdawī (Party of the National Progressive Unionist Rally), November–December 2005, 5–7.

illustration of the party's dire position by the end of the Mubarak years is found in an August 4, 2010, memorandum from the secretary general and president of the NPUR to local party secretaries:

> You all know, gentlemen, the financial hardships the party is experiencing, especially with the rising prices of goods and services, which has led to increased central spending on party offices and publications and party activities in general.
>
> Therefore, the party sees that it is urgent to be frank with you and our colleagues about this severe crisis, which will impact decisively the amount of spending on the upcoming parliamentary elections, especially as the number of the party's candidates will exceed eighty.
>
> Therefore, we wish to inform you that the central party will not be able to offer any financial support to any colleague among the candidates, and the party's support to each candidate will be strictly limited to the following:
>
> 1. Handbills and local programs in reasonable amounts, according to the party's capabilities.
> 2. Color posters: 2,000 copies.
> 3. Cloth for banners: 3 bolts of 30 meters.
> 4. Cards for distribution in front of polling stations: 5,000 cards.[47]

It stands to reason that a party that could not afford more than three bolts of cloth for each of its eighty candidates (out of a possible 444 seats) would find itself unable to compete with the ruling party and its millionaire affiliates. The atrophy of the party is further illustrated in Table 2.3, which lists the party's membership by governorate, and the total number of votes earned by its candidates in each of those governorates in 2005. As we can see, the party earned 145,000 votes in 2005 (or 1.6 percent of the total voter turnout of 8,790,708). Compared with the party's standing in 1984, when it had captured 4 percent of the vote, it is eminently understandable why, by the end of the Mubarak era, so many observers of the Egyptian scene had written off the left as a force in the country's political life.

2.3 Conclusion

This chapter has argued that the left's defeats under Mubarak were not functions of the unattractiveness of leftist ideology or to excessive repression by the authoritarian state or to the left's alleged coziness with that state, but rather due to electoral dynamics that severely disadvantaged opposition parties generally and leftist parties in particular. Though regime interference in voting processes and ocassional outright manipulation of the results harmed all opposition parties, leftist parties found themselves particularly unable to compete with the ruling

47 Memorandum from Sayyid ʿAbd al-ʿAl, Secretary General, and Rifʿat al-Saʿid, President, National Progressive Unionist Rally, to governorate party secretaries, August 4, 2010; available from the author.

Table 2.3 *NPUR Members, Branches, Candidates, and Voters, 2005*

Governorate	Members	Branches	Candidates	Votes
Cairo	6,054	9	4	11,100
al-Gīza	2,342	5	3	15,800
al-Qalyūbiyya	7,213	4	1	11,200
Matrūh	152	1	1	2,400
Alexandria	3,537	4	5	7,100
al-Buhayra	2,751	2	2	5,700
al-Gharbiyya	2,820	2	3	5,900
al-Minūfiyya	964	3	4	4,400
al-Sharqiyya	4,675	4	3	16,500
al-Daqahliyya	5,225	5	4	13,400
Kafr al-Shaykh	2,876	3	2	1,800
Damietta	1,011	1	1	1,500
Port Said	2,745	1	2	13,100
Suez	390	1	1	2,300
al-Ismāʿīliyya	152	1	1	1,900
North Sinai	82	1	0	—
Aswān	4,715	3	0	—
Qinā	672	4	4	16,100
Suhāg	508	2	1	3,400
Asyūt	425	2	3	6,300
al-Minyā	2,117	4	1	2,900
Banī Suwayf	76	1	1	1,900
al-Fayyūm	1,442	3	1	1,100
TOTAL	52,944	66	48	145,800

party's offers of patronage or the blandishments of the many thousands of local notables and businessmen. Robbed of its core constituencies – the poor, the workers, and the peasants – the left was unable to establish itself as an electoral force, even if the ideas that animated the left remained highly legitimate among broad swaths of Egyptians. Thus, if anything killed the left, it was not the collapse of the Soviet Union or the alleged failures of Nasserism but, to put it crudely, elections themselves.

This long and depressing story has powerful reverberations beyond the end of the authoritarian period that produced it. For, as we shall see in subsequent chapters, party politics at moments of transition are powerfully shaped by party dynamics in the authoritarian period. During the Mubarak years, the impressive electoral victories of the Muslim Brotherhood and the equally depressing defeats of the left created an expectation – on the part of scholars, policy makers, political actors, and even voters – of inevitability around the former and enervation around the latter. And though the left's continued defeats in the post-Mubarak era would seem to confirm the view that the ideology of leftist parties has long been unwanted, this chapter has presented evidence that should, at the very least, cause us to question this view.

This chapter could be read as a story of unrequited love. The Egyptian left during the Mubarak era may have declared its love for democracy, but what little democracy that existed in Egypt did not seem to love it back. As we shall see, the left's repeated disappointments at the ballot box, and Islamism's repeated triumps, would eventually generate a loss of faith in, and great suspicion of, democratic processes that would have important repercussions after Mubarak's fall. But, for now, this chapter raises another, more immediate, question. If the dynamics of authoritarian elections were so destructive to the left, what was it about Islamists that enabled them to elude or transcend those dynamics? This is the question to which we now turn.

3

The Islamic Machine?

If the politics of patronage and clientelism during the Mubarak era decimated the Egyptian left, they seemed to have had rather less of an effect on the Muslim Brotherhood. In 1987, 2000, and 2005, the movement established itself as the largest opposition bloc in the Egyptian parliament. And in the elections where it failed to secure significant representation – 1990, 1995, and 2010 – it had either boycotted the elections outright (as in 1990) or was the subject of such a systematic effort by the regime to prevent its candidates from campaigning or its cadres from getting out the vote that it withdrew after the first round of balloting (1995 and 2010). In fact, when one considers the barriers that the Muslim Brotherhood had to overcome to participate in and win Egyptian elections, its performances are nothing short of remarkable.

The Brotherhood was officially banned by the monarchy in 1948 and again by Nasser's regime in 1954 (Mitchell 1993; Makram-Ebeid 1989). Though allowed to resume activities in the early 1970s, the ban on the group was never formally lifted, and its legal limbo thus allowed the regime to periodically arrest its otherwise law-abiding members on the Orwellian charge of being part of an illegal organization (albeit one that the regime allowed to run for and win seats in parliament). Moreover, the Brotherhood could not formalize its status by registering as a political party because Article 4 of the law regulating political parties (Law 40 of 1977) explicitly banned parties formed on the basis of religion (in addition to geography, gender, or other factional identities). Thus, when the Brotherhood did run candidates, they were forced to do so either on the ticket of a registered party (as in 1984, when it was the junior partner of the Wafd Party, and in 1987, when it was very much the senior partner in an alliance with the Labor and Liberal parties) or as nominal independents (as after 1990). However, the Mubarak regime seemed intent on blocking even this, and in March 2007, Article 5 of the country's constitution was rewritten to specify that "*no political activity shall be exercised* nor parties established on the basis of religion," seemingly opening the way for the regime to prevent the Brothers from any form of political engagement whatsoever. Given the regime's systematic inhospitality to the Brotherhood and the inauspicious electoral dynamics discussed in Chapter 2, how was this banned movement able to win so often when the deck seemed so stacked against it?

As we saw in Chapter 1, it is widely believed that the Muslim Brotherhood was carried into office by beating the regime at its own game, offering health, education, and welfare services to the beleaguered masses. For example, in the waning years of the Mubarak era, the *Washington Post* reported that "the Brotherhood has provided clinics, youth camps and other services that have won the organization support among the poor."[1] However, little systematic evidence has been gathered for such claims. There are few studies of the Muslim Brotherhood's alleged social-service provision efforts and almost none that could tell us what services were offered, who received them, and – most important – how they were translated into electoral support for the movement. During the Mubarak era, attempts to answer these questions invariably foundered on the Brotherhood's alleged need to maintain secrecy and protect its good works from the depredations of the authoritarian state. Thus, while many Muslim Brothers spoke to me in expansive terms about their movement's efforts to relieve the misery of Egypt's poor, it was difficult to see these good works up close. ʿIṣām al-ʿIryān – then head of the Brotherhood's political bureau and assistant secretary general of the Physicians Syndicate – responded to my frustration at being unable to identify Muslim Brotherhood charitable works by explaining that the scrutiny of the security services had forced the Brothers to obscure their links to the Islamic charitable associations through which the movement conducted such work. "I could have been a member in scores of charitable societies," he told me, "but now my name creates problems. Before, they used to consider my involvement as something that would encourage people to trust the organization enough to donate. But now my presence is a burden."[2]

Al-ʿIryān's testimony explains not only why it was difficult during the Mubarak era for researchers to plumb the depths of the Muslim Brotherhood's charitable outreach but also why it was difficult for the Brotherhood to engage in such outreach in the first place, at least to the extent often attributed to it in the literature. Accounts of the Brotherhood engaging in vast social-service operations by which it won the allegiance of the poor were insensitive, if not blind, to the dynamics of the authoritarian system within which the Brotherhood was forced to operate. Wiktorowicz (2000) has noted that authoritarian regimes heavily regulated what nongovernmental actors could do, making it difficult for Islamists or anyone else to engage in the sorts of broad, politically motivated service-provision activities that were often ascribed to them.

1 Ellen Knickmeyer, "Cairo Moving More Aggressively to Cripple Muslim Brotherhood: Government Seen Eliminating Opposition as Transition Looms," *Washington Post*, Monday, October 1, 2007, A14.

2 Interview with ʿIṣām al-ʿIryān, Physicians Syndicate, Cairo, January 2007.

In this chapter I trace the ways in which the Muslim Brotherhood's service-provision efforts were routinely and systematically thwarted by the regime, rendering such efforts of only limited value at election times. This chapter thus seeks to situate our discussions of Islamist outreach in the broader empirical and theoretical literature on authoritarianism, recognizing that such regimes constrain opposition organizing in ways from which Islamists, despite the extraordinary charitable feats attributed to them, were not immune. The chapter lays the groundwork for an alternative account of Islamist electoral success under Mubarak offered in Chapter 4.

3.1 Service and Subjugation

One of the principal reasons for the persistence of the image of the Muslim Brotherhood stealing hearts, minds, and votes from Mubarak and his henchmen by providing social services to the poor and disenfranchised is that it seems plausible. A visitor to Egypt – today or under Mubarak – could not help but be struck by the ubiquity of religious associations offering aid to the poor. And the Muslim Brotherhood, at least in conversations with Western reporters, often took credit for it all. For example, in 2006, ʿAbd al-Munʿim Abū al-Futūḥ, then a member of the Brotherhood's Guidance Bureau (before resigning from the movement and recasting himself as a liberal), testified that fully 20 percent of the charitable associations registered in Egypt at that time belonged to the Muslim Brotherhood.[3] ʿIṣām al-ʿIryān told me, "If you go to any place today ... you will find in your area charitable clinics, homes for the aged, orphanges – these are all our idea."[4]

Though Ismail (2001, 36) tells us that the Muslim Brotherhood "established Islamic charitable organizations, schools and clinics, all of which rival or [are] better [than] the state's social services," the reality is that no authoritarian regime worthy of the name would allow such a thing. Wickham (2003) has documented the avidity with which the Mubarak regime regulated the civic realm, with a view toward preventing precisely the kinds of activities in which the Brotherhood was thought to engage. Charitable associations (then, as now) required a license from the Ministry of Social Affairs, which could deny permission to organizations that might, in its view, "threaten national unity, violate public order or morality or advocate discrimination against citizens, on account of sex, origin, colour, language, religion or creed."[5] The ministry also enjoyed wide latitude in interfering with an organization's day-to-day operations and could reject candidates for a

[3] "Egypt: Social Programmes Bolster Appeal of Muslim Brotherhood," Integrated Regional Information Networks News Service, United Nations Office for the Coordination of Humanitarian Affairs, February 22, 2006; available at: http://www.irinnews.org/report.aspx?reportid=26150; accessed June 3, 2012.

[4] Interview with ʿIṣām al-ʿIryān, Physicians Syndicate, Cairo, January 2007.

[5] Arab Republic of Egypt, Law 84 of 2002 on Nongovernmental Organizations, part 1, chapter 2, Article 11. Similar stipulations existed in the predecessor laws: Law 32 of 1964 and Law 153 of 1999.

group's board of directors or expel those already serving (Agati 2007). Moreover, the law allowed the ministry to dissolve an organization for any one of a number of vaguely defined violations, such as using its funds for "purposes other than those designated" or violating "the public order or morality."[6]

A dramatic example of just how hemmed in the Muslim Brothers were and just how vigilant the state was in preventing the movement from delivering social services to the poor is offered by the story of a Muslim Brotherhood–affiliated organization, the Islamic Medical Association (al-Jamʿiyya al-Ṭibiyya al-Islāmiyya), and its grandly named but ill-fated Central Charitable Hospital (al-Mustashfā al-Khayrī al-Markazī).

The Islamic Medical Association (IMA) was founded in 1977 by Aḥmad al-Malṭ, a surgeon and Muslim Brotherhood member who had served as a medic with the Brotherhood's militias in Palestine in 1948 and who had risen to become the movement's deputy general guide by the time of his death in 1995. Though formally independent of the Brotherhood, the IMA's board has always been comprised of several prominent and lesser-known Brothers. A former president of the association, Luṭfī Shahwān, a professor of cardiology at al-Zaqāzīq University, was of sufficient stature within the Brotherhood to warrant a public statement on his death in 2007 by the movement's general guide, Mahdī ʿĀkif, and had been one of the movement's nominees for parliament in 1987.[7] Other prominent Brothers on the board have included, at various times, Gamāl Ḥishmat, a former Muslim Brotherhood parliamentarian and, after Mubarak's ouster, a member of the Freedom and Justice Party's National Committee; ʿAbd al-Munʿim Abū al-Futūh, at one time a member of the Brotherhood's guidance bureau; and Maḥmūd ʿIzzat, who, as of this writing, is the movement's deputy general guide.

The founding of the IMA came during a period of relative comity between the Muslim Brotherhood and the regime. Sadat had been bedeviled by criticism from the left for his departures from Nasser's policies and, according to Davis (1984, 152), viewed the Brothers as an effective "counterweight to the left." The regime was thus supportive of the IMA, and the Ministry of Defense gifted it a 22,000-square-meter tract of land for the construction of a large hospital (the aforementioned Central Charitable Hospital, or CCH) that would commemorate President Sadat's "victory" against Israel in the 1973 Yom Kippur war.[8] The groundbreaking ceremony was attended by the president as well as by then vice president Mubarak and "the minister of defense, prominent doctors and notable men of the country."[9] President Sadat placed the hospital's foundation stone himself.

The honeymoon between the Brotherhood and its patron, the self-styled "believing president (*al-raʾīs al-muʾmin*)" (Khadduri 1999, 99) was short-lived,

6 Law 84 of 2002, Part 1, Chapter 4, Article 42.

7 "*Al-Murshid al-ʿām yanʿī al-duktūr Luṭfī Shahwān* (The General Guide Mourns Dr. Luṭfī Shahwān)," *Ikhwan Online* (Cairo), September 9, 2007; available at: http://www.ikhwanonline.com/new/Article.aspx?ArtID=30863&SecID=0.

8 *Al-Jamʿiyya al-Ṭibiyya al-Islāmiyya, Al-Mustashfā al-Khairī al-Markazī*, n.d., 1.

9 Ibid., 2.

however, and the IMA and its grand hospital were to suffer accordingly. In response to the widespread criticism of the 1978 Camp David Accords and the 1979 Egyptian-Israeli Peace Treaty, Sadat in September 1981 ordered the arrest of more than a thousand opposition figures and shut down Muslim Brotherhood–affiliated organizations, including its magazine, *al-Daʿwa*, and the IMA (El Saadawi 2007; Makram-Ebeid 1989). Construction on the CCH was halted and did not resume again until April 1982, when a court found that the IMA "had no relationship with any acts of extremism that happened during this period."[10]

Progress on the hospital – which was to have 300 beds – proceeded slowly. By 1986, the concrete had been poured for the first three of four planned floors. However, the entire project was once again brought to a halt. A 2010 IMA document detailing the history of the CCH tells what happened:

> We were surprised by the military's seizure, once again, of the site, and the expulsion of the workers and engineers without giving any reason. The armed forces seized the architectural plans and forced the architects, Integrated Consultations Company, and the contractors, the Arab Contractors, to complete the hospital under their contracts with us and with the same plans. They put up multiple banners on the site, calling it the "Center for Rehabilitation of the Wounded During the October War."[11]

The seized hospital was finally opened shortly thereafter as the al-Galāʾ Military Hospital for the Families of Officers (Mustashfā al-Galāʾ al-ʿAskarī li-ʿāʾilāt al-ḍubbāṭ) and is widely known as a place where President Mubarak would receive his annual checkup. It's worth noting that this living testament to the lengths that authoritarian regimes will go to prevent Islamists from challenging their monpoly over the poor lies on the main road from Cairo International Airport into the city center and thus has likely been driven past by virtually every scholar of Egyptian politics over the past quarter century.

The story of the IMA does not end with seizure of the CCH, however. The association turned to the courts to retrieve its property, and in 1991, the Ministry of Defense offered the IMA a settlement, compensating the group with 500,000 Egyptian pounds and a smaller (8,500-square-meter) piece of land in the then-new suburb of Naṣr City. To make up for the tract's diminished size, the IMA was allegedly given permission to build eleven stories instead of four. The groundbreaking on the new iteration of the CCH took place in 1993 and was attended by the National Democratic Party (NDP)–affiliated head of the Egyptian Physicians Syndicate, Ḥamdī al-Sayyid, indicating, perhaps, that the hospital had the state's blessing once again.

However, between 1993 and 2006, the project stalled repeatedly both for lack of funds and because of bureaucratic hurdles thrown up by the municipal government of Naṣr City. In 1997, the city declared that the IMA's plans to build

[10] Ibid., 3.
[11] Ibid., 3.

to a height of thirty-six meters (eight stories) were in violation of local building codes and that the hospital would be limited to twenty-four meters (six stories). The IMA sued in court and won and by 2006 had finally neared completion on the main eight-story building, as well as on a smaller five-story outpatient clinic.[12] Once again, however, the city government declared that the building was in violation of the law and ordered its demolition. The case worked its way through the courts and was finally given a court date of December 10, 2009. The bulldozers showed up anyway:

> We tried to explain to those responsible for implementing [the city's] decision that there had been scheduled an emergency court date to look into staying the decision, and that [the city] must wait for the court's decision in order not to waste public funds [on the demolition]. But we found no one to respond to us. Instead, the demolition shovels continued for more than a month, using heavy equpment as if they were in a race against time.[13]

An administrative court issued a ruling freezing the demolition on December 17, 2009, but by then the damage had been done. The top floor and much of the floor beneath it had been demolished. When I visited the hospital in the summer of 2010, it lacked electricity, and several millions of pounds worth of medical equipment sat in its various rooms gathering dust. The project director, a Brotherhood physician named Muḥyī al-Dīn Zāyiṭ (who would later serve on the assembly that would write Egypt's first postrevolutionary constitution) was visibly heartbroken as he showed me the damage to the upper floors. It would not be until after the January 25, 2011, revolution that the hospital would finally open to the public.

What the story of the IMA and its CCH teach us is that it is exceedingly difficult for any independent political movement in an authoritarian regime to "rival the state." Opposition groups in authoritarian regimes that seek to make investments in fixed capital – such as schools, hospitals, day-care centers, and clinics – do so at great risk because the regime can, at a moment's notice, seize what it likes and destroy everything else. This does not mean that the Muslim Brotherhood and its members were not involved in the provision of social services during the Mubarak era. Many Muslim Brotherhood members involved themselves in the provision of social services through preexisting Islamic organizations and associations. However, as we will see in the following section, these activities were also strictly policed by the state, and their political potential consequently muted.

3.2 The Limits of Entryism

If the regime prevented the Brotherhood from developing "bricks and mortar" (Cammett and Issar 2010) operations, it would have to find other ways of reaching potential voters. One way to do this was the strategy of *entryism* – named after

12 Ibid., 4–6.
13 Ibid., 9.

the Trotskyist technique of infiltrating existing workers' organizations with the aim of changing them from within (Shipley 1977, Webber 2009). In this telling, the Muslim Brotherhood could attempt to reach the masses indirectly through preexisting Islamic social-service networks, thus eluding the watchful eye of the state.

One institution the Brotherhood was said to have penetrated during the Mubarak era was al-Jamʿiyya al-Sharʿiyya li-Taʿāwun al-ʿĀmilīn bil-Kitāb wa al-Sunna al-Muḥammadiyya (the Legitimate Society for the Cooperation of Those Who Work by the Book and the Muhammadan Traditions, here abbreviated JS), described in Section 1.3. One report in the (admittedly anti-Brotherhood) magazine *Rose al-Yūsif* recently declared, "As for the Jamʿiyya al-Sharʿiyya, it is well known that it is the mother that long cradled the idea of the Society of Muslim Brothers, for it was founded along with the Muslim Brotherhood at the same time."[14] Another (typically overheated) report, rendered prior to the 2010 parliamentary elections, declared that "from the founding of the JS nearly 70 years ago, it has been penetrated from the inside by the Society of Muslim Brothers" and warned of a Muslim Brotherhood plan to secure voting cards for recipients of JS aid and then to bus them to the polls on election day.[15]

Leaving aside the fact that the JS actually predates the founding of the Muslim Brotherhood by sixteen years, the evidence of ties between the Brotherhood and the JS is complex. The society has always claimed that it abstains from political activity. According to Salāma (2010), the JS "does not engage in politics, nor does it speak about it, nor does it take any political positions." Wickham (2001, 128) reports to us the assessment of the Jamʿiyya rendered by one Islamic activist: "It stays far away from politics. It focuses on spreading the reading of the *Qur'an*, religious commentaries, religious culture, and promoting a religious consciousness." So assiduously did the movement appear to avoid politics during the Mubarak era that the president of the JS in April 2011 confessed to the Egyptian newspaper *al-Jumhūriyya* that he had "refused to allow the youth of the JS to go down to Taḥrīr square on January 25."[16]

That said, there is an undeniable historical association between the Brothers and the JS. The Brotherhood's founder, Ḥasan al-Bannā, routinely wrote in the society's magazine, *al-'Iʿtiṣām* (*Steadfastness*), and when asked to explain the difference between his movement and the JS, he quipped, "The Ikhwān are in al-Darb al-Aḥmar [a neighborhood of Cairo], and the Jamʿiyya is in al-Khayāmiyya [another neighborhood]" – in other words, the only difference between the two

14 ʿIṣām ʿAbd al-Jawwād, "*Laʿbat shad ḥabl bayn al-Salafīyīn wa al-Ikhwān li-Istiqtab 8 milyūn ṣawt min Anṣār al-Sunnah* (Tug of War between the Salafis and the Brothers to Capture 8 Million Votes from Ansar al-Sunnah)," *Rose al-Yūsif* (Cairo), October 25, 2011.

15 ʿIṣām al-Asyūṭī, "*Khiṭṭat al-Ikhwān lil-sayṭara ʿalā aṣwāt al-'arāmil wa al-muṭalliqāt fi al-Jamʿiyya al-Sharʿiyya* (Plan of the Brotherhood to Capture the Votes of Widows and Divorcees in the JS)," al-Anbā' al-Dawliyya (Cairo), July 20, 2010; available at: http://www.alanbaa-aldawlia.info/the85/body.asp?field=kadaya&id=58.

16 *Al-Jumhūriyya* (Cairo), Friday April 15, 2011.

groups was where their headquarters were located.[17] Under Mubarak, as today, Muslim Brotherhood members were often active in the JS – although the extent to which this was part of a Brotherhood strategy of penetration or the natural result of the Brotherhood's and JS's overlapping interests is unclear. Nonetheless, this interpenetration did appear to have political benefits. Al-Muḥammadī ʿAbd al-Maqṣūd, a Muslim Brotherhood deputy from Ḥulwān in the 2005–2010 parliament, told me that he became known in his district through his work setting up a branch of the JS in his district.[18]

However, as with the IMA, the security services heavily policed any relationships between Islamic charitable associations and the Muslim Brotherhood. In a May 2011 interview with an Egyptian newspaper, the head of the JS reminisced about his organization's difficulties with the security services, which were keen to keep him away from the Brotherhood:

> If we speak about the harrassments of the security apparatus, they were many. But this did not stop us from pursuing our service activities. But State Security would investigate our intentions. The most prominent harassment from them was that they wanted to push us into the political realm, which runs contrary to our program of non-interference in politics. They asked us to send poor women in Giza to the ballot box in the last elections to vote for the National Democratic Party, but I refused this completely. They accused me of supporting the opposition and wishing ill for the NDP, and even said I was secretly a member of the Muslim Brotherhood due to the fact that one of the speakers in the mosques of the JS was a Brother. So I said to them, "Go to him and ask him and if it turns out that he is from the Brotherhood we will fire him immediately."[19]

Further evidence of the regime's efforts to prevent the Brotherhood from benefiting from its links to the JS can be found in the regime's policing of the (now-defunct) magazine *al-ʾIʿtiṣām*. Though the journal was never the property of the JS but was rather licensed in the name of one of its shaykhs, Aḥmad ʿĪssā ʿĀshūr (who also owned the Islamic publishing house Dār al-ʾIʿtiṣām), it at one point described itself as the *lisān ḥāl* (official organ) of the JS. The magazine appears to have been politically quiescent during the Nasser years, but under Sadat, it became a reliable and outspoken mouthpiece for Islamist causes in general and the Muslim Brotherhood in particular. In fact, so completely did it give itself over to supporting the Brotherhood that it is referred to throughout the English-language literature on Egypt in this period as a Muslim Brotherhood organ (Warburg 1982, 148–9; Davis 1984, 152; Makram-Ebeid 1989). Whether

[17] ʿAbduh Mustafā Disūqī, "*Al-Imām Ḥasan al-Bannā fī ʿuyūn muʿāsirīh* (Imām Ḥasan al-Bannā in the Eyes of His Contemporaries)," *Ikhwan Online*, February 13, 2008; available at http://www.ikhwanonline.com/Article.asp?ArtID=34462&SecID=372. We also read that someone asked al-Bannā why the Jamʿiyya builds mosques and the Brothers do not. He is said to have replied: "Their job is to build them, our job is to fill them."
[18] Interview with al-Muḥammadī ʿAbd al-Maqṣūd, Ḥulwān, July 2006.
[19] *Al-Jumhūriyya* (Cairo), Friday, April 15, 2011.

the magazine was genuinely part of the JS (let alone the Brotherhood) during this time or not is open to question, but what is clear is that Sadat was troubled enough by what appeared in the magazine's pages to shut it down during the crackdown on the opposition in September 1981. The magazine remained suspended until 1985.[20] Apparently unchastened by its four-year hiatus, in 1987 the magazine ran an extensive series of articles in support of the Muslim Brotherhood's candidates in that year's parliamentary election. An exhortation in the magazine's April 1987 issue is worth reproducing in full, both to give a flavor of the magazine's support for the Brothers and, given the discussion in Chapter 2, for its focus on the left (specifically, its attempt to brand the left with precisely the reputation for failure that scholars have long attributed to it):

> My brother the voter: Real and convincing temptations and promises and election bribes must not obscure the ugly face of those who abandoned God and his prophet, whether in the government or the opposition. So do not be fooled by what they do, and do not forget that Allah witnesses all things!! Brother voter, when you think of voting for a Nasserist or a Marxist even a bit, remember the prisons, the jails, the confiscations, the torturing of those who believe in God and those who preach the religion of Islam, and remember also the bitter and total defeats in the mountains of Yemen and the loss of the Sinai twice!![21]

A magazine with those political leanings could not expect to remain in operation for long, and it was thus unsurprising that it was closed for good in 1990, when the regime refused to renew its license after its owner's death. The JS went without an official magazine for fourteen years before finally publishing *al-Tibyān*, which was generally considered less partisan than *al-'I'tiṣam*.[22]

The regime's avid interference in the Brotherhood's relationship to the JS and its journal demonstrates the limits of the entryist strategy. But there is an additional reason why penetration of Islamic social-service organizations was unlikely to redound to the Brotherhood's electoral benefit. Quite simply, the allies of the regime could infiltrate such organizations as well. As Bin Nafīsa and ʿArafāt (2005, 213) pointed out, "Sometimes the presidents of local branches of the JS are members of the National Democratic Party." For example, ʿĀdil Abū Ṣulayb, an unsuccessful candidate in the 2005 and 2010 elections, was both the president of his local branch of the JS (in the Giza district of al-Haram) and a local secretary

20 Maḥmūd Khalīl, "*Al-shaykh Aḥmad ʿĪssā ʿĀshūr ... rā'id al-ṣaḥāfa al-Islāmiyya (1889–1990): 'Assis majalat al-'Iʿtiṣām liltaʿbīr ʿan qaḍāyā al-'umma* (Shaykh Aḥmad ʿĪssā ʿĀshūr ... Pioneer of Islamic Journalism (1889–1990): Founded the Magazine *al-'Iʿtiṣām* to Express the Issues of the Nation)," *al-Tibyān* (Cairo), No. 75, May 26, 2011; available at: http://www.alshareyah.com/index.php?option=com_content&view=article&id=1671:-1889-1990-qq-&catid=138:issue-75&Itemid=812.

21 *Al-'Iʿtiṣām*, April 1987, 21.

22 Ḥasan Salāma, "*Al-Salafiyūn fī Miṣr: Muʿḍila 'am ḥal?* (The Salafists in Egypt: Problem or Solution?)," *al-Dimūqrāṭiyya* (Cairo), April 1, 2010; available at: http://democracy.ahram.org.eg/UI/Front/InnerPrint.aspx?NewsID=378.

of the NDP.[23] In a mirror image of the accusations made against the Brotherhood, during the 2005 parliamentary elections, one news outlet reported that the regime and "security agencies" exerted "heavy pressures" on the JS "to ensure support for the candidates of the National Democratic Party" by compelling widows dependent on the association to vote for the ruling party.[24] (Though, as we have seen, the leader of the JS has said he was able to resist such pressures.)

Of course, the JS is but one Islamic charitable association, and members of the Brotherhood have been found to be affiliated with a wide variety of local-level associations that may, by virtue of their diminutive size, have been less legible to the authoritarian state. Perusing the biographies of Muslim Brotherhood parliamentary candidates in the 2010 elections, one sees repeated mentions of the candidates' membership in the JS as well as in numerous local Islamic charities, such as al-Jamʿiyya al-Tarbawiyya al-Islāmiyya (Islamic Training Association) in the al-Gharbiyya governorate, Jamʿiyyat al-Muwāsa al-Khayriyya al-Islāmiyya (al-Muwāsa Islamic Charitable Society) in al-Munūfiyya, Jamʿiyyat al-Risāla al-Khayriyya (The Message Charitable Society), and Jamʿiyyat al-Ḍiāʾ al-Khayriyya (The Luminance Charitable Society), to name just a few. However, there are several reasons why it is similarly unlikely that participation in these smaller associations could have been deployed to *clientelistic* purposes during the Mubarak regime. In addition to the simple fact of security services interference was the fact that many such charities were also co-opted by the regime and its allies. For example, in December 2007, the independent Egyptian newspaper *al-Miṣrī al-Yawm* published an exposé on the use of public funds by ruling-party deputies to pay for charitable projects in their home districts: a number of the ruling party's deputies dispensed their allotments through local Islamic associations.[25] In 2005 in the rural district of Bilbays, Maḥmūd Khamīs, an NDP candidate and part of the family that owns the multi-million-dollar carpet manufacturing enterprise Oriental Weavers Group (Majmūʿat al-Nassājūn al-Sharqiyūn), touted his donations to one Islamic association, Jamʿiyyat al-Khayr al-Islāmiyya, in neighborhood 15 of

23 Aḥmad Jamal, "*Nakhibu al-Giza: Lan nasmah biʿawdat al-fulūl* (Voters of al-Giza: We Will Not Permit the Return of the Remnants)," *Ikhwān Online*, December 10, 2011; available at: http://www.Ikhwānonline.com/Article.aspx?artid=96942&secid=250. It's worth noting that in 2011, he ran for parliament again and won – this time on the banner of the Nūr Party. However, he died shortly after his victory and without ever having taken his seat. See Mahmud Ramzi, "*Wafat Abu Sulayb, na'ib Ḥizb al-Nur ʿan da'ira Shimal al-Giza* (Death of Abu Sulayb, Parliamentary Deputy of the Nūr Party for the District of North Giza)," *al-Misrī al-Yawm* (Cairo), December 20, 2011; and Aḥmad Abu Salih, "*Wafat ʿudw majlis al-shaʿb ʿAdil Abu Sulayb* (Death of People's Assembly Member ʿAdil Abu Sulayb)," *al-Wafd* (Cairo), December 20, 2011.

24 Muhammad Rashīd, "*al-Watani yadghat lihashd aramil al-Jamʿiyya al-Sharʿiyya lil-taswit li-murashahih* (The National Democratic Party Pressures to Mobilize the Widows of al-Jamʿiyya al-Sharʿiyya to Vote for Its Candidates)," *al-Misriyun* (Cairo), December 5, 2005.

25 "*Bi al-mustanadāt wa al-arqām: Al-Misrī al-Yawm takshif tafāsīl rashāwī al-hukuma li nuwwāb al-Watanī* (With Documents and Numbers: *Al-Misri al-Yawm* Exposes Government Bribes to the Deputies of the National Democratic Party)," *al-Misri al-Yawm*, December 10, 2007; available at: http://www.almasry-alyoum.com/article2.aspx?ArticleID=85878.

10th of Ramadan City in his campaign literature, which boasts a photo of the candidate seated on a dais with leaders of the association.

On top of all of this is the fact that members of these associations – Brotherhood and non-Brotherhood alike – had powerful incentives to obscure any Brotherhood involvement in those associations, lest the regime deploy the provisions of the draconian law governing nongovernmental organizations. We have alread seen al-ʿIryān's testimony to this effect. However, while obscuring the Brotherhood's links to a particular charity may have protected it from the prying eyes of the state, it also would have by necessity rendered it of limited use as a vehicle for the building of electoral clienteles. After all, if a recipient of Islamic charitable services did not know that the organization that provided his or her blankets or free medicines had a Muslim Brotherhood member on its board, how likely was his or her receipt of such goods to make him or her vote for the movement at election time?

A dramatic example of the difficulty the Muslim Brotherhood faced in translating these subrosa poor-relief efforts into votes was offered during the 2005 elections by Amīr Bassām, a physician and Muslim Brotherhood candidate in Bilbays in the governorate of al-Sharqiyya (in the district neighboring that of then-parliamentarian, Mohamed Morsī). In the face of the tycoon Maḥmūd Khamīs' constant expenditures of money on beautification projects, garbage removal, and rumored payments to local notables, Bassām took to circulating a pamphlet detailing what he alleged were the Muslim Brotherhood's own contributions to the district. The document was entitled, "What the Muslim Brothers Have Given to the District of Bilbays, with the Cooperation of Those Who Do Good," and included a table purporting to show that the Brotherhood had spent more than 10 million L.E. in Bilbays over the previous five years (see Table 3.1). In his public speeches, though, Bassām was careful to note that this impressive amount did not come from the Brothers but rather from "you, the people of the district." When I asked him about this – how could he claim that the Brotherhood gave 10 million to the district and also say that the money came from the people of the district – he told me that the money was disbursed by local charitable organizations in which Brotherhood members were involved but in which their role was not well known. As expected, Bassām lost that contest (although he would finally be carried into office after the January 25, 2011, revolution).

Informal Service Provision

If entryism was of limited value for the building of electoral constituencies, is it possible that the Muslim Brotherhood engaged in more direct clientelistic efforts among the poor in informal realms not easily observed by researchers? My interviews with Muslim Brotherhood activists in al-Zaqāzīq and al-Gīza during the prerevolutionary period did suggest that a significant portion of the Muslim Brotherhood's outreach occurred in this way. Here is how a Brother from al-Zaqāzīq described to me the manner in which the movement provides aid to the town's poor:

Table 3.1 *Muslim Brotherhood's Claimed Charitable Works in Bilbays, 2000–2005*

Area of activity	Item	Amount (L.E.)
Poverty alleviation		
	Orphan sponsorship	2,500,000
	Aid to orphans	200,000
	Holiday gifts	150,000
Disaster relief		
	Material support	200,000
	Medical aid	250,000
	Winter blankets	575,000
Seasonal charitable projects		
Feasts	Meat and slaughtered cattle	1,275,000
	Hides	210,000
Ramadan	Ramadan baskets	2,600,000
	Holiday clothes	900,000
	Books and publications	23,000
Education		
al-Azhar schools	Desks	112,000
	Renovations	60,000
	Tuition	50,000
Public schools	Tuition	110,000
	Clothes	750,000
	Student aid	555,000
Marriage		
	Aid to 390 brides	225,000
TOTAL		10,745,000

> During Ramadan, someone who wants to do good will give us, say, 5,000 pounds and tell us to distribute it among the needy people in the district. He knows that we are in touch with the needy people, particularly the orphans and the widows. And we will make Ramadan baskets, worth 50 pounds each, with sugar and tea and blankets, and give one to each family.

When I asked him how the Brotherhood knew who was in need, he told me, "We usually find out who the needy are from elders in the mosques who know the situations in their neighborhoods well," which speaks of the informal nature of this kind of activity.[26]

26 Interview with Muslim Brotherhood activist in al-Zaqāzīq, February 15, 2007.

For a sense of the scale of these kinds of efforts, in 2007 I obtained from one of my Brotherhood informants a list of all the recipients of the society's aid in the *shiākha* of Abū Qatāda (part of Bulāq al-Dakrur and one of eleven *shiākhas* in Giza's third electoral district). The list was dominated by orphans – which in Egypt also refers to those with only one parent – but also included the mentally disabled, the terminally ill, widows without independent means of support, and families with sick children. In keeping with my al-Zaqāzīq informant's description of the manner in which the Brotherhood comes to know the district's poor, many of the entries have notations next to them indicating the individual who put the Brothers in touch with the recipient. For example, next to the entry for one woman, a widow with leukemia, we read, "from Yāssir Fārūq the shopkeeper." Yāssir's name also appears next to the entry for a divorcee with "an old fracture." More prolific middlemen (and women) on behalf of the Brothers include Ṣābir the clothes presser (twenty-four entries), a woman named Umm Barā' (thirty-four entries), and Hajj Abū Sāmī (forty entries). Twenty-five entries are attributed to the local secondary school, Madrassa Mustafā Kāmil, suggesting a Brotherhood supporter within the school – perhaps a social worker – who could identify needy cases.

Abū Qatāda is one of the poorest areas in the environs of Cairo. Approximately 32 percent of its 9,245 households contain just one or two rooms, and 34 percent of adults in the district are illiterate. And yet, according to the document I received, only 456 households received Brotherhood support. That is, the Brotherhood's poor-relief operation in this particular area reached about 5 percent of the population. Of course, given the small vote shares needed to win in Mubarak's Egypt, even these limited efforts at service provision might have been enough to tip the scales in a Muslim Brotherhood candidate's favor. And though the Brother who shared the document with me was anxious to tell me that the Brotherhood makes no effort to try to mobilize those who receive its support, telling me that "we do this for the face of God, not to win elections," it is hard to believe that the recipients of the Muslim Brotherhood's kindnesses are not expected to render votes in return. After all, the mere existence of the kind of spreadsheet described here is consistent with what we expect of political machines. If the Brotherhood were going to mobilize the recipients of its aid, it would want to keep track of them – and of the individuals who vouched for them – in precisely the way the spreadsheet does. However, it is worth noting that in 2005 the Brotherhood did not field a candidate in the electoral district in which Abū Qatāda falls. Moreover, it is not clear that the Brotherhood was each person's sole source of aid or whether the amount of aid received by each person was sufficient to engender political loyalty. As Clark (2004, 959) tells us, many recipients of Islamic aid in Jordan were guilty of "double dipping," which "challenges the assumption that the poor attribute some form of loyalty, ideological or otherwise, to the aid they receive. Although the poor could have multiple patron-client ties at the same time, it cannot be assumed that at election time (or at demonstrations), this will convert to ideological support for Islamists, as opposed to the government or other ideological groups." The same dynamic is likely to have operated in Mubarak's

Egypt, especially because the regime's periodic crackdowns against the Muslim Brotherhood may have rendered poor voters particularly unlikely to put themselves at risk by marking ballots for the movement, even if they occasionally received help from its members.

Finally, even if the regime could not observe transactions between Muslim Brothers and their potential clients, it could take actions to dry up the resources on which those transactions depend. For example, an American diplomat in 2010 wrote a revealing dispatch on the regime's attempt to squeeze the Muslim Brotherhood in the Nile Delta town of al-Mansura in advance of that year's parliamentary elections, and its particular focus on robbing the movement of the ability to provide social services:

> Amer Fares, a local businessman and director of a youth empowerment NGO, told us that the [Government of Egypt] has cracked down on Muslim Brotherhood (MB) businessmen in Mansoura to the extent that the MB can no longer provide social services in the city. He said the GOE began to run prominent legitimate MB merchants out of business six months ago to weaken the organization in advance of the 2010 parliamentary elections.[27]

What the foregoing discussion reminds us, if we needed reminding, is that Egypt prior to the 2011 revolution was an authoritarian regime – the oft-used *semi*-qualifier notwithstanding. Elections may have been somewhat more competitive than the conventional wisdom gave them credit for, but the relative absence of election-day fraud was made possible only by systematic efforts by the regime on every other day of the year to tilt the playing field in its favor. This not only involved capturing the poor with offers of patronage and services, but preventing other groups from doing the same. All of this makes the Muslim Brotherhood's electoral victories under authoritarianism even more remarkable.

Individual-Level Evidence

If the story told in this chapter is correct, we should find that receipt of social services from Islamic institutions should not have caused individuals to be more likely to cast ballots for the Muslim Brotherhood during elections in the Mubarak era. The absence of Muslim Brotherhood–branded social-service operations, the keenness with which Islamic service providers distanced themselves from (or obscured their links to) the Muslim Brotherhood, and the ability of the ruling party to repress or co-opt Islamic charitable organizations all should militate against the existence of a strong link between receiving Islamic services during the Mubarak era and voting for his Islamist challengers. In this section I attempt to test this hypothesis using individual survey data – collected in December 2011 – on healthcare provision and patterns of voting during the Mubarak era. I show

[27] "Power, Politics, and Civil Society in the Delta City of Mansoura," U.S. Embassy, Cairo, July 19, 2009; available at: http://wikileaks.org/cable/2009/07/09CAIRO1393.html.

Table 3.2 *Patterns of Healthcare Usage, Egypt 2011*

Type of facility	Percent reporting use
Mosque clinic	19.28%
Church clinic	7.88%
Islamic charitable society	12.30%
Christian charitable society	6.45%
Nonreligious charitable society	9.85%
Medical caravan	9.91%
Government hospital	78.03%
Private clinic or hospital	79.88%

that recipients of Islamic healthcare services were highly unlikely to vote for the Muslim Brotherhood and that as many recipients of such services reported voting for the ruling party as reported voting for the Islamists.

First, the survey asked respondents whether they had voted in the 2010 elections, and, if the answer was affirmative, which party they had voted for. Of course, these data are likely to be of limited reliability. The previous regime was so universally discredited after the revolution that to admit having participated in its rigged elections was likely a difficult thing for an Egyptian to do in those heady months after Mubarak's overthrow. Similarly, we would expect people who had voted for the now-dissolved NDP to be unlikely to admit it, and we might also expect people to be more likely to retrospectively claim to have voted for its main opponent, the Muslim Brotherhood, even when they had not. Further complicating any analysis of these data is that we would expect such retrospective revision to be more likely among poor voters, for whom the stigma of having sold votes or otherwise supported the widely reviled regime was likely to be particularly intense.

Respondents were then asked about the various healthcare services they have relied on in the past, without specifying a time frame. The options were "Health services through a mosque" (*khadamāt ṣiḥiyya tābiʿa li-masjid*), "Health services through a church or Christian house of worship" (*khadamāt ṣiḥiyya tābiʿa likanīsa aw dūr ʿibāda masīḥiyya*), "Islamic charitable society" (*jamʿiyya khayriyya islāmiyya*), "Christian charitable society" (*jamʿiyya khayriyya masīḥiyya*), "Nonreligious charitable society" (*jamʿiyya khayriyya ghayr dīniyya*), "Government health center or hospital" (*wiḥda ṣiḥiyya aw mustashfā ḥukūmī*), "Private clinic or hospital" (*ʿayāda aw mustashfā khāṣ*), and "Medical caravan under the auspices of one of the candidates in elections in your district" (*qāfila ṭibbiya taḥt raʿāyat aḥad al-mutarashaḥīn fī al-intikhābāt qurb dāʾiratak*). The full results are presented in Table 3.2. Of the sample of 1,675, 323 (19.28 percent) reported having used a mosque clinic, and 206 (12.30 percent) admitted to relying on an Islamic charitable society. The total number of respondents who used either of these two forms of Islamic healthcare provision was 347 (20.72 percent).

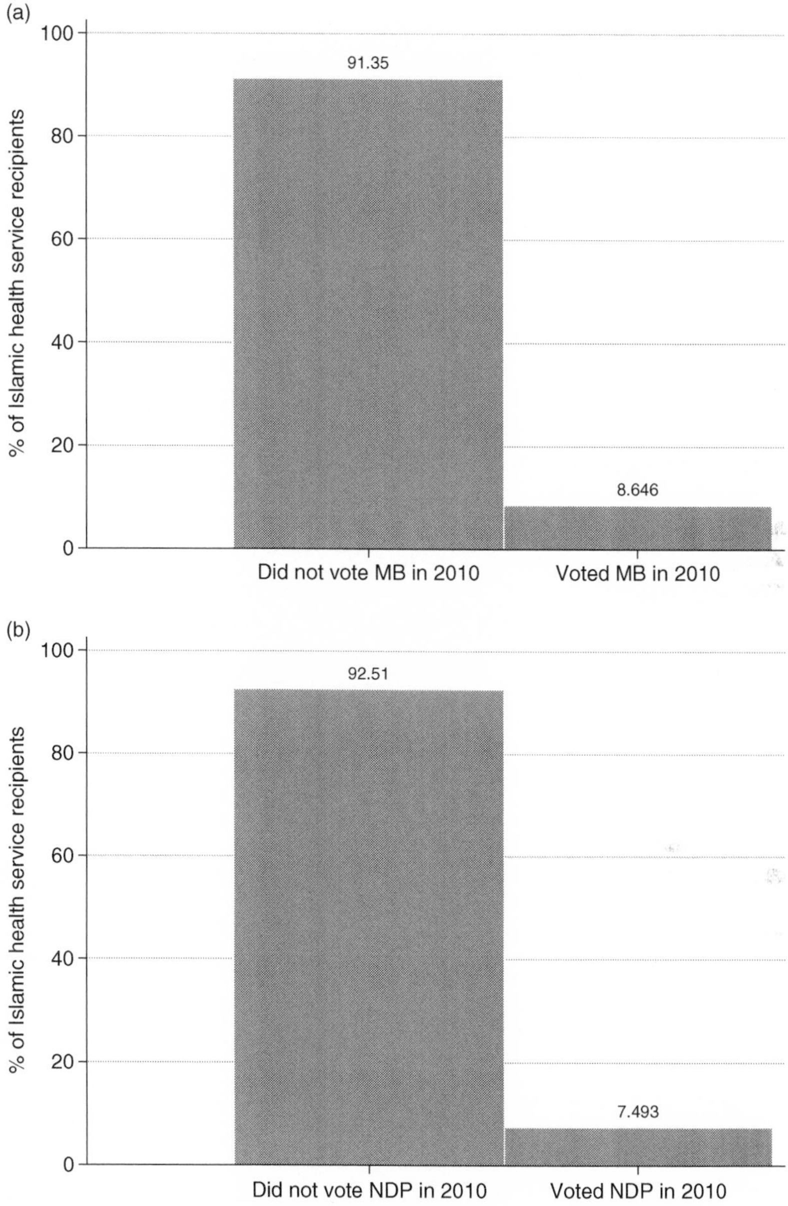

Figure 3.1 The limits of Islamic healthcare in yielding votes under Mubarak: (a) voting for the Muslim Brotherhood; (b) voting for the NDP.

How likely were recipients of Islamic healthcare services to have voted for the Brotherhood versus the ruling party in 2010? The share of recipients of Islamic healthcare services who voted for the Muslim Brotherhood in 2010 is shown in Figure 3.1*a*, and the share of those who voted for the NDP that year is shown in Figure 3.1*b*. All told, approximately 8 percent of recipients of Islamic healthcare voted for the Muslim Brotherhood in 2010, and a similar number voted for the NDP. In other words, not only were the vast majority of recipients of Islamic healthcare services unlikely to support the Muslim Brotherhood, but they were also as likely to support the ruling party as they were to support the Islamists who had allegedly provided those services.

These data, collected as they were at some remove from the 2010 elections – less in terms of actual time than in terms of the scope of political change that had occurred in the interim – must be interpreted with caution. But they do confirm the intuition of this chapter – that the Islamist movement's electoral victories during the Mubarak years could not have been built on a strong clientelistic component. Though the Muslim Brotherhood undoubtedly engaged in social-service activities during this period, these were too limited in scope and too vulnerable to regime depredations to have enabled the movement to compete with the ruling party on clientelistic grounds. If we want to explain how the Brothers were able to emerge as the principal regime opponent under the dome of parliament, we will have to look elsewhere.

3.3 Conclusion

During the 2005 parliamentary elections, the Muslim Brotherhood's newspaper at the time, *'Āfāq 'Arabiyya* (*Arab Horizons*), published a list detailing all the service activities of the seventeen deputies who had served in the previous parliamentary term and who, along with almost 150 of their fellow Brothers, were seeking election to the legislature that year:

- 600 medical caravans × 100 patients = 60,000 beneficiaries
- 250 celebrations for graduates × 100 students = 25,000 students
- 30,000 decisions for free healthcare [paid for by the government] × 2,000 L.E. = 60 million L.E.
- 250 meetings and debates to discuss scores of national issues
- 3,000 visits to agencies and institutions and workplaces
- 1,000 cataract surgeries in cooperation with al-Maghrabi Eye Hospitals
- 150 lessons for youth (computing, design, calligraphy, etc.) that benefited approximately 15,000 young men and women
- 75 literacy classes for approximately 2,500 men and women[28]

The rationale behind the publication of this list, one supposes, was to suggest that such efforts were but a small preview of what would come if voters

[28] See "*Al-Ikhwān taht qubbat al-Barlamān* (Brothers under the Dome of Parliament)," *Āfāq 'Arabiyya*, November 10, 2005, Election Supplement, 12.

put more members of the Brotherhood in office. But what struck me was something else entirely: the 1,000 cataract surgeries performed "in cooperation with al-Maghrabi Eye Hospitals." The chairman of that group of hospitals – one of the largest such establishments in the Middle East – was a well-known supporter of the Mubarak regime, and his brother served as the minister of housing in Mubarak's last cabinet. Moreover, the charitable program of cataract surgeries described in the Brotherhood's materials was not something specific to the Brothers but was rather a nationwide charitable effort conducted by the hospital in concert with members of parliament regardless of their political affiliation.[29] If the Brotherhood was indeed possessed of the vast social-service operations, the "state-within-a-state" (Davis and Robinson 2009, 1321) that was often ascribed to it, it is puzzling that its parliamentarians would instead tout as a singular achievement the free provision of healthcare by a private hospital owned by a family closely tied to the ruling regime.

In fact, one might even argue that the Brotherhood's electoral victories were less the result of service provision than they were an attempt to gain the ability to provide services. After all, as Hāzim Salāh Abū Ismāʿīl, then an unsuccessful Brotherhood candidate for the assembly from Duqī in al-Gīza in 2005, pointed out to me, "Communication through other channels is targeted by the security services. The charitable associations are shut down and dissolved. In mosques, they prevent sermons."[30] The good offices of the MP were often the only resource the Brothers could draw on to provide succor to citizens. For example, Gamāl Ḥishmat, who had served in parliament from 2000 to 2003 and who was running for election to the same seat in 2005, singled out as his achievements, securing 1 million L.E. worth of medical treatment for 897 people; obtaining direct subsidies from the prime minister for seven mosques (14,000 L.E.), two youth centers (4,000 pounds), and ten charitable associations (15,000 L.E.); getting a commitment from the governor of al-Buhayra governorate to dedicate 54,000 L.E. to the upkeep of sixty-two mosques in the district; and arranging for the inhabitants of "building number 8 on Midān al-Utubīs Street" to have their homes connected to municipal gas mains. (He also claims to have brought electricity to twenty settlements, erected 140 lamp posts, paved fifty-five streets, brought running water to five villages, filled twenty-six canals and drainage ditches, and secured the jobs of forty-five employees in the local cancer center.[31]) At one level, the list is unremarkable – constituency service is what a member of parliament is supposed to do. But the only mention of Islamic charities is not as dispensers of largesse but as recipients of it.

29 See, for example, former NDP parliamentarian Mahmud Abu Zaid's reference to free eye care provided by Maghrabi Eye Hospitals to constituents in his district: http://mahmoudabuzeid.info/about-me-ar.html.

30 Interview with Hāzim Salāh Abū Ismāʿīl, *al-Dukkī*, Giza, April 2007.

31 "*Dr. Muhammad Gamāl Hishmat: Injāzāt Tatahadath ʿan Nafsāha* (Achievements that Speak for Themselves), *āfāq ʿArabiyya*, November 10, 2005, Election Supplement, 4.

Ṣābir ʿAbd al-Ṣādiq, a former Brotherhood deputy from the northern governorate of Damietta, produced a similarly impressive list of things he had done for his district during the 2005 elections. His glossy, twenty-eight-page pamphlet – complete with corroborating memoranda from the various ministries he dealt with – informed constituents that he was the first representative of Damietta to establish an office to receive constituents, that his office processed 19,000 citizen requests over the previous five years, and that he was able to secure from the government 7 million L.E. worth of medical treatment for 3,000 constituents. He also claimed to have secured 5,500 L.E. for every urban youth center and 2,300 L.E. for every rural one in the district. But the supporting documentation for this claim – an undated form letter[32] from the Ministry of Youth – suggests that the disbursements were part of a nationwide government-sponsored program. In fact, then-parliamentarian Mohamed Morsi also claimed to have secured the exact same amounts for youth centers in his district. If the Muslim Brotherhood commanded a state within a state, it was one that exhibited a healthy dependence on, of all things, the state.[33]

Where does this leave us? If the Muslim Brotherhood could not win elections through clientelistic services to the poor, then how was it able to defeat the regime's patronage machine (at least in some districts) while the left foundered and failed? That is the subject of the next chapter.

[32] It appears to be a form letter because it is typed with blank spaces where the name of the addressee, his title, and district were filled in by hand.

[33] Ṣābir ʿabd al-Ṣādiq, "Ḥiṣād khamsa aʿwām taḥt qubbat al-Barlamān 2000–2005 (The harvest of 5 Years under the Dome of Parliament)," Election Pamphlet, Damietta, 2005.

4

Winning in the "Well-Run Casino"

Chapter 2 demonstrated how the politics of patronage and clientelism pose severe disadvantages for opposition parties under authoritarianism. Parties of the left find that their fervently-believed and passionately-delivered messages of redistribution fall on deaf ears, as the poor and rural constituencies to which they are directed are forced to vote for regime allies and local notables who can have a rather more direct impact on their daily lives. Chapter 3 investigated one popular explanation for how the Muslim Brotherhood was able to overcome these difficulties: sweeping up the hearts, minds, and votes of the poor with an array of services thought to be so extensive that they constituted a veritable state within a state. However, given the many ways in which the regime intervened in the civic realm to prevent precisely this outcome from occurring, it is unlikely that the story is this simple.

In this chapter I offer an alternative account of the Muslim Brotherhood's electoral victories under authoritarianism. The movement did not try to beat the regime at the game of patronage but rather played a different game entirely. Instead of competing with the regime for the votes of the poor, I argue that the Brothers instead won elections by mobilizing a small middle-class constituency. If elections in Mubarak's Egypt were, to use Benedict Anderson's (1988) evocative phrase, a "well-run casino," the Muslim Brotherhood had found a way of beating the house. It was not, of course, enough to change the settled order of things or to challenge the regime's dominance over the political landscape – the Brotherhood was too cautious and the regime too fierce to allow that to happen. But the constancy of the Brotherhood's victories did allow it to fix itself in the popular imagination as the likely inheritor of a democratic Egypt. And that prophecy, like all such prophecies, would prove to have a self-fulfilling quality.

This chapter examines the anatomy of the Muslim Brotherhood's electoral victories. After showing how it was able to win seats with just a small core of supporters, I try to identify who those supporters were. I find that they were largely drawn from the middle classes. First, I show how the movement's middle-class bias was reflected in the social backgrounds of Muslim Brotherhood elites, who were generally more highly educated than elites of other parties, and in the Brotherhood's heavy reliance (relative to other parties) on information technologies that were accessible only to voters of means. Then, using an original database of the socioeconomic characteristics of Egypt's 222 constituencies during 2005 and 2010 parliamentary elections, I show that the Muslim Brotherhood's electoral mobilization efforts were also skewed toward middle-class voters. Finally, I address the question of why other opposition parties did not adopt this middle-class strategy. Drawing on historical archival and econometric evidence, I show that the Brotherhood's middle-class appeal had its roots in the movement's early decades, rendering it particularly fit for competing in authoritarian elections.

4.1 Beating the House

In order to understand how the Muslim Brotherhood won elections in Mubarak's Egypt, we could do no better than to examine how Egypt's first democratically elected president, Mohamed Morsi, won *his* first election, running for parliament on the Brotherhood's ticket in the town of Zagāzīg in 2000. Recall that after 1990, Egyptian elections were conducted according to a majoritarian, open-nomination system that dramatically lowered the barriers to entry for would-be candidates. Nationwide, thousands of candidates entered the electoral arena, and Morsi's district was no exception. As we can see from Table 4.1, which gives the complete results for the first round of balloting in the 2000 parliamentary election in Zagāzīg, Morsi was but one of more than two-dozen challengers for one of the district's two parliamentary seats.

One of the small ironies of elections in Mubarak's Egypt was that the large number of candidates was accompanied by a relatively small number of voters. Zagāzīg, for example, had 161,504 eligible voters, but only 29,920 (18.53 percent) of them came out to vote, of which 1,131 were deemed to have cast invalid ballots. Therefore, the election was decided by 28,789 voters, who had to choose among 26 candidates. Recall that, in Chapter 2, at least one of each district's two seats had to go to a candidate certified as a "worker" or "farmer," of which there were eleven competing in Morsi's first election. Non-worker/farmer candidates, such as Morsi (a university professor), were classified as "fiʿāt," loosely translated as "belonging to other groups," but here rendered as "elites." There were fifteen such candidates in Morsi's district. Though Morsi (candidate 6 in the table) was the top vote-getter from among the elite candidates, he earned only 7,920 votes (27.51 percent of valid ballots and only 4.9 percent of registered voters). Because he outpolled all other candidates (but did not earn an outright majority), he entered into a runoff with the three other top vote-getters from among the elites: candidate 10, ʿĀṭif al-Maghāwrī of the National Progressive Unionist Rally (NPUR), and two National Democratic Party (NDP) members who had failed to earn their party's nomination

Table 4.1 *First-Round Results (November 2000), First District, al-Zaqāzīq, Sharqiyya Governorate*

Number	Candidate name	Category	Votes	Party
1	Muḥammad al-Musallamī	Elite/withdrew	299	NDP (official)
2	Rif'at Bayūmī	Elite	4,557	NDP (official)
3	Khālid Zurduq	Elite	5,176	NDP (independent)
4	Dr. Muḥammad Mūsā	Elite	3,270	Independent
5	ʿĀdil ʿUmar	Elite	99	Independent
6	Mohamed Morsi	Elite	7,920	Muslim Brothers
7	Aḥmad al-Fudalī	Elite	3,028	NDP (independent)
8	Maḥmūd Manṣūr	Worker	1,252	Independent
9	Ṣubḥi Shalabī	Worker	708	Independent
10	ʿĀṭif al-Maghāwrī	Worker	3,494	NPUR
11	Dr. Muḥammad ʿAbd Allāh	Elite	184	Muslim Brothers
12	Al-Sayyid Jarīda	Elite	2,794	Independent
13	Nagāt al-Ghamrāwī	Worker	2,509	NDP (independent)
14	Luṭfī Shaḥāta	Worker	5,197	NDP (independent)
15	Majdī ʿĀshūr	Elite	5,645	NDP (independent)
16	Ḥasan Aṭiyah Sayyid Aḥmad	Elite	785	Independent
17	Ḥasan Faḍl	Elite	217	
18	Salāḥ al-Dusūqī	Worker	555	
19	Alāʾ ʿAbd Allāh	Worker		
20	Tāriq Rushdī	Elite	871	Wafd
21	ʿAbd Allāh Badr	Worker	2,083	
22	Al-Sayyid ʿAbd al-Ḥāfiẓ	Elite	2,083	Liberal
23	Muḥsin Jumʿa	Worker	55	
24	Ismāʿīl Ghālī	Worker	1,788	
25	Majdī Muḥammad	Elite	1,178	Independent
26	Rifaʿat Abū al-Saʿūd	Worker	2,311	Independent

and so ran as independents: candidate 14, Luṭfī Shaḥāta, and candidate 15, Majdī ʿĀshūr. In the runoff, Morsi earned approximately 13,000 votes of 24,000 cast, enough to become one of the district's two representatives and one of seventeen Muslim Brotherhood members of parliament that year.[1]

What Morsi's first victory teaches us – aside from the fact that Egypt's first democratically elected president began his political life with a relatively modest showing – is that it was possible to do well in Mubarak's elections with relatively small vote shares. After all, only about 27 percent of actual voters (or 4.9 percent of eligible voters) cast their ballots for Morsi in the first round of the election that eventually put him in parliament. If we added up all the votes earned by candidates affiliated with the NDP – the two official candidates plus the many

[1] The other seat in al-Zaqāzīq was won by Luṭfī Shaḥāta, the NDP independent, who, of course, quickly reentered the party's fold and was its nominee in 2010.

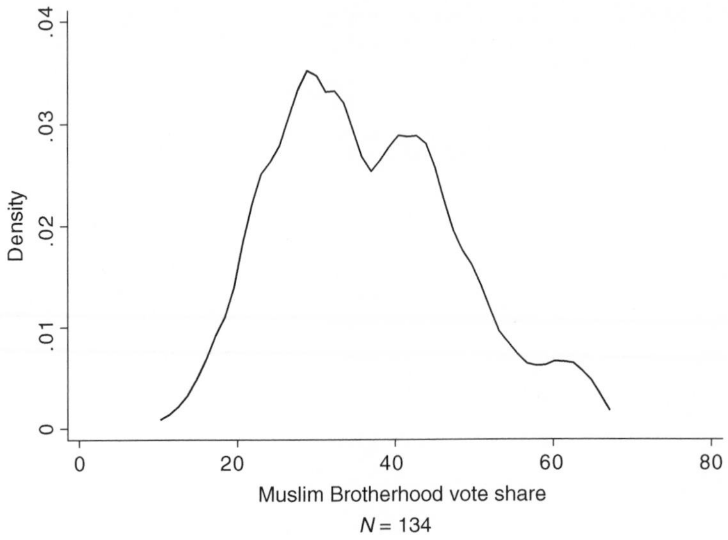

Figure 4.1 Muslim Brotherhood winners' vote shares (2005).

NDP members, such as Shaḥāta and ʿĀshūr, who ran as independents after failing to secure their party's nomination – they far exceed the number of Brotherhood votes. And though Morsi had to win a majority in a runoff election, his 13,000 runoff votes represented just over 8 percent of eligible voters. Thus the man who eventually succeeded the overthrown Mubarak (before being overthrown himself) won his first election not because most people in his district wanted him or his party, but because most people stayed home, and most of those who did vote ended up casting ballots for a heavily fragmented field. (As we shall see, this is a story that would be repeated in Morsi's presidential foray twelve years later.)

This is not a dynamic limited to Mr. Morsi, however. The same pattern – Brotherhood victories with small pluralities of voters – was evident during the 2005 parliamentary election, the apex of the Brotherhood's electoral success in Mubarak's Egypt. The Brotherhood had nominated 160 candidates in that election, 134 of whom either won outright or did well enough to enter a runoff election (of which 88 emerged victorious). The vote shares of Brothers who survived the first round in the 2005 election range from 11.49 to 64.66 percent, with a mean of 35.88 and standard deviation of 11.49 points. The distribution of these Muslim Brotherhood vote shares is shown in Figure 4.1. Though the Brotherhood won, it did so not by swaying majorities but by mobilizing minorities.

One might respond, of course, that these vote shares were likely depressed by the regime's acts of electoral manipulation. This is almost certainly the case. However, the 2005 elections were unique in that the way they were administered actually affords us the opportunity to control for electoral fraud, at least somewhat. In order to facilitate judicial oversight over the balloting, the elections had to be

Table 4.2 *2005 Vote Shares of Muslim Brothers Who Survived the First Round of the Electoral Competition, by Phase*

Phase	*N*	Mean	S.D.	Min	Max
All	134	35.88	11.49	8.50	64.66
1	46	33.73	10.20	8.50	62.32
2	53	40.94	12.23	12.81	64.66
3	35	31.07	8.97	15.97	47.22

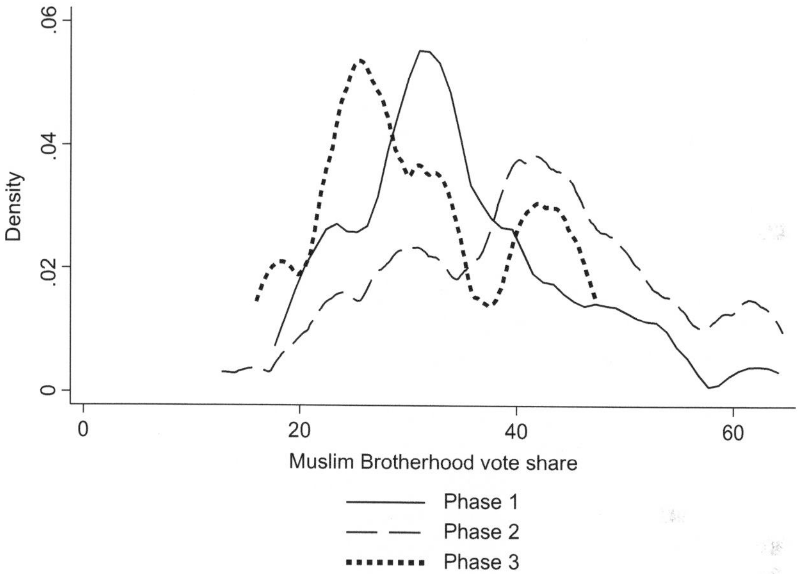

Figure 4.2 Muslim Brotherhood winners' vote shares, by electoral phase (2005).

staggered over three phases, with all of Egypt's judges migrating, en masse, from one part of the country to another every two weeks. The effect of this system was to allow the regime to calibrate its interventions based on its performance in the early phases. Thus, by all accounts, the regime engaged in almost no interference in the first phase, whereas the third and final phase was, in the words of one author, "akin to a war between the security forces and the people that were insistent on exercising their constitutional and electoral rights" (Abū Ṭālib 2006, 352).

The vote shares earned by Muslim Brotherhood candidates in each phase are presented in Table 4.2 and Figure 4.2. As we can see, there is little appreciable difference across the three phases, with the somewhat surprising exception that the Brotherhood seems to have done slightly better in the second phase than in the supposedly cleaner first phase. Thus, even when we control for possible electoral fraud, the Brothers' vote shares hovered around a third of voters on election day. And given that turnout was only 23 percent of eligible voters, the most one could say about the Brotherhood was that its greatest electoral victory in the Mubarak era was delivered to it by only 8 percent of eligible Egyptian voters. The question before us is, Who were those voters?

4.2 Competing for the Middle Class

Given the resource constraints under which opposition parties operate, the difficulty of competing with the ruling party for the suffrages of poor voters, and the regime's efforts to prevent its opponents from engaging in social outreach, it stands to reason that the most successful opposition parties would be those that did not rely on the votes of the poor. Instead, opposition parties should appeal to more affluent voters who are less likely to be wooed by promises of patronage and particularistic benefits, and more likely to vote on the basis of ideological commitments (be they Islamist or merely antiregime in nature). After all, the middle classes are unique in that they are neither poor enough to be captured by clientelism, nor wealthy enough to be beneficiaries of regime corruption. Instead, they are likely to oppose both of these things, and thus constitute a potential support base for oppositional politics. Though appealing to the relatively affluent was not likely to win any party a majority in a poor country such as Egypt, where approximately 40 percent of the population lives on less than three dollars a day, it is a viable strategy for a party in pursuit of the more modest aim of gaining a limited number of seats in parliament.[2] In this section I show that the Muslim Brothers during the Mubarak years focused primarily on just such a constituency.

One suggestive – but by no means definitive – piece of evidence for the claim that the Brothers drew on the middle classes for their core supporters is the class makeup of the movement's leaders. The Brotherhood has long recruited primarily from the most competitive university faculties, such as medicine and engineering. Accordingly, a comparison of the backgrounds of the movement's parliamentarians with those of the now-defunct NDP (Figure 4.3) reveals that 75 percent of Brotherhood parliamentarians in 2005 possessed college or postgraduate degrees compared with just 61 percent for the deputies of Mubarak's party. It is important to note here that whereas we might expect parliamentarians of all parties to be more highly educated than the average citizen, the analysis presented here compares the average Muslim Brotherhood member of parliament *not* with the average Egyptian but with the average representative of the former ruling party. The analysis thus indicates, at the very least, that the movement recruited members from a different – and more highly educated – pool than did the NDP. Further evidence of the Muslim Brotherhood's middle-class basis was its significant presence on the boards of professional syndicates for fields such as medicine and

[2] Income figure from the African Development Bank Group, http://www.afdb.org/en/countries/north-africa/egypt/human-and-social-development/; accessed, March 1, 2011.

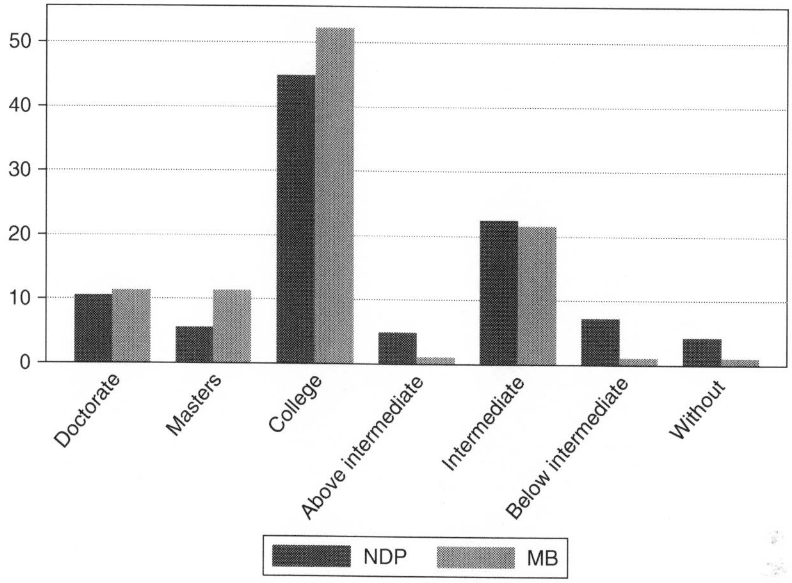

Figure 4.3 Educational attainment of NDP versus Muslim Brotherhood deputies, 2005. (*Source*: Rabīʿ 2006).

engineering and utter absence from the boards of labor unions, to which the NDP and NPUR had greater links (Fahmy 1998b; al Awadi 2004).

Another indicator – again, suggestive, not definitive – of the Brotherhood's middle-class outreach during the Mubarak years could be found in the work of its parliamentarians' district offices. Whereas much of the work of Muslim Brotherhood parliamentarians – like their counterparts in other parties during that period – involved securing access for their constituents to government services (such as prescription drug payments, business licenses, and scholarships), the Brotherhood's representatives also appeared to provide goods that appealed specifically to middle-class voters. In the district of Minā al-Baṣal in Alexandria, for example, Brotherhood parliamentarians circulated pamphlets promising first aid and CPR courses, instruction in the preparation of "eastern and western desserts," tutorials for lawyers on how to file tax forms, lessons in constructing Microsoft PowerPoint presentations, and a "self-improvement" course for those who want to "discover their potential and define their goals" – the kinds of offerings likely to appeal to more educated, sophisticated voters.[3] Many of the fliers circulated by Muslim Brotherhood parliamentarians included electronic mail and website addresses, suggesting an intended audience of sufficient means to at least be acquainted with those things.

[3] Newsletter of Ḥamdī Ḥasan and Ḥusayn Ibrāhīm, Fursān Mīnāʾ al-Baṣal (The Knights of Mīnāʾ al-Baṣal), April 2006.

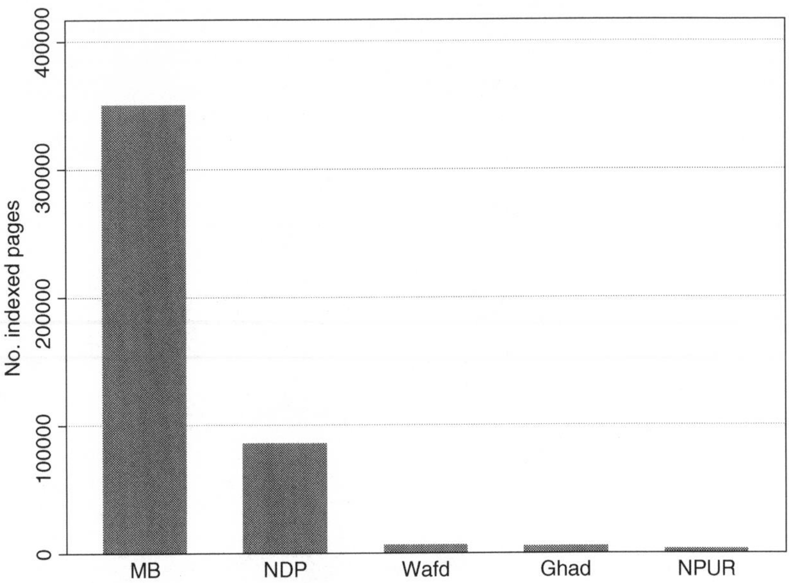

Figure 4.4 Internet presences of the Muslim Brotherhood, the ruling party, and secular opposition parties.

Indeed, the Muslim Brotherhood's wholehearted embrace of the Internet (see, for example, Lynch (2007) and Mehanna (2008)) is perhaps one of the clearest indicators of its fundamentally affluent social base. As of June 2009, Egypt had 12.5 million Internet users (or 16 percent of its population).[4] These individuals, as one would expect, are drawn disproportionately from the educated middle and upper classes. Of the 8 percent of respondents whom the *2005 World Values Survey* reports as having gotten their news from the Internet "in the last week," approximately 60 percent had university degrees, and an additional 30 percent had at least completed secondary school. And yet, despite the relative narrowness of Internet usage in Egypt, the Muslim Brotherhood put far more effort into this medium than did any other party. Figure 4.4 represents the total number of web pages, as of April 2010, indexed by Google for the Muslim Brotherhood, the ruling party, and three of Egypt's most prominent secular opposition parties at the time: the liberal Wafd, the al-Ghad Party (founded by Ayman Nur, a vocal opponent of the Mubarak regime), and the left-leaning NPUR.[5] As we can see, the Muslim Brotherhood's web presence dwarfed that of its competitors. Not only did it deploy many more websites (thirty-two, including several sites dedicated to local branches of the Brotherhood throughout Egypt's twenty-six governorates),

4 See http://www.internetworldstats.com/africa.htm#eg.
5 Website addresses available on request.

but the total number of pages (350,523) on its collected sites was several times greater than that of the ruling party and the major opposition parties combined.

The Brotherhood not only exerted more effort on the Internet, but it was also the recipient of more interest there as well. Figure 4.5 is a graph of the relative volume of Google searches conducted by Egyptians for various party names during two recent electoral periods.[6] Figure 4.5*a* shows the volume of searches from August 2005 to January 2006 – a particularly politicized period during which the country held its first multicandidate presidential elections (August 2005) and its eighth parliamentary election since 1976 (October–December 2005). As we can see, the two parties that garnered the most hits during this period were the al-Ghad Party, whose leader, Ayman Nūr, was running for the presidency, and the Muslim Brotherhood, which had fielded a large number of candidates in the parliamentary election. The interest of Egypt's educated classes in both these parties is understandable: both the al-Ghad and the Brotherhood were the clear antiregime choices in the 2005 presidential and parliamentary elections, respectively. (The Brotherhood was prohibited from fielding a presidential candidate by the fact that it did not possess a legal political party.)

Figure 4.5*b* shows the volume of searches that took place during the 2010 parliamentary election, from November to December 2010. Here too, despite a spike for the ruling party during the preelectoral period, the Muslim Brotherhood received the highest search volume. Of course, the impressive volume of Internet searches for the Brotherhood cannot be taken as straightforward evidence of middle-class support for the group – after all, one can look things up on the Internet because one hates them. But it is nonetheless highly suggestive.

The Islamist Machine, Redux

In Chapter 3, I documented the ways in which the Mubarak regime limited the Muslim Brotherhood's potential outreach to the poor by shutting down its health-care projects and preventing it from working through existing Islamic charities. The modest services that the regime did allow the Brotherhood to operate, however, all demonstrate not a concern for the poor but rather a focus on the middle classes (Clark 2004b).

Consider the activities of the Islamic Medical Association (IMA). Though Sullivan (1994, 13) tells us that the association has branches "throughout Egypt," the reality during the Mubarak years was somewhat short of this. The IMA's activities appear to have been concentrated in the greater Cairo area: As of 2009, it claimed to have seven facilities in Cairo, eight in al-Gīza, three in al-Qalyūbiyya, and one each in al-Minūfiyya, al-Buhayra, al-Ismāʿīliyya, and Asyūt. The nature of these facilities varies considerably. Many were small clinics, but others were more

[6] This is part of a larger project that explores Internet behavior patterns as unobtrusive measures of middle-class values around the world.

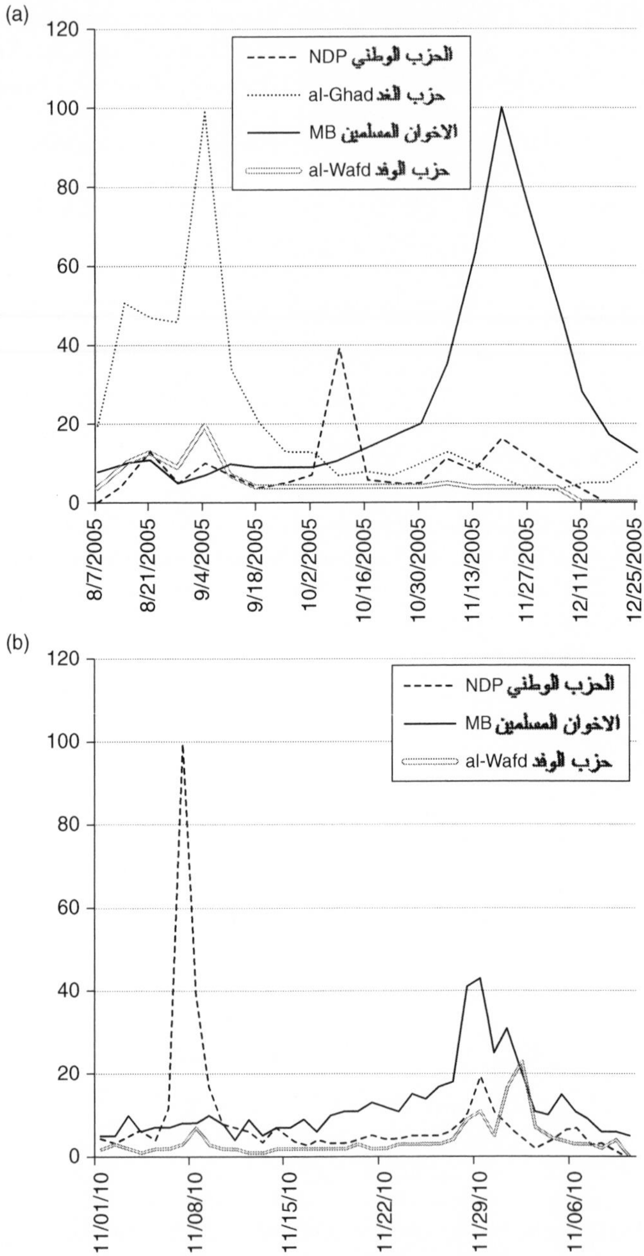

Figure 4.5 Egyptian Google searches for political parties during recent Egyptian elections: (*a*) Presidential and People's Assembly elections, 2005; (*b*) People's Assembly election, 2010.

extensive. The al-Fārūq Hospital, located in al-Ma'ādi in Cairo, boasted a dialysis facility with five beds and six dialysis machines, a unit for premature infants, a surgical department with four operating rooms, an intensive-care section with eight beds, and an outpatient x-ray facility. It employed around 225 individuals and offered a 20 percent discount on Fridays (itself a reminder that this is a paying hospital). The 'Umrāniyya Hospital in Giza was a larger, twenty-four-hour facility with a full imaging center with ultrasound and dental x-ray equipment, an inpatient department with thirty beds (of "different degrees to suit all [social] classes"), a pathology lab, and a surgical department with three operating rooms.[7]

According to unaudited figures released by the IMA, its hospitals in 2005 treated nearly 1.2 million people, or approximately 150 patients per day for each facility, and in 2005 performed more than 42,000 surgical procedures. Though these numbers are significant, they represent a minuscule portion of Egypt's overall health care market. Moreover – and most important for the purposes of this analysis – of the 1.5 million people served by the IMA in 2004, only 30,000 qualified for financial assistance, which, by the IMA's estimate, totaled 1 million L.E. per annum. In 2009, the IMA claimed to have provided free treatment to 42,612 Egyptians at a cost of 1,071,285 L.E.[8] The modesty of the IMA's charitable ambitions is also evident in a 2006 prospectus for the then-unfinished Central Charitable Hospital (CCH), which, as discussed in Chapter 3, is located in the upper-middle class district of Nasr City. Consider the "degrees of service" the hospital planned to offer (the language that follows is translated directly from the prospectus):

1. Free healthcare for the poor, whether they come to the hospital directly or are transferred from the clinics and hospitals of the association or referred by approved doctors throughout the republic, and spending for their treatment will be from the fund for the care of the poor.
2. Treatment at cost for the middle-class patients.
3. Treatment for well-off patients – which will achieve a margin of profit that can be spent in the free section or used to develop and improve service.
4. Treatment for our brothers of the Gulf Arabs and expatriates: They will receive care on the highest levels from the most highly experienced [doctors] and cutting-edge facilities [to rival] Western hospitals.[9]

This emphasis on serving the middle classes appears to confirm Clark's (2004b) finding that most efforts at Islamic healthcare are not directed primarily at the poor: "Vertical patron-client relationships within Islamic institutions are often

[7] Information on the two hospitals can be found on the IMA's website, available at http://www.imaegypt.net/.

[8] See "*Al-Jam'iyya al-Ṭibiyya al-Islāmiyya: Thalāthūn 'ām min al-'aṭā'* (The Islamic Medical Association: 30 Years of Giving)," IMA press release, October 2006. Figure from 2009 drawn from IMA Prospectus, 2010.

[9] See http://www.khieronline.com/PageView.asp?ID=508&SectionID=0 and http://www.darelsalam-eg.com/dc/tabid/102/ctl/Details/mid/433/ItemID/27/Default.aspx; accessed April 7, 2008.

weak, and the poor are generally not integrated into the institutions." Instead, Clark tells us, such services are deployed to expand and strengthn "middle-class networks, bringing Islamists and non-Islamists together," presumably making the latter more likely to vote for the former at election time (Clark 2004, 944).

4.3 Patterns of Electoral Mobilization

Finding a way to test the hypothesis here – that the Brotherhood drew, during the Mubarak years, on a more affluent support base – is not a simple matter. For example, though a voter survey conducted shortly before or after parliamentary elections might have been the most efficient means of ascertaining who voted for the Brotherhood, the agencies responsible for vetting all survey questionnaires – the Central Agency for Public Mobilization and Statistics and the Ministry of the Interior – explicitly prohibited survey researchers from fielding questions about the Muslim Brotherhood. In the absence of survey data, one might expect that the next best indicator of the movement's social base would be found in aggregate electoral returns. If the Muslim Brotherhood drew disproportionately on more affluent voters, we should be able to observe this through an ecological analysis of socioeconomic indicators and Muslim Brotherhood vote shares at the district level. This is possible for the 1984 election, when the state newspapers published detailed vote shares for each party. Examining the gross relationship between the Brotherhood-Wafd alliance's vote share in 1984 and the adult illiteracy rate (see Figure 4.6) in that election's forty-eight party-list districts, we see that, in

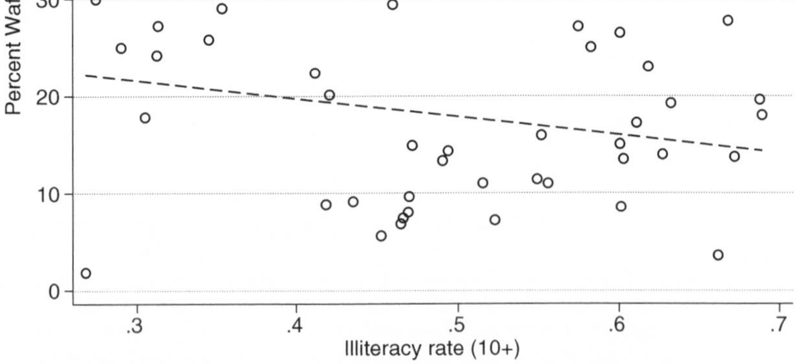

Figure 4.6 Illiteracy rate and Wafd/Muslim Brotherhood vote share, 1984.

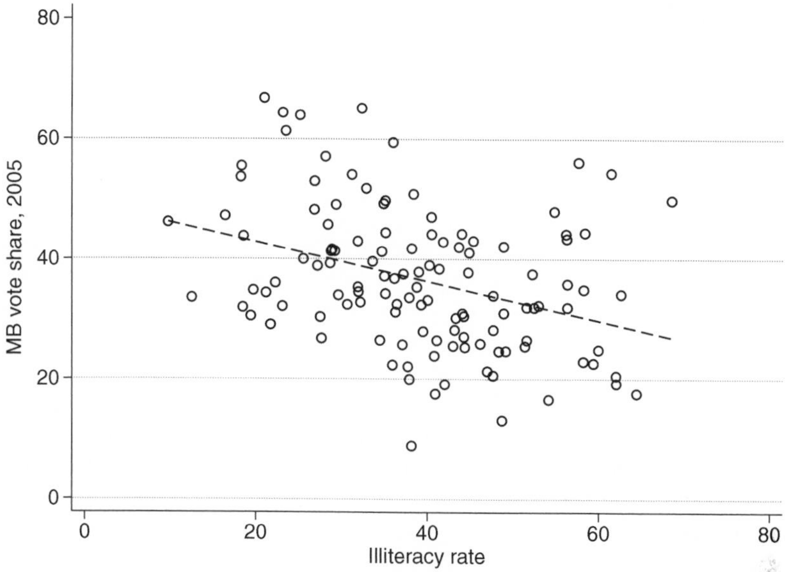

Figure 4.7 Muslim Brotherhood vote shares versus adult illiteracy rate, 2005.

general, the party did better in more affluent/urban districts, lending support to the narrative presented here.

But conducting a more detailed analysis using electoral returns from the post-1990 elections – in which the number of districts available for analysis is much larger, at 222 – is a more difficult matter. First, and most important, the Ministry of the Interior, which was responsible for administering elections prior to 2011, did not release complete electoral returns – the vote shares of losing candidates were simply not made public. Using only the data for the districts in which the Muslim Brotherhood candidates' vote shares were made public in 2005 – that is, districts where the Muslim Brotherhood either won or entered a runoff – we do observe the expected negative correlation between voting for the Muslim Brotherhood and affluence. This is revealed in Figure 4.7, which plots the Muslim Brotherhood's share of valid votes in the 120 districts for which its vote shares were available against the adult illiteracy rate (Pearson's coefficient = –0.35). However, the truncated nature of these data (which do not include Brotherhood candidates who lost in the first round of voting), and the regime's employment of fraud and intimidation against opposition candidates and their supporters, should render us cautious about using such official vote tallies for econometric analysis (Brownlee 2007).

One way of transcending this problem is to focus our analysis not on the *results* of Muslim Brotherhood electioneering but rather on the types of locales in which the Brotherhood fielded candidates. Though the Brotherhood participated in every Egyptian parliamentary election in the Mubarak era (save one), as Brown (2012) notes, it never fielded candidates for every seat in the legislature. In the 2010 elections – which would prove to be Mubarak's last – the Brotherhood nominated candidates in just over half of Egypt's 222 electoral districts; in 2005, it ran campaigns in two-thirds of the districts. One of the observable implications of the argument presented here – that the Brotherhood won by mobilizing middle class voters – is that the Brotherhood should have been more likely to field candidates in more affluent districts.

In order to test this conjecture, I constructed an original data set of the Muslim Brotherhood's electoral mobilization and the socioeconomic characteristics of Egypt's 222 electoral districts for the last two elections of the Mubarak period, in 2005 and 2010.[10] Did the Muslim Brotherhood concentrate its efforts in predominantly poor districts, competing with the ruling party's patronage machine, or did it focus instead on districts that were likely to be home to the kinds of middle-class voters who could afford to cast ballots for other than economic considerations? The dependent variable, Muslim Brotherhood mobilization, is a dichotomous variable coded 1 if the Muslim Brotherhood nominated a candidate in the district and 0 otherwise.[11] (I conduct the analyses of the 2005 and 2010 elections separately. Although the data would seem to lend themselves to a panel design, interelection gerrymandering means that the composition of the electoral districts in 2005 is different from those of 2010.)

The main independent variable in this analysis is the district's average socioeconomic status, as measured in the 2005 census estimates produced by the Central Agency for Public Mobilization and Statistics (CAPMAS). We want to observe the correlation (if any) between the Muslim Brotherhood's nomination patterns and the socioeconomic characteristics of districts. We might contend that this analysis runs into an ecological fallacy because of its use of aggregate data. However, the analysis here is not an attempt to infer individual behavior from aggregate data. Instead, it is attempting to understand the decision by a political party as to where to field candidates for parliamentary seats. That choice is certainly a function of the group's beliefs about the nature of its likely supporters, but it is nonetheless not an individual-level choice.

Measuring an electoral district's socioeconomic status is challenging because the Egyptian census does not collect – or at least report – straightforward income data. Thus I employ a number of proxies for this independent variable and run the analysis with each one. The proxies for socioeconomic status are as follows:

[10] The data set aggregates 2005 census estimates from Egypt's approximately 5,500 census tracts into electoral districts according to the precise district boundaries laid out by Law 206 of 1990 and its subsequent amendments.

[11] The analysis here makes no distinction between the handful of districts where the Brotherhood nominated two candidates (one for each of the two seats) and those in which it fielded just one candidate. Ordered probit regressions, in which the dependent variable could take on values of 0, 1, or 2 candidates, yielded substantially the same results as the logits reported here, with insignificant cut points between the categories for one and two candidates.

- *Crowding rate.* This measure is calculated as the number of inhabitants per household room. The Egyptian census reports the number of households with one room, two rooms, three rooms, four rooms, and five or more rooms. In order to estimate the crowding rate, I divide the district population by the total number of rooms $\sum_{i=1}^{5} X_i \cdot H_i$, where X_i is the number of rooms, and H_i is the number of reported households with X_i rooms. Because households with more than five rooms are lumped together in one category, we will overestimate the crowding rate at the top of the distribution. A positive relationship between Muslim Brotherhood mobilization and this variable would support the conclusion that the Muslim Brotherhood mobilized the middle classes electorally, whereas a negative coefficient would suggest that the Brothers mobilized the poor.
- *Percentage of workforce in agriculture.* This is a proxy for the level of urbanization (measured as the percentage of adults reported by the census as employed in agriculture, hunting, or fishing). We expect this variable to exert a negative effect on Muslim Brotherhood mobilization because rural dwellers are more likely than urbanites to be embedded in the kinds of clientelistic, patriarchal relationships that constrain their vote choices.
- *Illiteracy rate.* This is the percentage of citizens (aged ten and over) whom CAPMAS reports as illiterate. Though it is highly correlated with urbanization, it is used elsewhere in the literature as a proxy for socioeconomic status (Blaydes 2006, 2010).
- *Percent unemployment.* This is the percentage of the workforce that the census reports as "unemployed" or "newly unemployed." We often read of the Brotherhood's appeal among the unemployed (Kepel 1994). If this is the case, we should observe a positive coefficient on this variable. The relatively small mean (4.19) suggests that this variable is significantly underreported. Nonetheless, if the pattern of underreporting is either uniform or random, use of this variable still may allow us to explore the relationship between unemployment and our dependent variable.
- *Number of candidates.* I include this variable to capture differences among districts in the degree of political openness. The electoral districts of key regime allies, for example, were unlikely to be genuinely competitive, and consequently, potential candidates were likely to have been deterred from running in these districts. In 2010, for example, the district of the NDP's organizational secretary, Aḥmad ʿIzz, featured only 7 candidates. Thus, "closed" districts should have few candidates, and more "open" ones should have many candidates. Including the number of candidates in our analysis thus allows us to control for situations where the Muslim Brotherhood might have declined to field a candidate either because a certain competitor was difficult to overcome or because the regime was likely to interfere with the election to ensure victory for its candidate.
- *Logged district population.* To the extent that more densely populated districts are also urban, we might expect to see a positive correlation between

Table 4.3 *Descriptive Statistics*

Variable	$\bar{x}$	s	$x_{\min}$	$x_{\max}$
Rooms per household	3.6	0.35	2.51	4.44
Crowding rate	1.31	0.15	0.86	1.86
Percent three rooms or fewer	44.65	14.52	16.44	83.83
Adult illiteracy rate	40.54	13.63	9.76	70.33
Workforce in agriculture	14.73	9.45	0.14	34.56
Unemployment	4.19	1.50	0.70	8.56
Population (2005)	31,540	15,800	24,170	1,082,220
Number of candidates (2005)	23.38	9.09	7	53
Number of candidates (2010)	21.38	10.15	4	65

Note: $N = 222$.

this variable and the nomination of a Muslim Brotherhood candidate. That said, I have no strong prior theoretical expectations about the effect of a district's population on the Muslim Brotherhood's decision to field a campaign in that district.

As discussed earlier, the 2005 elections were staggered over three dates, each approximately ten days apart. I ran analyses of the 2005 results with and without fixed effects for the date on which a given district's elections were conducted. The results of those analyses were similar to those without fixed effects for election date and are not reported here.[12]

The results of these analyses (see Tables 4.3 through 4.5) suggest that in both the 2005 and 2010 elections, the Muslim Brotherhood was more likely to nominate candidates in more affluent districts than in less affluent ones. All specifications for both electoral years show a positive and significant effect of increasing socioeconomic status on the probability of observing a Muslim Brotherhood candidacy. In order to more easily illustrate the relationship between socioeconomic status and the Muslim Brotherhood's electoral mobilization, I use King, Tomz, and Wittenberg's (2000) Monte Carlo simulation routines to generate predicted probabilities of observing Muslim Brotherhood nominations

[12] The 2005 parliamentary election was staggered over the course of four weeks in November and December. The first phase was held on November 9 and included Cairo, al-Gīza, Minūfiyya, Banī Suwayf, New Valley, Asyūṭ, Marsā Matrūḥ, and al-Minyā. The second phase was held on November 20 and included Alexandria, al-Buḥayra, al-Ismāʿīliyya, Port Said, Suez, al-Qalyūbiyya, al-Gharbiyya, al-Fayyūm, and Qinā. The third and final phase was held on December 1 and included al-Sharqiyya, al-Daqahliyya, Kafr al-Shaykh, Damietta, Suhāg, Aswān, Red Sea, North Sinai, and South Sinai. Though this system of staggered elections was introduced in order to allow for adequate judicial oversight over the polling, in practice, it has allowed the regime to calibrate its level of interference in later phases depending on its performance in earlier ones. Most election monitoring organizations reported few violations in the first phase and then successively more violations in the second and third phases. In 2010, the elections were held on a single day with minimal judicial oversight.

Table 4.4 *Logistic Regression Results, Muslim Brotherhood Nominations in 2005 People's Assembly Election*

	(1)	(2)	(3)	(4)
Rooms per household	2.628***			
	(0.598)			
Crowding rate		−4.871***		
		(1.082)		
Households with three rooms			−6.990***	
or fewer			(1.399)	
Adult illiteracy (%)				−3.594**
				(1.544)
Average family size	−0.865**		−0.680	
	(0.434)		(0.435)	
Workforce in agriculture (%)	−0.0324	0.00604	−0.0366	
	(0.0280)	(0.0198)	(0.0279)	
Unemployment (%)	0.144	0.217*	0.104	0.212*
	(0.120)	(0.114)	(0.123)	(0.112)
Number of candidates per	0.0554**	0.0561**	0.0582**	0.0440*
district	(0.0233)	(0.0228)	(0.0236)	(0.0226)
Population	4.60e-06**	5.18e-06***	4.70e-06**	5.81e-06***
	(1.83e-06)	(1.76e-06)	(1.83e-06)	(2.05e-06)
Constant	−7.252***	3.449**	4.629**	−1.258
	(2.478)	(1.688)	(2.184)	(0.939)

Note: $N = 222$.
Standard errors in parentheses.
$^{***}p < 0.01$; $^{**}p < 0.05$; $^{*}p < 0.1$.

across the range of values for our key proxies of socioeconomic status (holding all other variables at their means).[13] The results of the simulations, using rooms per household and the adult illiteracy rate, are represented graphically in Figure 4.8. As we can see, in both 2005 and 2010, the likelihood of a Muslim Brotherhood nomination was positively correlated with socioeconomic status – districts with larger home sizes, or lower illiteracy rates were more likely to feature Muslim Brotherhood candidacies.

4.4 Historical Patterns of Recruitment and Mobilization

Instead of drawing on the support of the poor under Mubarak, the Muslim Brotherhood instead appeared to concentrate its efforts on the middle classes. Many

[13] The change in the probability of observing a Muslim Brotherhood nomination conditional on a change in X is represented by the following equation:

$$\triangle \Pr(\text{MB}=1)|\triangle X = \frac{\Pr(\text{MB}=1|X_{\text{high}}) - \Pr(\text{MB}=1|X_{\text{low}})}{\Pr(\text{MB}=1|X_{\text{low}})} \times 100$$

Table 4.5 *Logistic Regression Results, Muslim Brotherhood Nominations in 2010 People's Assembly Election*

	(1)	(2)	(3)	(4)
Rooms per household	1.497***			
	(0.547)			
Crowding rate		–1.998**		
		(0.983)		
Households with three rooms or fewer			–3.605***	
			(1.246)	
Adult illiteracy (%)				–3.230***
				(1.116)
Average family size	–0.0413		0.0799	
	(0.392)		(0.395)	
Workforce in agriculture (%)	–7.221***	–3.410**	–7.275***	
	(2.561)	(1.681)	(2.565)	
Unemployment (%)	6.483	13.12	4.829	12.10
	(10.96)	(10.17)	(11.16)	(10.11)
Number of candidates per district	–0.0148	–0.0139	–0.0146	–0.0159
	(0.0146)	(0.0149)	(0.0146)	(0.0147)
Population	3.76e-06***	4.22e-06***	3.83e-06***	4.35e-06***
	(1.14e-06)	(1.12e-06)	(1.14e-06)	(1.14e-06)
Constant	–5.136**	1.675	1.350	–0.0745
	(2.246)	(1.412)	(1.758)	(0.746)

Note: $N = 222$.
Standard errors in parentheses.
$^{***}p < 0.01$; $^{**}p < 0.05$; $^{*}p < 0.1$.

observers of the Egyptian scene attributed the Muslim Brotherhood's electoral victories in 2005 to protest votes cast by non-Islamists eager to throw stones at the regime. The most colorful exponent of this view, the gifted journalist Ibrāhīm ʿĪsā – who would later become a bitter opponent of the Muslim Brotherhood after the January 2011 revolution – put it this way:

> The citizen chooses the Muslim Brothers because [the Brothers] never held power and never used it to humiliate, never strangled the spirit, never imprisoned, never killed, never tortured, never plundered, never squandered, never mired the reputation of their country in the mud, never got beaten on every battlefield, never scored zero in every arena.[14]

This raises an important question: If beating the well-run casino was simply a matter of appealing to middle-class voters, why couldn't other parties do it? In

[14] Ibrāhīm ʿĪsā, "*Intahā al-dars yā Waṭanī* (Lesson Over, NDP)," *al-Dustūr* (Cairo), November 18, 2005.

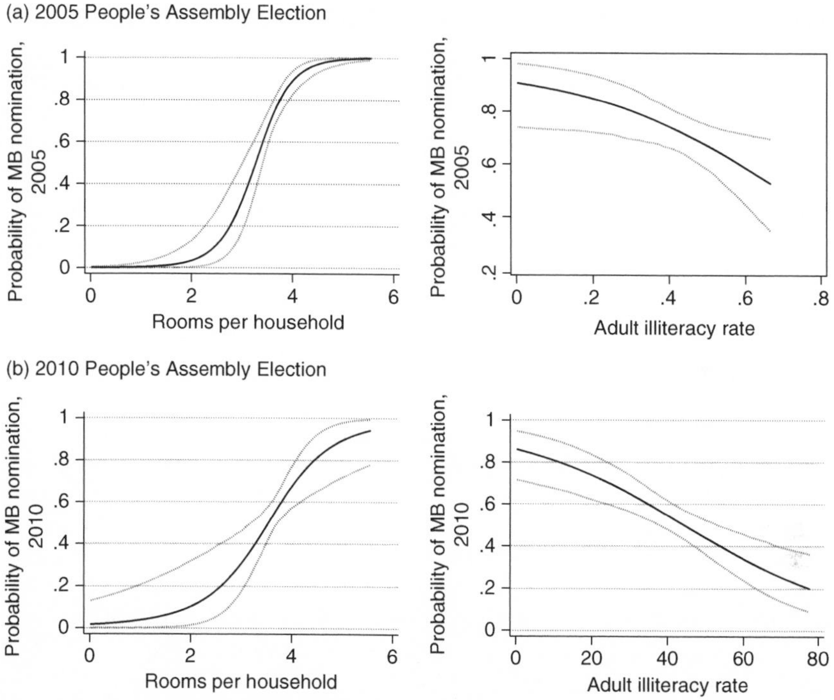

Figure 4.8 Effect of socioeconomic status on probability of Muslim Brotherhood nomination (dotted lines represent 95 percent confidence intervals).

the case of the NPUR, it is likely that its radically redistributive program was unpalatable to more affluent voters. Thus the party was caught in a double-bind. As we saw in Chapter 2, those who would have liked the party's program couldn't vote for it (captured as they were by the politics of patronage and clientelism), and those who could vote for the party did not like its program. As for the Wafd, in Section 2.2 we saw why it was unable to persist as an electoral force after the shift from party list to majoritarian elections: its history as a party of notables meant that the pillars of the party found it advantageous to defect when the change in the electoral system made it possible for them to gain access to the legislature without paying the costs of opposition party membership.

As for the Brotherhood, the embeddedness of its activists in middle-class networks of Islamic health and service provision (Clark 2004a) would have helped the movement build a reputation for probity with more affluent voters (Brown 2012). But the story of the Wafd's decline also indicates the importance of a party's historical antecedents. The evidence suggests that the Muslim Brotherhood's outreach to the middle class was less a strategic decision made by Muslim Brotherhood leaders in *response* to the incentives of elections than a long-standing feature of the group, akin to a random genetic mutation that happened to be "selected" by the electoral environment because it made the Brotherhood "fitter" than its competitors. A review of the historical literature reveals that the movement always drew heavily on members of the *affandiya* – the educated and professional stratum of Egyptian society (Lia 1998, 224). For example, in a 1954 memorandum to superiors in London, a British diplomat in Cairo could refer to the Brotherhood as a "middle class dominated movement."[15] Richard P. Mitchell, the great chronicler of the Brotherhood's history, describes attending gatherings of the Ikhwān in the 1950s and observing that "the student, the civil servant, the teacher, the clerk and office worker, and the professional in their Western suits" constituted "an overwhelming majority" of participants (Mitchell 1993 (1969), 330).

The Brotherhood's historically affluent social base is further illustrated by accounts of the movement's earliest electoral forays. Though the scholarly literature on the Brotherhood has generally dated its participation in elections to the Mubarak era, the movement had fielded candidates for Egypt's legislature – then called the Chamber of Deputies (majlis al-nuwwāb) – in 1945, and had attempted to do so in 1942 before being compelled to withdraw. Testimonials of the period note that the movement was not one of the poor and disenfranchised. Ṣāliḥ ʿAshmāwī, editor of the Muslim Brotherhood's newspaper, was in 1945 the Brotherhood's candidate for a seat in the district of Old Cairo. In a brief article recounting his battle for a place under the dome of parliament, he offered the following description of his campaign rallies:

> The Brothers that used to parade in the district were mainly university students and educated youth and noble civil servants and others, and this sight drew the attention of the people of the district, who were used to seeing parades made up of young boys and hirelings with their raggedy and tattered clothes. And one of the Brothers heard a man from the people of the district say to someone standing next to him: "The candidate of the Brothers must be very rich to be able to put together such a grand group of paraders." But this man did not understand that these were the soldiers of God and preachers of Islam and that all the money on earth could not buy or rent them, for faith is not for sale and hearts are not bought.[16]

During that election, as during the Mubarak era, one of the primary challenges the Brotherhood faced was overcoming the politics of patronage and clientelism. A Cairo law professor, lamenting the dominance of money and clan in Egyptian elections, wrote that as a result of the role of money in Egyptian elections, voting had become the sole province of the poor: "In Egypt, the educated are the most qualified for elections but are the least receptive to them and the least exercising

[15] Handwritten memo, Sir R. Stevenson, Cairo, No. 74(1012/4/54g) March 24, entitled "Muslim Brotherhood Activities from 25 July 1952 to 12 January 1954, When It Was Dissolved."

[16] Sālih ʿAshmāwī, "*Al-Maʿraka al-intikhābiyya: Fī dā'irat Miṣr al-Qadīma* (The Electoral Battle: In the District of Old Cairo)," *al-Ikhwān al-Muslimūn*, January 2, 1945, 3.

of their voting rights."[17] In January 1945, the Brotherhood published a ten-point list of its aspirations for that year's election. In an almost heartbreaking demonstration of how slowly moves the tide of progress, most of the points deal with the problem of vote buying in one form of another, which would continue to prove an obsession of Islamists to the present day:

> We want:
>
> 1. For the electoral battle to be a wonderful nationalistic spectacle in which the principles mix, and doctrines and views compete, so the people can understand and benefit, instead of a struggle around personalities and insults and libels and accusations.
> 2. Only those who are capable of serving the country to nominate themselves, for the position of deputy should not become a form of luxury and prestige, but rather service and struggle[18] and sacrifice.
> 3. For every candidate to comprehend the importance of the matter and not to deceive and lie and not to be hypocritical or to libel his rivals or to bribe the voters.
> 4. For every voter to exercise his voting right and not to take it for granted or to be cavalier in assigning his vote.
> 5. For every voter to know that he is performing a vital national duty, so he should plan and deliberate and give his vote only to him who deserves it from among the sincere and qualified men of high principles.
> 6. For every voter to be wary of dishonesty from hypocritical personalities, and not to be influenced by honeyed talk and polished speeches and enticing promises.
> 7. For every voter to respect his dignity and the dignity of his country and not sell his vote for money or offer it as a courtesy to he who does not deserve it.
> 8. For the elections to be free.
> 9. For the election results to reflect the popular will.
> 10. For the elections to reflect new qualifications and groups that can have a tremendous effect in directing the politics of the country.[19]

So pervasive was the problem of patronage and clientelism in elections in early twentieth century Egypt that even the Muslim Brotherhood's founder found his political ambitions thwarted by it. Ḥassān Ḥatḥūt, a young university graduate and acolyte of the Brotherhood's founder, Ḥasan al-Bannā, describes working on al-Bannā's own parliamentary campaign in al-Ismā'īliyya, the city in which the Brotherhood had been founded seventeen years earlier. In the initial round of balloting, Al-Bannā came in first, with 2,244 of 5,741 votes cast. His chief rival, with

[17] 'Uthmān Khalīl 'Uthmān, "*Arā' ḥurra: Ḥawl ta'dīl niẓām al-intikhāb* (Free Views: On Amending the Electoral System), *al-Ikhwān al-Muslimūn*, January 2, 1945, 6.

[18] The word used in the original Arabic is *jihād*. My translation of it as *struggle*, as opposed to *warfare*, is purely context-dependent and should not be interpreted as taking a stance on the extensive debate about this peculiar word.

[19] Ibn al-Saḥarā' (a pseudonym), "*Nurīd* (We Want)," *al-Ikhwān al-Muslimūn*, January 2, 1945, 5.

1,980 votes, was a physician and member of the Liberal Constitutionalist Party named Sulaymān ʿĪd. The two men then faced each other in a runoff. From the outset, the Brothers knew that ʿĪd would be a formidable competitor. Not only was ʿĪd wealthy and congenial to the British presence in the Canal Zone (the Muslim Brotherhood historiography claims that he was the chief purveyor to British forces in the area), he was also, as Ḥatḥūt put it, "one of the sons of Ismāʿīliyya," with a large family to support him (Ḥatḥūt 2000; see also Zakī 1980 (1952)). In order to defuse ʿĪd's advantage, Ḥatḥūt reports that members of the Brotherhood engaged in a bit of subterfuge: whenever a group of Brothers would find itself within earshot of townsfolk, they would pretend to be deep in conversation, during which one would say, in a loud voice, "Yes, it's true that Sulaymān ʿĪd is my relative, but I'm going to vote for Ḥasan al-Bannā." In this way, Ḥatḥūt writes, "we encouraged those who wavered between voting on principle and voting on the basis of clan loyalty." It didn't work. ʿĪd went on to beat al-Banna by 3,464 to 2,739.[20] But the story is eloquent both of the Brotherhood's long-standing reliance on educated members such as Ḥatḥūt (who went on to become an accomplished physician) and of its equally long-standing difficulty in reaching voters who are embedded in clientelistic networks based on family, clan, and the like.

Econometric Evidence from the Brotherhood's Early History

Is there more than just anecdotal evidence for the notion that the Muslim Brotherhood has always appealed to the more affluent? In this section, I present more systematic evidence that the Brotherhood's early mobilization patterns reflect its more affluent, or at least more educated, social base. In 1937, the Brothers published a complete list of the movement's 212 branches throughout Egypt (plus fourteen elsewhere in the Muslim world, including the Syrian town of Aleppo, the Moroccan city of Fez, and the island of Bahrain).[21] The same year, the Egyptian Statistical and Census Authority released a census of Egyptian towns and villages.[22] These data provide an opportunity to examine in more detail and in a somewhat more systematic fashion the socioeconomic correlates of the Muslim Brotherhood's institution-building efforts. If the testimony of contemporaneous observers is correct, we should find that the movement focused its work on more affluent areas just as it focused its electoral campaigns in more affluent areas more than sixty years later.

The Brotherhood report lists branches at the level of intermediate administrative districts. There are 145 of these in the 1937 census, and these, consequently,

[20] First-Round Results from *al-Ahram*, January 10, 1945, 2; runoff results from *al-Ahram*, January 15, 1945, 3.

[21] "*Bayān Mūjiz lil-Ikhwān al-Muslimīn*," *al-Ikhwān al-Muslimūn*, Cairo, June 11, 1937, 12–18.

[22] *Maslahat al-Ihsa' wa al-Ta'dad* (Statistical and Census Authority), *Ta'dād al-sukkān li sanat* 1937 (1937 Population Census). See Century Census Egypt, 1882–1996, Central Agency for Public Mobilization and Statistics and the Center for Economic, Judicial, and Social Studies and Documentation, Cairo, 2003.

are our units of analysis. We find that the Brothers established branches in ninety-eight of these units. The average number of branches per district is 1.78, with the largest number of branches (thirteen) being found in al-Manzalah in al-Daqahliyya. The proper way to model the process of establishing Muslim Brotherhood branches is to employ an event-count procedure. I use a negative binomial regression model to analyze the data because the mild overdispersion of the data (mean 1.48, variance 3.17) suggests that the more standard Poisson event-count model is inappropriate (i.e., there are more districts with large numbers of branches and more with none than a Poisson process would suggest).

What we are interested in learning is whether more affluent districts are more likely to have featured more (or any) Muslim Brotherhood branches than less affluent ones. One of the challenges with such an analysis is the absence of good proxies for socioeconomic status. As with later censuses, there is no direct measure of mean household income. Unlike the 2005 census, however, we do not even have the number of household rooms to serve as a proxy for income. Adult illiteracy, as noted earlier, is an imperfect proxy for income because of its high correlation with the rate of urbanization (the Pearson correlation coefficient for percentage of workforce in agriculture in 1937 and the adult illiteracy rate for that year is 0.8108).

The 1937 census does, however, include data on blindness. Approximately 1.5 percent of Egyptians were blind in one or both eyes during this period (see Figure 4.9 for the distribution of blindness across districts). In early twentieth-century Egypt, by far the leading cause of blindness was an infectious disease known as *trachoma*, caused by the bacterium *Chlamydia trachomatis*. Trachoma causes scars and bumps to form in the eyelids of its victims. These deformities of the eyelid, in turn, scratch the cornea of the eye, rendering it opaque and resulting – eventually – in loss of sight (Mozzato-Chamay et al. 2000). Though the disease is relatively widespread in the developing world, it is inextricably intertwined with Egypt. Europeans first encountered the disease during Napoleon's 1798 campaign in the country – hence trachoma's informal moniker, "Egyptian ophthalmia" (Inhorn and Lane 1988).[23] According to MacCallan (1913, 63), approximately 70 percent of all cases of blindness in early twentieth-century Egypt could be attributed to trachoma.

The literature on trachoma suggests that poverty is a primary risk factor for the disease. According to Cook and Mariotti (2011, 175), "Trachoma has always been linked to poverty, poor hygiene, and availability of water." More than 100 years ago, Boldt (1904, 127) wrote, "Trachoma most, and almost exclusively, affects the lower classes ... [I]t is distinctly a disease of the proletariat. Bad hygienic and social conditions, poverty, insufficient food, and still more want of cleanly habits, wretched houses, indolence and ignorance, promote the spread of

[23] According to Boldt (1904, 9), though Napoleon's armies in Egypt suffered from the usual catalogue of "military epidemics – plague, dysentery, scurvy, yellow fever, hepatitis, leprosy, sunstroke," it was trachoma that "was especially fatal to their efficiency as a fighting force."

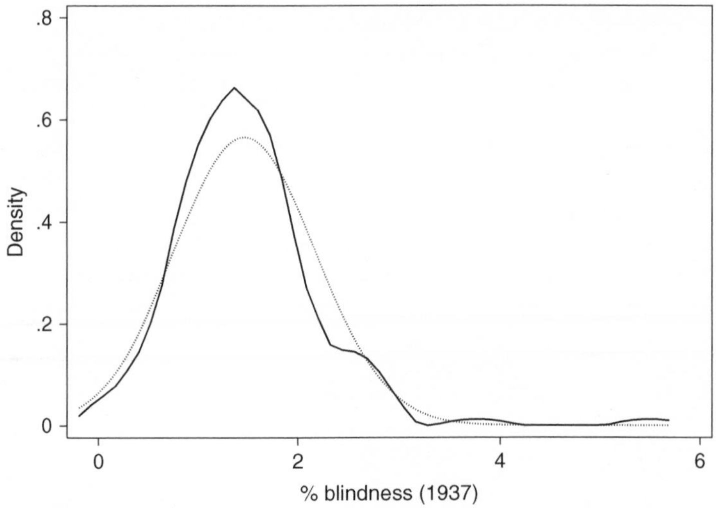

Figure 4.9 District-level distribution of blindness in Egypt, 1937. (Dotted line represents normal distribution.)

trachoma to an enormous extent." Egyptian ophthalmologist Abdel Aziz Elaguizy (1907, 3) wrote that the disease was particularly prevalent among the Egyptian poor because "our poorer classes, as a rule, wipe the surplus discharge by their fingertips, and, before washing their hands, touch ordinary household articles commonly used by everybody in the house. These articles become contaminated, and so transmit the disease in some form to the hands of those who, unconsciously, for some reason or other, touch their eyes, and in this way the disease slowly spreads." British ophthalmologist A. F MacCallan, who studied trachoma extensively during his tour as an ophthalmic surgeon with the Department of Public Health of Egypt from 1903 to 1923, elaborated thus on the causes of trachoma's prevalence among the poor:

> The upper ranks of society of any nation can be kept free from infection by trachoma provided care is taken to eliminate from the household all servants so affected, or at any rate to forbid entirely all contact between the children of the house and native servants. By these means it is possible to prevent children from becoming attacked, as has been shown to be the case during the last 40 years in the families of British officials in Egypt. Also in Egypt at the present time the upper classes of Egyptian society by one of these two means are preventing their children being exposed to the trachoma virus, and these children are usually now trachoma free, whereas in the past practically every child was infected within the first year or two of life. In the middle and lower strata of society the above-mentioned precautions are impossible. Among the predisposing causes to a general mass contagion are: (1) Bad houses with an unpaved floors, in hot countries kept as dark as possible in all weathers to reduce the plague of flies. (2) Absence of any regular water supply. In many parts of Eastern

Table 4.6 *Descriptive Statistics*

Variable	$\bar{x}$	s	$x_{\min}$	$x_{\max}$
Muslim Brotherhood branches	1.48	1.78	0	13
Muslim Brotherhood branches per 10,000	0.16	0.25	0	2.09
Blind in one or both eyes (%)	1.47	0.70	0	5.49
Workforce in agriculture (%)	25.10	16.81	0	48.24
Male unemployment (%)	13.44	4.19	5.20	30.85
Non-Muslim (%)	9.73	0.12	0.16	68.89

Note: $N = 145$.

> countries the women have to walk a mile or more to bring all water used from a river, canal, or well. (3) Overcrowding in many parts of the East is almost universal. (4) Dirt is all pervading in most trachomatous countries. (5) Poverty is obviously the origin of the above-mentioned predisposing causes [MacCallan 1931, 392].

The high association between blindness in Egypt and trachoma, and between trachoma and poverty, suggests that we may be able to use aggregate rates of blindness to proxy for socioeconomic status. The inherent noisiness of these data should render us cautious about attributing too much certainty to any resulting analysis. But, although the results are likely to be only suggestive, they promise a useful check on the ethnographic and anecdotal observations made in the contemporaneous accounts reported earlier. If we use the gross blindness rate as a proxy for poverty, then we should expect it to be negatively correlated with the incidence of Muslim Brotherhood branches. Because there are likely other factors that may be influential, we attempt to control for them here. As in our previous analysis, we control for urbanization, as proxied for the percentage of the workforce in agriculture. We also include controls for male unemployment and the percentage of non-Muslims in a given district, as well as a control for geographic region. Urban governorates were coded as 1, lower Egypt was coded as 2, upper Egypt was coded as 3, and the frontier as 4. This variable could be viewed as a rough proxy for a particular locality's distance from Cairo.[24] Given that transportation costs were not trivial in the early twentieth century, it is possible that the Brotherhood failed to establish branches in places that were simply too hard to get to. Descriptive statistics for the key variables in this analysis can be found in Table 4.6.

[24] The Egyptian Central Agency for Public Mobilization and Statistics carves up Egypt into four distinct geographic regions: urban governorates (comprising Cairo, Alexandria, Port Said, and al-Suways); lower Egypt (comprising the Nile Delta governorates of al-Buḥayra, al-Daqahliyya, Damietta, al-Gharbiyya, al-Ismāʿīliyya, Kafr al-Shaykh, al-Minūfiyya, al-Qalyūbiyya, and al-Sharqiyya); Upper Egypt (comprising the southern governorates of al-Minyā, Asyūt, Aswān, Banī Suwayf, al-Fayyūm, al-Gīza, Qinā, and Suhāg); and the frontier (comprising Matrūḥ, North Sinai, South Sinai, the Red Sea, and the New Valley).

Table 4.7 *Regression Results, Muslim Brotherhood Branches, 1937*

	Negative binomial (no. of branches)	OLS (branches per 10,000)	Logit (branch presence)
Blindness (%)	−0.635***	−0.0701**	−1.511***
	(0.195)	(0.0304)	(0.586)
Workforce in agriculture (%)	2.042**	−0.100	4.520**
	(0.809)	(0.162)	(2.138)
Male unemployment (%)	−3.871***	−0.0180***	−7.232*
	(1.434)	(0.00625)	(4.071)
Non-Muslim (%)	−2.494**	−0.275**	−2.513
	(1.138)	(0.134)	(2.281)
Population	1.98e-06		−3.02e-08
	(1.56e-06)		(4.89e-06)
Region	0.278**	0.0437	0.713**
	(0.118)	(0.0309)	(0.353)
Constant	0.247	0.210***	1.248
	(0.413)	(0.0577)	(0.969)
lnalpha	−1.865***		
	(0.708)		

Note: $N = 145$.
Standard errors in parentheses.
$^{***}p < 0.01$; $^{**}p < 0.05$; $^{*}p < 0.1$.

Moreover, in addition to the binomial regression model, we also reran the analysis twice using different regression models. First, we ran an ordinary least-squares regression using the same data, with the dependent variable transformed from a count of the number of branches into a continuous variable representing the number of branches per 10,000 inhabitants. Second, we generated a dichotomous dependent variable coded 1 if a Muslim Brotherhood branch is present and 0 otherwise, and we analyze it using a logistic regression model. The results of those analyses are presented alongside the negative binomial in Table 4.7. All show the same relationship between our proxy for socioeconomic status and the measure of Muslim Brotherhood presence – that is, districts with higher levels of blindness were less likely to feature Muslim Brotherhood branches.

Figure 4.10 shows the expected number of Muslim Brotherhood branches at different rates of blindness (holding all other variables at their means). The relatively wide 95 percent confidence intervals suggest that, whereas the relationship between our proxy for socioeconomic status is negatively correlated with the presence of Muslim Brotherhood branches, we can only be certain that a shift from very low socioeconomic status to very high produces a significant increase in the expected value of our dependent variable. Nonetheless, the relationship here is consistent with what historical accounts suggest – the Brotherhood's

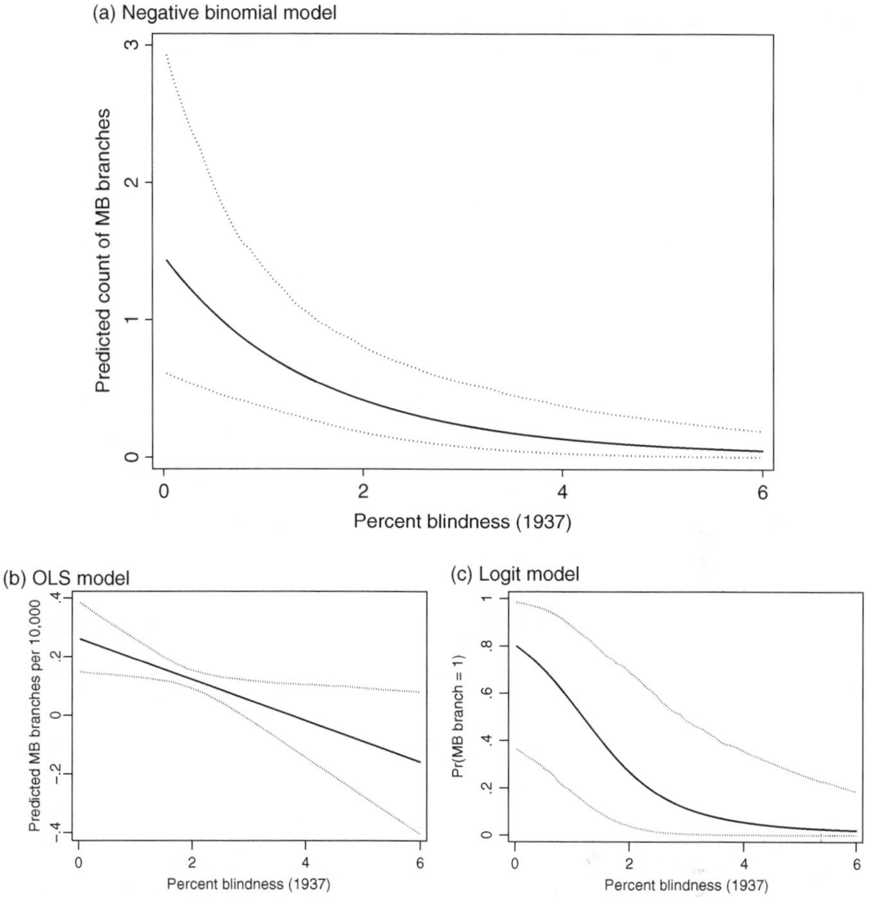

Figure 4.10 Relationship between average blindness rate and Muslim Brotherhood establishment of branches, 1937: (*a*) Negative binomial model; Dependent variable: number of branches. (*b*) OLS model. Dependent variable: branches per 10,000 population; (*c*) Logit model. Dichotomous dependent variable = 1 if Muslim Brotherhood branches present, 0 otherwise.

middle-class basis has it roots in the movement's early history. We thus should be unsurprised that the movement was able to continue appealing to this constituency during the Mubarak era.

4.5 Conclusion

One of the main aims of this and the preceding two chapters has been to demonstrate the importance of attending to the electoral environment in understanding the nature of Islamist electoral victories under authoritarianism. Traditional literature on political Islam has focused largely on individual-level cognitive processes that are thought to render voters hospitable to the Islamist message. Poverty, social strain, and the depredations of authoritarianism – all have been invoked to explain why individuals might join (or vote for) groups such as the Muslim Brotherhood (see Munson (2001) for a review). However, as valuable as these accounts are, they are blind to the ways in which authoritarian electoral environments shape the constituencies to which Islamists – or any opposition parties – can appeal. Where elections are about payoffs and patronage, the regime's superior ability to provide these things thwarts opposition parties' attempts to reach out to poor constituencies, even if those constituencies might be ideologically congenial to their messages. As Bayat (2007) has noted, "the poor cannot afford to be ideological." Even if desperate economic conditions would have made people more receptive to Islamist or Socialist or Nasserist appeals, those same conditions robbed the poor of "positive" or "substantive" freedom needed to act on them (Berlin 1959; Sen 1985). Instead, they were compelled to cast their ballots for regime candidates and others who could offer them material goods. Under this grim reality, the opposition parties that won seats were those that could appeal to middle-class voters – who could make their case to citizens who *could* afford to use their suffrages to express ideological preferences or strike blows against a corrupt ruling regime.

This was the case with the Muslim Brotherhood during the Mubarak era. As I have tried to document, the Muslim Brotherhood's pattern of electoral activism – from the outreach strategies it employed to the types of candidates it fielded to the types of districts in which it fielded those candidates – all focused on the middle classes. This finding echoes Magaloni's (2006, 88) study of the dominance of the ruling Institutional Revolution Party (Partido Revolucionario Institucional, or PRI) in Mexico during the latter half of the twentieth century. In that country, the PRI's control of the means of patronage meant that it "kept the support of the poorest localities, while the prosperous and wealthiest regions began to defect to the opposition, most notably to the PAN [National Action Party, Mexico's Christian Democratic Party]. This also echoes the findings of Chhibber's (1996) study of Algeria's 1991 legislative election. In that ill-fated contest, Chhibber argues, the opposition Islamic Salvation Front picked up the votes of middle-class Algerians (civil servants and small-business owners) who had defected from ruling National Liberation Front (FLN), whereas poor Algerians – captured by the regime's patronage machine – remained in the FLN fold.

Careful readers will ask: If the Brotherhood's victories and the left's losses were so exquisitely sensitive to the dynamics of authoritarian elections, what explains the continuation of those patterns after the collapse of the Mubarak regime? That is the subject of the second half of this book.

PART II

ISLAMISTS AND THEIR RIVALS AFTER THE "ARAB SPRING"

5

God, Mammon, and Transition

The 2010 parliamentary election – the last of seven such contests held during Mubarak's reign – by all accounts represented a bitter regression in Egypt's hitherto halting, eminently modest democratic "progress." The National Democratic Party (NDP) captured 473 of 504 elected seats,[1] dominating the legislature to an extent not seen since the opposition-wide election boycott of 1990. As the opposition reeled, the ruling party congratulated itself and its "organizational secretary," a steel magnate named Ahmed Ezz, for engineering such a stunning victory. Shortly after the conclusion of the elections, Ezz penned a series of articles in the state-owned newspaper, *al-Ahrām*, in which he declared that his party had won because it had "made a difference in the lives of the people." In a widely mocked (but, as far as this author can ascertain, empirically correct) paragraph, the magnate-cum-party leader – described unironically in his author biography as "the man behind the sweeping win by the ruling party in the recent parliamentary elections" – explained

> Overall, the standard of living for the Egyptian middle class has risen, as witnessed by 1.6 million students in private schools and their numbers are rising by 20 per cent a year. One million Egyptian bought new cars over the past five years (80 per cent of these cars cost less than LE 75,000), and permits for residential buildings rose by more than 10 per cent in 2009 alone. There are 39 private, joint and foreign banks in Egypt with more than 3,400 branches across the country. These banks, along with businesses in the fields of communications, computers, engineering consultancy and construction, provide thousands of job opportunities for the middle class, which means an increase in income.[2]

1 The legislature was comprised of 444 seats elected in 222 two-member districts plus 64 seats reserved for women, in addition to 10 elected seats. Elections in four districts had been suspended, bringing the total number of elected seats to 504.

2 Ahmed Ezz, "Parliament elections: a closer, more considered look," *Al-Ahram Online* (Cairo), December 24, 2010; available at: http://english.ahram.org.eg/News/2550.aspx.

Moreover, Ezz insisted, the party had created 4 million jobs since 2005, had presided over the doubling of average incomes, and had expanded access to sewage, potable water, and electricity for Egypt's vast rural population.[3] In addition to these alleged enhancements in Egyptians' welfare, the NDP apparatchik informed readers that his party had also upgraded its electoral machinery. According to Ezz, "We trained our cadres through the NDP Forum for Party Organizers in managerial skills, public issues, and the government's policies." The party, he wrote, had conducted repeated public opinion surveys and party primaries to select the most popular potential candidates. "We sought the opinion of two million Egyptians over five months before we decided whom to nominate to run for seats."[4] But, for all the talk of the regime's economic achievements, or the ruling party's judicious candidate selection and increased organizational discipline, the reality was that the regime had relied on more traditional methods – what journalist Robert Fisk called "the same old Egyptian magic" – for ensuring the ruling party's dominance.[5]

First was the simple fact that the regime made it much harder for Muslim Brotherhood nominees to get (or stay) on the ballot than it had in 2005. Ḥussayn Muḥammad Ibrāhīm, a Brotherhood candidate from the district of Mīnā al-Baṣal in Alexandria, was disqualified (along with three other Brotherhood candidates) by the Higher Elections Commission on the improbable charge of not being a registered voter in his district, despite the fact that he was its sitting member of parliament.[6] Likewise, a mere two weeks before the start of elections on November 29, 2010, the local elections commission in the southern governorate of al-Fayyūm disqualified four Muslim Brotherhood candidates after their NDP opponents filed complaints also alleging that they were not registered to vote in their districts.[7]

Brotherhood members of parliament who managed to stay in the race were confronted by an avid campaign of harassment by the security services. The relatively free atmosphere of the 2005 elections, which had seen the Brotherhood and other regime opponents organize large rallies and public events, had given way to a far more stifling one. I revisited al-Zaqāzīq during the 2010 elections, the home district of Mohamed Morsi, who had come close to winning in 2005

3 Ibid.

4 Ahmed Ezz, "Why We Won, and the Brotherhood Lost, in 2010," *al-Ahram Online* (Cairo), December 25, 2010.

5 Robert Fisk, "Egypt's Election Magic Turns the Opposition Almost Invisible," *The Independent* (London), November 29, 2010; available at: http://www.independent.co.uk/voices/commentators/fisk/egypts-election-magic-turns-the-opposition-almost-invisible-2146237.html.

6 Aḥmad Ṣabrī, "*Da'wā li-'ilghā' qarār istib'ād murashaḥī al-Ikhwān bil-'Iskandariyya* (Call to Cancel the Decision Disqualifying Brotherhood Nominees in Alexandria)," *Al-Ahrām* (Cairo), November 8, 2011.

7 "*Al-ṭa'n 'alā istib'ād 4 min murashaḥi al-ikhwān bil-Fayyūm* (Appealing the exclusion of 4 Brotherhood candidates in al-Fayyūm)," *Ikhwan Online* (Cairo), November 14, 2010; available at: http://www.ikhwanonline.com/Article.aspx?artid=74129&secid=460.

before the regime placed its thumb on the scales at the eleventh hour. This time around, there was no uncertainty about the final outcome. Morsi, who by then was a member of the Brotherhood's guidance bureau and one of its key political strategists, was not running. Instead, the seat was being contested by Aḥmad Fahmī, a mild-mannered professor of pharmacy whose son, ʿAbd al-Raḥmān, is married to Morsi's daughter.[8] Though Fahmī would, after the revolution, be elected to the upper house of parliament – of which he was the speaker until his in-law's ouster from the presidential palace in July 2013 – his first electoral foray was not so fortuitous. If Morsi's campaign had managed to stage grand marches through his district, attended by hundreds of Brotherhood activists, Fahmī's featured a few dozen and were almost invariably dispersed by the police shortly after they began. Predictably, he lost handily.

Though the disqualification of candidates and the suppression of campaign activities were likely sufficient to snuff out any potential Muslim Brotherhood victories, the regime did not stop there. In March 2007, it had amended the constitution and the law governing political participation to vacate the previously mandated requirement of direct judicial supervision of each of the country's more than 10,000 polling stations. According to the ruling party's Minister of State for Parliamentary Affairs, Mufīd Shihāb, this was only natural: "A judge is a man of justice, so how can you ask him to take on an administrative role like some employee?"[9] Instead, in a real-life version of placing the fox in charge of the henhouse, electoral oversight was put in the hands of local government employees, mainly from the Ministry of the Interior.[10] The Egyptian blogosphere lit up with surreptitious cell phone videos purporting to show pro-regime poll watchers stuffing ballots for the ruling party.[11] Opposition and Muslim Brotherhood members of parliament, refusing to accept the legitimacy of the elections that had resulted in their exclusion from office, announced the formation of a shadow "popular parliament" (*al-majlis al-shaʿbī*) to hold the government to account.[12] Mubarak's

8 Walīd Majdī, "*Dr. ʿĀdil Ḥassanayn ṭabīb al-raʾīs: Mursī kān yuʿānī min kīs dihnī fi al-raʾs tamat ʾizālatahu bi-Lundun wa al-jirāḥa najaḥat binisbat 100%* (Dr. ʿĀdil Ḥassanayn, the President's Doctor: Morsi Suffered from a Cyst in the Cranium Which Was Removed in London and the Surgery Was 100% Successful)," *al-Miṣrī al-Yawm* (Cairo), July 3, 2012; available at: http://today.almasryalyoum.com/article2.aspx?ArticleID=345081.

9 Basant Zayn al-Dīn, "*Mufīd Shihāb: al-Ishrāf al-qaḍāʾī ʿalā ṣanadīq al-intikhābāt yuhdar haybat al-qāḍī* ("Mufīd Shihāb: Direct Judicial Supervision over the Ballot Boxes Diminishes the Stature of the Judges)," *al-Miṣrī al-Yawm* (Cairo), September 28, 2010; available at: http://www.almasryalyoum.com/node/185565.

10 "Egypt's 2010 Elections: Fraud, Oppression, and Hope for Change," *Ikhwanweb* (Cairo), December 15, 2010; available at: http://www.ikhwanweb.com/article.php?id=27550.

11 See, for example, video entitled, *Faḍīḥat intikhābāt fī Bilbays* (The Scandal of the Bilbays Elections), uploaded on Nocember 28, 2010; available at: https://www.youtube.com/watch?v=T4HBUKkXyIc.

12 Muīr Adīb and Hānī al-Wazīrī, "*Al-Ikhwān tushārik fi 'al-barlamān al-shaʿbī' wa tarfuḍ musamayāt 'al-muwāzī' wa 'al-badīl'* (The Brotherhood Participates in the 'Popular Parliament'

response was to quip, "*Khalīhum yatsallū* [Let them amuse themselves]."[13] He would be overthrown fewer than eight weeks later.

It is too easy, of course, to trace the revolution that broke out in the opening weeks of 2011 to the rigged electoral contest of the closing weeks of 2010. The reasons for which people rise up against established orders are many, and social scientists may never capture them all. It is particularly worth noting that most scholars of Egypt and the Middle East did not at the time think that the NDP's sweeping victory in the 2010 elections would lead to an explosion of popular anger (Masoud 2011). What is clear is that those eighteen days of protest and the dictator's resignation were so unprecedented, so definitive a break with the past, that they seemed to open up previously unimagined possibilities. After all, despite all the predictions and prophecies of social scientists, the Mubarak regime, that poster child for durable authoritarianism (Brownlee 2007; Blaydes 2010), had fallen. We could have been forgiven, then, for allowing ourselves to think that other prophecies – such as the inevitability of Islamist dominion – might also fail to come true.

But come true they did. And in doing so, they reinforced the long-standing view of Egyptian politics as dominated by the question of *sharīʿa* and Islamic identity. In this chapter, and in the one that follows, I explore the roots of Islamist victories – and non-Islamist defeats – in Egypt's founding election. I argue that political competition during Egypt's democratic opening was less about religious ideology than it was about the economy. Islamists were voted into office not because of what they promised to do for God but because of what they promised to do with Mammon. Specifically, citizens voted for the Muslim Brotherhood's Freedom and Justice Party because they believed it would redistribute wealth and strengthen the welfare state. Why they thought Islamists, and not leftists, would be the ones to do these things explains why the dramatic events of January 25, 2011, would, from the perspective of the left, prove to be a revolution that changed everything and nothing at all.

5.1 A New Reality?

One could not help but conclude that the revolution of the winter of 2011 presented the Egyptian left with a promising new reality. The slogan of the revolution, "*Aysh, ḥurriya, ʿadāla ijtimāʿiyya* [Bread, liberty, social justice]," a riff on an old Leninist formulation (Lenin 2002 (1917)), could have been ripped from one of the campaign flyers of the National Progressive Unionist Rally (NPUR), and the party's headquarters just off Taḥrīr took on new life as a waypoint for

and Rejects Labeling It 'Parallel' or 'Alternative')," *al-Miṣrī al-Yawm* (Cairo), December 31, 2010; available at: http://www.almasryalyoum.com/node/283842.

13 Mohamed Abdel-Baku, "Shadow Play," *al-Ahram Weekly* (Cairo), No. 1028, December 23–29, 2010; available at: http://weekly.ahram.org.eg/2010/1028/eg6.htm.

activists on their way to and from the square.[14] Some of the most prominent personalities of the revolution were men and women of the left, such as the Ḥamdīn Ṣabāḥī, leader of a small Arab nationalist party known as al-Karāma (Dignity), the Nasserist writer ʿAbd al-Ḥalīm Qandīl, and the labor activist Kamāl Abū al-ʿĪṭa. Indeed, some analysts located the moment of the Mubarak regime's collapse not on January 25, when the first protests took place in Taḥrīr Square, nor on January 28, when the Muslim Brotherhood formally joined the demonstrations,[15] but to an explosion of workers strikes on February 8, 9, and 10 (Alexander 2012; Beinin 2012). The left had put its stamp on the revolution's image abroad as well – Jihān Ibrāhīm, who emerged in the Western media as a representative of the youth of Taḥrīr, was a member of a group calling itself the Revolutionary Socialists (*al-Ishtirakiyūn al-Thawriyūn*). To this author, watching Egypt closely during those eighteen days of revolution, it seemed that all of the energy was on the left.

Moreover, it appeared that the hearts of Egyptians were on the left as well. In a survey of 1,675 Egyptians conducted by the author a few months after the revolution, in December 2011, respondents revealed strong preferences for the kinds of welfare-statist redistributive policies that are the hallmarks of leftist-party platforms. For example, respondents were asked to place themselves along a continuum from 1 to 10, where 1 represented the belief that the welfare of individuals is the responsibility of the government, and 10 represented the belief that individuals should be responsible for their own welfare. The vast majority endorsed the statist view (see Figure 5.1). Similarly, when citizens were asked whether the government should focus on redistribution and equality or ignore equality and focus solely on economic growth, the vast majority displayed a strong preference for redistribution (see Figure 5.2).[16] Though the ruling party's Ahmed Ezz had tried to convince us that Egyptians were pleased with the results of his party's neoliberal economic policies, the evidence suggested that – regardless of whatever tangible improvements those policies had made – they were at odds with the sensibilities of the majority of his people.

14 Ulfat Madkūr, "*Fī Ūlā nadawāt al-tawthīq al-tārīkhī ḥawl thawrat 25 yanāyir* (In the First Conference on the Historical Documentation of the January 25th Revolution)," *al-Ahālī* (Cairo), April 6, 2011.

15 "*Al-Waṭan tanshur naṣ mudhakirat shabāb al-Ikhwān ʿan kawālīs ʿadam mushārakat al-jamāʿa yawm 25 yanāyir 2011* (Al-Waṭan Publishes the Text of the Brotherhood Youths' Memo Behind the Scenes on the Society's Abstention from the January 25 Protests)," *al-Waṭan* (Cairo), January 24, 2013.

16 In each question, respondents were presented with two contrasting policy options, each at either end of a ten-point scale, and asked where along that scale they would situate themselves. For the first question, the two poles were "The government should be responsible for the welfare of every citizen" and "Citizens should be responsible for their own welfare." In the second question, the two poles were "The government should raise taxes on the rich in order to give to the poor" and "The government should focus on economic growth and not social equality." Survey questionnaire is available at http://www.tarekmasoud.com/data/.

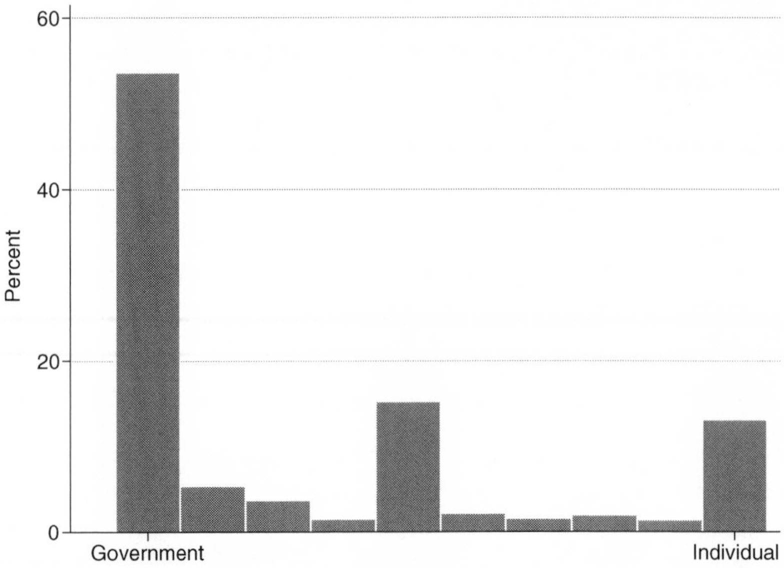

Figure 5.1 Most Egyptians believe that the government, as opposed to the individual, is responsible for citizens' well-being (December 2011).

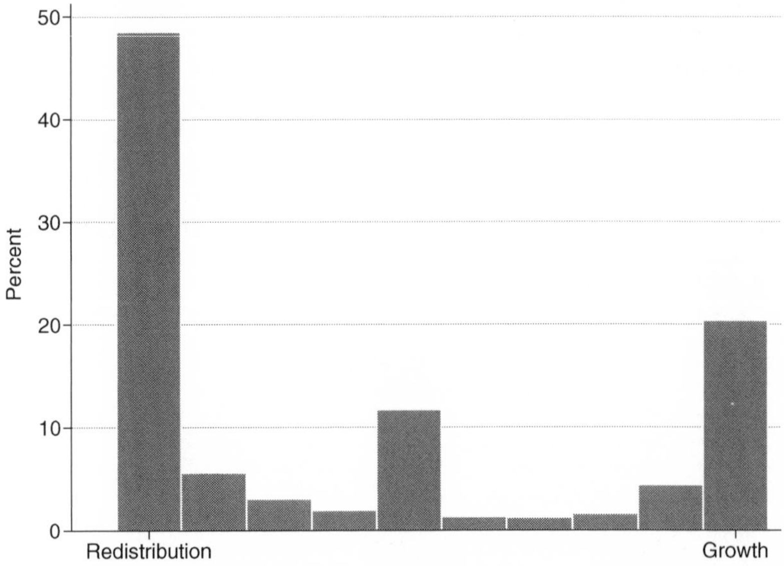

Figure 5.2 Most Egyptians want the government to focus on redistributing wealth rather than simply maximizing economic growth (December 2011).

If the so-called demand side seemed to favor the left, so too did the supply side. In the months that followed the revolution, much of the institutional framework that undergirded Mubarak-era elections and that made them rife with patronage and vote-buying was dismantled. In April 2011, an administrative court declared that the ruling party had been one of the "instruments" of the fallen regime, disbanded it, and ordered the state to seize its assets, which it declared the "property of the people."[17] In November of that year, an administrative court in the Nile Delta province of al-Manṣūra even banned former members of the party from running in that month's parliamentary elections, although that ruling was eventually overturned.[18]

Not that it would have mattered: the stigma of former association with the ruling party appears to have prevented many local notables from running in the first place. For example, in October 2011, the Abāẓa family of the governorate of al-Sharqiyya – which claimed among its members the minister of agriculture in Mubarak's last government – announced that it was not planning to nominate one of its members for a seat in the second district of Bilbays, which included the family seat Minyā al-Qamḥ and al-Tilīn and which had been held by an Abāẓa for more than seventy years.[19] In the district of Shubrā al-Khayma outside Cairo, the ʿAwda family, which typically fielded candidates in parliamentary elections, abstained in 2011 because the family's principal political personality, Muḥammad ʿAwda, a member of the 2010 parliament, faced charges of helping to organize attacks against protesters in Tahrir square.[20]

Moreover, even where NDP-affiliated local notables did run, the drying up of their access to sources of patronage – such as public-sector jobs for constituents

[17] Council of State, First District, Case Numbers 20030, 20279, and 20459, "*Ḥal al-Ḥizb al-Waṭanī al-Dīmuqrāṭī bi Miṣr* (The Dissolution of the National Democratic Party in Egypt," *al-Jazeera* (Doha), April 16, 2011; available at: http://www.aljazeera.net/news/pages/f159c235-7529-4253-9402-2ccf6317c65c; Muḥammad Asʿad, "*Al-ḥukm fī daʿwā ḥal al-ḥizb al-waṭani khilāl sāʿāt* (Decision in the Suit for the Dissolution of the NDP Expected in Hours)," *al-Yawm al-Sābīʿ* (Cairo), April 16, 2011; available at: http://www.youm7.com/News.asp?NewsID=392139.

[18] Sharīf Al-Dīb, "*Nanshur maswaddat ḥukm al-qaḍāʾ al-ʾidārī bi-manʿ ʾaʿḍāʾ al-ḥizb al-waṭanī min al-tarashuḥ* (We Print the Draft Ruling of the Administrative Court Prohibiting Members of the NDP from Running)," *al-Yawm al-Sābiʿ* (Cairo), November 1, 2011 ; Serene Assir, "Lifting of Ban on NDP Candidates: A Trojan Ballot Box?" *al-Akhbar* (Cairo), November 15, 2011; available at: http://english.al-akhbar.com/node/1515.

[19] Īmān Mahannā, "*ʿĀʾilat Abāẓa tahjar maqʿad Minyā al-Qamḥ liʾawwal marra mundh 70 ʿāmā* (The Abaza Family Abandons the Seat of Minyā al-Qamḥ for the First Time in 70 Years)," *al-Yawm al-Sābiʿ* (Cairo), October 15, 2011; available at: http://www.youm7.com/News.asp?NewsID=513249&.

[20] ʿĪd ʿAbd al-Jawād, "*Kubrā al-ʿāʾilāt al-barlamāniyya bil-Qalyūbiyya tughīb ʿan al-intikhābāt* (The Biggest Parliamentary Families in al-Qalyūbiyya Are Absent from the Elections)," *al-Misrī al-Yawm* (Cairo), December 12, 2011. As we shall see, however, the stigma of association with the National Democratic Party would have a short half-life, as evidenced by the 48 percent of the vote captured by former Mubarak-era official Aḥmad Shafīq in the second round of the May–June 2012 presidential election.

and expedited health and social services from the relevant government ministries – likely diminished their electoral prospects. For example, in the district of al-Zaqāzīq in al-Sharqiyya, former NDP-affiliated candidates with long records of service provision to their home villages – including three-time parliamentarian Luṭfī Shaḥata of the village of Banī Shibl, six-time parliamentarian and Ministry of Transportation official ʿIzzat Badawī – all fared poorly at the polls, and two-time NDP representative Rifʿat al-Bayūmī (1990-2000) withdrew his candidacy shortly before election day.[21] Stripped of the promise of preferential entrée to the patronage resources of a one-party state, many a local notable proved not notable at all.

Further putting paid to the prospect of a resurgence of the politics of patronage in that first post-revolutionary election was the electoral rule chosen by the Supreme Council of the Armed Forces (al-Majlis al-ʾaʿlā lil-quwwāt al-misalaḥa), which assumed the role of caretaker government after Mubarak's resignation. As noted in Chapter 2, from 1990 to 2010, Egypt employed a majoritarian, candidate-centric system with 222 two-member electoral districts. Each election featured several thousand candidates, the vast majority of whom were independents without party labels. As several observers have noted, this system encouraged the cultivation of personal votes (Carey and Shugart 1995) based on a candidate's ability to provide clientelistic benefits to his home district (Blaydes 2010). After Mubarak's overthrow, secular political parties lobbied for a shift to an electoral system based on proportional representation and closed party lists, believing that this would diminish the power both of old regime elites and Islamists (the two groups that had dominated under the old system). Sāmiḥ ʿĀshūr, leader of the Nasserist Party and former head of the Lawyers Syndicate, declared that "only the Muslim Brotherhood and the National Democratic Party want to keep *fardī* [candidate-centric] seats" and that only proportional lists would "ensure representation of all political and national forces in the parliament."[22] In the end, the military issued a compromise electoral law in which two-thirds of the parliament's 508 elected representatives would be elected on closed party lists in forty-six multimember districts, with the remaining third to be elected according to the old *fardī* candidate-centric system in eighty-two districts.[23] Though the

21 See Rūḥ al-Fu'ad Muḥammad, "*Al-intikhābāt bidawā'ir al-Sharqiyya* (Elections in the Districts of al-Sharqiyya)," *Jarīdat Akhbār al-'Iliktrūniyya* (Cairo), December 5, 2011; available at: http://akhbar.masreat.com/7581/; Imān Mahanna, "*Insiḥāb 4 murashaḥīn bi al-Sharqiyya baynahum nā'ib sābiq bi al-munḥal* (Withdrawal of 4 Candidates in al-Sharqiyya Including a Former Deputy of the Dissolved [NDP])," *al-Yawm al-Sabiʿ* (Cairo), December 7, 2011.

22 Maḥmud Saʿd al-Dīn and Maḥmud Ḥusayn, "*Al-Ikhwān yarfiḍūn mashrūʿ qanūn majlis al-shaʿb alathi 'aʿadahu al-majlis al-ʿaskari wa yasifūnahu bitashwih niẓām al-intikhābāt* (The Muslim Brothers Refuse the Draft People's Assembly Election Law Prepared by the Supreme Council of the Armed Forces and Describe It as Ruining the Electoral System)," *al-Yawm al-Sabiʿ* (Cairo), May 28, 2011.

23 *Qānūn raqam 120 lisanat 2011 bitaʿdīl baʿḍ aḥkām al-qānūn raqam 38 lisanat 1972 bi sha'n majlis al-shaʿb* (Law 120 of 2011, Mending Some of the Rulings of Law 38 of 1972 Concerning the People's Assembly), September 27, 2011.

persistence of a majoritarian tier raised fears that the old politics of patronage and vote buying and notability would be reenacted, the large size of these districts – two and a half times the size of the previous majoritarian districts – meant that it was much more difficult for candidates to buy their way into office.[24] The poor, previously locked up by the ruling party's patronage machine and the blandishments of the "whales of the Nile" (Sfakianakis 2004), now seemed ripe for the taking.

New parties of the left took advantage of the new opening. A center-left party calling itself the Egyptian Social Democratic Party (al-Ḥizb al-Miṣrī al-Dimuqrāṭī al-ʾIjtimāʿī), which declared its intention to "pass laws defending the rights of the poor and the weak," was formed in March 2011.[25] An even more left-leaning party called the Popular Socialist Alliance (Ḥizb al-Taḥāluf al-shaʿbī al-ishtirākī) was established in October 2011 by a thwarted claimant to the presidency of the NPUR, ʿAbd al-Ghaffār Shukr.[26] And in February 2011, labor leaders from several governorates and privatized companies gathered to form a Democratic Workers Party (Ḥizb al-ʿUmmāl al-Dimqrāṭī) that aspired to serve as "an independent platform to express the political and economic interests" of the working class.[27]

There were promising signs for other non-Islamist parties as well. In a March 2011 telephone poll conducted by the International Peace Institute (IPI), only 12 percent of Egyptians said that they would vote for the Muslim Brotherhood if the election were held immediately, whereas 20 percent said that they would vote for the Wafd Party. Similarly, a Pew poll conducted in March 2011 revealed that 20 percent of respondents believed that the Wafd Party should lead the next government, whereas only 17 percent thought that the Brotherhood should. A June 2011 follow-up poll by the IPI saw both the Wafd and Brotherhood parties tied at 12 percent. Thus, despite all the Brotherhood's alleged gifts, its long history, and its considerable electoral experience, the people seemed – if those

24 ʿAmr al-Shubaki, an Egyptian analyst and member of the now-dissolved 2012 People's Assembly, has proposed an electoral system with much smaller single-member districts, in part to increase the importance of candidates' personal connections to voters. See, ʿAmr al-Shubakī, "*Naḥw qānūn jadīd lil-intikhābāt al-barlamāniyya* (Toward a New Parliamentary Elections Law)," *al-Miṣrī al-Yawm* (Cairo), January 2, 2013.

25 "*Nash'at al-Dimuqraṭiya al-'ijtimaʿiyya wa taṭawuruhā wa mabādi'uha*, (The development of social democracy and its evolution and its principles)," website of the Egyptian Social Democratic Party; available at: http://www.egysdp.com/site/index.php?option=com_content&view=article&id=301&Itemid=141.

26 "*Al-Taḥāluf al-'Ishtirākī yuqaddam awrāq ta'sīsahu lilajnat al-aḥzāb* (The Socialist Alliance Presents Its Incorporation Papers to the Parties Committee)," Masrawy.com (Cairo), September 28, 2011; available at: http://www.masrawy.com/news/egypt/politics/2011/september/28/4464116.aspx.

27 *Mashruʿ birnāmij Ḥizb al-ʿUmmāl al-Dimuqrāṭī* (Draft Platform of the Workers Democratic Party), n.d., 1; Ibtisām Taʿlab, "*Al-'Iʿlān ʿan ta'sīs Ḥizb al-ʿUmmāl al-Dīmqrāṭī min mīdān al-Taḥrīr* (Announcement of Formation of the Labor Democratic Party from Tahrir Square," May 1, 2011; available at: http://www.almasryalyoum.com/node/419613.

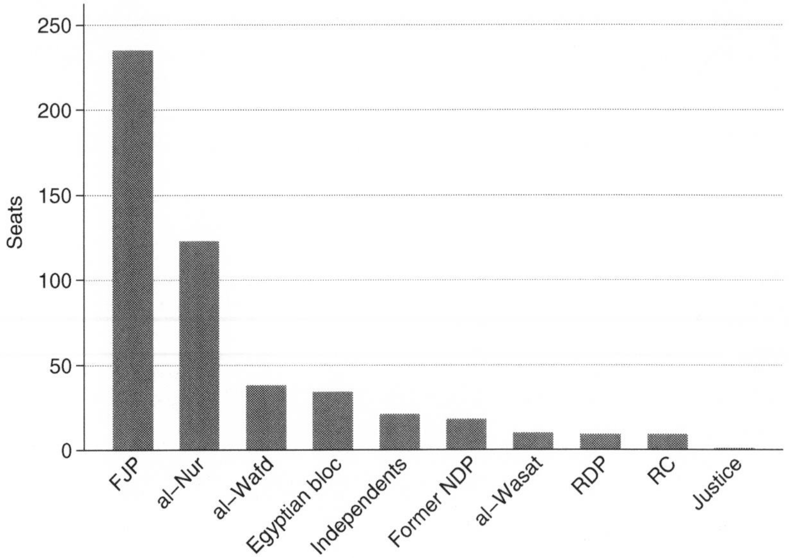

Figure 5.3 Results of Egyptian People's Assembly election, November 2011–January 2012.

early polls were accurate – to hold it in no greater esteem than they did a party that in the preceding two decades had never managed to place more than a handful of representatives in parliament.

As if in recognition of this fact, the Islamists seemed to grow more fragmented by the day. By June 2011, there were as many as seventeen identifiably Islamic parties.[28] Some, like the Movement for Peace and Development (Ḥarakat al-Salām wa al-Tanmiya) and the Center (Wasaṭ), Pioneer (al-Riyāda), Renaissance (al-Nahḍa), and Egyptian Current (al-Tayār al-Miṣrī) parties, were formed by breakaway members of the Brotherhood (the Center Party had been formed in 1996 and the others were established in the immediate aftermath of the January 25, 2011 revolution). Others, such as the Virtue Party (Ḥizb al-Faḍīla) and the Party of Light (Ḥizb al-Nūr), were formed by Salafi preachers, and still others, such as the Party of Construction and Development (Ḥizb al-Binā' wa al-Tanmiya) and the Party of Safety and Development (Ḥizb al-Salāma wa al-Tanmiya), emerged, respectively, out of the Islamic Group (al-Gamā'a al-Islāmiyya) and the Islamic Jihad (al-Jihād al-Islāmī), two Islamist militant organizations implicated in the assassination of Egyptian President Anwar Sadat in October 1981. Egyptian liberal commentator and journalist Ibrāhīm 'Īsa actually welcomed this

[28] Usāma 'abd al-Salām, "*Mumathilū 17 ḥizban islāmiyan yu'akidūn wasaṭiyyat al-Islām* (The Representatives of 17 Islamic Parties Affirm the Centrism of Islam)," *Ikhwan Online* (Cairo), July 20, 2011; available at: http://www.ikhwanonline.com/new/Article.aspx?SecID=230& ArtID=88080.

proliferation of Islamist parties, predicting that competition among them for the mantle of Islam would serve to split the Islamist vote and keep the Brotherhood from dominating the political arena.[29]

In short, in the immediate aftermath of the revolution, there were ample reasons for non-Islamist forces to be optimistic about their chances in post-Mubarak Egypt. As the months passed, however, that optimism gave way to the old fears of Islamist dominion. And when parliamentary elections were finally held and the dust settled on the new assembly, the worst of those fears had been realized. Not only had the Muslim Brotherhood emerged as the largest party in the new legislature – an outcome, perhaps, to be expected given the party's long history of winning elections under Mubarak – but an even more conservative party of Salafists emerged as a close second (see Figure 5.3). It appeared that Dekmejian (1995) had been right when he fretted, almost twenty years ago, that Egypt was "well on its way to becoming a near-Islamic state."

5.2 Voting for Islamic Law?

It was in March 2011 that the traditional fears of Islamist domination first re-emerged. When the Supreme Council of the Armed Forces (SCAF) assumed power on February 11, 2011, one of its first decisions was to suspend the 1971 constitution and to assemble a committee of eight jurists whose task would be to amend the existing constitution in order to facilitate a rapid transfer of power to an elected civilian government. The committee, chaired by Ṭāriq al-Bishrī, a jurist widely described as having "moderate" Islamist leanings (Ashour 2009, 151; Esposito and Voll 1996, 177; Murphy 2007, 318), worked up a set of amendments that strengthened judicial oversight of elections, established presidential term limits, opened up competition for the presidency, and trimmed presidential powers. The most important amendment, however, was one that stipulated that a new constitution would be written after the parliamentary elections by a constituent assembly chosen by the members of the new parliament.

Non-Islamists offered several objections to the plan. Some of these were technical. For example, Hishām al-Basṭawīsī, a judge who made his name opposing the Mubarak regime (and who would eventually become the NPUR's presidential candidate), argued that, since the role and powers of the parliament are determined by the constitution, it made no sense to elect the former before writing the latter.[30] Ḥasan Nāfiʿ, a Cairo University political scientist and leading member

[29] Ibrahim ʿĪsā, "*Sa aqūl lā liltaʿdilāt al-dustūriya li hādhihi al-asbāb* (I Will Say No to the Constitutional Amendments for These Reasons)," *Akhbar Live* (Cairo), March 16, 2011; available at: http://akhbarlive.com/news/4910.html.

[30] "Al-Basṭawīsī: al-Dustūr awalan, wa nāʾib al-raʾīs wa al-muḥāfaẓīn wa al-ʿumad bil-intikhāb (The Constitution First and the Vice President, Governors, and Mayors by Election," *al-Fajr* (Cairo), May 21, 2011; available at: http://www.masress.com/elfagr/19369.

of the pro-democracy National Association for Change, argued that the constitutional amendments would extend the transitional period needlessly because once the new constitution was passed, the parliament that produced it would have to be dissolved and a new one elected.[31] However, underlying such technical discussions was the concern that snap elections, held not a year after Mubarak's overthrow, would privilege the two groups that routinely won elections during his tenure – the ruling party and the Muslim Brotherhood. In a March television advertisement in which several leading Egyptian liberals – including former International Atomic Energy Agency Chief Mohamed ElBaradei and Amre Moussa, former foreign minister and secretary general of the Arab League – called on voters to reject SCAF's plan, Egyptians were told, among other things, that voting for SCAF's proposal would mean early elections, which would be won by Mubarak's National Democratic Party (NDP) and the Brotherhood, who would then control the writing of the new constitution.[32]

For their part, the Islamists campaigned hard to get out the vote in favor of the amendments. Three days before the referendum, the Jamʿiyya al-Sharʿiyya (JS), Egypt's largest and oldest Islamic charity, ran an advertisement on the front page of *al-Ahrām* declaring it "a religious duty for every Egyptian to take care to vote in favor of the amendments."[33] One author accused Islamists of "inciting the spectre of communal division over article 2 of the constitution" – which since 1981 had made "the principles of *sharīʿa* the principal source of legislation."[34] Thus, when the referendum passed on March 19, 2011, with 77 percent of the vote (amid approximately 40 percent turnout), it seemed to suggest an electorate fearful of a secularization of the state and thus poised to bring into office the defenders of *sharīʿa*. Emad Gad, an analyst for the Ahram Center for Political and Strategic Studies, in explaining the outcome, complained that the Muslim Brotherhood "made the referendum a matter of religion. They manipulated the people's ignorance and purported [*sic*] that approving the amendments was virtuous and would please God, and anyone who rejected the amendments was evil."[35] The narrative seemed to be advanced by the Islamists themselves. After the vote, Muḥammad Ḥusayn Yaʿqūb, a popular Salafist preacher, declared the

31 Ḥasan Nāfiʿ, "The Ones Who Fear for Democracy," *al-Miṣrī al-Yawm* (Cairo), March 27, 2011; available at: http://www.almasry-alyoum.com/article2.aspx?ArticleID=291694&IssueID=2087.

32 The advertisement can be viewed at http://www.youtube.com/watch?v=fRDs7iu1C1E.

33 "*Bayān al-Jamʿiyya al-Sharʿiyya al-Raʾīsiyya bi-shaʾn al-istiftāʾ ʿalā al-taʿdīlāt al-dustūriyya* (Statement of JS Headquarters in the Matter of the Referendum on the Constitutional Amendments)," *al-Ahram* (Cairo), March 16, 2011, 1.

34 Hishām ʿAbd al-Ghaffār, "*Kashf al-mastūr fī taʿdīl al-dustūr* (Uncovering the Secrets of the Consititional Amendments," *al-Yawm al-Sābiʿ* (Cairo), March 17, 2011; available at: http://www.youm7.com/News.asp?NewsID=371764.

35 Emad Gad, "Political Participation for Egyptians," *al-Ahram Weekly* (Cairo), April 27, 2011; available at: http://english.ahram.org.eg/NewsContentPrint/4/0/10904/Opinion/0/Political-participation-for-Egyptians.aspx.

result a victory for the faith and is reported to have announced, "That's it, the country is ours."[36]

There are reasons to doubt, however, that voters experienced the referendum as a battle over *sharīʿa*. First is the simple fact that the ruling party – which by then had not yet been dissolved – was a strong supporter of the amendments as well.[37] Muḥammad Ragab, the party's secretary general, declared that the amendments "achieve constitutional legitimacy and a transition to a new phase of national action" and urged his party's adherents to head to the polls and vote yes.[38] In fact, when one examines the distribution of yes votes across the country's localities, it seems to match the largely rural vote base that characterized the ruling party in the past. Figure 5.4 is a plot of the share of voters in each of Egypt's 345 *marākiz* and *aqsām* who voted yes in the referendum plotted against adult illiteracy. As with the pattern of voting for the ruling party in previous elections explored in Chapter 2 (see also Blaydes 2010), there was a positive relationship between illiteracy and support for the referendum. Thus it is impossible to know whether support for the amendments represented popular anxiety over the status of *sharīʿa*, a desire to move quickly out of Egypt's constitutional limbo and back to "normal" politics (which was the argument most often made by the Muslim Brotherhood), or simply a popular endorsement of the military council that was then ruling Egypt.

Of course, the fact that the Muslim Brotherhood and the Salafi Nūr Party later went on to capture a majority of the seats in the legislature gave added ballast to the idea that Egyptian voters were finally acting out a long-standing desire to implement Islamic law. That Egyptians would turn to faith so soon after a revolution built on "bread, liberty, and social justice" was unsurprising to those who had always argued that Egyptians were closet Islamists. We were reminded of how, during the periodic surveys of Egyptian public opinion that had been conducted throughout the Mubarak years, one of the few empirical regularities that emerged was a popular desire for the application of *sharīʿ*a. For example, in 2000, the World Values Survey found that almost 80 percent of the 3,000 Egyptians they surveyed agreed with the statement, "The government should implement only the laws of the *sharīʿah*."[39] And, more recently, in the summer of 2011, the *Arab Barometer* found that almost 80 percent of Egyptians agreed with the statement

36 "Popular Salafi Claims Victory for Religion in Referendum," *al-Miṣrī al-Yawm* (Cairo), March 22, 2011; available at: www.almasryalyoum.com/en/node/369373.

37 Muḥammad Ḥasan Shaʿbān, "*Al-Miṣriyūn yarsimūn al-yawm malāmiḥ mustaqbalhum fī al-istiftāʾ ʿalā al-taʿdīlāt al-dustūriyya* (Today Egyptians Sketch the Outlines of Their Future in a Referendum on Constitutional Amendments), *al-Sharq al-Awsat* (London), March 19, 2011; available at: http://www.aawsat.com/details.asp?section=4&article=613224&issueno=11799#.Uc3gRj7SMbY; Muḥammad Gamāl ʿArafa, "*al-Taʿdīlāt: naʿm am lā?* (The Amendments, Yes or No?)," *al-Wafd* (Cairo), March 16, 2011; available at: http://www.alwafd.org/index.php?option=com_content&view=article&id=24276.

38 "*Al-Ḥizb al-Waṭanī yadʿū ʾaʿḍāʾihi litaʾyīd al-taʿdīlāt al-dustūriya* (The NDP Calls on Its Members to Support the Constitutional Amendments)," Masrawy.com (Cairo), March 13, 2011; available at: http://www.masrawy.com/news/egypt/politics/2011/march/13/national_party.aspx.

39 World Values Survey, third wave, Egypt, 2000; available at: http://www.worldvaluessurvey.org/.

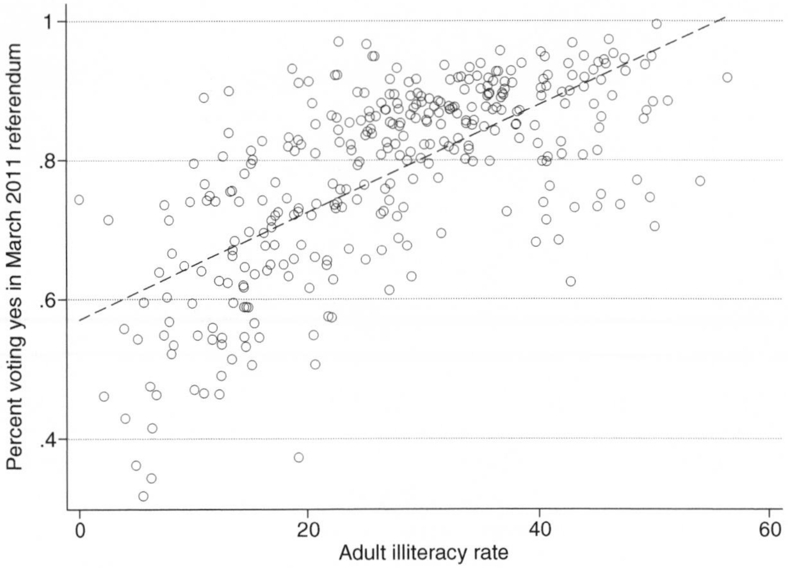

Figure 5.4 Department-level percentage of yes votes versus adult illiteracy, Egyptian constitutional referendum, March 2011.

that "Government and parliament should enact laws according to the *sharīʿa*" (Figure 5.5). Scholars had long noted that the country was in the midst of a broad Islamic "revival every bit as encompassing as ... the religious revival in mid-nineteenth century Christendom" (Rodenbeck 1998, 178). Signs of this revival were everywhere – from the expanding number of mosques (Gaffney 1994, 47), to the increasing hours of religious radio and television programming (Abu Lughod 2006, 11), to the tendency of Muslim women to don headscarves (Abdo 2000, 149–61). Given decades worth of data and ethnographic observation, it was perhaps little wonder that the partisans of *sharīʿa* would receive the suffrages of the people in a free and fair election.

However, if we examine what Egyptians actually had been thinking about during the eighteen months following their revolution, it is difficult to sustain the image of voters primarily concerned with enshrining the *sharīʿa* and defending it against so-called secularists. For example, in June–July, the *Arab Barometer* asked a sample of 1,220 Egyptians to name their country's two most important challenges. Almost 85 percent cited the economy – including such issues as poverty and unemployment. Another 7.5 percent cited "financial and administrative corruption" (see Figure 5.6). In a survey of 1,200 Egyptians conducted by the Ahram Center for Political and Strategic Studies shortly after the parliamentary elections in May 2012, 68.5 percent of respondents said that the economy was the most urgent issue facing Egypt – only 2.5 percent said writing the final version of the constitution was, and only 2.3 percent said applying Islamic law

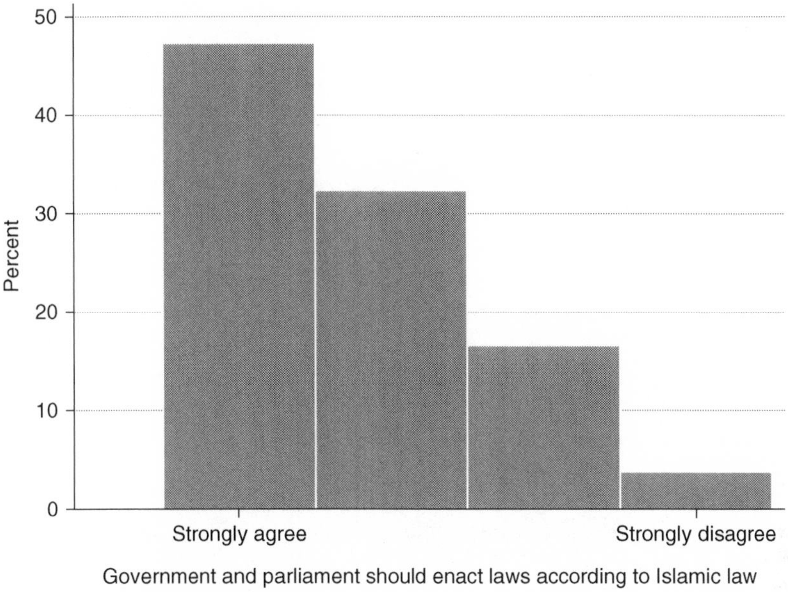

Figure 5.5 Support for *sharīʿa*, Egypt, June–July. (*Source: Arab Barometer Second Wave.*)

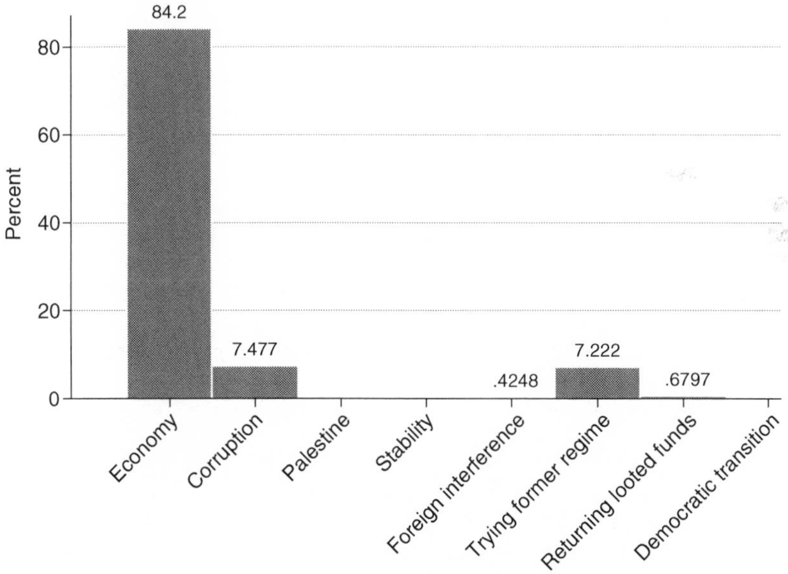

Figure 5.6 Concerns of Egyptians after the 2011 revolution. (*Source: Arab Barometer Second Wave.*)

was the most important issue facing the country.[40] The same pattern is evident in another al-Ahram poll conducted twelve years earlier: the vast majority of 1,600 respondents in a 2000 survey also identified economic issues as Egypt's primary challenges, with more than a third citing the "labor market" and another quarter citing the "economic situation." In fact, only around 15 percent of those polled pointed to "social problems" (*mashākil ijtimā'iyya*) – an admittedly vague category, but one that comes closest to encompassing the issues of moral decay with which Islamists are supposed to be concerned.[41] The overwhelming impression conferred by these data is that, whereas vast majorities of Egyptians pay an easy lip service to *sharī'a*, only for a small minority is their political calculus dominated by it.

In fact, this is something that the Islamists themselves seem to have grasped intuitively. During the 2011 election, the Muslim Brotherhood's candidates focused on matters other than the question of *sharī'a* or who would get to write the country's constitution. For example, one campaign flier summarizing its program identified four goals: "security, job opportunities, education, and health."[42] Another flier laid out a six-point program – focusing on security, public services, employment, education and culture, health, and communication between representatives and voters. And though one might have expected the latter flier's discussion of education to include a strong religious component, it is worth reproducing it here in full:

Education and culture

1. Establishing a program to raise the standard of education in the district through competition among the schools of the district.
2. Establishing new schools in order to reduce overcrowding in the classrooms, especially in the new settlements.
3. Activating public libraries and establishing new ones in places deprived of them and providing them with electronic books.
4. Activating the role of cultural, literary, and political salons to raise the intellectual level and political awareness of the youth and giving them the incentive to participate in public life.
5. Holding debates and artistic and cultural and literary competitions to discover, nurture, and support talents and raise public tastes.
6. To work to improve wages for teachers in the ministry of education

40 Ṣubḥī 'Isaila, "*al-Iqtiṣād wa al-amn ... al-matlabān al-aham lil-miṣriyīn* (The Economy and Security ... the Two Most Important Demands of Egyptians)," in "*Kayf Yufakir al-Miṣriyūn*? (How Do Egyptians Think?)," *al-Ahrām* (insert), June 14, 2012.

41 The sample included 747 men (46.69 percent) and 853 women (53.31 percent). Sample is stratified with respect to governorate. Cairo and Alexandria account for 24.38 percent of sample; Nile Delta governorates for 44.38 percent and Upper Egypt for 31.25 percent.

42 *Min Birnāmijunā al-Intikhābī li'ām 2011* (From Our Electoral Program for the Year 2011), Ḥizb al-Ḥurriya wa al-'Adālah (Freedom and Justice Party, Dā'irat Sharq al-Qāhira (District of East Cairo), November 2011.

7. To establish training sessions for teachers in modern methods of teaching and establish quality programs, in addition to honoring model teachers in each of the district's schools.[43]

When one reads the full party platforms put forward by both the Muslim Brotherhood and the more religiously conservative Salafists, one is struck by the extent of their emphasis on issues of economic development. The platform of the Nūr Party, for example, begins not by declaring the importance of returning to the path of Allah or the method of the Prophet, but by noting three forms of corruption that characterized the Mubarak regime and that the party comes to combat: electoral fraud, the theft of national resources, and the use of the security services to defend the regime instead of the people.[44]

The Islamists' focus on the economy is further revealed by a statistical analysis of the 2011 electoral platforms of both the Nūr Party and the Muslim Brotherhood.[45] The most frequently mentioned word in the Nūr Party's 8,876-word platform is not *sharīʿa* (which appears five times) or *Islam* (which, in its various forms, appears twenty-five times) but *economy* (*iqtiṣād*), which appears fifty-eight times in its various forms. Similarly, the Muslim Brotherhood's 12,639-word parliamentary elections program only mentions sharīʿa fourteen times, whereas *economy* appears thirty-five times. In Mohammed Morsi's 15,000-word presidential campaign platform, *Islam* earned only thirty-six mentions and *sharīʿa* only eight, whereas *development* (*tanmiya*) in its various forms was mentioned 178 times and *economy* 158 times. Moreover, when these parties talk about the economy, they appear to be addressing it as it relates to citizens' welfare, and not simply railing against the ways in which the modern economic system departs from Islamic strictures. For example, though Kuran (1996, 438) asserts that the prohibition on interest (*ribā*) is the "centerpiece of Islamic economics," both the Nūr Party and Freedom and Justice Party platforms call for the replacement of interest only gradually (*tadrījiyan*). In August 2012, Yusrī Ḥammād, official spokesman of the Nūr Party, even went so far as to declare that the interest charged by international financial institutions such as the World Bank and the International Monetary Fund – both of whom were in the process of negotiating loans with Egypt – did not constitute *ribā* but should instead be viewed as "administrative fees."[46]

43 *Al-Birnāmij al-Intikhābī limurashaḥī dā'ira Miṣr al-Jadīda, al-Nuzha, al-Shurūq, Badr, Fardī* (Electoral Program of the Candidates in the District of Miṣr al-Jadīda, al-Nuzha, al-Shurūq, Badr, Fardī, Individual Seat), Ḥizb al-Ḥurriya wa al-ʿAdāla (Freedom and Justice Party), 2011.

44 *Birnāmij Ḥizb al-Nūr al-Salafī* (Program of the Salafi Nūr Party), n.d., Cairo 2011.

45 The analysis was conducted using *TextSTAT*, which allows the user to generate word frequencies and concordances for any text document. Available at: http://neon.niederlandistik.fu-berlin.de/en/textstat/.

46 Islām Ẓarīf, "*Ḥammād: Fawā'id al-bank al-dawlī laysat ribā inama maṣārīf idāriyya* (Hammad: World Bank Interest Is Not *Ribā* but Rather Administrative Fees)," *al-Miṣriyūn* (Cairo), August 25, 2012; available at: http://www.almesryoon.com/permalink/22432.html.

The reason that Islamist parties focused on the economy rather than Islamic law is simple: for the vast majority of Egyptians – including non-Islamist parties – the position of *sharīʿa* as the foundation of all law was a settled issue. Article 2 of the constitution, which since 1981 had declared that "Islam is the religion of the state and the principles of the *sharīʿa* are the main source of legislation," had garnered wide acceptance. Ḥamdīn Ṣabāḥī, a Nasserist politician and leader of the Dignity (Karāma) Party, in September 2011 declared that "I am with the Islamic *sharīʿa* and article 2 of the constitution" and that Egyptian law should not violate "that which is clear cut in the *Qurʾān* and *sunna*."[47] In March 2011, prior to the constitutional referendum, a writer in the newspaper of the Wafd Party declared that the second article of the constitution was "the soul of the constitution and one of its most important articles" and affirmed that "it is not right under any circustances for Islamic Egypt to be governed by laws that conflict with God's law."[48] In fact, the opening section of the Wafd's platform, which outlines the party's "fixed principles [*thawābit*]" begins with the declaration that "Islam is the religion of the state and the principles of the *sharīʿa* are the principal source of legislation, and for the followers of other revealed religions is the right to be governed by their own religious law in personal and religious matters."[49] This language is almost identical to the language employed by the Salafī Nūr Party in its program, which, in affirming *sharīʿa*, also declares the right of Christians to be governed by their own religious law in personal status and religious matters. We see the same language yet again in the program of the Free Egyptians Party: "The party believes that we must maintain the second article of the constitution, adding the right of members of other religions to be governed in their personal matters by their own religious law."[50] Though the NPUR's platform does not discuss the issue of *sharīʿa*, the party put forward a draft constitution in July 2012 that declared, "Islam is the religion of the state, Arabic is its official language, the principles of Islamic *sharīʿa* are its principal source of legislation, and non-Muslims are to be governed in their personal matters by their own religious laws."[51] As columnist and editor ʿImād al-Dīn Ḥusayn has written, even "the very liberal Free Egyptians [and] the very leftist NPUR" had declared their acceptance

47 Isrāʾ Badawī, "*Ḥamdīn Ṣabāḥī: nurīd dawla yaqūl fīhā al-Miṣriyīn raghbatihim, wa ana maʿ al-sharīʿa al-Islāmiyya wa al-māda al-thāniya min al-dustūr* (Ḥamdīn Ṣabāḥī: We Want a State in Which Egyptians Can Declare Their Desires, and I Am with Islamic Law and Article 2 of the Constitution)," *Kilmitī* (Cairo), September 22, 2011.

48 Aḥmad Abū Zayd, "*Al-māda al-thāniya rūḥ al-dustūr* (Article 2 Is the Soul of the Constitution)," *al-Wafd* (Cairo), March 16, 2011; available at: http://www.alwafd.org/index.php?option=com_content&view=article&id=24183.

49 *al-Birnāmij al-Intikhābī li-Ḥizb al-Wafd* (Electoral Program of the Wafd Party), November 9, 2011.

50 *Birnāmij Ḥizb al-Miṣriyīn al-Aḥrār* (Program of the Free Egyptians Party), n.d; available at: http://www.almasreyeenalahrrar.org/PartyProgram.aspx.

51 Maḥmūd Jāwīsh, "*Al-Tajammuʿ yaṭraḥ mashrūʿ dustūr yuʾasis lidawla madaniya dimuqrāṭiyya* (NPUR Proposes Constitution to Establish Civilian Democratic State)," *al-Miṣrī al-Yawm*, July 16, 2012.

Table 5.1 *Determinants of Vote for Parties, 2011–2012 Elections, List Proportional Representation Districts*

	FJP	Nur	Wafd	Egyptian Bloc	RC
Crowding rate	−10.79	−17.56	−12.02*	31.32***	−22.52**
	(10.18)	(23.40)	(6.464)	(10.74)	(8.560)
Percent agriculture	0.0280	0.345*	0.0224	−0.319**	−0.0377
	(0.131)	(0.188)	(0.0828)	(0.148)	(0.0806)
Logged population	1.220	−3.959	−0.768	1.479	−0.683
	(1.560)	(6.025)	(0.934)	(1.287)	(1.017)
Constant	30.09	99.12	33.34*	−43.71*	39.09**
	(26.33)	(101.6)	(17.55)	(22.65)	(14.97)
Observations	46	44	45	41	22
R^2	0.060	0.093	0.064	0.249	0.418

Standard errors in parentheses.
$^{***}p < 0.01$; $^{**}p < 0.05$; $^{*}p < 0.1$.

of Article 2 of the constitution and the position of *sharīʿa* as the principal source of legislation.[52]

There is thus reason to doubt that the cleavage between two imagined communities, a secular Egypt and an Islamic one, drove political outcomes in the months after Mubarak's ouster. A preliminary analysis of the aggregate results of the 2011 parliamentary elections is even more suggestive. Table 5.1 presents the results of a regression analysis of the demographic bases of voting in Egypt's forty-six list proportional representation districts, for the Brotherhood's Freedom and Justice Party (FJP), the Salafist Nūr Party, the conservative Wafd Party, the Egyptian Bloc (which contained the NPUR), and the left-leaning Revolution Continues coalition.[53] The main variables in this analysis are the crowding rate (i.e. the number of inhabitants per household room) and the share of the workforce in agriculture (a proxy for lack of urbanization). As we can see from the statistically insignificant regression coefficients on these variables for both the FJP and the Nūr Party, both of those Islamist groups appeared to capture districts from across the socioeconomic spectrum. Recall that in Chapter 1, the so-called secularization thesis posited that religion was more likely to be politically salient among the poor and rural. The fact that Islamists in Egypt's founding election appeared to appeal to more than just those traditionally-minded constituencies suggests that

52 ʿImād al-Dīn Ḥusayn, "*Man yaqif ḍid al-sharīʿa* (Who Stands against the *Sharīʿa*?), *al-Shurūq* (Cairo), February 16, 2013.

53 In order to conduct this analysis, I first collected census data on second-level administrative units (qism and markaz) from the Central Agency for Public Mobilization and Statistics. This data was then aggregated into 46 party list districts according to the provisions of law 109/2011. The provisions of this law as they relate to the assignment of second-level administrative units to electoral districts can be viewed at: http://www.almasryalyoum.com/node/491975

voters endorsed them for reasons other than their purported fidelity to the faith. In the following section I delve into the individual-level determinants of voting for Islamist parties in those elections, showing that for Muslim Brotherhood voters at least, economic concerns trumped moral ones.

5.3 Economics, Faith, and Voting for Islamists

The suggestive nature of the evidence presented earlier is reinforced by analysis of the vote preferences of respondents in a nationally representative survey conducted during the 2011 parliamentary elections (we have already seen those voters' economic preferences in Figures 5.1 and 5.2).[54] If voters cast ballots for Islamists out of a concern for religion, we should observe that the voters' perceived "distance" from Islamists on religious issues (such as the status of women or the need to preserve public morality) should be much more important determinants of vote choice than the voters' perceived distance from Islamists on state provision of welfare and redistribution. In order to test this, I employ the method developed by Gelman and Cai (2008). My data are voters' placements of themselves and Islamist political parties on economic and social issues.

As described earlier, voters were asked two questions about the economy and two questions about social/moral policy. In each question, they were presented two contrasting policy options – each at the end of a ten-point scale – and asked to indicate where they stood along the scale and where they placed key parties and groups, including the Brotherhood's FJP, the Wafd, the leftist NPUR, the Free Egyptians Party, the Revolutionary Youth Coalition, and the Reform and Development Party. The economic policy questions were described in Section 5.1, and voters' reponses were displayed in Figures 5.1 and 5.2. The two social/moral questions covered two key pillars of the Islamist program – the role of women in public life and the regulation of personal freedom in the service of maintaining moral observance. To be more specific: for the first question, respondents were presented with two polar opposites "Women are unsuited to assume public positions," which was scored 1, and "Women must be allowed to assume public positions," which was scored 10. For the second social/moral question, the two poles were "Government should limit personal freedoms in order to protect public morality" (scored 1) and "Government should not interfere with personal freedoms as long as they are not hurting anybody" (scored 10).[55]

For this analysis, I am interested in determining the relative importance of economic versus social/moral policy positions in respondents' decisions whether or not to vote Islamist. As a first step, I collapse the two economic policy questions into a single economic dimension by summing each respondent's self-placements to the two questions, yielding the respondent's self-placement on a two to twenty scale. I do the same for the two social policy questions. I then repeat this for

54 Survey conducted in cooperation with Ellen Lust of Yale University and Hamid Latif of the Egyptian Research and Training Center.

55 Survey questionnaire is available at http://www.tarekmasoud.com/data/.

each respondent's placement of the two Islamist parties. We thus emerge with six data points for each respondent: their self-placement on the two-to-twenty point economic scale, self-placement on the two-to-twenty point social/moral scale, placement of the FJP on the two-to-twenty economic scale, placement of the FJP on the two-to-twenty social/moral scale, placement of the Nūr Party on the two-to-twenty economic scale, and placement of the Nūr Party on the two-to-twenty social scale. The party placements are displayed in Figure 5.7, and self-placements are displayed in Figure 5.8. Low scores on the social/moral dimension connote greater conservativism, and low scores on the economic dimension can be taken to connote a more leftist economic orientation.

Having generated social and economic positions as judged for the country's two religious parties as well as voters' self-assessments, I then define, for each survey respondent *i*, the distance between himself or herself and each party *p* on the two dimensions:

$$EconDistance_i^p = |EconPlacement_i^p - EconPlacement_i^{self}|$$
$$SocialDistance_i^p = |SocialPlacement_i^p - SocialPlacement_i^{self}|$$

I then estimate two logistic regressions predicting a voter's party preference given his or her ideological distance from the parties on each dimension.

$$Logit(PartySupport_i^p = 1) = \beta_0 + \beta_1 EconDistance_i^p + \beta_2 SocialDistance_i^p + \beta' X + \varepsilon_i$$

Where $PartySupport_i^p$ is the likelihood that voter i supports party *p*.[56] $EconDistance_i^p$ is the voter's self-judged proximity to party *p* on economic issues, and $SocialDistance_i^p$ is the voter's self-judged proximity to party *p* on social issues. X is a vector of covariates including the respondent's education level, age, gender, religion, and whether he or she lives in an urban or rural area. The dichotomous dependent variables are, respectively, support for the Muslim Brotherhood (or its Freedom and Justice Party) and support for the Salafists (or the Nūr Party). For each party, I run three regressions – the first is a regression of party support against perceived distance from the party on economic issues, the second is a regression of party support against perceived distance from the party on social/moral issues, and the third is a regression of party support on both distance variables. Each specification includes the entire vector of demographic covariates. The results are presented in Table 5.2.

Negative coefficients on the measures of social or economic distance mean that greater perceived proximity between voter and party on those dimensions increases the likelihood of voting for the party. As we can see in the first two

[56] Respondents were asked which party or group they trusted most to move Egypt forward. Those who named the Muslim Brotherhood or the Freedom and Justice Party are coded as Brotherhood supporters; those who named the Salafi Call Society or its political arm, the Nūr Party, were coded as Salafi supporters.

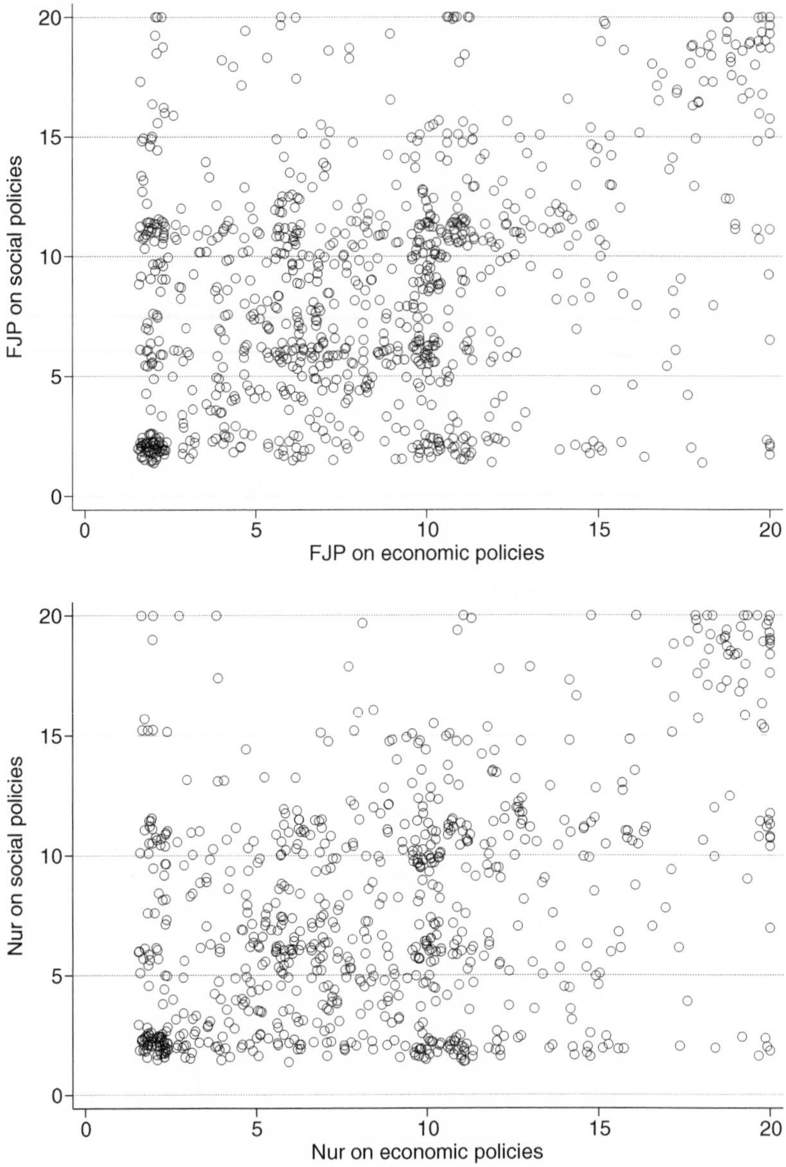

Figure 5.7 Economic and social positions of Freedom and Justice and Nūr parties, as judged by respondents in December 2011 (points jittered to avoid overplotting).

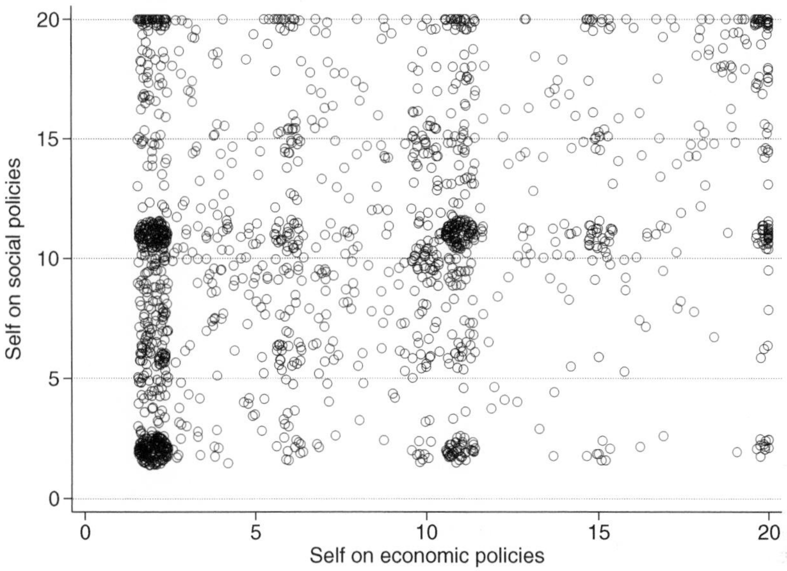

Figure 5.8 Voter self-placements on economic and social policies, December 2011 (points jittered to avoid overplotting).

columns of Table 5.2, when *EconDistance* and *SocialDistance* are each included separately as determinants of support for the Muslim Brotherhood, the coefficient on each is negative and significant, although *EconDistance* is significant at the 99 percent level and is larger than the coefficient on *SocialDistance*, which is significant at the 95 percent level. Including both these terms in the regression (column 3), *EconDistance* remains significant at the 99 percent level, whereas the coefficient on *SocialDistance* loses significance. What this suggests is that moral/social concerns were less important determinants of voting for the Muslim Brotherhood than economic ones.

The case of the Salafi Nūr Party is more complex. The variables *EconDistance* and *SocialDistance* are negative and significant at the 99 percent level in all three specifications, and the size of the coefficient on *SocialDistance* is larger than the size of the coefficient on *EconDistance.* What this suggests is that religious concerns mattered more than economic ones in determining support for the Salafis. Though the negative and significant relationship between *EconDistance* and support for the Salafis suggests that assessments of the Salafists' economic positions were not inconsequential (otherwise, we would have seen an insignificant coefficient on this variable), we cannot rule out the possibility that a desire to avoid cognitive dissonance may have simply caused religion-minded voters to assign high congruence to the Salafis on the economic dimension.[57]

[57] Readers will notice that the number of observations in each of these six specifications fluctuates this is due to missingn responses to the economic and social questions. Given the inferential

Table 5.2 *Logit Regressions of Islamist Support against Voter's Estimation of Social and Economic Policy Congruence between Voter and Party*

	MB/FJP			Salafi/Nur		
EconDistance	−0.0794***		−0.0720***	−0.0808***		−0.0659***
	(0.0188)		(0.0198)	(0.0232)		(0.0255)
SocialDistance		−0.0369**	−0.0237		−0.102***	−0.0962***
		(0.0154)	(0.0177)		(0.0240)	(0.0270)
Education	−0.0506	−0.0253	−0.0456	0.0693	0.0871	0.0863
	(0.0451)	(0.0428)	(0.0470)	(0.0563)	(0.0545)	(0.0580)
Urban	−0.0398	0.0124	−0.00903	−0.174	−0.112	−0.0444
	(0.139)	(0.130)	(0.146)	(0.182)	(0.177)	(0.195)
Female	0.0889	0.0162	0.0740	−0.372**	−0.314*	−0.320*
	(0.134)	(0.126)	(0.140)	(0.181)	(0.172)	(0.191)
Age	−0.00483	−0.00345	−0.00410	−0.0153**	−0.0178***	−0.0173***
	(0.00474)	(0.00447)	(0.00494)	(0.00637)	(0.00607)	(0.00670)
Non-Muslim	−0.968***	−1.128***	−1.025***	−1.752**	−1.735**	−1.533**
	(0.311)	(0.309)	(0.342)	(0.717)	(0.708)	(0.694)
Constant	0.551**	0.204	0.561*	−0.401	−0.406	−0.136
	(0.278)	(0.262)	(0.291)	(0.343)	(0.327)	(0.359)
Observations	978	1,103	910	863	1,021	801
pseudo-R^2	0.0235	0.0164	0.0241	0.0414	0.0578	0.0649

Standard errors in parentheses.
$^{***}p < 0.01$; $^{**}p < 0.05$; $^{*}p < 0.1$.

What these data reveal is that for the largest Islamist party in Egypt, economic concerns appear to have trumped social ones in determining whether voters would cast their ballots for it. Thus, at least in Egypt's so-called "founding election," it appears that the longstanding belief that Islamists such as the Muslim Brotherhood earn votes by causing voters to sublimate their economic interest on the altar of fealty to God is largely a myth.

5.4 Are Islamists Leftists?

If economic concerns trumped social/moral ones in determining votes for the Muslim Brotherhood and were as important as social ones in determining votes for the Salafists, what kinds of economic policies do voters think those parties represent? Figure 5.9 provides the mean self-placement of survey respondents and the mean perception of where some of the principal parties stand on each of the two economic policy issues discussed earlier (i.e., welfare provision and redistribution). I have included the two Islamist parties – the Brotherhood's Freedom and Justice Party (FJP) and the Salafi Nūr Party – the secular Free Egyptians Party (*Ḥizb al-Miṣriyīn al-Aḥrār*, here abbreviated as FEP), the leftist NPUR, and the Wafd Party. I have also magnified the scale to more easily discern the differences between average party scores.

As is evident in both parts of the figure, Egyptians, on average, placed themselves to the "left" of all political parties, Islamist or otherwise. But, among the political parties, they identified the FJP and the Nūr Party as being the most left-leaning. In other words, Egyptians appear to think that the Islamists favor redistribution over growth, and they think that Islamists believe that the government is responsible for the welfare of individuals. More important, respondents appeared to think that Islamists are *more redistributive* and *more welfare-statist* than parties such as the NPUR, a party that describes itself as "the party of workers and farmers"[58] and whose current program declares that it "puts its thought and its struggle in the service of the millions who suffer under current conditions,

problems involved in analyses of missing data, I constructed a different measure of respondent-party proximity that would allow the use of all 1,675 cases. Instead of coding "don't knows" as missing responses, I recode them as neutral ones, placing them on the mid-point (5.5) of the ten point scale for each of the two questions used to measure economic and social distance from each party. A replication of the analysis in Table 5.2 using these measures, not reported here, further suggests that economic issues were more important determinants of support for the Brotherhood than social ones: though the new measures of both economic and social proximity were found to be significant determinants of Brotherhood support, the magnitude of the coefficient on economic proximity was larger than that of the coefficient on social proximity. It was also significant at the 99% level, while the coefficient on social proximity was significant at the 95% level. Both social and economic proximity were equally significant predictors of support for the Salafists.

58 Party flyer entitled, "*Ḥizb al-Tajammu' al-taqadumi al-Waḥdawī: Man naḥnū?* (The National Progressive Unionist Rally: Who Are We?)," 2011.

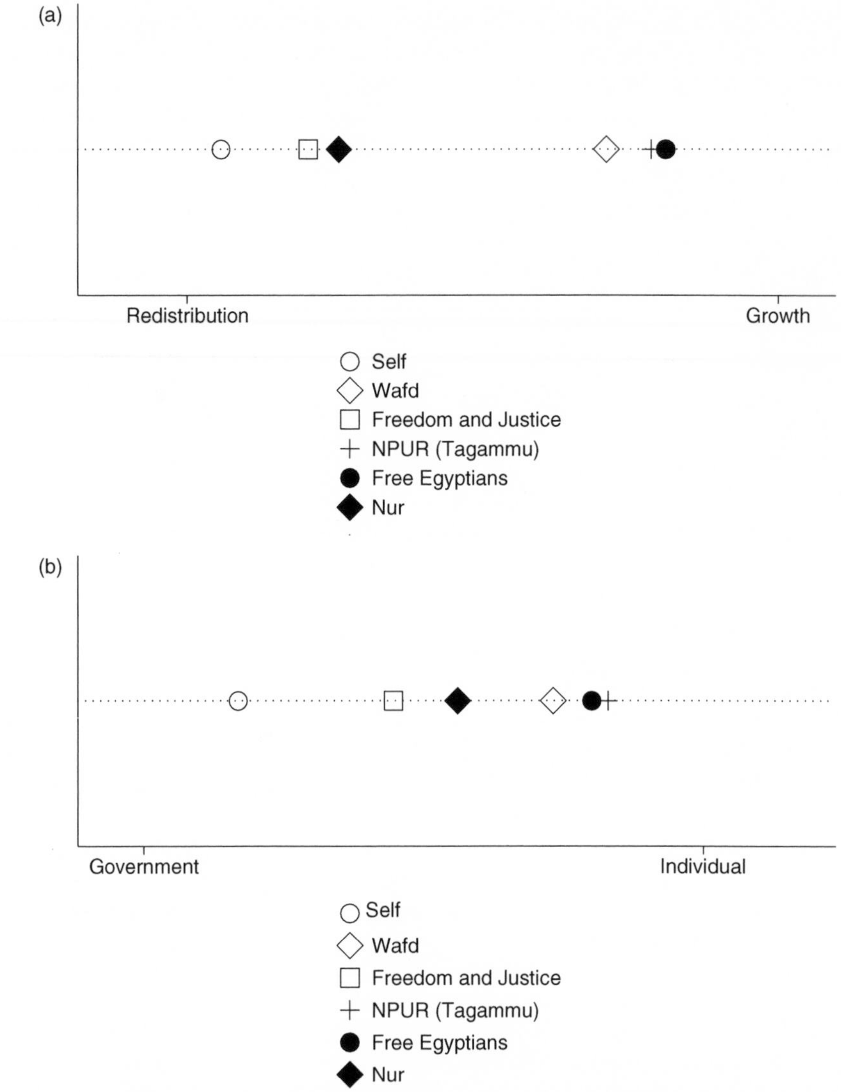

Figure 5.9 Mean placement of parties and mean self-placement on economic issues: (*a*) redistribution versus growth; (*b*) government versus individual responsibility.

especially the working classes."[59] Are they right? Could it be that Islamists win because they are, in fact, better leftists than the left?

59 "Building a Society of Popular Participation (*Binā' Mujtama' al-Mushāraka al-Sha'biyya*)," National Progressive Unionist Rally, October 1, 2012; available at: http://altagamoa.com/index.php/2012-06-30-00-38-17/2012-06-30-00-36-39/472-2012-10-01-15-01-07.

The evidence on this score is mixed. On the one hand, Brotherhood parliamentary candidates frequently deployed populist language – railing against high prices, unemployment, and inequalities of wealth – and the FJP's electoral platform promised to remedy the latter problem by passing "a law specifying a minimum wage and also a maximum wage."[60] However, the Brotherhood has also staked out policy positions that put it at odds with the sentiments of a majority of Egyptian voters. For example, the *New York Times* reports that in a March 2012 meeting with a group of American lawmakers (including Republican Senator Lindsey Graham of South Carolina), the Muslim Brotherhood's Deputy General Guide Khayrat al-Shāṭir "assured them of the group's commitments to free-market capitalism."[61] Thus, after the Brotherhood won a plurality of seats in last year's parliamentary elections, the head of a major Egyptian bank reported that the Brotherhood's rise did not trouble him because the FJP was "capitalist in its thinking."[62]

In fact, if we widen our temporal aperture, we see that the Brotherhood has long championed "capitalism and private property" (Abu Lughod 1995, 54) and has traditionally tended to resist state interventions in the economy. For example, according to Abed-Kotob (1995, 327), in the 1970s, the Brotherhood's leaders supported Sadat's policies of opening Egypt to trade (popularly known as *infitāḥ*) and paring down the massive public-sector buildup during the rule of his predecessor, Gamal Abdel Nasser (1954–1970). According to Lesch (1995, 231), the Brotherhood's electoral programs featured economic demands that were "congruent with the government's own approach, including the call to decrease the size of the public sector and reinforce the private sector as the backbone of the economy." Given these contradictory signals, the most that can be said of the Brotherhood's commitment to the core economic beliefs of the average Egyptian voter is that it is unclear.

The same is true of the Salafi Nūr Party. As with their Muslim Brotherhood counterparts, Salafi candidates beat the populist drum on the campaign trail, speaking of "just distribution of wealth" and "expanding the umbrella of social insurance."[63] However, the party's economic program appears remarkably market-oriented. In July 2011, three months before the parliamentary elections

60 Available at: http://www.hurryh.com/Party_Program.aspx.

61 David D. Kirkpatrick, "The New Islamists: Keeper of Islamic Flame Rises as Egypt's New Decisive Voice," *New York Times*, March 12, 2012. In the same article, Muhammad Habib, a former Muslim Brotherhood leader (who had once served with al-Shatir as co-deputy general guide), declared that al-Shatir "tightened the screws on anyone" who did not share his business-friendly understanding of Islam.

62 Aḥmad Ya'qūb, "*Al-Sibā'ī: Ṣu'ūd al-Islāmiyīn lan yu'athir 'alā al-bunūk* (Al-Sibā'ī: The Rise of Islamists Will Not Affect the Banks)," *al-Yawm al-Sabi'* (Cairo), January 4, 2012.

63 "*Al-Birnāmij al-intikhābī wa al-sīra al-dhātiyya lil-murashā Sayyid Maghāwrī al-Jiyūshī* (Electoral Program and Biography of the Candidate Sayyid Maghāwrī al-Jiyūshī)," Nur Party flyer, October 2011. al-Jiyushi was a candidate in Giza's third district, covering Imbaba, Duqi, and al-'Aguza.

that would give it the second largest share of seats in the legislature, the party convened a conference that laid out a plan for Egypt's economic renaissance. It called for establishing an "Islamic chamber of commerce" that would "attract owners of capital from among the party's sons"; setting up an Islamic bank; encouraging businessmen to fund small projects and micro loans; helping "to transmit the voices of Islamic businessmen to decision-making circles"; and preparing "economic legislation to ... lift the tariffs and tax burdens that grievously harm the Egyptian economy."[64]

Further evidence that Islamist economic preferences may not be in line with those of most Egyptians can be found in the constitution passed by the Islamist-dominated constituent assembly on November 29, 2012. Although it was the religious provisions of Egypt's 2012 charter that received the most attention, the document also appeared to advance a capital-friendly vision for the economy, including restricting the establishment of independent trade unions and limiting official unions to "one per profession" (Article 53),[65] enabling legal restrictions on the right to strike (Article 63), and – most notably – withdrawing the state's long-standing commitment to provide free healthcare for all, instead offering the more modest promise to provide *gratis* care only "to those who are unable to pay" (Article 62).[66]

But even if one wishes to claim that Islamists deserve to be placed on the left of the economic spectrum, there is simply no credible account that could put a party such as the NPUR on the right. The party has long identified itself with the interests of Egypt's poor and long championed robust state interventions in the economy. In contrast to those who contend that Egyptian opposition parties are devoid of ideological platforms (Zaki 1995; Blaydes 2006), the NPUR is explicitly and unabashedly socialist in its orientation. For example, the party's 2005 platform demanded that the state "take on a direct and active role in the arena of productive investments and not simply create an environment that encourages the private sector." It calls for "preserving what remains of the public sector ..., [e]nding the policy of trade liberalization ..., revising tariffs to limit unnecessary imports and to protect domestic industry from unfair competition ..., and [e]nding the policy of unfettered reliance on the market." Instead, it calls for

64 Hanā' Abū al-'Iz, "*Ḥizb al-Nūr al-Salafī Ya'qid Mu'tamaruhu al-Iqtiṣādī al-Awwal* (The Salafi Nūr Party Holds its First Economic Conference)," *al-Yawm al-Sābi'* (Cairo), July 24, 2011; available at: http://www1.youm7.com/News.asp?NewsID=460599&SecID=296&IssueID=0; and Nādir Bakkār, "*Waṣiyāt Mu'tamar Ḥizb al-Nūr al-Iqtiṣādī al-Awwal* (Advice of the Nūr Party's First Economic Conference)," July 28, 2011; available at: http://thenokhba.blogspot.com/2011/07/1.html.

65 It can be argued that the establishment of industrywide unions will actually increase wages (Calmfors and Driffill 1988), although empirical work by Golden (1993) suggests that industry-level unions of the kind envisioned by the Egyptian constitution can work to moderate wage demands if they are small in number and have monopolies over their members, which the Egyptian constitution of 2012 attempted to guarantee.

66 The text of the 2012 Egyptian Constitution, passed on December 23 with 64 percent of the vote (33 percent voter turnout), is available in Arabic at: http://dostour.eg/ and in English at: http://www.acus.org/egyptsource/unofficial-english-translation-egypts-draft-constitution.

"overarching national planning ... of the direction of the economy," with an emphasis on industrial development. Finally, the program urged the state to "take on a fundamental role in revising the distribution of income to the advantage of the poor and those of limited income through the policies of taxes and subsidies and wages."[67] In a section entitled, "How We Will Find the Financial Resources Necessary to execute This Program," the party outlined how it expected to pay for all of this (the material that follows is quoted verbatim from the party's platform):

1. Reforming the income tax structure set by the recent tax law, in order to increase the number of tax brackets and their prices in such a way as to achieve a reasonable level of progressiveness and which will lead to more revenue and the ability to redistribute wealth to the advantage of the poor and those of small incomes.
2. Increasing the revenue that the state earns from fees, by forcing the owners of apartments and buildings and land and automobiles and other assets to register their property within a specific time frame and to pay the fees owed, with a discount in registration fees and simplification of the process in order to encourage registration.
3. Imposition of a tax on the profits of capital based on the trading of shares, speculation in the Bourse, the sale of real estate, and other non-productive activities.
4. Increasing taxes on luxury goods and on imports of goods that compete with domestic production, and this is for the protection of national industry.
5. Increasing the recently reduced taxes on the revenue of hotels and tourist resorts and increasing the registration fees of luxury automobiles and on licenses for the agents of foreign companies.
6. Collecting all revenues earned by public bodies and agencies into the general budget of the state and making spending priorities clear, allowing for the distribution of spending in favor of productive projects and improving wages and raising the standard of public services.[68]

Contrast this with the Muslim Brotherhood's generally neoliberal, antistatist stance on the economy, articulated in a pamphlet circulated shortly after the 2005 elections:

> Economic matters are by their nature complex and intertwined and require great detail, but in general terms we believe that the economy develops and flourishes in the shadow of freedom and security and stability, and therefore we must achieve political reform in order to achieve economic reform. We also believe in the right

[67] *Al-Birnāmij al-intikhābī al-ʿām: Birnāmij lī al-taghyīr al-siyāsī wa al-iqtisādī wa al-ijtimāʿī* (The General Electoral Program: A Program for Political, Economic, and Social Change), Ḥizb al-Tajammuʿ al-Waṭanī al-Taqaddumī al-Waḥdawī (Party of the National Progressive Unionist Rally), November–December 2005, 5–7.

[68] Ibid. 7–8.

> to private property and its inviolability, provided it is from Islamically permissible sources and activities that violate neither God nor the society and therefore we believe in the urgency of creating a space that encourages investment in the broadest scope and therefore achieve the free economy (without monopolies) on one hand, and at the same time we see that there are some grand projects that individuals are unable to undertake because they are not profitable even though they are vital for the nation such as military and heavy production so the state should support and own them.[69]

We emerge from all of this with two conclusions. First, the Muslim Brotherhood and its religious counterparts are not be the foremost champions of redistribution or of the role of the state in the economy – at least in comparison with the NPUR. Second, despite this fact, voters clearly *perceive* them to be. The fact that Islamists have long resisted the kinds of state interventions in the economy that the NPUR has repeatedly called for and for which voters demonstrate an enormous thirst does not register (Abu Lughod 1995, Abed Kotob 1995, Lesch 1995). Even if one wishes to argue that Islamists have moved leftward in recent years, what is remarkable is less that voters *may* be getting Islamist economic positions wrong and more that they are *certainly* getting leftist ones wrong.

The ignorance of voters regarding the substantive policy positions of leftist parties is further illustrated in Figure 5.10, which indicates the percentage of those surveyed who responded, "Don't know," when asked to place themselves or the various political parties on the questions of redistribution and government responsibility for welfare. Approximately 60 percent of respondents declared ignorance of the NPUR's position on the two economic issues, whereas only around 40 percent of respondents declared ignorance of the stances of the Nūr Party (which had only been established six months before), and only 36 percent said that they did not know where the Brotherhood's FJP stood. (For comparison's sake, I have included the percentage of individuals who responded, "Don't know," when asked to indicate their own policy preferences on the two questions.) Thus it seems clear that few voters know where leftist parties stand, and when they think that they do know where these parties stand, they are invariably wrong.

Would more Egyptians vote for leftist parties (and fewer for Islamists) if they actually knew what those parties stood for and how proximate those parties are to voters' own ideal points? This is a difficult question to answer definitively, but it seems self-evident that voter ignorance about leftist parties' economic positions cannot help the left's cause. For example, Pepinsky, Liddle, and Mujani (2012) demonstrated that voter uncertainty about Indonesian parties' economic platforms redounded to the benefit of Islamists and that this advantage disappeared once voters knew more about parties' economic positions. Given the congruence

69 Maḥmūd Ghuzlān, "*Na'm, al-Islām huwa al-ḥal* (Yes, Islam Is the Solution)," Muslim Brotherhood pamphlet, December 2005.

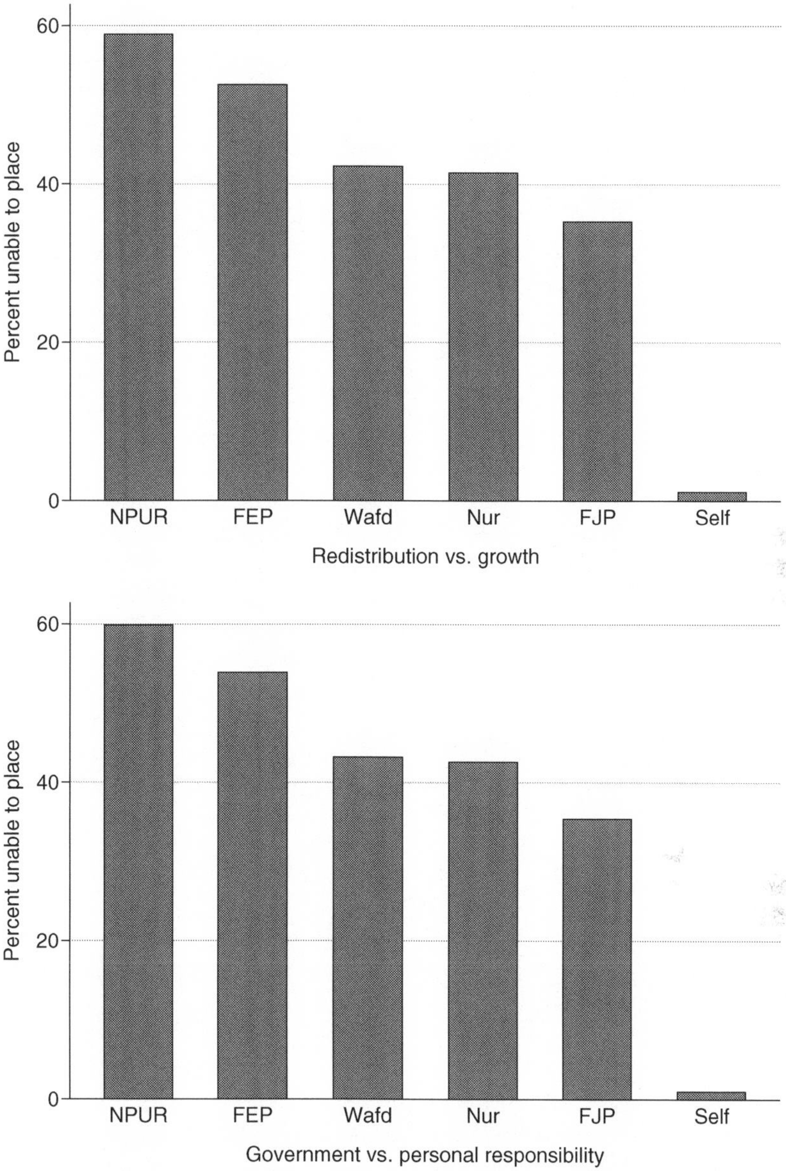

Figure 5.10 Egyptians feel that they know more about Islamist parties' economic positions than about those of their rivals, especially leftist ones.

between voters' economic attitudes and those of leftist parties, it is reasonable to assume that leftist fortunes could not help but be buoyed by increased public recognition of this fact. The question for us, then, is why the uncertainty regarding the preferred economic policies of leftist parties – and the misplaced certainty regarding the preferred economic policies of Islamists – exists in the first place? In an election dominated by concerns over the economy, and in which voters yearned for precisely the kinds of policies that left parties have been promoting for years, why were those parties unable to emerge victorious? We take up that question in the next chapter.

6

Islam's Organizational Advantage? Or, Why Voters Think Islamists Are Leftists

In Chapter 5, we examined evidence that suggested that the victory of political Islam in Egypt's founding elections was driven less by a desire to implement the *sharīʿa*, or to protect the second article of the Egyptian constitution from the grasping hands of infidel politicians, than by beliefs about Islamists' economic policies. This was particularly true of the Muslim Brotherhood, but economic policy was also a significant determinant of support for the Brotherhood's Salafi counterparts. Furthermore, when we investigate Egyptians' perceptions of the economic policy stances of these parties, we see that they believe those parties to be *more* committed to redistribution and the expansion of the welfare state than leftist parties such as the National Progressive Unionist Rally (NPUR), which has made such policies the centerpiece of its program for the better part of half a century. In fact, we saw that most voters confessed ignorance of what the NPUR stood for, and those who thought they knew, more often than not believed the party to be opposed to redistribution and to the state's role in caring for citizens. Given the stunning failure of the left to make its preferences known, it is worth asking what they are doing wrong. If leftists are losing despite the fact that most voters seem to want what they want, are they simply worse than Islamists at communicating their policy preferences to voters? Why can't a pro-poor party win elections in a poor country?

At this point, readers may protest, given the dynamics explored in Chapter 2, that it is too much to expect leftist parties to bounce back from decades of systematic disadvantage. A thirty-year legacy of losing elections, with all the reputational costs that entails, cannot be transcended easily, especially when such a legacy is pitted against an equally long Islamist record of leaping over the barriers of the authoritarian state and into the halls of parliament. If voter choices are based not only on a party's policy positions but also on voter estimates of competence and effectiveness – admittedly a proposition for which we have not gathered systematic evidence – then the legacy of the Mubarak era is one that will take the left, and non-Islamist parties more generally, a long time to overcome.

For many, though the problem of the left and its secular counterparts lies not in the abuses of the Mubarak era but in the parties themselves. For while the scholarly and popular literature is replete with references to the Muslim Brotherhood as the "most organized"[1] and "most disciplined"[2] Egyptian political group, leftist and secular parties are routinely derided as "ineffectual," "feckless," "divided," "disorganized," "lazy," and – in one particularly memorable formulation – "cartoon parties."[3] In this telling, Islamists trounce the left at the ballot box because they do what it takes to win elections, where as non-Islamists do nothing. This is not a new complaint. During the Mubarak era, Hamzawy and Ottaway complained that secular parties "neglected grassroots mobilization and constituency building for a long time," failed to develop "emotionally appealing, simple political slogans," and "have not developed the funding methods to sustain the staff required to carry out systematic organizing work."[4]

The two years since Mubarak's ouster seemed to put all the Brotherhood's organizational powers and the secular left's organizational dysfunctions on full display. During the country's "founding elections," the Muslim Brotherhood and its religious allies appeared determined to lose no time making up for decades of political repression. Though, as we saw in Chapter 3, Mubarak's security services had once worked assiduously to prevent the Brotherhood from engaging in clientelistic electioneering, the end of that regime suddenly made such a strategy possible. Thus, while we found that only 8.7 percent of recipients of Islamic healthcare services surveyed in December 2011 had voted for the Muslim Brotherhood in the 2010 parliamentary election (see Section 3.2), nearly 45 percent of them indicated an intention to vote for the Brotherhood in the first postrevolutionary election. During the March 2011 constitutional referendum, the Brotherhood was reported to have distributed bottles of cooking oil and bags of sugar in an attempt to sway citizens to vote in favor of the proposed package of constitutional

1 See, for example, Anthony Shadid, "Egypt's Path after Uprising Does Not Have to Follow Iran's," *New York Times*, February 12, 2011; Condoleezza Rice, "The Future of a Democratic Egypt," *Washington Post*, February 16, 2011; Kristen Chick, "Egypt Vote Is On, Despite Deadly Protests. How Will the Muslim Brotherhood Do?" *Christian Science Monitor*, November 27, 2011; among many others.

2 See, for example, "Protest in Egypt: Another Arab Regime under Threat," *The Economist*, January 27, 2011; "Egypt's Revolution: Mubarak now Has Few Good Options for Retaining Power," *Wall Street Journal*, January 29, 2011; Jeffrey T. Kuhner, "Obama's Anti-Israel Agenda," *Washington Times*, February 17, 2011; and Hamza Hendawi and Sarah El Deeb, "Raucous Start to Egypt's Newly Elected Parliament," Associated Press, January 24, 2012, among many others.

3 See, for example, Dina Salah Eldin, "As Egypt Prepares to Vote, Only One Side Seems Organized," National Public Radio, December 14, 2012; Marina Ottaway, "The Unfinished Egyptian Transition," *The National Interest*, January 25, 2013; Amir Taheri, "Will Egypt's Democrats Get Serious?" *New York Post*, February 27, 2013; Gert Van Langendonck, "Egypt's Opposition Still Hopeful, Despite Many Defeats," *Christian Science Monitor*, December 31, 2012.

4 Amr Hamzawy and Marina Ottaway, "Fighting on Two Fronts: Secular Parties in the Arab World," *Carnegie Papers*, Carnegie Endowment for International Peace, No. 85, May 2007, p. 21; available at: http://carnegieendowment.org/files/cp85_secular_final.pdf.

amendments.[5] During the parliamentary election, the Brotherhood's "charitable machine" reportedly went into overdrive, opening shops to sell "discounted meat and vegetables" to cash-strapped families.[6] On the second anniversary of the January 25 revolution, amid widespread demonstrations against President Morsi, the Brotherhood announced that it would organize a nationwide volunteer campaign to offer health services and school improvements.[7] In one district, al-Haram in the governorate of al-Gīza, the Brotherhood's Freedom and Justice Party even offered free cram courses for secondary-school students, in keeping with a longstanding pattern of providing services to middle-class voters.[8]

What did non-Islamists do in the face of the Brotherhood's avid efforts at grassroots mobilization, service provision, and outreach? The conventional wisdom is that they did very little. As one liberal Egyptian party member lamented, "No party will succeed if they sit around and talk politics ... which is what all the parties are doing except for the Muslim parties. What we should do is take the way that they are reaching the people and use it. We need to do what they're doing."[9] In a July 2012 speech to the Carnegie Endowment for International Peace, a visibly exasperated Secretary of State Hilary Clinton echoed the notion that the political marginalization of the non-Islamist field was a function of their own organizational inadequacies:

> I am urging those who are concerned, not only Christians, but also moderates, liberals, secularists, to organize themselves. This is something that I started talking to the Tahrir Square veterans about shortly after the fall of Mubarak. It has been my experience that when democratic space opens up, when freedom opens up, with authoritarian regimes falling, those who are unorganized will not be successful. How's that for a profound statement? ... In a democracy you have to get out there and work to elect people who represent your views, otherwise you are going to be sidelined.[10]

5 Rāmī Nawwār, "*Taqrīr huqūqī yarṣud tawzī' al-Ikhwān al-zayt wa al-sukkar 'alā al-nākhibīn* (Legal Report Details the Brotherhood's Distribution of Oil and Sugar Among Voters)," *al-Miṣrī al-Yawm* (Cairo), March 19, 2011; available at: http://www.youm7.com/News.asp?NewsID=372852.

6 Leila Fadel, "Muslim Brotherhood Sells Cheap Food Ahead of Holiday and Egypt Parliament Vote," *Washington Post*, November 5, 2011; available at: http://articles.washingtonpost.com/2011-11-05/world/35283999_1_muslim-brotherhood-eid-al-adha-new-party.

7 Muḥammad Ismā'īl, "*Mu'tamar saḥafī lil-ikhwān al-muslimīn litadshīn miliyuniya al-khadamāt al-thulathā'* (Press Conference to Inaugurate a Million-Man Service Campaign on Tuesday)," *al-Yawm al-Sābi'* (Cairo), January 20, 2013; available at: http://www.youm7.com/News.asp?NewsID=915312.

8 "*Bi al-ṣuwar: al-Ikhwān tukathaf taḥarukātihā lilḥashd fī intikhābāt al-barlamān* (In Pictures: The Brotherhood Intensifies Its Movements to Mobilize in the Parliamentary Elections)," *al-Maṣrāwī*, January 11, 2013; available at: http://www.masrawy.com/news/egypt/politics/2013/january/11/5487402.aspx

9 Evan Hill, "Do Egypt's Liberals Stand a Chance?" *Foreign Policy*, November 16, 2011.

10 Speech by Secretary of State Hilary Rodham Clinton, "International Religious Freedom," Carnegie Endowment for International Peace, July 30, 2012; available at: http://www.c-spanvideo.org/program/307322-1.

In this chapter, I ask why Islamists seem not to need Secretary Clinton to tell them what to do, whereas non-Islamists seem unable to follow her advice. I argue that the answer lies less in the decisions or nondecisions of party leaders than in structural factors that gave the Muslim Brotherhood and other Islamists greater opportunities than their non-Islamist rivals to reach voters during Egypt's first post-Mubarak elections. Egyptian leftists are smart enough to know that grassroots organizing and providing social services to voters works. But, as we saw in Chapter 1, the social infrastructure available for them to do so is dwarfed by that available to Islamists. Voters thus have plenty of opportunities to hear Islamist candidates assure them of their fealty to redistribution and the welfare state and relatively few opportunities to hear what the left has to offer.

The chapter proceeds as follows. First, I explore a related, but analytically distinct, argument from the one presented here – that the Islamist organizational advantage is a function of their superior discipline, better recruitment strategies, and emphasis on obedience. In this telling, the Muslim Brotherhood and its ilk are better at providing services and doing what it takes to win elections because the organization is less a political party than a secret society, with all that the term entails of deep commitment and organizational cohesion. I argue that the literature has feitishized Muslim Brotherhood internal practices while neglecting evidence that militates against assigning such factors causal weight. Instead, I show, using a combination of aggregate and individual-level evidence, that the Islamist electoral advantage, and leftist disadvantage, lies not in party's internal organization but in the social networks of its members. To put it plainly: In the battle to build linkages to voters after the fall of the Mubarak regime, Islamists simply had a richer fund of social ties to draw on than their lefist counterparts.

6.1 The "Organizational Weapon"

As we saw in Chapter 1, one oft-cited explanation for the Brotherhood's superior ability to, in Secretary Clinton's words, "get out there and work" is the movement's internal discipline and cohesion. In a society marked by decayed and inefficient institutions, the Muslim Brotherhood stands out as a well-oiled machine, with disciplined cadres able to act in concert when other parties seem unable to act at all. Indeed, one of the most common slurs against the movement, particularly in vogue after the January 25 revolution, is to twist their moniker from "*al-Ikhwān*" (brothers) to "*al-Khirfān*" (sheep) – a backhanded testament to the unity of the movement and the absolute obedience of its members to their superiors.

The source of these qualities is often located in the process by which the movement recruits its cadres. Frequently likened to a Leninist vanguard party (see, e.g., Rubin 2007; Halliday 2007; see also Nasr 1994), the movement has always conceived of itself as a kind of "outstanding minority," drawing on university students – particularly those in competitive faculties such as medicine and engineering – for much of its membership base and subjecting potential members to a relatively stringent selection process that is thought to exclude all but those who are prepared to commit themselves fully to the organization and its goals.[11] A candidate for membership – informally called an "admirer" or *muḥib* – is, according to the movement's bylaws, to "spend at least one year under examination." After demonstrating his commitment to the "resonsibilities of membership," "knowledge of the purposes and means" of the Brotherhood's mission, his "respect for its procedures," and his commitment to "realize its goals," a *muḥib* is admitted to the probationary status of "regular" Brother (*akh muntaẓam*). Only after three years as a *muntaẓam* is the initiate considered for full admission as an "active" Brother (*akh ʿāmil*), at which time he swears the following oath:

> I swear to Allah the great, my commitment to the rulings of Islam, and to jihad for His sake, and to fulfilling the duties and conditions of membership in the Society of Muslim Brothers, and to obeying without question its leaders to the best of my abilities in matters pleasant and distasteful so long as they are not sinful, and I declare my allegiance with God as my guarantor.[12]

As is evident in the Brotherhood's loyalty oath, unquestioned obedience (*al-samʿ wa al-ṭāʿa*) is a value to which the movement attaches a great deal of importance. Ḥasan al-Bannā spoke of obedience as "total compliance with and immediate execution of commands, whether in hardship and in ease, whether [the task is] appealing or hated."[13] The emphasis on obedience and loyalty, while thought to be a secret of the group's success, has long opened up the Brothers to charges that it is a fundamentally antidemocratic, authoritarian movement. The movement's third general guide, ʿUmar al-Timissānī, felt compelled to respond to such accusations by noting that the Brotherhood's attempts to cultivate member loyalty were not unique to the movement but standard democratic practice: "Members of all political parties in any country of the world raise their right hands and swear loyalty to the party" (Al-Tilmissānī 1985, 101).

In addition to processes of member recruitment and promotion intended to select for and inculcate obedience, scholars have located the roots of the Brotherhood's discipline in how it manages its members. A member's commitment to

[11] This description of the Muslim Brotherhood as a "select" or "excellent" minority is inspired by Greene's (2007) description of Mexico's principal Christian Democratic party, *Partido Acción Nacional* (PAN). According to Greene (2007, 188), "The PAN considered itself a party of 'excellent minorities' where membership was restricted to ideologically compatible activists of high quality." The term *outstanding minority* (sometimes rendered *select minority*) comes from the Spanish philosopher Ortega y Gasset, who believed that human progress was always the function of the exertions of a small elite. See accounts by Maldonado-Denis (1961) and Dobson (2009).

[12] This and all previous quotes in this paragraph are taken from *Al-Niẓām al-ʿĀm li al-Ikhwān al-Muslimīn* (Statute of the Muslim Brotherhood), Section 3, Article 4; available at http://www.Ikhwānonline.com/Article.aspx?ArtID=58497&SecID=211. An earlier version of these bylaws, dating from July 1982, is reprinted in Al-Nafīsī (1989, 401–16). One difference between the 1982 version and the current one is that the period of examination for new members in the earlier version was "at least six months" long, whereas it is now "at least a year."

[13] Quoted in Maḥmūd (1991, 693).

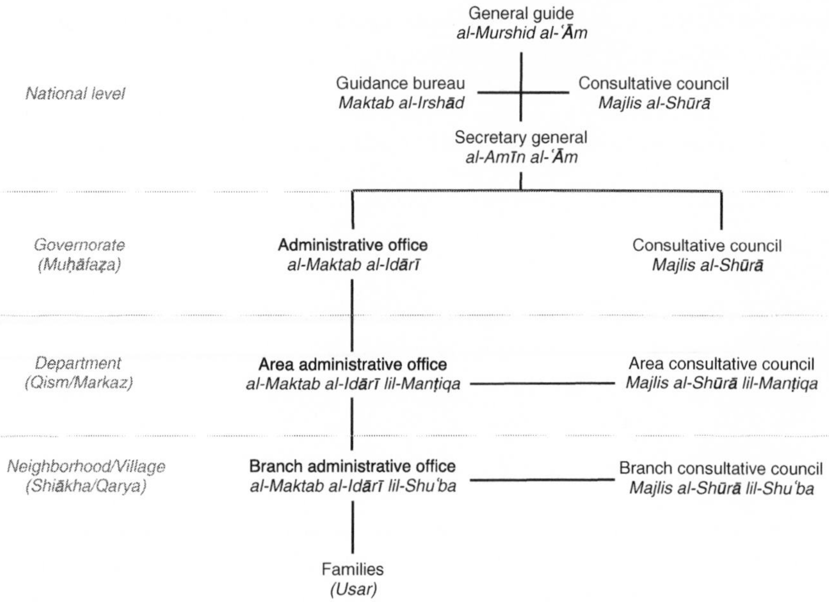

Figure 6.1 The Muslim Brotherhood's organizational hierarchy.

the group and its aims is thought to be forged and deepened within its system of clandestine cells or "families" (*niẓām al-usar*). Each "family" (*usra*) consists of five or six individuals – one of whom (typically the most senior) is designated as the *usra's* leader, or *mas'ūl*. The members of an *usra* often live in the same vicinity, and the *mas'ūl* is in charge of presiding over weekly study circles (in which they will read everything from religious texts to self-help books such as Stephen R. Covey's *Seven Habits of Highly Effective People*), assessing and reporting on the performance of the *usra's* members, and directing its activities – such as distributing baskets of food to the neighborhood's needy in Ramadan or leafletting mosques and local businesses during election times. The Brotherhood's organizational structure is detailed in Figure 6.1. Cells are grouped into branches (shu'ab, singular shu'ba), which are grouped into areas (manāṭiq, singular manṭiqa), each with its own administrators. These are accountable to a governorate-level administrative office, which in turn is accountable to the movement's secretary general and, through him, to its general guide.

The Muslim Brotherhood's founder, Ḥassan al-Bannā, did not call this the "system of *families*" by accident. It was his intention to bind his men emotionally as well as organizationally. In an essay on *niẓām al-usar*, he wrote, "Islam is keen to create families out of its people, to direct them to the high ideals and to strengthen their bonds and raise their brotherhood from the level of talk and abstractions to the level of deeds and actions. So take care, my brother, to be a righteous brick in this structure (Islam)." Al-Bannā (n.d., 323–4) exhorts the members of each cell to do three main things:

> 1. Get to know each other: This is the first pillar of this system. Get to know and love each other in the spirit of God, and feel the true meaning of complete Brotherhood in what is between you, and strive to ensure that nothing clouds the purity of your relationship, and always represent the noble verses and sayings of the Prophet, keep it always in mind and remind each other of God's words, "For all believers are brothers," and His words, "And hold fast by the rope of God and be not divided," and the sayings of the Prophet, peace be upon him, "The believer to the believer is like a building, [each part] reinforcing the other." "The Muslim is the brother of the Muslim, he does not oppress him or give him up [to enemies]." "Muslims in their love and mercy and sympathy for each other are as a single body." ...
>
> 2. Understand each other: This is the system's second pillar. Remain true to the program of truth, and do what God has commanded you to do, and avoid that which He has commanded you to avoid. And hold each other to a precise account on [matters of] obedience and sin. Each one of you should advise his brother whenever he sees in him any fault. And the brother should accept the advice of his brother with happiness, and should thank him for it. Similarly, the advice-giver should be warned not to allow the feelings of his heart to change even a hair's breadth with regard to the brother he has advised, and is to be warned not to deem [his brother] lacking, nor to think himself superior to him. Rather, he should conceal [his brother's behavior] for an entire month, and not tell anyone what he noticed [of his brother's behavior] except the head of the family alone if he is beyond reform. And even after that he should continue to love his brother and value him .... The advisee is warned to refrain from stubbornness or rebellion or changing his heart towards his brother even by a hair's breadth, for the love of God is the highest order, and advice is a pillar of the the faith: "Religion is advice." May God fasten you together, enrich you in His obedience, and keep from you the devil's plots.
>
> 3. Be responsible for each other: This is the third pillar .... Each of you must shoulder the burden of the other, and this is the essence of faith and the kernel of brotherhood. So you should pledge yourselves to ask after and support each other, and to take the initiative to help [each other] by any available means. And see the words of God's messenger, peace be upon him: "For one among you to walk with his brother in need is better than to spend an entire month in this mosque of mine." "He who brings happiness into the home of one of the Muslims will not see from God any reward except heaven." And may God bind your hearts with His spirit, for He is the the most wonderful of masters and the most wonderful of supporters.

Al-Bannā urged his brethren to "take care to attend all meetings, regardless of the excuse" and to "endeavor to pay dues to the family treasury." He encouraged them to bare their secrets to each other and said that the *usras* should use their weekly meetings to discuss personal problems faced by each Brother (although he says "there is no place in the *usra* for argument or challenging or raising of voices"). "In order to increase the ties between the Brothers," al-Bannā even offers a list of activities that the members of each family should engage in, including trips to visit "antiquities and factories," sport outings, rowing, hiking in "the mountains, deserts, or fields," bicycle tours, weekly or biweekly fasts, and praying the dawn prayer together at least once a week. Moreover, al-Bannā says, "Brothers must take care to spend the night together once a week or every two weeks." (al-Bannā n.d., 325).[14]

As Wickham (2003, 16) explains in her learned study of Islamic activism in Mubarak's Egypt, the Brotherhood's "integration of new recruits into the close-knit nuclei of movement networks reinforced their new Islamic commitments and weakened the hold of competing loyalties." [Wickham (2013) would later point out that "encapsulating" Brothers within the movement in this manner also had the effect of blinding them to the opinions of those outside of it, with disastrous effects once they came to power.] Moreover, by embedding each Brother in a small group of peers, the *usra* system helps the movement to monitor and deter free-riding (Olson 1965; Chong 1991). In fact, according to Richard Mitchell, the finest chronicler of the Brotherhood's early history, the chief virtue of *niẓām al-usar* was the way in which it enabled movement leaders to exert control over the rank and file:

> The new system, the structure within which it operated, and the ideas it transmitted to its members were in fact the real basis of the power of the Society of Muslim Brothers; permitting, as it did, authority to express itself through a well-recognized, clearly defined, and tightly knit chain of command, the system became the fundamental instrument through which the leadership expressed its will [Mitchell 1993, 198].

As impressive as such practices are, however, there are several reasons to doubt that they are the source of Islamist success. First, Egyptian communist organizations (Ismael and Saʿīd 1990) also employed systems of clandestine cells and emphasized obedience and secrecy among their members and yet were unable to become anything more than fringe groups in Egyptian political life. Second, the Salafi party, Ḥizb al-Nūr – the second-most popular party in the 2011–2012 parliamentary elections – does not apply the Brotherhood's organizational model. The pietist movement on which it is largely based, the Salafi Call Society (Jamāʿ*at* al-Daʿwa al-Salafiyya), displays neither the Brotherhood's selectivity with respect to new members nor its cellular structure. On the whole, Salafi movements are far less routinized and bureaucratized than the Brotherhood, with the emphasis being on the individual's adoption of and adherence to orthodox practices (*iltizām*) rather than formal membership in an organization (Wiktorowicz 2001; Trager

14 Article 10 of the Brotherhood's bylaws (1982 version) elaborates on the norm of mutual assistance that the movement tries to instill in its members: "It is the responsibility of members to take care of each other, and to promise to look after and provide for each other, and for each to take the initiative to help his brother if he finds a way to do so, as Islam ordered them, and this is the heart of faith and the core of Brotherhood." See Al-Nafīsī (1989, 401–16).

2013). And though Ḥizb al-Nūr has a seemingly Brotherhood-like tiered membership structure and demanding criteria for promotion to higher levels within the party, this appears to be relatively standard practice among all Egyptian political parties.[15] For example, the internal regulations of the secular Free Egyptians Party (FEP) detail three levels of membership – the "friend of the party," "member," and "active member." To be an active member in the FEP, the recruit must undergo a probationary period of six months with at least 100 hours of voluntary service to the party.[16] It is unnecessary to point out that tiered membership, thought to be key to the Muslim Brotherhood's success, worked no similar effect for the FEP.

In any case, recent events have provided cause for caution with respect to our estimations of Islamists' internal discipline and cohesion. The reality is that the Muslim Brotherhood has experienced more than its fair share of fractures. For example, a brief survey of the current Egyptian partisan landscape reveals no fewer than six parties formed by breakaway elements of the Brotherhood (Table 6.1). Among the most prominent of these is the Egyptian Current Party (Ḥizb al-Tayār al-Miṣrī), which was founded shortly after the 2011 revolution by five members of the Brotherhood's youth wing, who were subsequently expelled from the organization.[17] The fourth-place finisher in the 2012 presidential elections, ʿAbd al-Munʿim Abū al-Futūḥ, had once served on the Muslim Brotherhood's governing body, the Guidance Bureau (Maktab al-Irshād), but was expelled from the movement when he announced his presidential candidacy in defiance of the Brotherhood's stated intention not to field a candidate in that election (a decision it later reversed, to lasting effect). Moreover, Ḥāzim Abū Ismāʿīl, son of the Brotherhood's first member of parliament – Ṣalāḥ Abū Ismaʿīl, elected in 1976 – and himself a Brotherhood parliamentary candidate in 2005, not only ran for president in 2012 (before being disqualified by the courts) but in 2012 established his own political party (Ḥizb al-Rāya). The Salafists, too, have fractured. In December 2012, the founder of Ḥizb al-Nūr, ʿImād ʿAbd al-Ghafūr, quit to form a rival organization, Ḥizb al-Waṭan (Nation Party), accusing his former party of having lost touch with the people and declaring that his new party would be free "of the concept of obedience present in the Salafi Call movement" and open to "a diversity of views."[18]

[15] *Al-lā'iḥa al-dākhiliyya li-ḥizb al-Nūr* (Internal Regulations of the Nūr Party), Section 2, Articles 6 to 26; available from author.

[16] *Al-Nizām al-asāsī li-ḥizb al-misriyīn al-aḥrār* (Statute of the Free Egyptians Party), Section 3 "*ʿaḍā' al-ḥizb* (Party Members)," especially Articles 75 and 76; available at: http://www.almasreyeenalahrrar.org/Rules/Statute.aspx.

[17] Jamāl ʿIṣām al-Dīn, "*Ḥizb al-Tayār al-Miṣrī yaʿqad ijtimāʿahu al-taʾsīsī al-ʾawwal* (The Egyptian Current Party Holds Its Founding Meeting)," *al-Ahram* (Cairo), June 22, 2011; available at: http://gate.ahram.org.eg/News/85796.aspx.

[18] Muṣtafā Sulaymān, "*Rasmiyan … ʿImād ʿabd al-ghafūr yastaqīl min al-Nūr wa yu'assiss al-Waṭan* (ʿImād ʿabd al-ghafūr Officially Resigns from the Nūr Party and Forms the Waṭan Party)," *al-ʿArabiyya*, December 29, 2012; available at: http://www.alarabiya.net/articles/2012/12/29/257655.html.

Table 6.1 *Islamist Parties in Egypt (as of October 2012)*

Party	Antecedent Movement
Liberty and Justice (Ḥizb al-Ḥurriya wa al-ʿAdāla)	Muslim Brotherhood (MB)
Pioneer Party (Ḥizb al-Riāda)	MB offshoot
Renaissance Party (Ḥizb al-Nahḍa)	MB offshoot
Egyptian Current Party (Ḥizb al-Tayār al-Miṣrī)	MB offshoot
Movement for Peace and Development (Ḥarakat al-Salām wa al-Tanmiya)	MB offshoot
Center Party (Ḥizb al-Wasaṭ)	MB offshoot
Strong Egypt (Miṣr al-Qawiyya)	MB offshoot
Party of Construction and Development (Ḥizb al-Bināʾ wa al-Tanmiya)	Islamic Group (al-Jamāʿa al-Islāmiya)
Party of Safety and Development (Ḥizb al-Salāma wa al-Tanmiya)	Islamic Jihad (al-Jihād al-Islāmī)
Party of Light (Ḥizb al-Nūr)	Salafi Preaching Society (Jamāʿa al-Daʿwa al-Salafiyya)
Party of the Nation (Ḥizb al-Waṭan)	Salafi
Party of the Banner (Ḥizb al-Rāya)	Salafi
Party of Virtue (Ḥizb al-Faḍīla))	Salafi
Party of Authenticity (Ḥizb al-Aṣāla)	Salafi
Party of Reform and Renaissance (Ḥizb al-Iṣlāḥ wa al-Nahḍa)	Salafi
Party of the Community (Ḥizb al-Umma)	Nominally Islamist, Mubarak-era opposition party

Though we might be tempted to attribute the recent fragmentation of the Muslim Brotherhood to the strains of a new, more open postauthoritarian period, there is evidence that the movement has faced periodic crises of cohesion throughout its history. In 1939, the founder himself, Ḥasan al-Bannā, faced a leadership challenge that saw the defection of a sizable contingent of Brothers known as Muhammad's Youth (Lia 1997, 255). In 1996, another group of Brothers split off to form the Waṣat Party (Stacher 2002; Wickham 2004), which in 2011 was able to capture approximately 10 percent of seats in parliament. An even more dramatic split occurred in 2009, when elections to a vacant seat on the Brotherhood's Guidance Bureau led to a bitter procedural dispute that caused the movement's general guide, Mahdī ʿĀkif, to threaten to resign. A few months later, his deputy, Muḥammad Ḥabīb, quit the movement in a smilar dispute. In the words of Khalīl al-ʿAnānī, these episodes, played out in the media, "pierced the MB's aura of being somehow more principled than their opponents by exposing the squabbling, bartering, and back room deals that plague all Egyptian political parties."[19] During the heavily disputed 2010 elections, Majdī ʿĀshūr, a Muslim Brotherhood member of parliament from ʿIzbat al-Nakhl in Cairo, defied the organization's order to boycott the second round of the contests. He was then allegedly kidnapped by the Brothers and forced to make a videotape declaring his intention to comply with the organization's request – which he promptly ignored once they set him free.[20] Such are not the hallmarks of a well-oiled machine.

Where does all this leave us? How can we explain the inability of leftist parties to make their case to voters if not with reference to Islamists' superior organizational talents? One answer, often encountered in the prodigious political commentary on this issue, is that non-Islamists simply lack strategic acumen. For example, a leading Egyptian jurist recently accused the Brotherhood's secular opposition of suffering from "political stupidity."[21] In 2005, after the Muslim Brotherhood captured a 88 of 444 seats in the Egyptian parliament (while non-Islamist opposition parties captured a total of nine), a U.S. embassy dispatch declared that the secular opposition parties were "done in by their ineptitude."[22] Carothers and Ottaway (2004) tell us that secular parties possess "little capacity – and less inclination – to translate abstract ideas into programs with mass appeal"

[19] Khalil El-Anani, "When the Alternative Is Not So Different After All," *al-Ahram Weekly*, January 28–February 3, 2010; available at: http://weekly.ahram.org.eg/2010/983/op32.htm. See also Shaʿbān Hadiya, "*ʾAnbāʾ ʿan istiqālat ʿĀkif wa qiyām Ḥabīb biʾaʿmālahu* (News of ʿĀkif's Resignation and Ḥabib's Taking Over His Duties)," *al-Yawm al-Sābiʿ* (Cairo), October 18, 2009; available at: http://www.youm7.com/News.asp?NewsID=146836.

[20] "*Bayān Majdī ʿĀshūr li-muqāṭaʿat intikhābāt al-ʾiʿāda* (Statement of Majdī ʿĀshūr on Boycotting the Runoff Elections," Decemer 3, 2010; available at: http://www.youtube.com/watch?v=sIrJ39j6op4.

[21] Sayyid Aḥmad, "*Raʾīs maḥkama al-istiʾnāf: al-muʿāraḍa tuʿānī min ghabāʾ siyāsī* (Chief of the appeals court: The Opposition Suffers from Political Stupidity)," *al-Dustūr* (Cairo), December 9, 2012.

[22] "2005 in Egypt: Serious Change Raises Serious Resistance," U.S. Embassy, Cairo, Egypt, December 15, 2005; available at: http://wikileaks.org/cable/2005/12/05CAIRO9314.html.

and "talk to Western organizations and each other more than to their fellow citizens" – a bad strategy for winning elections. Almost twenty years ago, Egyptian scholar Moheb Zaki (1995, 98) wrote that the weakness of secular opposition parties during the Mubarak era was "a consequence of their political incompetence and lack of realism."

Of course, without being able to conduct psychometric tests on members of different parties, we cannot know whether there are in fact differences in the intelligence and strategic sophistication of party leaders (let alone whether these differences, if measurable, can explain differences in party behavior). But it is difficult to take this notion seriously. If parties behave differently, it seems more reasonable to begin from the assumption that they do so because they face different opportunity and incentive structures, not because their leaders have different cognitive capacities. Though activists and political pundits may be frustrated by the fact that leftist and liberal parties do not copy the Islamist playbook, it may be that these parties' failures are less due to stupidity or short-sightedness than to factors that reside beyond their control.

6.2 Opportunity Structures

In Chapter 2, we saw that parties of the left were at a disadvantage in the elections of the Mubarak era because the types of voters such parties sought to attract were captured by offers of patronage and material benefits by the ruling party and the local notables who ran for office as independents. After the fall of the Mubarak regime and the concurrent disruption of many networks of notability, parties of the left still could not manage to win votes and seats, despite the fact that Chapter 5 has shown that most voters seem to have wanted the policies that leftist parties were offering. I argue that the left's failure to capitalize on the political opening posed by the post-2011 period is not due to their alleged fecklessness or other deficiencies but because they face fewer opportunities for making their case to voters than do Islamist parties.

As Desai (2002, 624) points out, political parties in new democracies "are presented with structurally defined possibilities" that include "prior forms of association [and] preexisting networks of social action." These preexisting forms of collective activity can be powerful resources for political parties in newly democratizing systems. Given the compressed time period between autocratic collapse and a country's founding elections – in Egypt, it was a mere ten months – parties face the almost-insurmountable challenge of generating the kinds of linkages that will enable voters to recognize the party's policy stances and trust that it will implement them if elected to office. But establishing the institutions and mechanisms of linkage – such as base units, social-service operations, community centers, and the like – is both costly and time-consuming. As a result, the more embedded a party – or, more accurately, its members – within these prior forms of association, the greater is its potential for capturing the votes of similarly embedded citizens.

As we saw in Chapter 1, the associational landscape confronting Egyptian political parties at the end of Mubarak's rule was one dominated by traditional forms of collective life, rooted in the family and in the faith, but with comparatively little in the way of civic organization rooted in class or occupation. Political parties seeking to win in that country's founding elections thus had to embed themselves within Egypt's encompassing familial and religious organizations and networks, and this was harder for some than for others.

For example, some networks were ostensibly open to the highest bidder, such as the family networks that had been co-opted by the National Democratic Party (NDP) and that were now potentially available to be harnessed by parties across the ideological spectrum – as long as they could afford it. It practically goes without saying that parties of the left, with their emphases on redistribution and state control over the economy, were neither attracted nor attractive to these economic elites. This was less of a problem for other parties. The Wafd Party, for example, nominated on its slate a woman named Saḥar Ṭalʿat Musṭafā, who was the sister of NDP tycoon and former upper house member Hishām Ṭalʿat Musṭafā and presumably possessed of a large bank of retainers whose votes could be brought over to the party.[23] Similarly, in the district of Qalyūb in the governorate of al-Qalyūbiyya, the Muslim Brotherhood's Freedom and Justice Party nominated Muḥammad Hānī, the scion of a large family in the district and the son of a former high-ranking official of the NDP.[24]

In the districts of the southern Sinai, which are dominated by bedouin tribes – such as the Ḥuwayṭāt, Qararsha, and ʿAlayqāt – several parties sought to capture tribal votes by putting tribe members at the top of their electoral lists.[25] During the 2012 presidential election, Sinai tribal leaders emerged as key power brokers because several presidential candidates made pilgrimages to seek their endorsements (and their vote banks).[26] For the parliamentary elections that had been scheduled for the summer of 2013 – but which are as of this writing postponed

23 Aḥmad ʿAbd al-Jalīl, "*Al-Aḥzāb tuṭālib bil-ʿazl al-siyāsī wa turashah fulūl al-waṭanī ʿalā qawāʾimuhā* (The Parties Call for Political Exclusion While Nominating the Leftovers of the National Democratic Party on Their Electoral Lists)," *Al-Fajr* (Cairo), October 15, 2011; available at: http://www.elfagr.org/dailyPortal_Print_News_Details.aspx?nwsId=69866&secid=1.

24 ʿĪd ʿAbd al-Jawād, "*Kubrā al-ʿāʾilāt al-barlamāniyya bil-Qalyūbiyya tughīb ʿan al-intikhābāt* (The Biggest Parliamentary Families in al-Qalyūbiyya Are Absent from the Elections)," *al-Misrī al-Yawm* (Cairo), December 12, 2011; available at: http://www.almasryalyoum.com/node/575811.

25 Nabīl Siddīq, "*Qabāʾil al-Mazīna wa al-Qararsha wa al-ʿAlayqāt wa al-Jibāliyya wa al-Ḥuwayṭāt tataṣāriʿ ʿalā 6 maqāʿid bi-junūb Sīnāʾ* (The Tribes al-Mazina, al-Qararsha, al-ʿAlayqāt, al-Jibāliyya, and al-Ḥuwayṭāt Wrestle for 6 Seats in South Sinai)," *al-Ahram* (Cairo), December 26, 2011.

26 Nāṣir Abū Ṭahūn, "*Qabāʾil junūb Sināʾ tubāyaʿ Musa raʾīsan li-miṣr wa aḥad shuyukhiha yaqul lahu uṭālibuk bi-ʾan taqtaḍī bisayyidnā Mūsā* (The Tribes of Southern Sinai Pledge Allegiance to Musa for president of Egypt and one of their leaders says to him, I ask you to emulate the prophet Moses)," *al-ʿArabī* (Cairo), February 24, 2012; Maryam ʿAbd Allāh, "*Hal yaḥṣud Mursi aṣwāt qabāʾil Sīnāʾ?* (Has Morsi Harvested the Votes of Sinai's Tribes?)," *al-Dustūr* (Cairo), May 26, 2012; Huda al-Misri, "*Qabāʾil Sīnāʾ yastabdilūn ʿAmr Mūsā bi-daʿm Aḥmad Shafīq* (The Tribes of Sinai Trade Amr Musa for Aḥmad Shafīq)," *Rose al-Yūsuf* (Cairo), June 16, 2012.

until 2014 – the southern Sinai branch of the Brotherhood's Freedom and Justice Party (FJP) had declared its intention to nominate candidates from the tribes of al-Mazīna and al-Ḥamāḍa.[27]

Just as the collapse of the ruling party made it possible for political parties to compete for the allegiances of local notables and family blocs, so too did it increase the space for parties to try to link to voters through religious institutions. And in this, Islamists had a natural advantage – not because they "owned" the "parallel Islamic sector" (Wickham 2007) but rather because, as we saw in Chapter 4, they were embedded in it. As ʿAbd al-Wahhāb (2011) has written,

> Many of the Brotherhood candidates who won maintained deep relationships with branches of these associations in their electoral districts. There are some who gave sermons in its mosques, or who supervised or participated in overseeing some of its charitable social projects, or who took on important roles in its *zakāt* collection committees, and through these associations, candidates linked to scores of hospitals and clinics and orphanages and literacy programs and training sessions and social centers.

Though the embeddedness of Islamist activists in Islamic social organizations and institutions meant that they and their parties were more likely to be able to reach out to voters through these institutions than their secular rivals, it also meant that they had to compete with each other within those organizations. For example, during the 2011 parliamentary campaign, the (admittedly anti-Islamist) publication *Rose al-Yūsif* described a "tug-of-war" between the Muslim Brotherhood and the Salafists for the votes of members of Egypt's largest Islamist associations. For example, though the Muslim Brotherhood may have wished to monopolize organizations such as the JS, Nūr Party candidates reportedly "had a great deal of credit with the members of al-Jam'iyya al-Shar'iyya due to the fact that many members of al-Daʿwa al-Salafiyya would frequent its mosques."

But these challenges were minor compared with those faced by the left. Though the fall of Mubarak could open up new opportunities for parties to gain access to voters through preexisting networks, it could not create new networks where they did not exist. Though the leftist NPUR had long cultivated ties to the Egyptian labor movement, the narrowness of this movement and the general lack of occupational organization among Egypt's poor meant that the networks within which leftist activists were embedded were limited in scope. The revolution could not change the occupational structure of Egypt, moving workers from the informal sector to the shop floor or from the fields to the factory. Perhaps in recognition of this fact, Egypt's foremost labor leader, Kamāl Abū ʿĪṭa, a former member of the NPUR and founder of the Egyptian Federation of Independent Trade Unions,

[27] "*Al-Ḥurriya wa al-ʿadāla yaʿlan qāʾimat murashaḥīh li-intikhābāt al-nuwwāb bi-junūb Sīnāʾ wa al-Nūr yarfud al-tansīq maʿhum* (Freedom and Justice Announces Its Nominees for Elections to the Chamber of Deputies in Southern Sinai, and al-Nur Refuses to Coordinate with Them)," *al-Mashhad* (Cairo), January 8, 2013; available at: http://al-mashhad.com/Articles/145893.aspx.

acquiesced in 2011 to run on the FJP's "Democratic Alliance" list in the district of North Giza despite his misgivings about the party's parent organization.[28] The alternative would have been to risk exclusion from parliament entirely.

6.3 Empirical Analyses

This chapter has argued that Islamists outperformed leftist parties during Egypt's founding elections in part because Islamist activists were embedded in religious social networks that enabled them to reach large numbers of voters. In contrast, the labor-based organizations that could offer analagous linkage opportunities to leftists were weak – a product both of a long legacy of state control and a workforce that is largely agrarian and informal. Consequently, while Islamists were able to find opportunities to convince voters of their commitment to the economic policies voters cared about, leftists were relatively isolated, a fact reflected most poignantly in the voter ignorance and misapprehension of leftist economic policy stances we saw in the previous chapter. In this section I test the argument with aggregate and individual-level data from recent Egyptian elections.

Religious Institutions and Islamist Voting in Cairo and Alexandria Neighborhoods

One of the observable implications of the argument advanced here is that Islamist vote shares should be positively correlated with the density of Islamic institutions. There are obviously potential confounds that would have to be controlled for – most notably, both Islamist vote shares and the density of religious institutions could be functions of some deeper variable, such as popular religiosity. As a first cut at assessing the plausibility of the argument, though, I examine the correlation between voting for Islamists and the distribution of religious institutions – specifically, mosques – in Egypt's two largest cities, Greater Cairo and Alexandria, after the "Arab Spring."

Though we are interested in exploring the effect of Islamic institutions on voting for Islamists, spatial data on such institutions are limited. Therefore, we focus primarily on the relationship between mosques (for which spatial data are available) and Islamist voting.[29] Mosque coordinates were collected from the Google Places database, in which houses of worship were queried at every 0.0025 degree of latitude (to obtain the nearest twenty houses of worship every 750 feet). Though the Google Places database – which draws on Egyptian government sources and

[28] ʿAbd al-Laṭīf Ṣubḥ, "*Abū ʿIṭa yujammad ḥamlitahu al-intikhābiya iḥtijājan ʿala aḥdāth tal-Taḥrīr* (Abū ʿĪṭa Suspends His Campaign in Protest at Events in Taḥrir)," *al-Yawm al-Sābiʿ* (Cairo), November 24, 2011; available at: http://www.youm7.com/News.asp?NewsID=539452.

[29] Based on my admittedly unsystematic observations, there is a high coincidence between mosque presence and the presence of Islamic charitable associations. Moreover, since 2002, the Ministry of Religious Endowments has stipulated that all newly build mosques must dedicate space for social services, thus ensuring further spatial convergence between these two types of Islamic institutions over time.

directories – is reasonably comprehensive, it is not exhaustive. For example, coverage is thin outside of Cairo and Alexandria, forcing us to restrict our analyses to neighborhoods in those two cities.[30] Another cause for caution is the fact that even within Cairo and Alexandria, the database's mosque coverage is incomplete. According to the Ministry of Religious Endowments, the number of large mosques in those two cities is 4,772, and the total *zawāyā* are 9,203. However, the total number of mosques obtained from the Google database is 6,594, and a spot check of the locations of those mosques leads us to conclude that the database captures most large mosques but severely undercounts *zawāyā*. Figure 6.2 displays the spatial distribution of mosque density (calculated as the number of mosques per 10,000 inhabitants).

Our principal dependent variable is the share of votes cast for Islamist parties and candidates. Here, too, we run into data limitations. Though ideally we should analyze the results of Egypt's first postauthoritarian parliamentary elections, returns for that contest are not available at the neighborhood level but instead are reported only at the level of the electoral district. As described earlier, the electoral system employed in that election was comprised of two tiers – a list tier of forty-six multimember districts and a constituency tier of eighty-three dual-member districts. Together, Cairo and Alexandria were allocated six districts in the list tier and thirteen in the constituency tier – neither offering a large enough sample for econometric analysis. Consequently, the analysis in this section is restricted to elections for which it was possible to obtain data at a lower level of aggregation (in this case, the second-degree administrative unit, or *qism*, of which Greater Cairo and Alexandria together make up more than sixty). There are three elections for which *qism*-level data were available. These were

- *The March 19, 2011, constitutional referendum.* That referendum asked Egyptians to vote on a package of nine amendments to the country's 1971 constitution, which had been suspended after Mubarak's departure. The amendments were written by a committee of legal experts, chaired by Islamist-leaning jurist Ṭāriq al-Bishrī, and were endorsed by the Muslim Brotherhood and the major Salafi associations. As described in Chapter 5, three days before the referendum, the Jamʿiyya al-Sharʿiyya (JS), Egypt's largest Islamic association, took out an advertisement in Egypt's largest newspaper, *al-Ahram*, declaring that it was "a religious duty for every Egyptian to take care to vote in favor of the amendments."[31] Therefore, I use the percentage of yes votes to proxy for Islamist support, recognizing that it is at best an imperfect proxy and also captures support for the old ruling party

30 The data set includes twenty *aqsam* from the governorate of al-Giza, which are considered part of Greater Cairo.

31 "*Bayān al-Jamʿiyya al-Sharʿiyya al-Raʾīsiyya bi-shaʾn al-istiftāʾ ʿalā al-taʿdīlāt al-dustūriyya* (Statement of al-Jamʿiyya al-Sharʿiyya Headquarters in the Matter of the Referendum on the Constitutional Amendments)," advertisement in *al-Ahram* (Cairo), March 19, 2011, 1.

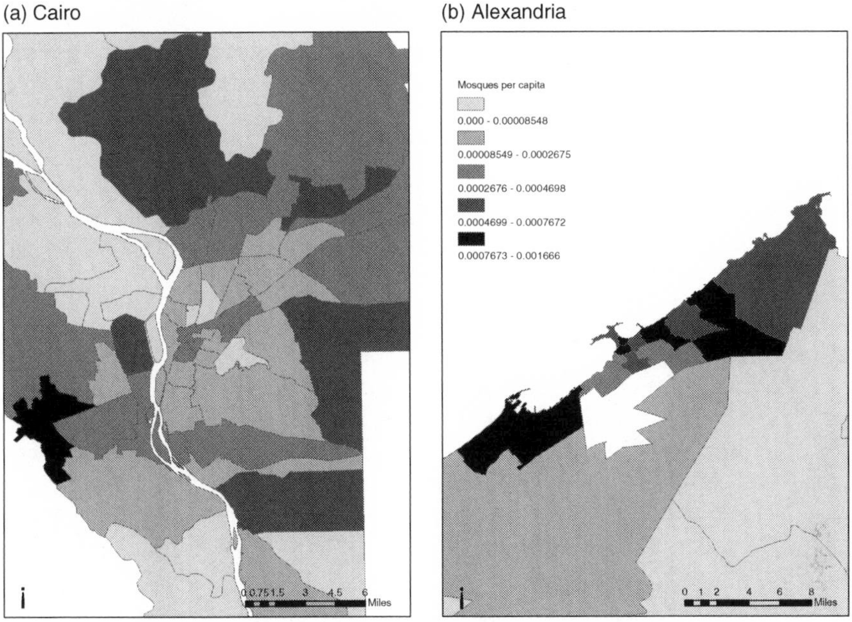

Figure 6.2 Mosque density in Cairo and Alexandria.

(which favored the amendments) and for the interim military government (Masoud 2011, 30).

- *The first round of the most recent presidential election, conducted on May 23 and 24, 2012.* In this contest, each of the country's two major Islamist parties – the FJP and the Nūr Party – supported a different candidate. The FJP supported its party leader and member of the Brotherhood's executive committee, Mohamed Morsi, and the Nūr Party supported ʿAbd al-Munʿim Abū al-Futūḥ, a former member of the Brotherhood who departed the movement shortly after the Egyptian revolution. Though Abū al-Futūḥ was widely considered more liberal than his Salafi supporters (and than his Brotherhood rival), seventy-four of the Nūr Party's 123 members of parliament voted to support him for president, as did eight of the eleven members of the Party's high committee.[32] According to the Nūr Party's secretary, ʿImād ʿAbd al-Ghafūr, the party supported Abū al-Futūḥ in order to prevent the Muslim Brotherhood from monopolizing power.[33]

32 Bāhī Ḥasan, "*Ḥizb al-Nur yaʿlan rasmiyan daʿm al-Futūḥ li-riʾāsat al-jumhūriyya* (The Nūr Party Officially Announces Its Support for al-Futuh for President of the Republic)," *al-Misri al-Yawm* (Cairo), April 28, 2012.

33 See "*ʿAbd al-Ghafur: Ḥizb al-nur qad yadʿam Abu al-Futuh li-riʾāsat Miṣr* (ʿAbd al-Ghafur: The Nūr Party May Support Abu al-Futuh for the Presidency)," *al-Misri al-Yawm* (Cairo), April 25,

- *The second round of the presidential election, held on June 16 and 17, 2012.* Egyptian electoral law requires a runoff between the top two vote-getters if no candidate earns more than 50 percent of the vote. The FJP's Morsi faced Aḥmad Shafiq, a former air force general who had held the posts of minister of civil aviation and prime minister under Mubarak.

In order to determine whether aggregate voting patterns in those three elections was a function of mosque density, I estimate a regression of the form

$$IslamistVote_i = \beta_0 + \beta_1 MosqueDensity_i + \beta' X + \varepsilon_i$$

where *IslamistVote* is the vote share captured by Islamists in *qism i*, and *MosqueDensity* is a measure of the number of mosques in the *qism* per 10,000 people, and *X* is a vector of covariates including the percentage of workforce in agriculture (in order to capture the extent of urbanization), the unemployment rate, the average number of inhabitants per household room (to proxy for socioeconomic status), and the logged *qism* population. All demographic variables are drawn from the 2006 population census conducted by the Egyptian Central Agency for Public Mobilization and Statistics (al-Jihāz al-Markazī lil-Taʿbiʾa al-ʿĀmma wa al-Iḥṣāʾ).[34]

I run four models, each with a different proxy for the dependent variable – model 1 employs as its dependent variable the percentage yes votes in the March 2011 referendum; models 2 and 3 use vote shares in the first round of the presidential election for Morsi and Abū al-Futūḥ respectively; and model 4 uses vote shares for Morsi in the presidential election runoff. Summary statistics for the key variables are listed in Table 6.2. The results of all four regressions are reported in Table 6.3. Figure 6.3 contains marginal-effects plots of increasing mosque density on the predicted (*a*) yes vote, vote shares for (*b*) Morsi and (*c*) Abū al-Futūḥ in the presidential election's first round, and vote share for (*d*) Morsi in the runoff.

As is apparent from Table 6.3 and the marginal-effects plots, the effect of mosque density is positive and statistically significant only in two of the four models – vote share for Abū al-Futūḥ in the first round of the presidential election and vote share for Morsi in the runoff. The relationship is positive but not significant when the dependent variable is the share of referendum yes votes, perhaps reflecting the fact that the 77 percent of voters who approved them were responding not only to Islamist appeals but also to appeals of the former ruling party (which had not yet been dissolved), as well as appeals of the country's military rulers, who were then basking in the glow of public acclaim for safeguarding the revolution. The insignificant, and negative, coefficient on Morsi's first-round vote share and the positive and significant coefficient on Abū al-Futūḥ's may reflect differences in the ability of the Muslim Brotherhood and the Salafi Daʿwa

2012; and "Egypt Salafis Back Abol Fotouh for President," al-Jazeera, April 29, 2012; available at: http://www.aljazeera.com/news/middleeast/2012/04/2012428234136158208.html.

[34] *Qism* and *markaz* level 2006 census data are available here: http://www.censusinfo.capmas.gov.eg.

Table 6.2 *Summary Statistics, Cairo and Alexandria* Aqsām

Variable	N	mean	S.D.	X_{min}	X_{max}
% Yes, March 2011 referendum	65	66.45313	15.61887	31.81979	96.66718
% Voting Abū al-Futūḥ, May 2012	65	17.45343	6.04029	7.563471	39.75454
% Voting Morsi, May 2012	65	18.303	9.206028	5.261542	49.01502
% Voting Morsi, June 2012	65	46.73913	13.13418	21.43329	77.4473
Mosques per 10,000	65	3.813501	3.985515	0	16.65809
% Workforce in agriculture	65	1.796357	4.513779	.0143012	25.65077
% Unemployed	64	4.220124	1.392295	1.360469	8.455105
Log population	65	11.9869	1.049632	8.962904	13.97182
Crowding rate	65	1.09832	.1434814	.5762787	1.512419

Table 6.3 *OLS Regressions of Correlates of Pro-Islamist Voting over Three Elections, Cairo and Alexandria*

	% Yes (3/19/11)	**% Morsi (Round 1)**	**% Futuh (Round 1)**	**% Morsi (Runoff)**
Mosques per 10,000	0.581	−0.191	0.346***	0.766***
	(0.431)	(0.170)	(0.118)	(0.273)
% Workforce in agriculture	1.611***	1.077**	0.758**	1.703**
	(0.442)	(0.413)	(0.321)	(0.699)
% Unemployed	0.172	0.514	−0.378	0.784
	(1.218)	(0.817)	(0.479)	(1.245)
Log population	−1.372	1.129	1.522*	2.486*
	(1.247)	(0.972)	(0.768)	(1.453)
Crowding rate	79.73***	25.64***	−4.245	29.02***
	(10.97)	(4.824)	(3.708)	(8.448)
Constant	−10.53	−26.75***	2.838	−24.13*
	(14.87)	(8.847)	(7.335)	(14.57)
Observations	64	64	64	64
R^2	0.716	0.617	0.408	0.552

Standard errors in parentheses.
*** $p < 0.01$; ** $p < 0.05$; * $p < 0.1$.

to use mosques to get out the vote for their candidates. Though both the Brothers and the Salafis employed mosques for linkage, the Salafis may have had a superior ability to do so, based on the fact that their quiescence during the Mubarak regime meant they were traditionally allowed more room to maneuver in mosques. The

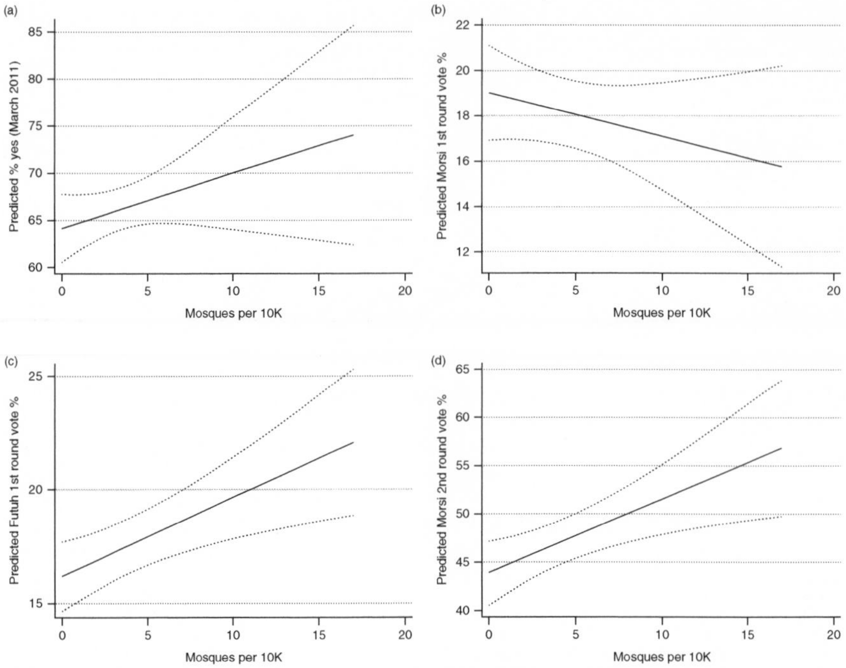

Figure 6.3 Marginal effects of mosque density on Islamist voting in Cairo and Alexandria; (*a*) Percent yes, March 19, 2011, referendum; (*b*) vote percent for Morsi, May 13–14, 2012; (*c*) vote percent for Abū al-Futūḥ, May 13–14, 2012; (*d*) vote percent for Morsi, June 16–17; 2012.

fact that mosque density is a positive and significant predictor of Morsi's second-round vote share may reflect the rallying of all Islamists behind him as the only Islamist candidate.

However, as noted earlier, aggregate data of this nature can only be suggestive. In addition to the fact that we are unable to control for potential confounds – most notably, the baseline level of religiosity in a given *qism* – we are also confronted with the problem of inferring individual behavior of aggregate data (King 1997). But most important, though correlations between the presence of Islamic institutions and support for Islamist parties are consonant with the argument presented here, they actually do not get at the core mechanism this chapter attempts to explore – specifically, how Islamic institutions provide Islamist parties with greater access to voters and how this allows them to shape voter perceptions of where those parties stand economically.

Individual-Level Evidence

As noted earlier, though the economic agenda of the Egyptian left appears highly congruent with the preferences of Egyptian voters, the latter are unaware of this fact and instead believe that Islamists – whose stances toward welfare and redistribution are complicated at best – most share their views. The explanation offered here is that leftists have few channels through which to convince voters otherwise, whereas Islamists can make use of dense webs of mosques and religious associations to make their case to voters. In order to probe this argument, I further analyze the survey data explored in Chapter 5, which allowed us to determine that Muslim Brotherhood voters cared more about the party's stance on the economy than its defense of religious mores. That survey, of 1,675 respondents, was conducted in the midst of Egypt's first free parliamentary elections. If the theory outlined here is correct, we should observe that voters who are embedded in Islamic social networks – mosques, charities, and religious lessons – are more likely to believe that Islamists are welfare-statist and redistributive. Similarly, those embedded in networks of labor activism – which bring them into contact with leftist party activists – are more likely to assign such preferences to parties of the left.

To test this hypothesis, I first code respondents on how they placed the FJP, Nūr, NPUR, Wafd Party, the Free Egyptians Party, and the Revolutionary Youth Coalition with respect to economic policy (i.e., whether they believed the party endorsed government responsibility for citizens' welfare and redistribution of wealth or not). For each party, I generate a dichotomous variable equal to 1 if the respondent failed to place that party on the "left" end of the economic spectrum (i.e., if he or she gave the party a score of greater than five or don't know on each of the two ten-point economic policy questions) and 0 otherwise. I then estimate a logistic regression of the form

$$Pr(\sim Left_{p_i} = 1) = \frac{e^{\beta_0 + \beta' Embeddedness_i + \gamma' X}}{1 + e^{\beta_0 + \beta' Embeddedness_i + \gamma' X}}$$

where $\sim Left_{p_i}$ is a dichotomous variable connoting whether respondent *i* placed party *p* on the right of the economic spectrum (or did not know), and *Embeddedness* is a vector of covariates capturing the key independent variables in this study, which are measures of a respondent's membership in religious and labor-based associations. We want to know if a respondent's embeddedness in particular forms of association influence his or her information about and assessments of different political parties. The embeddedness measures are

- *Frequency of mosque attendance*, coded 1 if the respondent attends mosque at least once a week and 0 otherwise. If mosques are thought to be a prime channel through which Islamist parties communicate with voters, then we should expect that voters who attend mosque more frequently to have greater access to Islamist party messages and thus to have a greater propensity to trust or vote for those parties.
- *Reliance on Islamic healthcare services*. As described in Section 3.2, this is a dichotomous variable in which all respondents who reported receiving health services either through a mosque (*khadamāt ṣiḥiyya tābiʿa li-masjid*)

or Islamic charitable society (*jam'iyya khayriyya islāmiyya*) were coded 1, and all others were assigned a score of 0. Given the embeddedness of Muslim Brothers in particular in networks of religious charity, we might expect that voters who have relied on such services would be more likely to believe in the welfare-statist and redistributive orientation of the Brotherhood.

- *Religious and scriptural studies*. Respondents were asked whether they attend religious lessons or sessions (*durūs aw jalasāt dīniyya*) or attend an instutue for memorizing the *Qur'an* (*maqra'a*). A dichotomous variable was created, coded 1 if respondents answered yes to one or both of these questions and 0 otherwise. We should expect participants in such lessons to be more likely to place Islamist politicians and parties on the "left" end of the spectrum.
- *Union membership*. Respondents were asked whether they were enrolled in a labor union or syndicate. Those who answered affirmatively were coded 1; all others received a score of 0. If leftist parties and political activists are embedded in labor unions, we should find that citizens who are similarly situated actually should be able to place leftist parties on the left end of the economic spectrum. The total share of respondents who admit to being union or syndicate members is 6 percent, considerably lower than the 12 percent union density. One potential explanation for this is that awareness of union membership is low because of the state's control over and enfeeblement of the General Federation of Egyptian Trade Unions (GFETU). In his study of construction workers in Cairo, Assaad (1993, 934) noted that "virtually all the workers I interviewed have had no interaction or involvement with the union other than the occupational certification test and the payment of the required three years of dues. Most do not even know what the union is."

In addition to measures of embeddedness, I include a vector of covariates X_i to control for potential confounding influences on a respondent's placement of political parties. These include education, unemployment, urbanization, gender, and age.[35] The results of the six regressions are presented in Table 6.4.

In column 1, the dependent variable is the respondent's placement of the Muslim Brotherhood's FJP. The coefficients on the measures of mosque attendance and reliance on Islamic health services both have the expected negative sign – meaning that people who pray in the mosque often or who received medical treatment through Islamic networks were less likely to fail to place the FJP on the left economically – but they are not statistically significant. The latter is particularly puzzling, given that Islamic healthcare activities would provide the Brotherhood's party both access to voters and a demonstration

[35] Diagnostics for collinearity reveal low variance inflation factors on all variables (< 2.05) and a condition number of 12.34, indicating that collinearity is not a serious concern. See discussion in Snee and Marquardt (1984).

Table 6.4 *Determinants of "Right" Party Placement*

	FJP	Nur	NPUR	Wafd	RYC	FEP
Prays in mosque ≥ once weekly	−0.0261	−0.0715	−0.0124	0.0378	0.196	0.0527
	(0.125)	(0.124)	(0.129)	(0.122)	(0.122)	(0.124)
Recipient of Islamic healthcare services	−0.0447	−0.00295	−0.0903	−0.249**	0.0102	−0.212*
	(0.125)	(0.124)	(0.131)	(0.123)	(0.123)	(0.125)
Religious lessons	−0.419**	−0.324*	0.00987	−0.184	−0.256	−0.109
	(0.185)	(0.178)	(0.184)	(0.174)	(0.173)	(0.176)
Union member	−0.0823	−0.351	−0.571***	−0.198	−0.284	−0.124
	(0.220)	(0.219)	(0.213)	(0.211)	(0.208)	(0.210)
Education	−0.124***	−0.117***	−0.0255	−0.0999***	−0.0864**	−0.0820**
	(0.0359)	(0.0356)	(0.0379)	(0.0356)	(0.0357)	(0.0366)
Urban	−0.127	−0.0425	0.169	0.112	0.0736	−0.0592
	(0.107)	(0.105)	(0.112)	(0.105)	(0.104)	(0.107)
Female	0.273**	0.358***	0.321**	0.347***	0.215*	0.319***
	(0.119)	(0.119)	(0.126)	(0.118)	(0.118)	(0.121)
Age	0.00542	0.00658*	0.00186	0.00224	0.00123	0.00385
	(0.00367)	(0.00364)	(0.00385)	(0.00359)	(0.00361)	(0.00372)
Non-muslim	0.248	0.511**	−0.245	0.0645	−0.247	−0.626***
	(0.208)	(0.210)	(0.207)	(0.203)	(0.203)	(0.204)
Constant	−0.244	−0.0765	0.601**	0.108	0.221	0.567**
	(0.227)	(0.227)	(0.241)	(0.225)	(0.227)	(0.235)
N	1,675	1,675	1,675	1,675	1,675	1,675
pseudo-R^2	0.0192	0.0250	0.0112	0.0138	0.00917	0.0146

Standard errors in parentheses.
*** $p < 0.01$; ** $p < 0.05$; * $p < 0.1$.

of their commitment to social welfare. However, there are two potential explanations. First, because recipients of Islamic health services appear, on average, to be less educated than nonrecipients (32.6 percent report no formal education compared with 25.9 percent for nonrecipients; 19.6 percent of recipients report at least some college education, whereas 21.7 percent of nonrecipients do not), it may be the case that this subset of the population is simply less able to assess political parties for their policy positions. Second, it may be that the causal mechanism through which Islamic service provision works to promote voting for Islamists is purely clientelistic, involving no shaping of voters' beliefs about the parties' preferences for redistribution or the welfare state.

There is, however, a negative and significant relationship between a respondent's attendance at religious lessons or Qur'anic sessions and the likelihood of not considering the FJP left wing economically. In order to quantify the magnitude of the effect, I employ King, Tomz, and Wittenberg's (2000) Monte Carlo simulation routines to estimate the difference in the probability that a respondent will consider the Brotherhood's party non-left conditional on attendance at religious lessons or sessions (holding all other variables constant at their means).[36] The results of the simulation are presented graphically in Figure 6.4*a*, which contains two smoothed histograms of the simulated probabilities that a respondent will fail to place the FJP on the left. The dotted line represents the distribution of simulated probabilities for respondents who do not attend religious lessons, the solid line is the distribution of simulated probabilities when religious lessons are attended. On average, an individual was found to be between 14 and 32.6 percent *less* likely to fail to place the FJP on the left if he or she attended religious lessons than if he or she had not. In other words, attendees at religious lessons seem more likely to deem the FJP welfare-statist and redistributive.

Column 2 of Table 6.4 displays the results of the same analysis for the Salafist Nūr Party. As with the FJP, the coefficients on mosque attendance and reliance on Islamic healthcare are insignificant, but the coefficient on participation in religious instruction is negative and significant at the 90 percent level. The effect of religious instruction on respondents' propensity to consider the Nūr Party welfare statist and redistributive is represented graphically in Figure 6.4*b*. On average, an attendee at religious lessons and Qur'anic sessions was found to be between 8 and 25 percent less likely than a nonattendee to fail to place the Nūr party on the left.

If religious embeddedness renders voters more likely to think religious parties are redistributive and welfare-statist, does embeddedness in labor-based organizations cause voters to think the same of leftist parties? It appears so. The coefficient on union/syndicate membership is, as expected, negative and significant,

36 Due to a statistical coding error discovered after the first edition went to press, the discussion of the results in the previous version of this section was not accurate. Instead of calculating the probabilities that respondents would place parties on the right, this analysis instead shows only the probability that respondents would *not* place parties on the left with respect to the welfare state and wealth redistribution.

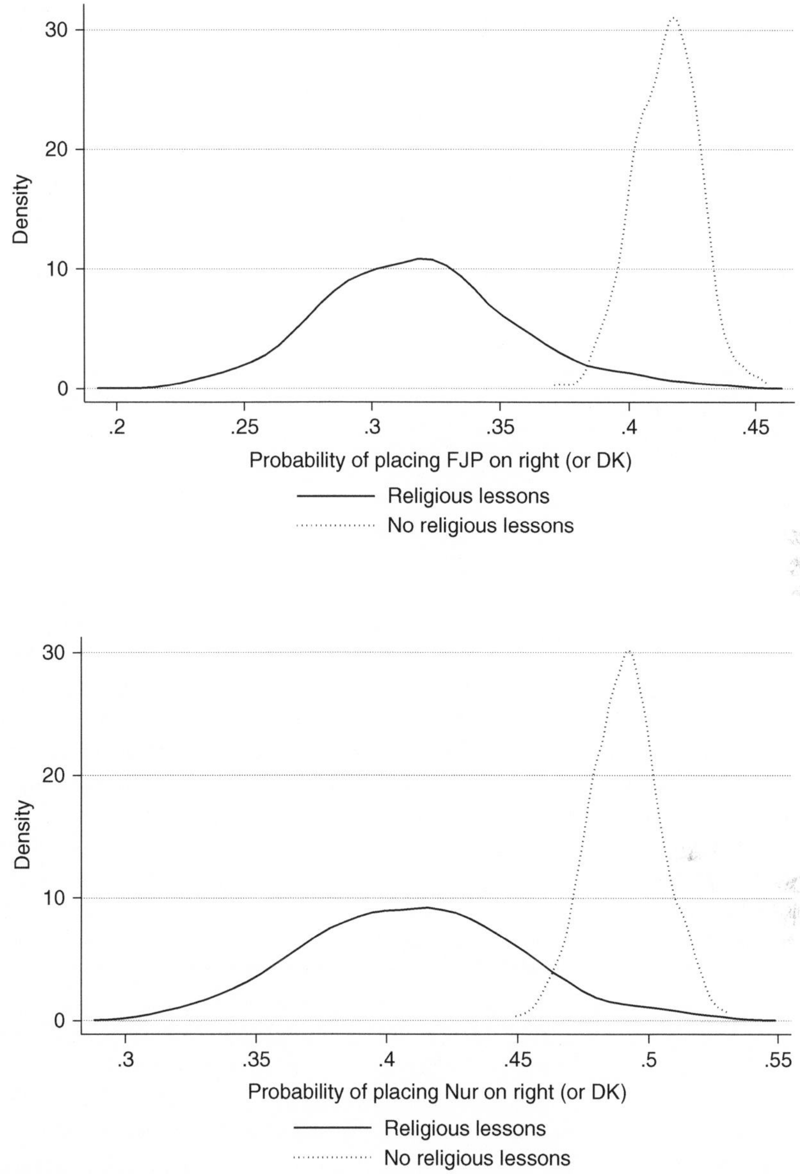

Figure 6.4 Simulated effect of religious lesson attendance on probability of identifying Islamist parties as nonredistributive and antiwelfare-statist: (*a*) Freedom and Justice Party; (*b*) Nūr Party.

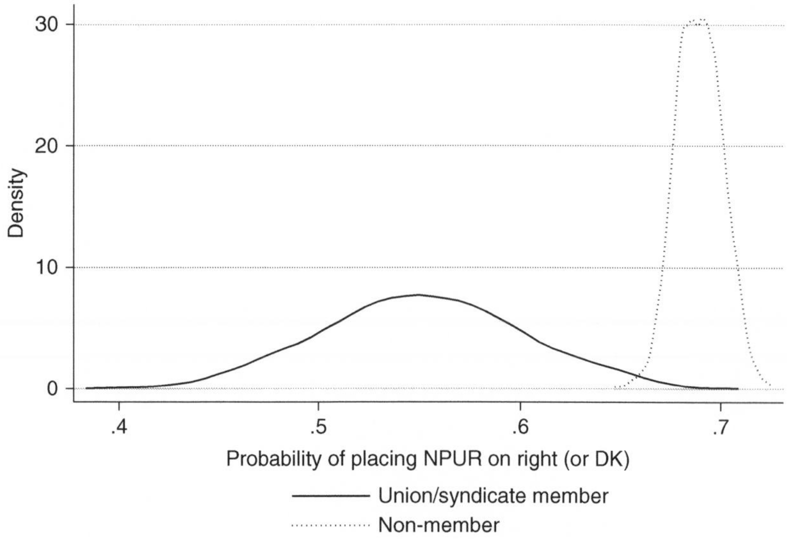

Figure 6.5 Simulated effect of union membership on probability of identifying NPUR as nonredistributive and antiwelfare-statist.

suggesting that membership in these organizations reduces the represented probability that a respondent will not think of the NPUR as a left party (column 3, Table 6.4). On average, a union member was between 12.5 and 27.4 percent less likely to deem the NPUR non-left than was a nonunion member (represented graphically in Figure 6.5). Union membership was not a significant predictor of the likelihood of identifying any other party as non-left.

More work is needed to tease out the causal mechanisms by which voters arrive at assessments of the economic policy stances of political parties, but the evidence gathered in this section suggests that an important part of the story are the associations and organizations in which voters are embedded. Voters who are members of labor-based organizations, in which activists from left parties are also likely to be embedded, are more able to come to accurate assessments of the economic positions of those parties. It is the limited extent of such organizations in Egypt that is the cause of the left's inability to reach voters – not the indolence of leftist party members, the insufficiency of their party apparatuses, or the special genius of the Islamists.

6.4 Conclusion

In Chapter 5, we saw that most people who voted for the Brotherhood in the 2011 parliamentary elections did so not because they wanted to legislate some conservative interpretation of God's law, but on the basis of their economic policy stances. We also saw that the kinds of economic policies these voters want are highly redistributive and accord the state a primary role in welfare provision. They vote for the Muslim Brotherhood (and, to a lesser extent, the Salafists) because they believe that the Brotherhood and the Salafists are more faithful to those policies than the leftists who have long championed them. In this chapter we have tried to understand why the left has proven so maladept at communicating its policy preferences to voters, investigating the claim that what leftists lack and what Islamists have is the organizational discipline and cohesion needed to mount national electoral campaigns and take their case to the grassroots. We find that, despite the large body of testimonials to the Islamists' superior cohesion, this alone is unlikely to explain the failures of left parties to put their policy proposals and positions on the public agenda.

Instead, I have argued that the leftists' disadvantage lies not in the practices of parties but in the social landscapes within which those parties are embedded. Long-duration political and developmental processes have generated a social landscape rich in religious networks and poor in networks of social action based on class or occupation. As a result, Islamists possess multiple opportunities to communicate with voters and convince them of their fealty to their interests, whereas leftists – who actually may be truer to those interests – simply lack equivalent opportunities to make their case. Thus, though the majority of poor Egyptian voters prefer significant redistribution and a large welfare state, they are unable to connect these preferences with the parties that most espouse them, voting instead for Islamist politicians who, by virtue of their embeddedness in dense networks of religious organizations, are able to speak to voters in ways that leftists are not.

The argument shares much with that of Tsai (2007), who shows that elites who are embedded in religious solidary organizations are more receptive to their communities. Here I have explored a complementary phenomenon, also seen by Thachil (2011) in India – that common embeddedness in solidary groups makes communities more receptive to political elites. It is important to note that the embeddedness of parties in associational structures is not necessarily the result of purposive strategies by party leaders but instead emerges organically from the affiliation decisions of party activists. ʿAlī Fatḥ al-Bāb, a Muslim Brotherhood member of the upper house of parliament, argued that although the Brotherhood benefited from his organic ties to the community, it did not generate them:

> I am already present in the middle of the people. I am here twenty-four hours a day, my house is here. Going and coming I am among them. I buy my vegetables, my bread in the morning, by myself. I stand in line with everyone else. I pray with the imam of the mosque every day. If he has a problem, I talk to him about it. If I can help him in something, I help him. And so on. These relationships are, by their nature, present, even before I became a Muslim Brother.[37]

[37] Interview with ʿAlī Fatḥ al-Bāb, al-Tibīn, Cairo, January 2006.

The type of individual likely to join the Muslim Brotherhood is also the type who is likely to donate some of his or her spare time to a local Islamic charity or to regularly attend the mosque. As we saw in Chapter 3, Brotherhood activists' embeddedness in religious networks was of only limited electoral utility during the Mubarak era, both because voter turnout was low, and because religious associations were forced to avoid the kinds of politicization that could invite unwanted regime attentions. But, with the advent of more open political competition, Islamist parties found themselves with a fund of linkages that leftists, who had no analogue to such networks of faith-based institutions, could not match.

Those concerned with boosting the fortunes of leftist parties (and non-Islamists in general) might conclude that the situation is largely hopeless. If Islamists possess an informational and communication advantage that is conferred on them by nothing less than the structure of civil society, what hope do secular parties have? But recall that in the argument presented here, religious networks don't shape voter preferences; they merely provide Islamists channels for convincing voters that they share those voters' already extant preferences. These channels matter most in the low-information environment of a founding election, where few parties have national reputations, and those who do have such reputations nonetheless lack track records of policy making. There are two observable implications of this argument. The first is that candidates who have alternative connections to voters – such as those based on family or clan – should be able to trump the Islamists' advantage (at least at the local level). The second is that, as Islamist parties brought into office during initial postauthoritarian elections prove unable to deliver on their promises, voters will update their assessments accordingly. In other words, the importance of religious networks as means of conveying information about candidates is heavily bounded, and so, consequently, is the Islamist electoral advantage. We examine this proposition in Chapter 7.

7

Connections, Not Creed: Further Evidence from Egypt and Beyond

In the previous chapters, I showed that Egyptians voted for Islamists not primarily because they wanted the application of God's law, but because they saw Islamists as champions of the redistributive policies that the majority of them crave. The reason that citizens attributed such policy commitments to Islamists rather than to leftist parties lies in the ability of Islamists to make their case to voters through religious social networks within which large numbers of Egyptians are embedded. In this chapter, I offer additional evidence for this proposition. Specifically, I argue that two facts of recent Egyptian political life are consistent with the story offered here. The first is the constriction of the Islamist vote base after their initial victory in the 2011 parliamentary elections. The second is the strong performance of non-Islamist candidates in pockets of the country where they were able to draw on local solidarities that could provide them channels to voters that matched those available to Islamists.

This chapter proceeds as follows. First I trace the eighteen months after the Muslim Brotherhood's victory in the 2011 parliamentary elections to demonstrate the speedy defection of large numbers of Egyptians from the Islamist camp, a fact that is inconsistent with the hypothesis that Islamist victories represent a popular desire for the rule of Islamic law. By the time of Mohamed Morsi's election in June 2012, it was clear that political Islam's long run of dominance had nearly run its course. The informational advantage that Islamists enjoyed in the opening moments of Egypt's new democratic era had withered rapidly as the Brotherhood and its partners racked up a record in the legislature that voters could assess (and rail against). The chapter then offers a subnational analysis of results in Egypt's 2012 presidential elections, demonstrating that Islamist candidates were particularly vulnerable in locales where opposing candidates could tap into alternative, nonreligious social networks. The people in these locales were no less pious than their Islamist-voting counterparts, no less embedded in Islamic networks and institutions, but they could vote for non-Islamist candidates because they had means of learning about those candidates directly. The analysis suggests that connections, and not creed, are what mattered in determining the results of Egypt's early post-Mubarak elections.

The chapter then considers the dynamics of Islamist victories outside the Egyptian case. It begins by examining the postrevolutionary constituent assembly elections in Tunisia, in which an Islamist party, Ḥizb Ḥarakat al-Nahḍa (Renaissance Movement Party), captured 89 of 217 seats. Al-Nahḍa's performance reinforced the impression that Muslims were driven primarily to vote on the basis of a concern over religious identity, but a closer examination of the results reveals that, as with Egypt, embeddedness mattered more than ideology. As we shall see, Al-Nahḍa performed best where it could rely on a preexisting religious infrastructure that its candidates could deploy to reach out to voters. And it was defeated in places where its opponents had nonreligious networks of their own that they could mobilize. In short, the Tunisian example demonstrates that ties of tribe, kinship, and local belonging can neutralize the Islamist advantage. I then explore the applicability of the theory outside the Arab world. If the dominance of Islamists is a function of the density of religious networks, how can we explain the relatively poor fortunes of Islamist parties in such countries as Indonesia and Pakistan, both of which are broadly similar to Egypt demographically and developmentally? I argue that in both of those places, the poor performance of Islamists reflects the fact that, even with the advent of competitive politics, traditional clientelistic networks continue to dominate the electoral calculus of most voters, creating relatively few opportunities for Islamists. This is in sharp contrast to Egypt, where Mubarak's overthrow ruptured the clientelistic networks that had been co-opted by his ruling party, and created the opening that Islamists were poised to take advantage of.

The chapter concludes by exploring what the dynamics explored here portend for the emergence of a more pluralistic politics in Egypt and countries like it. Given the Muslim Brotherhood's stunning ejection from power on July 3, 2013, what will emerge to replace it (assuming, of course, that electoral life resumes in earnest)? Though it seems likely that Islamists will not be able to reenact their initial, post-Mubarak electoral performances, the question for us is, from whence will a new pluralism emerge? Will we witness a progressive politics that seeks the genuine uplift of Egypt's poor, the reconstitution of the old ruling party's networks of privilege, or the emergence of a crude and opportunistic populism?

7.1 The end of the monopoly

When Mohamed Morsi was elected to Egypt's presidency with 52 percent of the vote in June 2012, it was easy to forget how hard fought and narrowly won the victory was, and to fit it instead into the established narrative of inevitable Islamist dominion. This would have been a mistake. For, although the two years following Mubarak's ouster may have looked like one long Islamist winning streak, it was one that was made up of increasingly narrow victories, suggesting that the informational advantage enjoyed by Islamists in Egypt's "founding" moment had

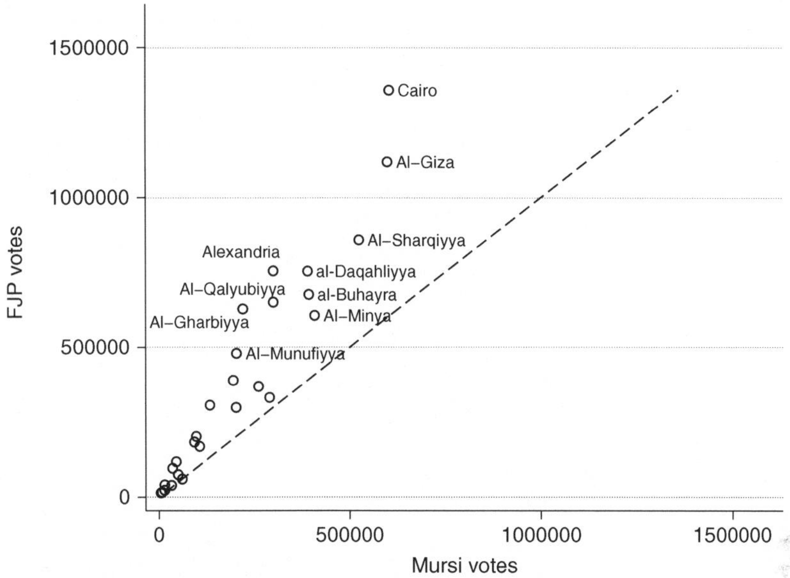

Figure 7.1 Voting for FJP versus voting for Mohamed Morsi.

steadily evaporated. For example, if we compare the number of votes cast for the Muslim Brotherhood's Freedom and Justice Party (FJP) in the legislative contest to the number of votes cast for its candidate, Mohamed Morsi, in the presidential one, we see that in every one of the country's governorates, the Muslim Brotherhood actually lost supporters. This is represented in Figure 7.1, where the *Y* axis represents the number of votes in each governorate cast for the FJP, and the *X* axis is the number of corresponding votes for Mohamed Morsi in the first round of the presidential election in May 2012. The dotted, 45-degree line is where all data points would lie if the same number of people voted for Morsi as had for the FJP. If Morsi had managed to get *more* votes than the FJP, the data points would all lie *below* the dotted line. Instead, however, we see that all governorates lie above the dotted line, indicating a sizeable voter exodus from the FJP between the two elections.

Of course, the FJP was not the only Islamist party in the parliamentary elections, and Morsi was not the only Islamist candidate in the presidential one. Could it be that voters who left the Brotherhood turned to other guardians of the Islamic cause? Thirteen candidates contested the 2012 presidential election's first round, including two identifiably Islamist candidates in addition to Morsi: a scholar named Muḥammad Salīm al-ʿAwā and ʿAbd al-Munʿim Abū al-Futūḥ, a former member of the Brotherhood's guidance bureau who decided to run for president at a point when the Brotherhood had declared that it would not field a candidate. As noted in Chapter 6, it is worth asking whether Abū al-Futūḥ could be called an Islamist candidate at all, since his campaign spent a considerable

Table 7.1 *Candidate Vote Shares in First Round of 2012 Presidential Election*

Name	Party	Votes	%
Mohamed Morsi	Freedom and Justice	5,764,952	25%
Aḥmad Shafīq	None (former NDP)	5,505,327	24%
Ḥamdīn Ṣabāḥī	al-Karāma	4,820,273	21%
ʿAbd al-Munʿim Abū al-Futūḥ	Independent (Nūr party)	4,065,239	17.5%
Amre Moussa	None	2,588,850	11%

amount of time emphasizing his differences with the Brotherhood, whom he criticized for mixing religion and politics. However, he is included here because he was endorsed by the Salafi Nūr Party, in a tactical move designed to thwart Muslim Brotherhood dominance.

Vote shares of the top 5 candidates in the first round of the 2012 presidential election are presented in Table 7.1 In an illustration of how far the Brothers had fallen, Morsi only secured 25 percent of the more than 23 million votes cast – not enough to win outright, but enough to enter a runoff. Careful readers will recall from Chapter 4 that Morsi's modest vote share in the presidential election echoed his first foray into the electoral arena, when as a parliamentary candidate in al-Zaqāzīq, he earned just 27 percent of the vote. A May 2012 survey of 1,200 Egyptians conducted by *al-Ahrām* and the Danish Egyptian Dialogue Institute, and designed in collaboration with the author, found that most of those who declared an intention to vote for Morsi were religious conservatives, indicating that the broad coalition that had supported the FJP in November 2011 had dissipated.[1]

The rest of the Islamist field performed no better. Abu al-Futūḥ earned only 17.5 percent, and Salīm al-ʿAwā recorded just 1 percent of the vote. In fact, a majority of votes went to non-Islamist candidates, including to Mubarak protégé and former prime minister Aḥmad Shafīq (almost 24 percent of the vote), the Karāma Party's Ḥamdīn Ṣabāḥī (with 21 percent of the vote), and former foreign minister Amre Moussa (11 percent). Though the runoff in the presidential election eventually brought Morsi to power, it was only on relatively narrow margin (52 percent to 48 percent), and against a figure widely reviled as a pillar of the regime Egyptians had overthrown a mere seventeen months earlier. Moreover, it is worth noting that voter turnout in that election was approximately 46 percent, which means that the Brotherhood candidate's eventual 52 percent of voters represents only around a quarter of eligible voters.

[1] See Masoud, et al, "*Al-Intikhabāt al-Riʾāsiyya fi Miṣr: Man ʾaʿṭā ṣawtahu li man, wa limāthā?* (Presidential elections in Egypt: Who voted for whom, and why?" in *Kayf yufakir al-Miṣriyūn? Istiṭlāʿāt al-raʾy al-ʿām* (How do Egyptians think? Public opinion surveys), *al-Ahrām* (Cairo), June 14, 2012 (insert).

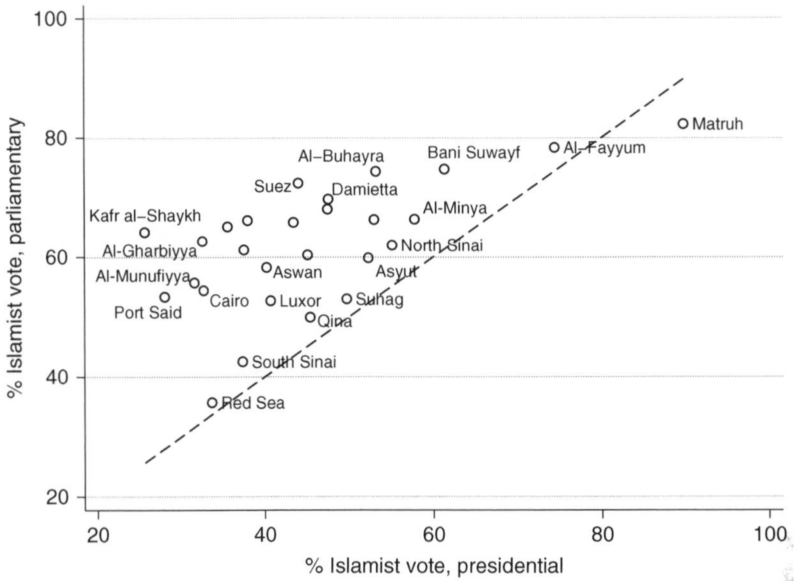

Figure 7.2 Comparison of Islamist vote shares in parliamentary and presidential elections (2011–12).

To illustrate the extent of the Islamists' regression in the first five months of 2012, Figure 7.2 is a scatterplot of the share of votes captured by all Islamist candidates in the May 2012 first-round presidential election against the vote share captured by all the country's Islamist parties, the FJP, Nur, and the more liberal Wasaṭ Party, in the parliamentary election concluded in January 2012. The scatterplot shows a precipitous decline in the Islamist vote share between the two elections across practically every governorate (the only exception being Maṭrūḥ, where the Nūr party could call on tribal loyalties cultivated through its parent movement, the Salafi Call Society).[2] This dramatic reduction in support for Islamist candidates is entirely inconsistent with a view of Egyptian politics that

[2] Though the Nūr Party's capture of nearly 80 percent of votes in the district of Matrūḥ, a western border region dominated by tribal solidarities, would seem to militate against the logic of the argument here, it actually illustrates it. The electoral success of the movement is based not on supplanting tribal loyalties, but on incorporating them. During the 2011 parliamentary election, the party was keen to ensure that key tribal leaders found slots on its electoral lists. The exquisite sensitivity of the party to Matrūḥ's tribal dynamics was demonstrated in April 2012, when the party's parent movement, the Salafi Call Society, instructed the party to halt planned internal elections for fear of igniting "sedition and volatility." In an official statement, the SCS declared that it had decided to appoint the leaders of the party's general secretariat in Maṭrūḥ directly, "in order to reflect the tribal and demographic map." See: "*Al-Da'wa al-Salafiyya fī Maṭrūḥ tarfuḍ intikhābāt al-Nūr al-Dākhiliya* (The Salafi Call Society in Maṭrūḥ rejects the Nūr Party's internal elections)," *al-Rāī* (Kuwait), April 9, 2012; available at: http://www.alraimedia.com/ArticlePrint.aspx?id=376024

ascribes the dominance of Islamists in founding elections to a popular passion for religion. The results of that presidential election should have demonstrated definitively that Egyptians will not automatically vote for Islamists, that the Muslim Brotherhood's vaunted organizational machine clearly had its limits, and that a dramatic reckoning lay in the movement's future.

Family and Regional Connections in the 2012 Presidential Elections

It is little surprise that one lesson that many took from the result of Egypt's first presidential election is that non-Islamists must put aside their differences and unite in order to defeat the Muslim Brotherhood and its allies. However, the results are more instructive for what they say about the nature of political competition in that country. For while it is perhaps unremarkable that the top two candidates in Egypt's first real presidential election were a Muslim Brother and a member of the *ancien régime*, the genuine surprise to many observers of the Egyptian political landscape was the third-place finish of Ḥamdīn Ṣabāḥī, a journalist and head of the small Arab nationalist Karāma Party (which in the 2011 parliamentary election had joined the Muslim Brotherhood's slate and earned six seats in the bargain). How did the leader of a fringe party manage to emerge within striking distance of both the vaunted Muslim Brotherhood and the putative leftovers of Mubarak's machine?

One possible account is that Ṣabāḥī, who positioned himself as a believer in the Nasserist project of restoring Egypt's leadership abroad and reestablishing the statist, redistributive social contract at home, had earned his votes from the poor and disenfranchised to whom he seemed to address himself. After all, the candidate's campaign slogan, "*wāḥid minina* (one of us)," was eloquent of his pretensions to represent the common man.[3] His official campaign biography waxed extensively about his commitment to workers and the poor. Whereas Mohamed Morsi's campaign flyers emphasized the future president's technical credentials – a doctorate from the University of Southern California and an alleged stint working on space shuttle engines for the National Aeronautics and Space Administration – Ṣabāḥī's biography spoke of his participation in protests (led, incidentally, by the National Progressive Unionist Rally (NPUR)) against an unpopular 1990s land-reform law that eliminated Nasser-era protections for tenant farmers (Kienle 2001, 92).[4] Voters were informed that Ṣabāḥī was subjected to "a string of arrests, among them when he led demonstrations in 1997

[3] Muḥammad al-Khūlī, "*Ḥamdīn Ṣabāḥī: Murashaḥ al-'ummāl wa al-falāḥīn wa al-ṭalaba* (Ḥamdīn Ṣabāḥī: Candidate of workers, farmers, and students)," *al-Akhbār* (Cairo), May 22, 2012.

[4] The Muslim Brotherhood's position on the reforms was one of muted assent. As one Muslim Brotherhood supporter put it to a Western journalist at the time, "Islam protects property rights [...] therefore the law is good." See Deborah Horan, "Egypt: State fails to tar Muslim Brotherhood with 'terrorism' brush," Inter Press Service, October 24, 1997. Tingay (2006, 22) calls the Brotherhood an "oustpoken supporter" of the law, and one socialist writer noted at the time that, although the Brotherhood was "timid" in its show of support for the law, it nonetheless "stood clearly on the side

with the farmers of Egypt, who had been harmed by the land tenancy law, a law that expelled millions of poor farmers from their land, in a brazen return to the feudal system."[5]

However, when one examines the social correlates of Ṣabāḥī's vote share, it does not appear that his victories were concentrated in rural or impoverished areas populated by the people on whose behalf he is alleged to have fought. Table 7.2 contains the results of regression analyses of *qism*- and *markaz*-level vote shares for Morsi, Shafīq, Ṣabāḥī, Amre Moussa, and ʿAbd al-Munʿim abū al-Futuh (abbreviated AMAF here) in the first round of the presidential election, conducted on May 23 and 24, 2012 (I have also included an analysis of Morsi's vote share in the runoff election). The key independent variables in the analysis are the crowding rate (a proxy for socioeconomic status, defined as the average number of inhabitants per household room), the share of the adult workforce in agriculture (a proxy for urbanization), and the logged district population. Though one must be cautious about inferring individual behavior from aggregate data (King 1997; 1999; Cho 1998; Cho and Gaines 2004), the negative correlation between Sabāḥī's vote share and both the crowding rate and percentage of the adult workforce in agriculture seems to suggest that he appealed primarily to a more affluent, urban constituency. However, it is worth noting that one of the governorates in which Ṣabāḥī dominated his opponents was the relatively small industrial center of Port Said, a hotbed of labor activism (and one of the few places where the NPUR under Mubarak reliably won a seat in the legislature). Based largely on the strength of his appeals to Port Said's workers, Ṣabāḥī earned 35 percent of the vote in Port Said, in contrast to 15 percent for the second-place finisher in that governorate, Mohamed Morsi. Still, the largely urban support base of Ṣabāḥī and Morsi's other main rival, Aḥmad Shafīq, would seem to support the notion that the election represented an existential struggle over the nature of the regime, with the traditional countryside pitted against the cosmopolitan urban areas in a pitched battle for the soul of Egypt.

A closer look at these results paints a different picture, however. Figure 7.3 is a scatterplot of votes for Ṣabāḥī at the *qism* level, plotted against the percentage of the adult workforce in agriculture (our proxy for urbanization or, rather, the lack thereof). Though the relationship appears to be weakly negative, we observe a set of outliers where Ṣabāḥī's vote share exceeded 50 percent, even in highly rural areas. These places all turn out to be located in Ṣabāḥī's home governorate of Kafr al-Shaykh. Presumably, the inhabitants of the villages of Kafr al-Shaykh are no less religious than other rural dwellers. What distinguishes them from their counterparts who voted for the Muslim Brotherhood's Morsi is probably less their

of large landowners and capitalists." See Rafīq Ẓahrān, "*al-Ḥaraka al-falāḥiyya wa qānūn ṭard al-mustaʾjirīn* (the peasants movement and the law of expulsion of tenants)," *al-Sharāra*, September 1997; available at: http://www.e-socialists.net/node/5502

5 Al-Birnamij al-Intikhabi lil-Murashah Ḥamdīn Ṣabāḥī (Electoral Program of the Candidate Ḥamdīn Sabahi), 2012.

Table 7.2 *Determinants of Vote for Candidates, May–June 2012 Presidential Elections*

	Morsi 1st round	**Shafīq 1st round**	**Ṣabāḥī 1st round**	**Moussa 1st round**	**AMAF 1st round**	**Morsi 2nd round**
Crowding rate	23.49***	−7.581**	−19.04***	0.270	0.650	27.90***
	(2.475)	(3.098)	(3.642)	(3.024)	(2.844)	(4.399)
% agriculture	0.661***	−0.245***	−0.544***	−0.0511	0.120	0.633***
	(0.0691)	(0.0621)	(0.0886)	(0.0402)	(0.0790)	(0.0745)
Logged population	0.355	2.663***	0.243	−1.957***	−1.241**	−1.483**
	(0.354)	(0.431)	(0.432)	(0.433)	(0.623)	(0.618)
Constant	−12.33**	0.702	43.12***	36.09***	30.65***	32.82***
	(4.897)	(6.490)	(7.233)	(6.586)	(8.319)	(9.163)
Observations	332	332	332	332	332	336
R-squared	0.481	0.130	0.234	0.121	0.050	0.326

Standard errors in parentheses.
*** $p < 0.01$, ** $p < 0.05$, * $p < 0.1$.

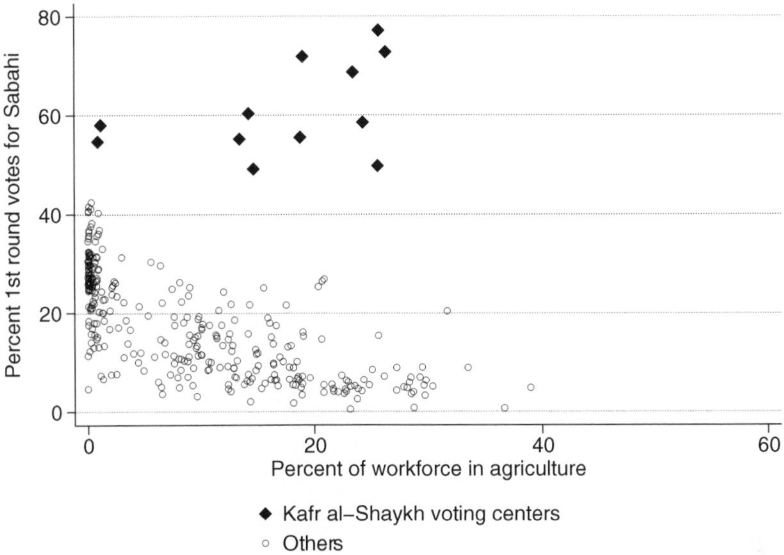

Figure 7.3 *Qism*-level vote share for Ḥamdīn Ṣabāḥī, May 23–24, 2012.

ideology than their information – Sabāḥī's embeddedness in his home governorate simply meant that voters knew enough about Ṣabāḥī to vote for him over the Muslim Brotherhood, despite the latter's attempts to reach out to voters through the religious infrastructure. Careful readers will recall how this result echoes a result observed during the 1984 elections, when the NPUR's best showing against the ruling party was in the home district of the party's founder, Khālid Muḥyī al-Dīn, in the governorate of al-Qalyūbiyya (see Section 2.2).

We observe a similar pattern with Aḥmad Shafīq's vote share in that election. Figure 7.4 is a scatterplot of Shafīq votes at the *qism* level, plotted against the agricultural workforce. The locales at the very top of the vote distribution are all located in the governorate of al-Minūfiyya, birthplace of Shafīq's mentor, ousted president Hosni Mubarak. Again, al-Minūfiyya is not significantly different demographically or socially from other rural governorates. Its inhabitants are not somehow less religious than their fellow citizens elsewhere. In fact, the governorate has the highest proportion of Islamic private voluntary organizations in Egypt. And yet it went overwhelmingly for the opponent of the Muslim Brotherhood on the strength of his ties to the governorate's favorite son. It's further worth noticing that another governorate in which Shafīq won an outright majority of votes was Morsi's home governorate of al-Sharqiyya. Though to some this suggested that the Interior Ministry had engaged in fraud on the former air force general's behalf, the more likely explanation is that, as a son of al-Sharqiyya himself, Shafīq was able to call on networks of family loyalty in that governorate that could rival Morsi's. Moreover, Shafīq could also count on former NDP loyalists from among the governorate's notability to get out the vote on his behalf. Indeed,

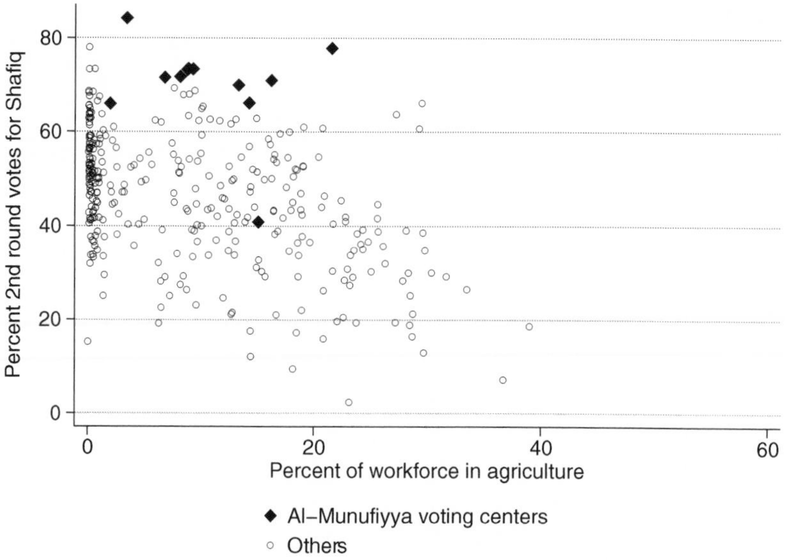

Figure 7.4 *Qism*-level vote share for Aḥmad Shafīq, May 23–24, 2012.

the Egyptian newspaper, *al-Miṣrī al-Yawm,* reported in August 2011 – almost a full year before the presidential election – on a Ramadan dinner held for Shafīq by "the big families of al-Sharqiyya," who "asked Shafīq to announce his candidacy for the presidency of the republic."[6] Though these big families lacked the clout they once had under Mubarak, they would nonetheless help Shafīq give Morsi and the Brotherhood a run for their money in a governorate that many thought of as an Islamist stronghold.[7]

Probing the electoral results from al-Sharqiyya more closely confirms the intuition that ideology had little to do with the way that voters in the governorate chose between those two candidates. Villages that were identical across a range of socioeconomic factors ended up voting in very different ways, depending on the embeddedness of the candidates within them. Figure 7.5 displays the percentage of voters in each of al-Sharqiyya governorate's second-level administrative units (*marākiz* and *aqsām*) who selected Shafīq over Morsi in the two rounds of the 2012 presidential election. One of the locales that went most heavily for Shafīq in both rounds was called Markaz al-Ibrāhīmiyya. Shafīq beat Morsi there by 10.5 percent in the first round, and by 20 percent in the second. One of the districts that went most heavily for Morsi, in contrast, was Markaz Hihyā, where

6 "Shafīq fī ḍiyāfat ahālī al-Sharqiyya (Shafiq is the guest of the families of al-Sharqiyya)," al-Miṣrī al-Yawm (Cairo), August 27, 2011; available at: http://www.almasryalyoum.com/node/490517

7 See, for example, "El-Sharqia: Circulated ballots reappear," ikhwanweb.com December 1, 2005; available at: http://www.ikhwanweb.com/article.php?id=5268; and Omar Ashour, "Egypt's Salafi Challenge," Project Syndicate, January 3, 2012; available at: http://www.project-syndicate.org/commentary/egypt-s-salafi-challenge

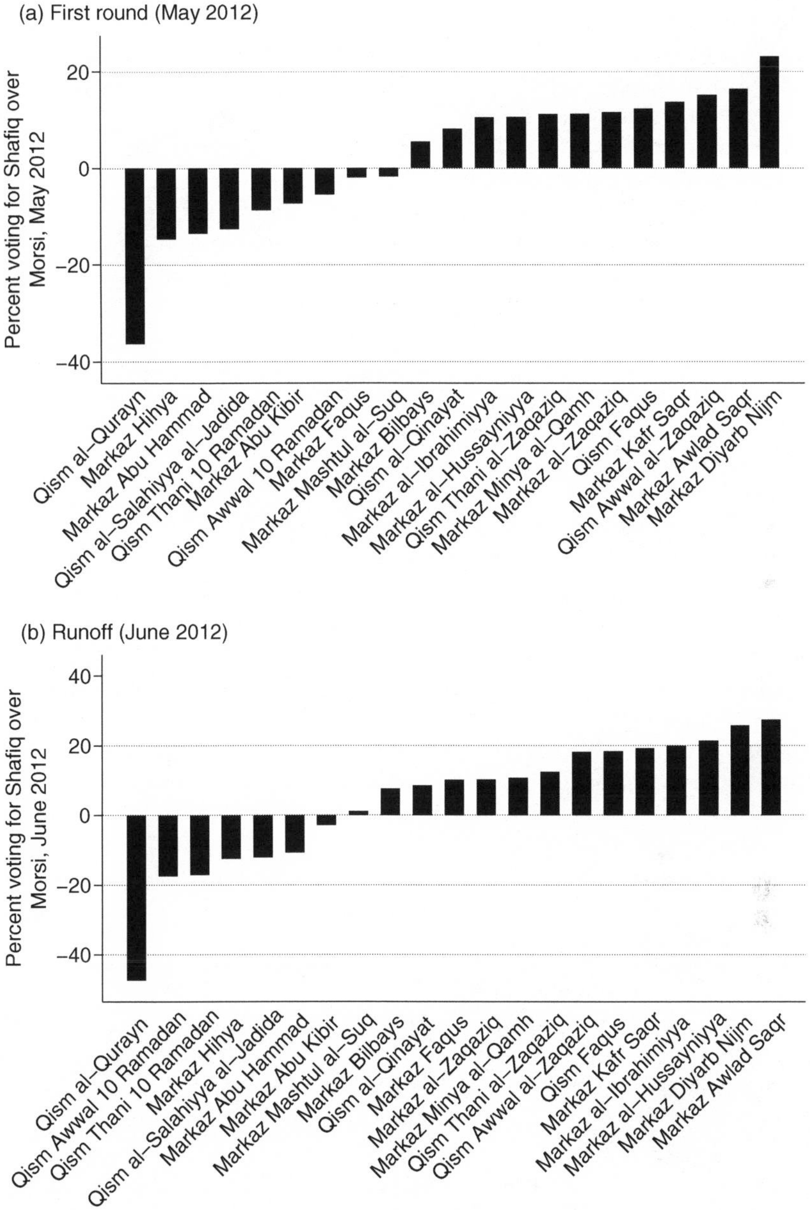

Figure 7.5 Vote difference between Shafīq and Morsi, al-Sharqiyya Governorate, 2012 presidential election.

the Islamist surpassed his opponent by 14.6 percent and 12.4 percent in the first and second rounds, respectively. Little distinguishes Markaz al-Ibrāhīmiyya from Markaz Hihyā. Both feature high illiteracy – 35 percent in al-Ibrāhīmiyya and 30 percent in Hihyā. The share of the workforce employed in the agricultural sector is 11 percent in Hihyā and 18 percent in al-Ibrāhīmiya. Almost 85 percent of the inhabitants of the pro-Morsi Markaz Hihyā, and 87 percent of inhabitants of the pro-Shafīq Markaz al-Ibrāhīmiyya voted for the March 2011 constitutional amendments. What does distinguish these places, however, is that Markaz Hihyā contains Morsi's home village of al-ʿUdwa, whereas Markaz al-Ibrāhīmiyya contains Shafīq's home village of Qaṭīfa Mubāshir.[8] Similarly, the district where Morsi performed best over the two rounds, Qism al-Qurayn, is indistinguishable from Markaz al-Zaqāzīq, where he performed far worse. In Qurayn, 94 percent of citizens had voted for the March 2011 constitutional amendments, whereas 91 percent had in Markaz al-Zaqāzīq. Of the six Muslim Brotherhood activists in al-Sharqiyya that I asked, none could offer me a convincing explanation for why al-Qurayn had favored them so heavily and Markaz al-Zaqāzīq went so definitively against them. One suggested that al-Qurayn's proximity to Morsi's home district may have played a role, but others rejected this assertion, pointing out that other locales bordering Markaz Hihyā had gone against its most famous son. All however, in groping for answers, suggested that the Brothers in al-Qurayn had simply done a better job of reaching out to citizens (and families) there than the old NDP allies who mobilized support for Shafīq, whereas the reverse was true in Markaz al-Zaqāzīq. It is thus difficult not to conclude that, within al-Sharqiyya as across the country, Egypt's presidential election seems to have been less about who stood for or against Islam, and more about who stood closest to the voter.

7.2 Beyond Egypt

The patterns described here – in which electoral outcomes are functions not of competition over the role of Islam in public life, but rather of the relative embeddedness of parties and candidates in local communities – are not restricted to Egypt. We observe the same phenomenon in the October 2011 elections to Tunisia's constituent assembly. There, the Islamist party Al-Nahḍa won 41 percent of 217 seats and emerged as the single largest bloc in the body tasked both with governing Tunisia and crafting its future constitution. The dominant description of that result in the West was as one more sweeping victory for Islamists, and one more demonstration of an insatiable Arab thirst for *sharīʿa*. However, close examination of those results reveals that, like Egypt, this outcome was not primarily attributable to the political salience of the role of faith in public

[8] Faṭhiyya al-Dīb, "*Shafīq yataqaddam fi masqaṭ ra'sahu biqaryat qaṭifa al-sharqiyya* (Shafīq advances in his hometown, the village of Qaṭīfa in al-Sharqiyya)," *al-Yawm al-Sābiʿ* (Cairo), May 24, 2012, available at: http://www3.youm7.com/News.asp?NewsID=687741.

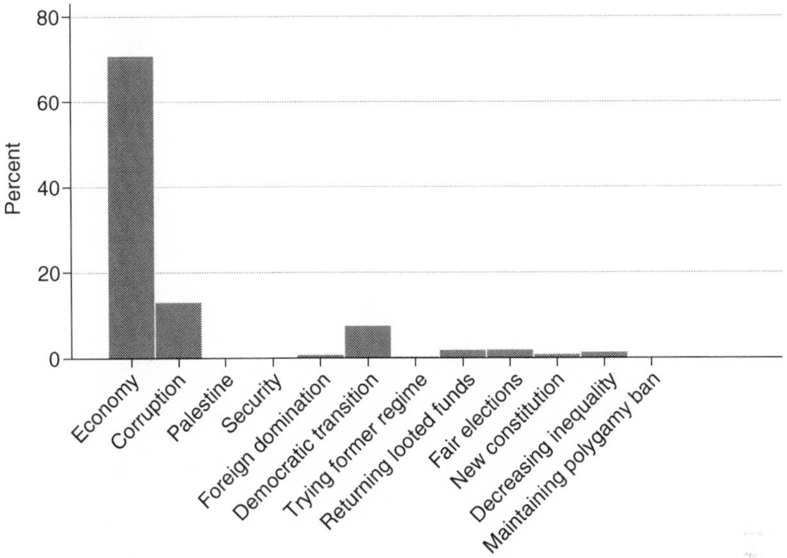

Figure 7.6 Concerns of Tunisians after the 2011 revolution.

life, but rather to differences in the ability of different parties to reach primarily economics-minded voters where they lived.

An initial indication that Tunisian voters were not gripped by anxiety over the role of religion in public life is offered by the results of an *Arab Barometer* survey of 1,200 Tunisians conducted in advance of that country's constituent assembly elections.[9] As in Egypt, respondents were asked what issue they thought constituted the most important challenge facing their country. More than 70 percent named the economy, whereas fewer than 1 percent mentioned the new constitution or concern over maintaining (or reversing) the country's longstanding ban on polygamy (see Figure 7.6). When Tunisians were asked what their second highest priority was, fewer than 3 percent named the constitution and fewer than 2 percent the polygamy ban, with most voters naming internal security (23 percent), corruption (21 percent), and returning funds looted by the Bin ʿAlī regime (15 percent). As two gifted scholars of the Middle East and North Africa put it, "Tunisians voted for jobs, not Islam."[10]

However, if Tunisians did indeed vote for jobs, why did they believe that Islamists were the best guarantors of those jobs? The theory offered here would suggest that Islamists earn the benefit of the doubt because they are able to reach

9 The author thanks Amaney Jamal for generously sharing this data.

10 Michael Robbins and Mark Tessler, "Tunisians voted for jobs, not Islam," Foreign Policy Middle East Channel, http://mideast.foreignpolicy.com/posts/2011/12/07/tunisians_voted_for_jobs_not_islam; See also Issandr al-Amrani, "Tunisia moves to the next stage," MERIP http://www.merip.org/mero/mero110811

voters through religious institutions, while their secular and leftist opponents are restricted to relatively more limited networks of labor organizing. Though union membership in Tunisia (taken as a percentage of the population and not, as is standard practice, as a percentage of the nonagricultural and formal workforce) is 50 percent higher than in Egypt (4.7 percent to 3.0 percent), it remains low in absolute terms.[11] The Tunisian General Labor Union (al-Ittiḥād al-ʿām al-Tūnisī lil-shughl, abbreviated UGTT after its French name, Union Générale Tunisienne du Travail) claims 500,000 members. And though the UGTT appears to have played a more important role in the revolution that brought down Bin ʿAlī than its Egyptian counterpart played in the revolution that unseated Mubarak, this may have been less because of differences in the extent of union membership than because of structural differences between the two organizations. The UGTT, like its Egyptian counterpart was dominated by the regime (see Posusney 1997), but as Kamāl ʿAbbās, an Egyptian labor activist, argued, "the most important difference between the UGTT and the ETUF is that the representatives of the former are chosen via direct elections."[12] Similarly, a 2006 U.S. State Department cable written in advance of the UGTT's twenty-first general congress noted that "despite the leadership's pro-government stance, the UGTT is almost universally recognized as the most democratic Tunisian organization."[13] However, while this may have ensured the union's militance during the revolution, the relatively narrow vote base the UGTT represented suggested that the left's ability to cultivate suffrages through it would be limited. It's worth noting that in the Arab Barometer's 2011 survey of Tunisians, only 3 percent indicated membership in a labor union or syndicate.

If networks of labor activism were limited in Tunisia, those based on religion were not. Although the Tunisian regime tightly regulated the religious realm in order to prevent the emergence of Islamic challengers, the departure of Bin ʿAlī on January 14, 2011 meant that the country's religious infrastructure suddenly became available for Islamists to use to engage voters. Thus, as in Egypt, the density of religious networks should serve as a strong predictor of al-Nahḍa's eventual vote share. In order to test this proposition, I constructed a dataset of Tunisia's 262 second-level administrative units (*muʿtamadiyāt*, or delegations) that includes their socioeconomic characteristics, measures of mosque density, as well as the votes captured by each party in the October 2011 constituent assembly elections. I then conduct six ordinary least squares regressions, one for each of six major Tunisian political parties, in which the dependent variable is the party's vote share, and the key independent variables are measures of average socioeconomic status and mosque density. The six parties whose vote shares are analyzed are:

[11] Figures drawn from the website of the Tunisian General Labor Union: http://www.ugtt.org.tn/

[12] Jano Charbel, "State's union control keeps Egyptian labor quiet," Egypt Independent, January 21, 2011; available at: http://www.almasryalyoum.com/en/node/301820

[13] http://www.cablegatesearch.net/cable.php?id=06TUNIS2887

- *Ḥizb Ḥaraka al-Nahḍa* (Renaissance Movement Party): Founded in the early 1970s by independent Islamic thinker Rached al-Ghannouchi as the "Islamic Group," and in 1981 renamed the "Movement of the Islamic Trend," before becoming Ḥaraka al-Nahḍa (Renaissance Movement) in 1988, the movement was originally viewed by Habib Bourguiba's ruling Constitutional Socialist Party as a useful counterweight to the left (for the movement's history and development, see Hamdi (1998)). After winning close to 15 percent of the vote in Tunisia's 1989 parliamentary elections, the group was subject to a brutal crackdown, particularly after it was alleged that some of its members launched an armed attack against an office of the ruling party in 1991. Ghannouchi went into exile, and by some estimates, close to 25,000 members of al-Nahḍa were thrown into Bin ʿAlī's prisons. And though al-Nahḍa members are thought to have continued to operate underground during that period, allegedly infiltrating the country's main labor union (Alexander 2000), by all accounts the party's street presence was limited prior to Bin ʿAlī's resignation. As of July 2013, the party held eighty-nine seats in the 217-member constituent assembly.
- *al-ʿArīḍa al-Shaʿbiyya lil-Ḥurriya wa al-ʿAdāla wa al-Tanmiya* (Popular Petition for Freedom, Justice, and Development): Founded by former al-Nahḍa member Mohamed Hachmi Hamdi in 2011, this party – or, more accurately, electoral list – is often described as "populist" (Zeghal 2013), and appears to combine al-Nahḍa's demand for "respect for the Arab and Islamic identity of Tunis" (al-ʿArīḍa's campaign materials begin and end with the traditional Islamic greeting) with two worker-friendly demands: unemployment benefits and free healthcare for all. The list won twenty-six seats in the constituent assembly.
- *al-Muʾtamar min ajl al-Jumhūriya* (Congress for the Republic): Founded by Moncef Marzouki, a "left wing physician who went into exile after his party was banned in 2001" (El Amrani and Lindsey 2011), the party won twenty-nine seats in the constituent assembly. In December 2011, Marzouki was selected by the assembly to serve as the country's first postrevolutionary president.
- *al-Takattul al-Dimuqrāṭī min ajl al-ʿamal wa al-ḥurriyāt* (Democratic Forum for Labor and Liberties): Described as a "socialist" party (El Amrani and Lindsey 2011; El-Khawas (2012b)), the party won twenty seats in the constituent assembly elections.
- *al-Ḥizb al-Dimuqrāṭī al-Taqadumī* (Progressive Democratic Party): Led until 2012 by the feminist and human rights activist Maya Jribi, the party is described as "center-left" (Brody-Barre 2013) and holds sixteen seats in the assembly.
- *Ḥizb al-ʿUmmāl al-Shiyūʿī al-Tūnisī* (Tunisian Workers Communist Party): The party, whose ideological inclinations are perhaps self-evident, captured three seats in the October 2011 elections.

The independent variables are the share of the workforce in agriculture, the unemployment rate, the crowding rate (defined as the number of inhabitants per household room), the logged population, and, in order to capture the density of religious networks, the number of mosques per 10,000 inhabitants.[14] The results of the regression analyses are presented in Table 7.3. Though Zeghal (2013) argues that "the secularist parties' and al-Nahdha's constituencies are not necessarily that different in terms of their socioeconomic characteristics," the results of our regression analysis reveal that al-Nahḍa was more definitively urban than its competitors. The party seems to have cut across class lines, however, as revealed by the insignificant coefficient on our proxy for poverty, the crowding rate. For the purposes of our analysis here, however, the key variable of interest is mosque density. We find a positive and significant relationship between that variable and al-Nahḍa's vote share, whereas the relationship is insignificant for most parties, and is negative and significant at the 99 percent level for the leftist al-Takattul party.

Readers might object that mosque density is actually a proxy for religiosity, and that what this analysis shows is not that Islamists won by canvassing voters through pre-existing religious networks, but that places that were more religious tended to vote for al-Nahḍa. The only way to rule this out would be to demonstrate that the process by which mosques were generated and distributed in Tunisia was unrelated to the distribution of religiosity. After all, as we know, the Tunisian state heavily restricted all forms of religious activity, and was particularly likely to police so-called Islamist strongholds more heavily than others. A 2008 report indicates that the state required anyone wishing to build a mosque to demonstrate that the area in which they proposed to build was underserved relative to some arbitrary, state-determined ratio of mosques to people.[15] This regulation might mean that the most religious locales were ones – at least since 2008 – with the fewest, not most, mosques . All of this suggests that we cannot take mosque density as a straightforward indicator of popular religiosity, and that the correlation between mosque density and al-Nahḍa's vote share may be attributable to more than just the likelihood that more mosques signify more religious people.

Another, more powerful demonstration of the importance of local networks in determining vote shares can be found when we examine the spatial distribution of votes for some of al-Nahḍa's key competitors. Several commentators, for

[14] Thanks to Duncan Pickard and Safia Trabelsi for data assistance. Demographic data is drawn from the 2004 census conducted by the Tunisian National Institute for Statistics (al-Maʿhad al-Waṭanī lil-ʾiḥṣāʾ). Mosque data was provided by the Tunisian Ministry of Religious Affairs (Wizārat al-Shuʾūn al-Dīniyya). Both available from the author. Mosques are divided into two types: *masājid* (sing. *masjid*), which connotes smaller mosques akin to the Egyptian *zawāya* described in Chapter 6, and *jawāmiʿ* (sing. *jāmiʿ*), which are large mosques in which Friday prayers are offered.

[15] "*Tūnis tafriḍ shurūṭ jadīda li-bināʾ al-masājid minhā dhikr madā al-ḥāja* (Tunisia imposes new conditions on building mosques, including demonstrating need)," *al-Fajr* News (Tunis), April 6, 2008; available at: http://www.turess.com/alfajrnews/3680

Table 7.3 *Correlates of Party Vote Shares in Tunisian Constituent Assembly Election, October 2011*

	al-Nahḍa	al-ʿArīḍa	CPR	al-Takatul	PDP	CP
percent agriculture	−0.283***	0.158***	−0.0104	−0.00600	0.0202*	0.0421***
	(0.0364)	(0.0301)	(0.0157)	(0.0135)	(0.0110)	(0.0118)
percent unemployment	−0.101	0.0356	−0.0866**	−0.0442	0.0223	0.0454**
	(0.107)	(0.0722)	(0.0368)	(0.0345)	(0.0219)	(0.0200)
log population	1.878*	2.000***	0.881**	0.302	-0.278	−0.296
	(1.080)	(0.648)	(0.396)	(0.376)	(0.218)	(0.385)
Crowding rate	4.073	8.811***	−6.613***	−9.621***	-2.886***	−1.792***
	(2.604)	(2.054)	(1.170)	(1.140)	(0.730)	(0.668)
Mosques per 10K	0.796***	0.157	0.0474	-0.289***	−0.0601*	−0.0952
	(0.152)	(0.112)	(0.0920)	(0.0983)	(0.0336)	(0.0592)
Constant	11.27	-32.27***	9.435**	19.82***	10.61***	6.436
	(12.87)	(7.853)	(4.562)	(4.899)	(2.781)	(4.965)
Observations	262	262	262	262	262	239
R-squared	0.275	0.373	0.253	0.462	0.110	0.139

Standard errors in parentheses.
*** $p < 0.01$, ** $p < 0.05$, * $p < 0.1$.

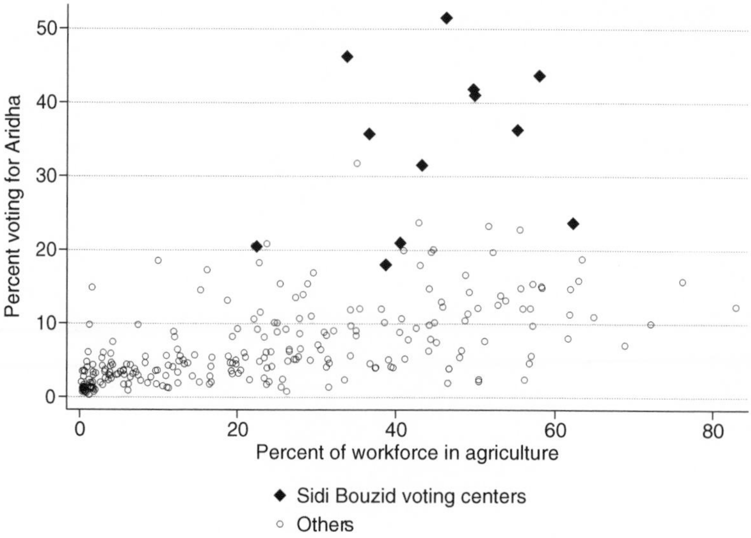

Figure 7.7 Vote share for al-ʿArīḍa al-Shaʿbiyya across Tunisian *muʿtamadiyyāt*, October 2011.

example, have noted that al-Nahḍa performed poorly in Sidi Bouzid, the central Tunisian province in which the December 17, 2010 self-immolation of a fruitseller, Muḥammad Abū ʿAzīzī, is thought to have sparked the uprising that led to the ouster of Bin ʿAlī scarcely one month later (Schraeder and Redissi 2011). According to the brilliant scholar of Islamism and North Africa, Malika Zeghal, al-Nahḍa's loss in the poor, rural Sidi Bouzid "speaks to a crucial line of [class] cleavage that is often ignored."[16] However, examining the distribution of votes for the list that performed best in Sidi Bouzid – al-ʿArīḍa al-Shaʿbiyya – suggests a different, and more mundane story. Figure 7.7 is a scatterplot of al-ʿArīḍa's vote share across Tunisia's 262 second-level administrative units, against the share of the workforce employed in agriculture. As we can see, al-ʿArīḍa's performance in Sidi Bouzid is a clear outlier – nowhere else was the party able to capture anywhere near a majority of the vote. The reason for this voting pattern is not mysterious – the party's founder, Hicham Hamdi, is a native son of Sidi Bouzid (Lindsay and El-Amrani 2011) and was very likely able to call on local loyalties at election time.

The same, incidentally, is true of voting for the second largest party in the constituent assembly, Marzouki's Congress for the Republic (CPR). Figure 7.8 is a scatterplot of CPR's vote shares across the country, against the share of the workforce in agriculture. As with al-ʿArīḍa's vote share, there is a clear set of outliers – this time in the southwestern province of Kebili. The reason for CPR's

[16] "The Arab Spring: What Next?" *Bulletin of the American Academy of Arts and Sciences*, Summer 2013, p. 19

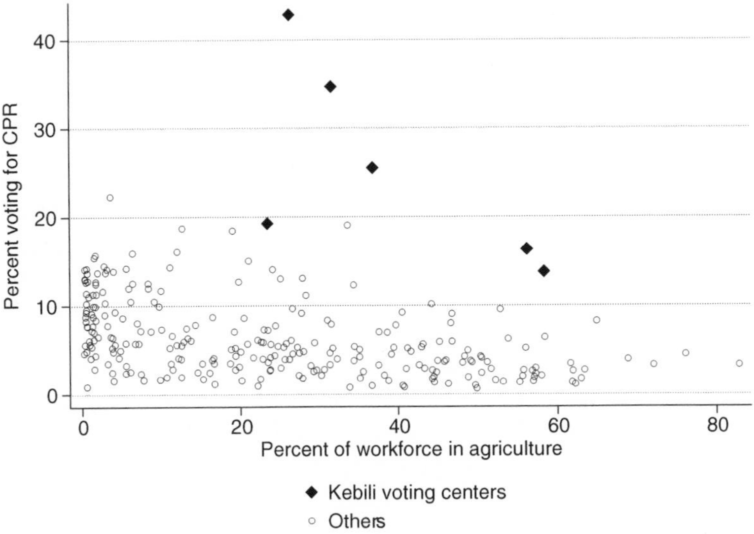

Figure 7.8 Vote share for CPR across Tunisian *mu'tamadiyyāt*, October 2011.

remarkably strong performance in that locale is not that voters there were somehow more ideologically receptive to leftist appeals, but that Marzouki hails from the Marāzīq tribe based in Douz, a town in Kebili. An illustration of the political importance of Marzouki's belonging to Douz and to his tribe is offered by a December 2012 speech that the Tunisian president gave on a visit to that district, in which he promised to address the region's chronic water shortages, and concluded with the rousing declaration, "Have faith in God, have faith in yourselves, have faith in Douz, and have faith in the Marāẓīq!"[17] What this all suggests is that, in the calculus of Tunisia's voters, ideology matters less than a candidate's or party's ability to credibly commit to serving voters, and the credibility of that commitment is greater the more embedded in the locality the candidate or the party is (Lust 2006). Interpreting the results of such elections through the lens of grand social cleavages, rather than through the connections parties have to voters, obscures as much as it illuminates.

Islamist weakness in Indonesia and Pakistan

The importance of mosque-density as a predictor of voting for Islamists in Tunisia, and of local connections as a predictor of voting for the CPR and al-ʿArīḍa al-Shaʿbiyya, reinforce the argument of this book – that Islamist victories

[17] Mosaique FM, "Al-Munṣif al-Marzūqī: Thiqū billāh, thiqū bi-dūz, thiqū fi al-marāzīq (Moncef Marzouki: Have faith in God, have faith in Douz, have faith in the Marāzīq," December 24, 2012; available at: http://www.youtube.com/watch?v=slHHjbqkdbg

are in part due to social landscapes in which religious forms of organization are dense and encompassing – a common feature of rural, agrarian societies like Egypt. But, given the broad similarity of other Muslim countries, such as Indonesia and Pakistan, to Egypt in terms of their levels of industrialization and the relative density of religious organizations, how can one account for the fact that democratic politics in both of those countries has failed to bring analogues of the Muslim Brotherhood to power? In Pakistan's 2002 National Assembly elections, the coalition of Islamic parties known as the United Action Front (Muttahida Majlis-i-Amal) earned 11.3 percent of the vote; but by the 2008 contests, that had declined to 2.2 percent (on account of a boycott by the Brotherhood-affiliated Jamaat-e-Islami). In 2013, the parties that had made up the Islamic coalition together earned 5.3 percent of the vote. In Indonesia's 2004 parliamentary elections, only 7.3 percent of voters cast ballots for the Muslim Brotherhood offshoot Partai Keadilan Sejahtera (Islamist Prosperous Justice Party), whereas in 2009, the PKS managed only a slight uptick in its vote share, polling at 7.88 percent.

However, far from undermining the theory presented here, these Islamist failures are of a piece with it. After all, as noted in Chapter 2, nonindustrialized societies are likely to be rich in both religious and clientelistic networks. The latter are rooted in family, clan, and relations of economic dependence (i.e. toward employers, landowners, local notables, agents of the state or ruling party). In Egypt, clientelistic networks built up during the authoritarian era were disrupted in the immediate aftermath of the January 2011 revolution, due to a judicial decision to dissolve the ruling National Democratic Party (which had integrated co-opted local notables), and a decision by the country's interim military rulers to shift the electoral system to one in which a majority of representatives were selected on the basis of party lists in geographically large districts. This move diminished the ability of candidates to call upon local vote banks in Egypt's founding elections. This reduction in the importance of traditional clientelistic networks could not help but to magnify the importance of the only other types of institution that existed in considerable density throughout Egypt – religious ones.

The case of Indonesia offers a stark contrast. In 1998, that country's strongman, Suharto, who had ruled since 1967, was forced to step down by protests remarkably similar to those of the "Arab Spring." The name that Indonesians gave to that event, however, was not revolution (or *revolusi* in Bahasa Indonesia) but rather reform (or *reformasi*). Where Egyptians put their dictator on trial and dissolved his ruling party, Indonesians allowed Suharto to retire from public life, and resisted calls to dissolve his ruling party, Partai Golongan Karya (the Party of Functional Groups) or Golkar for short. That party has won approximately 20 percent of the vote in each of the three legislative elections since Suharto's fall, and has been included in every post-Suharto cabinet but one. In other words, where Indonesia departs from Egypt is in the maintenance of the old ruling party's clientelistic networks. Tomsa (2009, 187) has written of Golkar's "extensive patronage networks that reach down to the remotest villages in South Sulawesi," and has suggested that even after Suharto's fall, "this pattern had essentially remained the same" (see also Tomsa 2008). The implication of the argument presented here is that if Golkar had been dissolved as the NDP was, the dynamics we observe in Egypt would have obtained there too: voters loosed from established clientelistic networks would likely have voted for candidates embedded in the religious networks they inhabit.

Moreover, if we look beyond Indonesia's Muslim Brotherhood-based party and instead examine vote shares of all Islamist parties in that country's first post-Suharto election, we see that Islamists have actually captured a significant share of legislative power. Religious life in Indonesia is dominated by two large Islamic societies – Nahdat-ul-Ulama (Renaissance of the Scholars, abbreviated NU), which boasts 40 million members, and the Muhammadiyah (which boasts 20 million). After Suharto's overthrow, each of these movements spawned a political party – NU gave rise to the National Awakening Party (Partai Kebangitan Bangsa, PKB), while Muhammadiya gave rise to the National Mandate Party (Partai Amanat Nasional, or PAN). In addition to these parties, the Islamist space was rounded out by the precursor to the Muslim Brotherhood's PKS (then called the Justice Party), as well as the Suharto-era Crescent Star and United Development parties. Together, these Islamists captured 33 percent of the vote, constituting the largest bloc in parliament, with 164 seats (Woodward 2008; Tanuwidjaja 2010).

Pakistan, like Indonesia, represents a case in which old clientelistic networks have remained undisrupted by expansions or constrictions of the country's volatile political space. As several scholars have noted, Pakistan today is a feudal society dominated by large landowners, and patron-client relations in rural areas continue to dominate voting behavior (Keefer, Narayan, and Vishwanath 2005; Tanwir 2002). There is little reason, then, to expect Islamist parties to be able to pierce these clientelistic relations. The extent of Pakistani feudalism is illustrated in Table 7.4, which indicates the breakdown of land ownership in Egypt, Indonesia, and Pakistan (data is drawn from the UN's Food and Agriculture Organization). The average size of landholdings in Pakistan is much larger than either Egypt or Indonesia, and the percentage of landholdings over 2 hectares (a threshold that appears in the literature to distinguish large from small-scale farming) is 4 times larger than in Indonesia, and 10 times larger than in Egypt. If Pakistan's feudal clientelistic networks had suffered the same kind of disruption as the patronage-based networks of the NDP in postrevolutionary Egypt, we might very well expect Islamist parties to pick up the slack through their superior embeddedness in the religious social institutions that exist in considerable density throughout that country (Weinbaum 1996).

7.3 Progressivism or populism?

One of the most important implications of this study has been to problematize settled narratives of the left's political enfeeblement in Egypt and the Arab world more broadly. Where most have located the source of leftist weakness in the

Table 7.4 *Patterns of Landholding in Indonesia, Pakistan, and Egypt*

Country	No. holdings	Total area (ha)	Avg. size (ha)	No. over 2 ha	% over 2 ha	year
Indonesia	24,868,675	19,673,412	0.79	2,801,627	11.27	2003
Pakistan	6,620,224	20,437,554	3.09	2,805,261	42.37	2000
Egypt	4,541,884	3,750,699	0.83	188,831	4.16	2000

"failed" legacies of Arab socialism or the collapse of the Soviet Union or in the purposive actions of the authoritarian state, this book has argued that the left's problem is not ideological but developmental. Vast majorities of Egyptian citizens, after all, articulate economic preferences that could have been torn from the pages of Marx and Engels, giving the lie to the notion that they believe the economic programs of the left to have been tried and failed. The reason that leftist parties appear unable to convert this palpable demand for redistributive and welfare-statist policies into actual political power is that, unlike the Islamists, they possess precious few avenues for communicating their policy commitments to the voting public. A party's proximity to the median voter on matters of economic policy is of little moment when the median voter is unable to discover this fact.

What does this mean for Islamists in future elections? It may seem quaint to inquire after the electoral prospects for non-Islamist parties in the wake of a military coup and subsequent crackdown that seems likely to prevent Islamists from competing in future elections at all, but electoral life is almost certain to resume in Egypt, and it is worth asking what pro-poor parties can do to become genuinely competitive. Readers of this book might come to one of three conclusions. The first is that if parties of the left want to win future elections, they must don religious garb, get themselves to the nearest mosque, and adorn their rhetoric with Islamic embellishments. The great Egyptian leftist and NPUR activist, Muhammad Sid-Ahmed (1982, 19), proposed just such a strategy more than thirty years ago: "We cannot leave this [religious] arena to the fanatic forces. We should have our own presence within it, with the people, speaking its language." But his description of the contours of this strategy is eloquent of its ultimate limits. Sid-Ahmed – speaking in 1982 – reports that, "Throughout the month of Ramadan, both last year and this year," his party was "very active at the nightly gatherings that follow the days of fasting. [...] We would begin with one sheikh talking, and then our activists would speak" (1982, 22). Given his party's lamentable performance in subsequent parliamentary elections, it appears that such stage-managed, overtly political interventions in religious social networks are likely to be inferior to the organic embeddedness of Islamic activists in everyday networks of religious activity.

The second conclusion, based on our analysis of the local bases of presidential candidates' vote shares, is that parties should attempt to embed themselves more deeply in local networks of kinship and notability, particularly by recruiting candidates with their own vote banks. As we have seen, this happened to a limited extent in Egypt's founding election, and is almost certain to increase in the coming period, as former regime allies who had been sent into disarray by the dissolution of the ruling party – and perhaps momentarily tainted by their association with it – have now had a decent interval in which to regroup. The strong performance of Aḥmad Shafīq in the 2012 presidential election, in which former ruling party networks were deployed to mobilize votes on his behalf, might thus be a prelude to the resurrection of the politics of patronage and local notability. But while this would introduce a measure of pluralism into an electoral environment once dominated by Islamists, it is unlikely to be encouraging to the left. For, just as the politics of clientelism strangled pro-poor parties during the Mubarak years, so too can it be expected to suffocate them in the future.

The third conclusion would be that the only hope for the emergence of a genuine pro-poor alternative in Egypt is for that country to enact laws to make it easier for the country's workers to organize collectively. As noted in Chapter 1, Egypt's main labor federation has long been tightly controlled by the state, and as a result labor militancy has generally had to occur outside of it (Beinin 2005, 2012). During its brief reign, the Muslim Brotherhood sought to regulate labor activism, both in order to assuage capital and to prevent the emergence of an organizational base through which leftists could pose a challenge to Islamist dominance. In 2012, for example, the Brotherhood-led ministry of manpower introduced a bill that would eliminate independent trade unions and impose harsh punishments on striking workers.[18] Reversing such regulations would undoubtedly help the cause of labor in Egypt, but we should not expect this to fundamentally change the balance of power in Egyptian politics. Unless informal workers and small-holding farmers are also organized collectively – a notoriously difficult task (Sanyal 1991; Garay 2007) – the labor movement cannot encompass more than a small minority of citizens. What all of this suggests is that the road before progressives is likely to be a long one, and that the fall of Islamists will no more lead to the rise of the left than did the fall of Mubarak.

Have the Islamists really fallen, anyway? And is their descent likely to be permanent? The evidence is inconclusive. On the one hand, it is a measure of how intense popular passion against the Muslim Brotherhood had become that, by the end of Morsi's time in power, the movement had begun to lose its preferential access to the religious social institutions with which it had worked for so long. For example, in March 2013, the Egyptian newspaper *al-Shurūq* reported that in elections to the board of directors of the JS in the town of al-Sanṭa in al-Gharbiyya, the Muslim Brotherhood's candidates for the five open slots were

[18] Muḥammad Māhir, "al-ʿUmmāl fi ʿahd Mursī (Workers in the reign of Morsi)," al-Miṣrī al-Yawm (Cairo), June 29, 2013; available at: http://www.almasryalyoum.com/node/1893026; Cam McGrath, "Morsi Slams New Lid on Labour Rights," Inter Press Service, January 24, 2013; available at: http://www.ipsnews.net/2013/01/morsi-slams-new-lid-on-labour-rights/

all defeated, having collectively captured just under a third of the 610 votes cast.[19] On the other hand, the current resurgence of the former ruling party's supporters should serve as ample testament to the possibility of bouncing back from what appears to be national rejection. The economic challenges that (at least partially) inspired the revolution against Mubarak – high unemployment and a retrenchment of state commitments to social welfare – and which stoked dissent against Mohamed Morsi are likely to persist. We should not be surprised if Islamists are eventually able to capitalize on them.

Even if the alternative that Egyptians settle on is not Islamist, it's unlikely to be leftist. Given the foregoing analysis, the emergence of progressive forces seems less probable than the emergence of populist ones. The maintenance of Egypt's presidential system means that personal charisma and money will play an important role in the shaping of that country's future political landscape. Presidential elections, after all, are ultimately contests between persons. Organizational factors may matter on the margins, but the extensive media coverage provided to presidential candidates can enable them to compensate for their organizational deficits with their personal attributes. The Muslim Brotherhood may have been able to dominate local elections, where the movement's politicians were more embedded, but those advantages diminish in presidential contests, where a few favorable television interviews can make a previously little-known presidential aspirant such as Ḥamdīn Ṣabāḥī as much a household name as the storied Muslim Brotherhood.

Readers, of course, are unlikely to be buoyed by the suggestion that personalistic, presidential politics offer the best hope for non-Islamist politics in Egypt. If a nonsectarian, pro-poor politics is doomed to failure unless yoked to the charisma of a populist political entrepreneur, can it truly be considered progressive? And if such stunted pluralism requires presidentialism – a system whose dysfunctions are well known (Linz 1990), and that all seem to have been on display in Egypt in the year following Morsi's election – is it worth the price?

[19] ʿAlāʾ Shibl, "Khusārat murashaḥī al-Ikhwān fī intikhābāt al-Jamʿiyya al-Sharʿiyya bil-Gharbiyya (Defeat of the candidates of the Brothers in the elections of the JS)," al-Shurūq (Cairo), March 30, 2013; available at: http://shorouknews.com/news/view.aspx?cdate=30032013&id=7f35aa05-f62f-4ee1-a32a-7775580db35d

8

Conclusion

This book has been an attempt to discern how much Islam "counts" in explaining the steady victories of Islamist parties in Egypt over the past 30 years. The conventional wisdom has held that Egypt's politics have long been marked by an existential struggle between a great majority that desires the application of God's law, and a small minority, empowered and armed by the West, that has sought to deny that majority its fondest ambition. This book, in reanalyzing the last several decades of Egyptian political history, and by exploring variation in Islamist performance over time and across space, offers an alternative account. It argues that the persistence of Islamists in electoral politics of the authoritarian era, and their dominance in the elections that took place after the end of that era, were born not of a grand passion for Islam, but of structural factors that are on the one hand more quotidian, but on the other just as profound in their effects.

As we have seen, the Brotherhood won elections under authoritarianism by appealing to affluent voters who could afford to cast their ballots as paper stones against an authoritarian regime. The poor, contrary to the expectations of the great body of theorizing, voted not for Islamists, but for those close to the regime who could promise to deliver to them the material benefits they so desperately needed. When the democratic floodgates were thrown open, the Brotherhood and its Islamist allies were able to capture these voters as well, benefiting from the superior opportunities for linkage offered by the country's dense religious networks, and for which parties of the left had no analogue.

This resource asymmetry between Islamists and their rivals, I have argued, is largely a function of development. In a poor, nonindustrialized country full of religious social institutions, and relatively deprived of those based on class or occupation, it was natural that politicians embedded in those institutions would have ready-made conduits for reaching out to voters, and for convincing them that Islamist parties would not just be good for the faith, but good for the finances as well. Put simply, the dominance of Islamist parties in Egypt's founding elections was less about the structure of conflict in that society than it was about the structure of communities.

The argument presented here challenges our understanding of the relationship between political parties and social cleavages. Scholars dating back to Lipset and Rokkan (1967) have argued that the structure of a country's party system is somehow reflective of the fundamental lines of conflict over values in that society. For example, the rise of socialist parties is thought to reflect underlying class cleavages (Hechter 2004); the emergence of confessional parties is thought to reflect the salience of sectarian identities (Kalyvas 1996); and the rise of Green parties in the latter half of the twentieth century is said to reflect the newfound importance of concerns over the environment (Kitschelt 1989). Scholars have of course problematized this account. They have asked, for example, whether social cleavages are exogenous to parties, or are created and reinforced by them (Przeworski and Sprague 1986; Bartolini 2007; Desai 2002). And they have investigated the conditions under which parties "evolve" from their roots as ideologically committed warriors on one side of a particular social cleavage to become "catch-all" parties, appealing beyond the narrow sectional interests in which those parties were incubated (Kircheimer 1966). But what binds all of these accounts is their assumption that party systems are – if only at their moments of formation – eloquent of the structure of mass opinion in a given society. The evidence in this book suggests that, at least in the case of Islamist politics in postrevolutionary Egypt, such an assumption is mistaken.

There are three important implications of this argument. The first is that the spectacular dominance of Islamists in Egyptian and Arab electoral politics was always far more fragile than it appeared. Built on worldly promises, it would ultimately prove highly sensitive to Islamists' ability to fulfill those promises. This would not be the case if the voters who catapulted Islamists into office did so primarily because they were in search of guardians of the faith who would ensure the primacy of sharīʿa and the centrality of Islam to Egyptian identity. If a passion for Islam is what drove voters in Egypt's founding elections, the Muslim Brotherhood and its allies might still be in power today. Instead, we saw that voters defected from Islamists almost as soon as they elected them, once the Brotherhood and its allies began to build up a record of policymaking that could be assessed against their outsized oaths. The argument presented here therefore provides an important theoretical underpinning to Kurzman and Naqvi's (2010) observation that Islamist parties tend to lose votes after founding elections. Since Islamist victories are primarily the function of superior opportunities for reaching voters during founding moments, and since what those voters care about is not *sharīʿa* but their material well-being, the contraction of support for the forces of political Islam is as unsurprising as their initial rise to power was.

The second implication of this argument, however, is that the transience of Islamist dominance does not mean that the left's political lassitude is similarly impermanent. This is not because there is no popular desire for the policies and programs of the left. Though Bassam Tibi (2009) may have been correct to describe the Arab left as a "*quantité négligeable*" with "no enduring effect," we have seen that there is a large constituency for the redistributive and welfare-statist policies that are supposedly the special province of left parties. The reason that such parties are unable to capitalize on this unmet demand is not because faith trumps economic interest, or because leftist ideology is unattractive, or because left party leaders are strategically and organizationally inept, or because leftist parties were the recipients of disproportionate attention of autocratic coercive apparatuses, but because those parties operate under severe structural disadvantages born of underdevelopment itself. Consequently, though this book comes to offer some measure of redemption to the much maligned Arab left, it is, ultimately, closer to a counsel of despair. Islamists may have been thrust out of office, but the structural disadvantages that made the left unable to benefit from Mubarak's ouster unfortunately persist. As the examples of Pakistan and Indonesia attest, even in the absence of Islamists, as long as the poor remain encapsulated in traditional clientelistic networks, they will more often than not be trapped into trading their suffrages for material succor.

Finally, in addition to shedding light on the rise (and fall) of political Islam, the argument in this book also helps us to understand the reasons for the collapse of Egypt's democratic experiment (or, to put it more optimistically, the end of that experiment's first phase). On June 30, millions of Egyptians took to the streets to demand President Mohamed Morsi's resignation, and when this was not forthcoming, on July 3rd the minister of defense, ʿAbd al-Fattāḥ al-Sīsī, announced the suspension of the constitution and Morsi's removal from office. In the remainder of this chapter, I demonstrate how the actions of both the Islamists and their opponents in the months preceding the president's overthrow are consistent with the dynamics explored in this book. I conclude by examining the likelihood that Islamists will avenge the abrogation of their victory at the ballot box by turning away from elections and toward violence. I contend that, partially due to the Muslim Brotherhood's long history of electoral participation, there is a much greater fund of democratic commitment within that movement than many of its critics give it credit for. Whether that will be enough to keep the Islamist movement from embracing death is an open question.

8.1 Causes of the Collapse

Some might argue that the mass movement that prefigured Morsi's overthrow casts doubt on my contention that the dominant cleavage in Egyptian politics is not a religious one. To many, the so-called *tamarud* (rebel) movement, which organized the anti-Morsi protests of June 30, 2013, was not simply an expression of discontent with his and the Muslim Brotherhood's inability to manage the country's affairs, but was a popular rejection of the Brotherhood's religious nature as well. This new narrative of the sources of popular antipathy to the Muslim Brotherhood is the mirror image of the older story of popular acclaim for the movement. Where once we were told that Egyptians were mainly Islamists, now we are told that they see in the Islamist agenda a threat to their very identity.[1] There are as many reasons to doubt this new narrative as there were to doubt the old one. Although the *tamarud* movement certainly included those whose opposition to the Morsi government, and the Muslim Brotherhood more broadly, was built on an antipathy to the Islamist project, the movement's public statements make little mention of Islam or *sharīʿa*. The *tamarud* petition provides seven reasons to justify its call for Morsi's ouster, and opposition to *sharīʿa* figures nowhere in them:

> Because security has still not been restored … we don't want you
>
> Because the poor one still has no place … we don't want you
>
> Because we still beg from abroad … we don't want you
>
> Because justice for the martyrs has still not been achieved … we don't want you
>
> Because there is no dignity for me or my country … we don't want you
>
> Beause the economy has collapsed and has become based on begging … we don't want you
>
> Because Egypt is still dependent on the Americans … we don't want you.[2]

But if the *tamarud* petition illustrates that Brotherhood's championing of the *sharīʿa* was not the reason millions of Egyptians rose up against it, it also illustrates why the movement's dedication to *sharīʿa* was unable to keep it in power. As we have seen throughout this book, the Brotherhood's claim to rule was always based not on claims of superior fidelity to the faith, but on claims of superior ability to do well by Egypt, to deliver to Egyptians the economic development and egalitarianism that had eluded them for the past 30 years. When the movement failed to do this, it mattered little that it was the self-styled vanguard of *sharīʿa*. In a country where everyone pays a healthy and sincere lipservice to the role of Islam in public life, wrapping oneself in the mantle of Islam is insufficient to distinguish oneself, let alone stay in power. If religious purity were the thing voters thought they were purchasing with their suffrages, we would expect those voters to insist on keeping Islamists in office, regardless of the slowing of the economy, the decay of public services, or the steady erosion of public order. If religion were truly possessed of the totemic power that observers of the Muslim world have long assigned to it, then it would take a great deal more than a few months of fuel shortages, blackouts, or inflation to cause the faithful to turn their backs on it.

But turn their backs on it they did. As noted in Chapter 7, the Muslim Brotherhood had forfeited much popularity in the months since that first

[1] See, for example, Wael Nawara, "It's the Egyptian Identity, Stupid," Al Monitor, July 2, 2013; available at: http://www.al-monitor.com/pulse/originals/2013/07/egyptian-identity-stupid.html

[2] For the most sophisticated treatment of the dynamics of anti-Americanism in the Arab world, in which all sides of any conflict almost invariably believe the United States to be behind their opponents, see Jamal (2012).

post-Mubarak victory. A measure of how much ground the Muslim Brotherhood had lost is offered by a comparison of the results of two surveys, conducted by the Egyptian Research and Training Center, almost two years apart – the first in December 2011, the second in June 2013 (see Figure 8.1).[3] In both surveys, respondents were asked to state how much confidence they had in the Muslim Brotherhood. In the 2011 survey, conducted in proximity to the country's first parliamentary elections, more than 40 percent of respondents claimed to be "very confident" in the movement, with only around a quarter of voters claiming to have "no confidence." In the second survey, conducted in proximity to the mass anti-Morsi protests and subsequent military coup, the share of respondents claiming to have no confidence in the Brotherhood had swelled to more than 60 percent.

All of this raises a question, however. Given the massive public discontent with Morsi, why did the opposition support a military coup, rather than dedicating its energies to capitalizing on this anger against the Islamists at the ballot box? A close examination of the demands of the opposition and of the government in the months leading up to the coup suggests that the opposition *did* want an election – just not the kind of election that the government wanted. In fact, I argue that the battle between Islamists and their opponents is properly understood not as a struggle over the place of religion in public life. Instead, it was a battle over a relatively narrow institutional matter – whether to have presidential or parliamentary elections. Morsi and the Brotherhood naturally preferred the latter, and had tentatively scheduled the parliamentary contest for April 2013 (before these plans were derailed by the Constitutional Court, which rejected the proposed electoral law).[4] Shortly after the army's announcement of the coup, Morsi once again called for the "rapid conduct of the upcoming parliamentary elections so that we can create a parliament in accordance with the already extant Egyptian constitution."[5] The president's opponents, on the other hand, wanted a presidential contest. United in a temporary National Salvation Front (*Jabhat al-Inqādh al-Waṭanī*) – led by Mohamed ElBaradei and former presidential candidates Ḥamdīn Ṣabāḥī and Amre Moussa – they refused anything short of a reset of the presidential election that had brought Morsi to power a year earlier.[6]

3 Thanks to Dr. Hisham Hellyer, director of the Tahrir Trends Project that commissioned the June 2013 survey, for sharing this data. See http://tahrirsquared.com/node/5561.

4 "Mursī yadʿū li-intikhābāt barlamāniyya ʿalā arbaʿ marāḥil tabdaʾ 27 Ibrīl (Morsi calls for parliamentary elections in four stages beginning April 27)," al-ʿArabiyya, February 21, 2013, available at: http://www.alarabiya.net/articles/2013/02/21/267451.html. See also, "Egypt court rejects election law, may delay poll," Reuters, February 18, 2013, available at: http://www.reuters.com/article/2013/02/18/us-egypt-election-idUSBRE91H08820130218

5 Translation available at: http://austingmackell.wordpress.com/2013/07/04/morsis-post-coup-speech-translated/

6 "*Jabhat al-inqādh: lā badīl ʿan al-intikhābāt al-riʾāsiyya al-mubakira* (Salvation Front: No Substitute for Early Presidential Elections," *al-ʿArabiyya,* June 27, 2013.

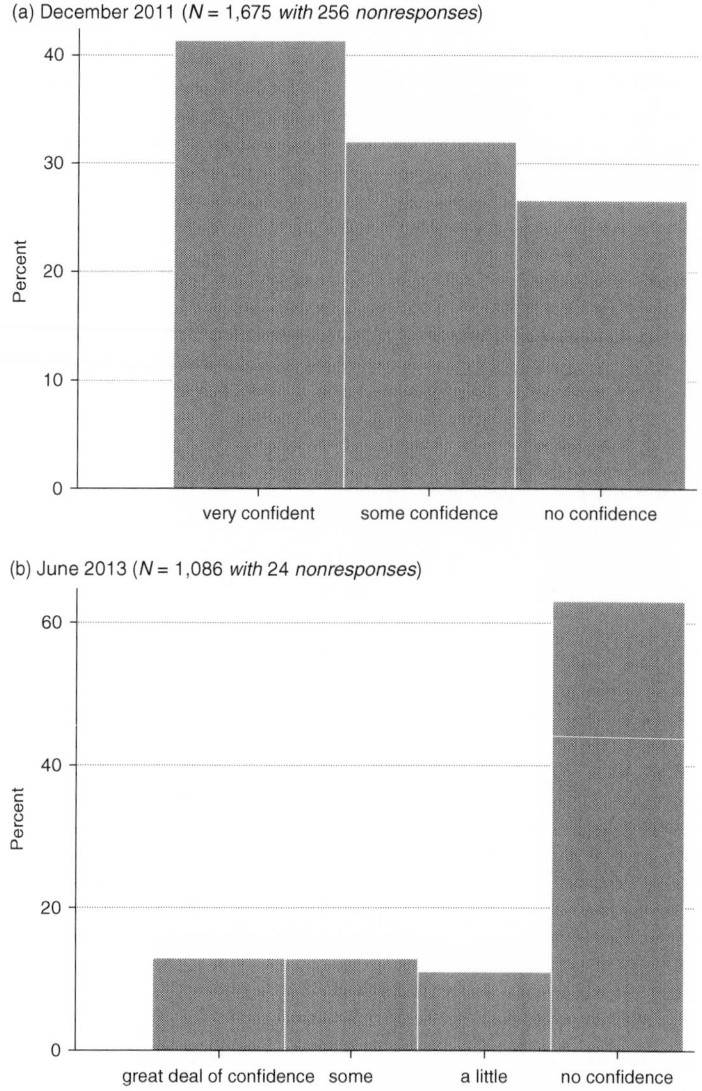

Figure 8.1 Voter confidence in the Muslim Brotherhood in the post-Mubarak era.

What explains each side's preferences, and why was each side so intransigent? Non-Islamists have argued that they could not risk allowing Morsi three more years to consolidate power.[7] The scholar Jason Brownlee has described how the

[7] Amīn Ṣāliḥ and Īmān ʿAlī, "*al-Barādʿī li-CNN: Mursī ʿaṭal al-dimuqrāṭiyya* (ElBaradei to CNN: Morsi has stalled democracy)," *al-Yawm al-Sābiʿ* (Cairo), July 5, 2013, available at: http://www1.youm7.com/News.asp?NewsID=1149250#.UoFtQZTXRcl

ousted president "used a familiar bag of dirty tricks against his opponents while his partisans captured the state."[8] But opposition fears of the "Brotherhoodization of the state" (*akhwanat ul-dawla*) are undermined by the fact that an opposition victory in Morsi's proposed parliamentary elections would have given the opposition a surfeit of instruments with which to thwart the president's alleged designs. If the opposition had run for parliament and earned a majority, article 139 of the constitution – passed in December 2012 by the Muslim Brotherhood-dominated legislature – would have allowed it to select the prime minister and the cabinet, thus enabling the opposition to isolate the president almost entirely. Moreover, article 152 of the constitution would have even made it possible for them to expel the president from office, if they could get two-thirds of the vote in the legislature. It is thus difficult to credit the argument that early presidential elections were necessary to prevent Morsi from consolidating power. An opposition success in the parliamentary elections that Morsi called for would have offered it ample opportunities for clipping Morsi's and the Muslim Brotherhood's wings.

The common response to this argument is that legislative elections held under a Morsi presidency were sure to be manipulated.[9] Tharwat al-Kharabāwī, a self-described former Muslim Brotherhood member and one of the foremost critics of the group, warned in March 2013 that the Muslim Brotherhood was planning to rig parliamentary elections, and likened the movement's assurances of "international and civil society monitoring to ensure the fairness of elections" to the empty promises made in "Banana Republics."[10] Shortly after the coup, the writer Waḥīd ʿAbd al-Magīd elaborated on the opposition's fears:

> No one outside the Muslim Brotherhood and its supporters trusted in the fairness of any parliamentary elections under Morsi and the government of [Prime Minister] Hishām Qandīl. It is clear enough that preparations for rigging these elections had begun in earnest through the [Brotherhood's] hegemony over the relevant ministries and executive agencies. The rigging of parliamentary elections would have yielded results that contradicted the true balance of power on the ground, and which would have weakened in turn the legitimacy of the call for early presidential elections.[11]

It is not possible for us to know whether the fears of the president's opponents were well-founded, although it is worth asking why they believed that early presidential elections were less likely to be rigged than parliamentary ones.

8 Brownlee, "Morsi Was No Role Model for Islamic Democrats," Middle East Institute, July 17, 2013.

9 "Radan ʿalā shāʾiʿāt tazwīr al-intikhābāt al-muqbila (In response to rumors that coming elections will be rigged)," www.fjp.com (website of the Freedom and Justice Party), June 1, 2013; available at: http://fj-p.com/article.php?id=64321

10 Samāḥ al-Gamāl, "*al-Kharabāwī: Akhshā min tazwīr al-intikhābāt* (al-Kharabāwī: I fear the rigging of elections)," *al-Ahrām* (Cairo), March 16, 2013; available at: http://gate.ahram.org.eg/News/321583.aspx

11 Waḥīd ʿAbd al-Majīd, "*Ijtihādāt Hishām Qandīl: Shukran?* (The judgements of Hishām Qandīl: Thank you?)," *al-Ahrām* (Cairo), July 30, 2013; available at: http://digital.ahram.org.eg/Policy.aspx?Serial=1364428

And, given the Egyptian military's subsequent muscular intervention in domestic politics, one is further left to wonder why the opposition did not just call for the military to safeguard the parliamentary election process. That task would certainly have been far less costly for all involved than the overthrow of Egypt's first democratically elected president.

If the opposition's reasons for rejecting Morsi's call for parliamentary elections are unconvincing, Morsi's and the Muslim Brotherhood's reasons for refusing to budge are equally problematic. In an interview with a British newspaper, Morsi argued that acquiescing to the opposition's demands would do violence to the principal of constitutionalism: "If we changed someone in office who [was elected] according to constituitional legitimacy – well, there will be people opposing the new president too, and a week or month later they will ask him to step down."[12] This argument runs contrary, however, to the many peaens to the notion of "people power" offered by the president and other Brotherhood leaders throughout Egypt's transitional period. For example, in a June 2012 interview with the Egyptian writer ʿImād Adīb, then-candidate Morsi explicitly invited voters to take to the streets to hold him accountable, declaring, "Trust me, for I will never betray you, nor betray God, and the Square is available [to you] otherwise."[13]

The real reason that the opposition rejected parliamentary elections and Morsi rejected a presidential one is that neither side thought it could win the elections favored by the other. The opposition resisted parliamentary elections because they feared that the Muslim Brotherhood's unpopularity might not be enough to overcome the Islamists' still-considerable resource advantage. After all, the revolution of 2011 had not changed the fundamental alchemy of Egypt's politics or its associational life. The non-Islamist opposition remained bereft of the infrastructure that would allow it to reach the vast majority of voters. They faced the formidable challenge of identifying non-Islamist candidates in each of the country's electoral constituencies who could call on local allegiances to match those of the Islamists, incorporating them all into a national opposition front, and waging district-by-district campaigns against Muslim Brotherhood and Islamist candidates who, for all of the flaws of their parties or their president, remained deeply embedded in local communities.

A presidential election, from the opposition's standpoint, was a different matter. It was much easier for the opposition to envision coordinating around a single presidential candidate, a charismatic figure such as Ḥamdīn Ṣabāḥī or a "wise man" such as Amre Moussa, who could reap votes simply by serving as the focus

[12] David Hearst and Patrick Kingsley, "Egypt's Mohamed Morsi Remains Defiant as Fears of Civil War Grow," *The Guardian* (London), June 30, 2014, available at: http://www.theguardian.com/world/2013/jun/30/egypt-mohamed-morsi-defiant-civil-war

[13] Muṣṭafā al-Rāmiḥ, "Mursī lil-Miṣriyīn: Lan akhūnakum abadan wa idhā ḥadath al-mīdān mawjūd (Morsi to Egyptians: I will not betray you ever, and if I do, the Square is available)," *al-Badil* (Cairo), June 8, 2012, available at: http://www.el-balad.com/184969.aspx

of popular anger with Mohamed Morsi. After all, when respondents in the June 2013 survey cited above were asked whether their lives had improved or worsened since Morsi's election to the presidency, more than 63 percent said their lives had worsened. Only 11 percent said their lives had improved. For his part, the president was probably aware of his dwindling popularity. The anger in the streets, not to mention the narrowness of his electoral victory a year prior against former Mubarak protégé Aḥmad Shafīq, likely convinced him that he could not prevail in a new electoral contest. Rather than risk an election, then, Morsi chose instead to put Egypt's fledgling democracy at risk. Brandishing his claim to democratic legitimacy like a weapon, he was soon to find that it could not help but prove impotent in the face of the real weapons carried by the men in uniform.

8.2 Recquiescat in Pace?

Twenty years ago, Edward Djerejian, a former American diplomat, famously worried that Islamists would exploit democratic elections to come to power, after which they would replace democracy with Islamic theocracy. Instead of "one man, one vote," he said, Islamists would usher in "one man, one vote, one time."[14] Of course, it is easy now to say that Djerejian was wrong, that the decades we spent fretting over the democratic commitments of Islamists were wasted, that what we should have been doing was inquiring after the democratic commitments of so-called liberals and secularists. Though the Egyptian novelist Alaa al-Aswany has written that Morsi "climbed the democratic ladder to power only to kick it away after him so that no one else could join him up there," it is hard not to conclude that something very different happened.[15] Islamists didn't kick the democratic ladder out behind them; so-called liberals pulled the democratic rug out from under them.

Of course, one might counter that the Muslim Brotherhood's conduct during its year in power offers considerable evidence that Djerejian and al-Aswany were right. The bill of particulars against President Morsi is vague, but central to it is a lack of "inclusivity." For example, in a statement on the military coup and subsequent slaughter of pro-Morsi protesters, U.S. President Barack Obama declared that, "While Mohamed Morsi was elected President in a democratic election, his government was not inclusive and did not respect the views of all Egyptians."[16] The coup's architect, General ʿAbd al-Fattāḥ al-Sīsī, complained to the *Washington Post* on August 3 that Morsi's removal was necessary because the Muslim Brother was "not a president for all Egyptians, but a president representing his

[14] Edward Djerejian, "The US and the Middle East in a Changing World," Dispatch (U.S. Department of State), Vol. 3, No. 23, June 8, 1992 (http://dosfan.lib.uic.edu/ERC/briefing/dispatch/1992/html/Dispatchv3no23.html

[15] Alaa al-Aswany, "Egypt's Two Front War for Democracy," *New York Times*, November 10, 2013

[16] "Remarks by the President on the Situation in Egypt," August 15, 2013, Chilmark, Massachusets; available at: http://www.whitehouse.gov/the-press-office/2013/08/15/remarks-president-situation-egypt

followers and supporters." In an August 18 speech to members of the police and armed forces, al-Sīsī swore that the Muslim Brotherhood had revealed to him "that they came to rule for 500 years."

One of the most damning actions taken by Morsi during his year in power was his decision, in November 2012, to issue a series of unilateral amendments to the Egyptian constitution, in which he declared that his word was "final and binding and cannot be appealed by any way or to any entity," and that he was empowered to "take the necessary actions and measures to protect the country and the goals of the revolution."[17] According to Jason Brownlee, this was the equivalent of an *auto-golpe,* an abrogation of democracy every bit as egregious as his ouster at the point of a gun eight months later.[18] Though Morsi was ultimately forced to rescind that decree, to many it revealed something fundamentally authoritarian about the president and the movement of which he was a part, and thus legitimated a popular, extra-constitutional movement to oust him.

The president's supporters, in contrast, justify his actions as necessary to protect Egypt's fledgling democracy against the depredations of the leftovers of the Mubarak regime, particularly within the judiciary. For example, the president's supporters charge that Morsi's had to declare himself above judicial review because the judiciary had proven itself eminently hostile to Egypt's democratic experiment. Most notably, on the eve of Morsi's election in June 2012, the Supreme Constitutional Court dissolved the Islamist-dominated lower house of parliament that had been elected six months earlier.[19] By the time of Morsi's November constitutional declaration, it appeared as if the court was preparing

17 "Naṣ al-ʾiʿlān al-dustūrī al-jadīd aladhi aṣdarahu Mursī (Text of new constitutional declaration issued by Morsi)," al-Taḥrīr (Cairo), November 25, 2012; available at: http://tahrirnews.com/news/view.aspx?cdate=22112012&id=dc690e5c-b4a7-4c60-a7ae-f8d2089022ce

18 Jason Brownlee, "Morsi Was No Role Model for Islamic Democrats," Middle East Institute, July 17, 2013; available at: http://www.mei.edu/content/morsi-was-no-role-model-islamic-democrats

19 See *"Iṣdār al-ḥukm fī qaḍiyat raqam 20 lisanat 34 qaḍāʾiyya dustūriyya* (Issuance of ruling in case number 20 for the 34th judicial year," *al-Jarīda al-Rasmiyya* (Official Gazette), No. 24, June 14, 2012. It is beyond the scope of this book to critique the logic of the ruling, but this author believes that it was fatally flawed. To summarize, the court ruled that the parliament must be dissolved because the electoral law under which it was constituted violated article 7 of Egypt's interim constitution, which mandated that all citizens must have equal opportunities to participate in politics. The critical issue was the fact that the electoral law, which divided Egypt into two electoral tiers – a party list tier with two-thirds of the seats, and an individual candidacy (*fardī*) tier with the remaining third – allowed *both* partisans and non-partisans to run in the individual candidacy tier. The court believed that allowing partisans to run in the individual candidacy tier meant that partisans were being given greater political opportunities than non-partisans. The court had used this logic before, to dissolve both the 1984 and 1987 parliaments (the former, readers will recall, had been elected on an all-party list system, while the latter had reserved approximately 10 percent of seats for independents).

However, this author argues that the court's logic was inapplicable to the 2012 parliament, because the interim constitution then in effect was different in important respects from the 1971 constitution on which the court had based its earlier rulings. Specifically, although article 7 of the interim constitution did call for equality, article 38 of the same document specified *explicitly* an electoral system in which partisans were allocated more seats than nonpartisans (i.e. two-thirds to to dissolve the 100-member committee that was then writing the country's new constitution, as well as the sole remaining democratically elected legislative body, the upper house of parliament, or Consultative Council (*Majlis al-Shūrā*). Supporters of the president argue that the *specific* decisions Morsi wished to protect from the judiciary were those mandating the continuation of both of those democratically legitimated bodies.[20] To many, Morsi's constitutional declaration was not an attempt to destroy democracy, but to save it.

Regardless of whether one believes Morsi or his opponents, Djerejian was right in another sense. Islamist victories in democratic contests *did* endanger democracy, just not because Islamists were imperfect democrats. Instead, democracy was imperiled by the same factors that contributed to Islamist dominance – a dense Islamic social infrastructure, and a thin non-Islamic one. For, though the Muslim Brotherhood's opponents were legion (and growing), they lacked a means of channeling collective discontent through constitutionally legitimate political processes. When the Brotherhood failed to acquiesce in their demands, mass protest was the only option available. Given the structural determinants of the fortunes of both Islamists and their opponents, it is difficult to escape the conclusion that both sides in Egypt's political drama were players in a tragedy whose plot was set before they even took the stage.

8.3 Counting Islamists Out?

Regardless of how one interprets the causes of Morsi's removal and the subsequent crackdown on the Muslim Brotherhood, both no doubt have powerful implications for the country and for the movement that has played such an important role in its modern history. Some have worried that the Muslim Brotherhood will now conclude that democracy is a fool's game, that future elections that might bring them once again to power will never be respected by so-called liberals or by the men with guns. One commentator fretted that "supporters of the Brotherhood will ask, with good reason, whether democracy still has anything to offer them," that "Mr. Morsi's removal will breathe new life into the ideological claims of radicals," and that the Brothers will conclude "violence is the only path."[21] Despairing of the ballot box, the Brothers, in this telling, would finally return to the path of violent revolution, fully embracing the jihadist ideology of Sayyid

one-third), which is by definition unequal. The only way to harmonize these two articles is to reason that the framers did not believe that apportioning more seats to party lists than to individuals violated equality of treatment (especially since every citizen theoretically enjoyed an equal opportunity to join a party). Though the author would not go so far as to argue that this illogic reveals the fundamentally *political* nature of the ruling, it is understandable why some supporters of the Muslim Brotherhood saw it as such.

20 The constituent assembly had not been directly elected, but was chosen by the elected parliament before its dissolution, in accordance with the provisions of the interim constitution issued by the Supreme Council of Armed Forces on March 30, 2011.

21 Shadi Hamid, "Demoting Democracy in Egypt," *New York Times*, July 5, 2013.

Qutb (1964), who preached that this thing called democracy was an abomination and an illusion. Events in Egypt in the aftermath of Morsi's ouster seemed to confirm these fears, as a spate of church-burnings, police station firebombings, and other acts of violence have been attributed to supporters of the ousted president.

As of this writing, it is unclear what the final disposition of this conflict will be. On August 15, 2013, Egypt's interim government authorized a brutal crackdown on two Muslim Brotherhood demonstrations in greater Cairo, and reports pegged the number of dead at more than 1,000. In the aftermath, dozens of senior Muslim Brotherhood leaders were arrested, including the movement's general guide, Muḥammad Badīʿ, and his leading deputy (and the organization's erstwhile presidential candidate) Khayrat al-Shāṭir. Muslim Brothers describe the current crackdown as being every bit as brutal as the one that befell them sixty years ago, when Gamal Abdel Nasser embarked on a bloody campaign of repression against the movement. That earlier period of repression was thought to have given rise to the radical jihadist strand of Islamism that undergirds groups such as al-Qaeda. It is thus not entirely unreasonable to worry that the current moment of brutality will have similarly disturbing repercussions.

Given the uncertainty about Egypt's present, let alone its future, it is premature to try to divine whether the Brotherhood will embrace the path of violence, or seek integration into Egypt's new political space. But, as the movement charts its trajectory, it must wrestle with two distinct strands in its heritage – one that accepts, even urges, the use of violence in the service of its cause, and another that holds that the ballot box, even when rigged, is the only legitimate means of advancing the movement's goals.

The Muslim Brotherhood's use of violence during its early history is well documented. For example, in the 1940s, the Egyptian Muslim Brotherhood established a (now defunct) "special apparatus," which has been blamed for the assassination of Prime Minister Maḥmūd Fahmī al-Nuqrāshī in 1948. However, the scholar Ḥassanayn Tawfīq Ibrāhīm (1998, 63) has argued that the Egyptian Brotherhood's "special apparatus" was part of a political landscape in which "many political trends … had their own armed militias." According to the historian Yunan Labib Rizk, both the Wafd and Young Egypt parties, inspired by the fascist shirt organizations in Germany and Italy, established paramilitary organizations – called, respectively, the Blue Shirts and the Green Shirts.[22] And though the movement has never fully acknowledged nor atoned for its role in the Nuqrashi assassination, it is worth noting that the Brothers were not alone in their use of political assassination during that particularly turbulent period of Egypt's colonial history. Anwar Sadat – who in 1970 became Egypt's president – in 1945 and 1946 participated in assassination attempts against then-Prime Minister Muṣṭafā

[22] Yunan Labib Rizk, "The Colour of Shirts," Al-Ahram Weekly, no. 748, June 23–29, 2005; available at: http://weekly.ahram.org.eg/2005/748/chrncls.htm. According to Rizk, the newspaper of the Wafdist Blue Shirts was even called al-Jihad. See also Marius Deeb, *Party Politics in Egypt: The Wafd and Its Rivals 1919–1939*, London: Ithaca Press, 1979, pp. 350–354

al-Naḥḥās (which failed) and pro-British Finance Minister Amīn ʿUthmān (which succeeded).[23] Thus, the Muslim Brotherhood was not unique in deploying violence in Egypt in the 1940s.

The Muslim Brotherhood's next flirtation with violence occurred during the Nasser regime. Though the Brothers had initially supported the Free Officers' coup of 1952, the movement quickly fell out of official favor, and in 1954 was accused of attempting to assassinate Nasser at a public rally in Alexandria. The years that followed saw the Brotherhood hounded out of political and social life, its leaders imprisoned, executed, and exiled. One of those leaders was Sayyid Quṭb, who during his prison years penned a volume, *Maʿālim fī al-Ṭarīq* (usually translated as *Milestones*), that encouraged Muslims to wage jihad against regimes that, on account of their refusal to implement God's law, were Muslim in name only. According to Zollner (2007), Quṭb became the leader of an armed, activist vanguard within the Brothers (later called the Organization of 1965), which was rounded up by Nasser in 1965 on charges of plotting revolution. Quṭb was executed the following year, and in the season of bitter subjugation that followed, the Brotherhood's General Guide, Ḥassan al-Huḍaybī (who had succeeded the founder, al-Bannā, upon the latter's assassination in 1949) penned a volume, *Preachers Not Judges*, intended to refute Quṭb's call to militancy (Zollner 2008; Ashour 2009). Upon the Brothers' release from Nasser's prisons in the 1970s, the idea of advancing its political project through violence seems to have been largely abandoned.

Any account of the Brotherhood's abandonment of violence or its commitment to peaceful means will likely be met with one of two rejoinders. The first, often repeated by nonspecialists, is that the Brotherhood continued to engage violence even after ostensibly forswearing it, most notably participating in the assassination of Egyptian President Anwar Sadat in 1981 (see, for example, Krause 2001; Welner 2007).[24] However, there exists little evidence for this assertion. The men convicted of Sadat's assassination were all members of a violent organization known as the Islamic Jihad. Juergensmeyer (1995) refers to the Islamic Jihad as "a radical fringe group of the Muslim Brotherhood," leaving readers with the impression that it was a faction of the Brotherhood, and not a separate organization, that carried out that deed, but the basis of that assertion is unclear. The founder of Islamic Jihad, Muhammad ʿAbd al-Salām Farāj, is described as "a former Muslim Brotherhood member," but one "who was disillusioned by its passivity" (Zeidan 1999), suggesting that he had departed the movement precisely because it was nonviolent.

23 See Donald M. Reid, "Political Assassination in Egypt, 1910–1954," *International Journal of African Historical Studies*, 15, no. 4, 1982: 625–651.

24 For examples outside of the scholarly literature, see Andrew C. McCarthy, "Fear the Muslim Brotherhood," National Review, January 31, 2011; Ahmed Sobhy Mansour, Testimony to Congressional Subcommittee on Terrorism, Humint, Analysis, and Counterintelligence, April 13, 2011.

The second rejoinder is that the Muslim Brotherhood's appetite for violence is on full display in the statements of its founder, and in its endorsement of acts of terror by Palestinians against Israeli civilians. This is a more serious claim. Ḥasan al-Bannā, in his epistle on jihad, argued that "the people who perfect the production of death, and know how to die the noble death, is given by God a precious life on earth and eternal bliss in the hereafter."[25] Anticipating an argument that would be made by Sayyid Quṭb decades later, al-Bannā argued against those who declared that military jihad was somehow a "lesser" jihad, subordinate to a "greater" jihad of the perfection of personal virtue. He writes:

> It is commonly said among many Muslims that fighting the enemy is the lesser jihad and that there is a greater jihad that is the jihad of the self. And many of them prove this with the reported saying of the prophet: "We have returned from the lesser jihad to the greater jihad." They said, "What is the greater jihad?" He said: "The jihad of the heart or the jihad of the self." And many of them try with this to deter people from the importance of fighting and preparing for it and the intention of jihad doing what is necessary for it.[26]

According to al-Bannā, there is little textual support for the idea that self-improvement is a greater jihad than fighting Islam's enemies. He says that the tradition of the prophet on which it is based is allegedly apocryphal. Instead, al-Bannā argues, jihad is to be undertaken for two reasons – first, to spread the faith, and second, to defend the lands of the faithful from invaders. In the first instance, jihad is a *farḍ kifāya* – an obligation that individual Muslims are relieved of if enough of their number undertake it. In the second instance, defense against encroachers, jihad is a *farḍ ʿayn* – incumbent on all Muslims. It is to this latter form of jihad that he devotes the greatest attention. He writes:

> Muslims today as you know are subjugated by others and ruled by nonbelievers. Their lands have been trampled and their sanctities violated. Their enemies govern their affairs, and their faith is disrupted in their own homes, in addition to their neglect of spreading their faith. And so it is incumbent on all Muslims without exception to prepare, and to settle upon the intention of jihad and prepare for it until the opportunity arises that Allah might accomplish that which must be done.[27]

This emphasis on jihad to defend against what it sees as domination clearly explains the Brotherhood's uncompromising support of the use of terror by Palestinian groups such as the Islamic Resistance Movement (Hamas). In fact, Brotherhood leaders often refer to Hamas as their movement's "military wing,"

[25] Ḥasan al-Bannā, "Risālat al-Jihād (Epistle on Jihad)," n.d; available at: http://hassanalbanna.yoo7.com/t20-topic

[26] Ibid.

[27] Ibid.

and the Brotherhood's website even lists the website of Hamas' ʿIzz al-Dīn Qassām Brigades in its compendium of "Brotherhood websites." The question for us in this chapter, however, is whether this deeply troubling belief in the legitimacy of jihad abroad signifies a willingness to use it at home, especially in the face of as massive a trauma as the ouster of Mohamed Morsi.

If the story told throughout this book is any guide, it is unlikely that the movement will abandon elections and democracy entirely. Mohamed Morsi's ouster is not the first time an election that went in favor of the Brothers has been ignored or overturned – this was a common occurrence during the Mubarak years, as Morsi himself experienced with his 2005 reelection "defeat." And yet, even when, as Brown (2012) memorably put it, "victory [was] not an option," the Brothers continued to put their efforts and resources into the electoral game. As ʿUmar al-Tilmissānī, the Brotherhood's General Guide from 1972 to 1986, put it:

> All people should know that entering parliament is not one of the [main] goals of the Society of Muslim Brothers. Rather, it is an instrument for spreading our message. And the day that we have realized that hope that occupies the most shining place in our minds and efforts, we will be able to say that we have achieved what we set out to do and reached our ultimate aim. And after that, it matters not to us who rules, or whether the Society endures or not (al-Tilmissānī 1985, 186-187)

It is easy to dismiss such lofty sentiments as disingenuous, and to conclude that the Brotherhood's commitment to elections extends only so far as whether those elections will deliver them to the halls of power. And yet, ʿIṣām al-ʿIryān, the former director of the Brotherhood's political bureau and later a high-ranking member of the Freedom and Justice Party, in explaining the decision to run in Mubarak's rigged elections, drew a distinction between the Brothers and its political rivals that may prove important. He argued that political parties, whose raison d'etre is the seeking of power, are justified when they decide not to participate in the limited elections of the Arab world. They are, he tells us, simply "being honest with [themselves and their] members." But the Brotherhood, he declared, is not a political party – it is a movement that seeks to reform society by all means available to it: "political, economic, social, cultural, philosophical, humanitarian, and artistic."[28] For the Brotherhood, al-ʿIryān wrote, elections, even rigged ones, are:

> [A] great workshop. A workshop for training thought and action, for decision-making and execution, for following up, for measuring efforts and individuals, for pumping new blood into the life of the Brotherhood, and for renewing its cells which require activation and resuscitation. A workshop for preparing agendas, studying

[28] ʿIṣām al-ʿIryān, "Al-Ikhwān al-Muslimūn wa intikhābāt Majlis al-Shūrā ... Limādhā nushārik? (The Muslim Brotherhood and the Elections to the Consultative Assembly ... Why Do We Participate?)" http://www.egyptwindow.net/modules.php?name=News&file=article&sid=5340 (Last Accessed February 19, 2008)

> problems, and presenting solutions. A workshop for connecting with society, for explaining our ideal, stating our program, and attracting notice to the ideas and not the organization. A workshop for dealing with the regime, the security [services], judges, administrators, politicians, partisans, and others. A workshop for innovation and creativity, for overcoming obstacles, surmounting barriers, and leaping over hurdles in the race for hearts and minds, not simply votes or seats.[29]

It remains to be seen whether the Brotherhood (or, for that matter, al-ʿIryān, who was imprisoned in October 2013) still believe in the utility of elections. But even if not, the movement has in recent years made too many rhetorical investments in democracy to abandon it entirely. For example, in an October 2005 attempt to put to rest doubt about the Brotherhood's commitment to nonviolent political participation, the movement's general guide at the time, Mahdī ʿĀkif, declared, "We believe in and call for the peaceful alternation of power via ballot boxes within the framework of a constitutional parliamentarian republic."[30] A stronger statement was offered by Yūsif al-Qaraḍāwī (reported to have twice declined the Egyptian Muslim Brotherhood's top post)[31], who more than ten years ago wrote:

> It is strange that some people judge democracy to be an abomination and a form of disbelief when they do not know what it is. ... Democracy, which is called for by all of the world's people, on whose behalf have worked multitudes in both East and West, which the people reach after bitter struggles with tyrants in which blood was spilled and thousands – nay, millions – of lives were sacrificed as in Eastern Europe and elsewhere, and which many Islamists see as an acceptable means of curbing the excesses of dictatorship and trimming the claws of political domination which have burdened our Muslim peoples. . . . [Is this] an abomination or a form of disbelief, as is repeated by the superficial and the rash?[32]

Many observers have described the Brotherhood's avid electoralism during the Mubarak years as evidence of the movement's "evolution," a signal of its "moderation," of its gradual coming to terms with the ways of modern life. As one observer wrote, "One of the most important political developments of recent years was the decision of Islamist parties to make peace with democracy and commit to playing by the rules of the political game."[33] But this assumption that Islamist parties begin life in as violent, antidemocratic, revolutionary organizations, and only gradually mature enough to lay down their arms and take up the

29 Ibid.

30 http://www.ikhwanweb.com/article.php?ID=13336&SectionID=89 (accessed, June 25, 2011).

31 Owen Bowcott and Faisal al Yafai, "Scholar with a Streetwise Touch Defies Expectations and Stereotypes," The Guardian, Friday, July 9, 2004; available at: http://www.guardian.co.uk/politics/2004/jul/09/religion.immigrationpolicy (accessed April 12, 2008).

32 Quoted in Mustafa Muhammad al-Tahhan, al-Fikr al-Islami al-Mu'asir: Dirasa fi Fikr al-Ikhwan al-Muslimin [Contemporary Islamic Thought: A Study in the Thought of the Muslim Brotherhood], Cairo: Dar al-Tawzi'awal-Nashr al-Islamiyya, 2002, p 294.

33 Shadi Hamid, "Demoting Democracy in Egypt," New York Times, July 4, 2013

ballot box, is divorced from historical reality. As Brown (2012, 24) has noted, the Muslim Brotherhood's "decision to participate [in elections] is old and well established," dating to the early years of the movement. The Brotherhood's first electoral foray, after all, took place in 1942, when the movement was just 14 years old. According to Lia (1998, 69, 183), the Brotherhood's founder, Ḥassan al-Bannā, made the decision to contest elections even earlier than that, in 1938. Of the movement's nine general guides, four had at one point in time stood as parliamentary candidates – al-Bannā in 1942 (before being forced to withdraw) and 1945 (in which, as we saw in Chapter 4, he was defeated), al-Tilmissani in 1945, Ma'mūn al-Huḍaibī in 1984, and Mahdī 'Ākif in 1984 and 1987. In explaining why the Brotherhood had decided to run for parliament, Ḥassan al-Bannā opined that running in elections was a religious duty, declaring that it was "incumbent on the Brotherhood to press with their sermons and message to this pulpit [of parliament] in order to raise from atop it the word of their message, and reach the ears of the representatives of the people."[34]

This enthusiasm for elections is part of a larger, often underappreciated, commitment by al-Bannā to democratic (but not, I would argue, liberal) procedures and institutions. For, although the founder was critical of Egyptian political parties of his time and of the divisiveness of partisanship, he endorsed the idea of democratic, constitutional government. In a statement to Brotherhood members in 1939, he explained:

> The truth is, Brothers, that when the inquirer looks at the principles of constitutional government, which can be summarized as the preservation of all forms of personal freedom, consultation, the derivation of all authority from the people, the responsibility of leaders in front of the masses and holding them accountable for all that they do, and the setting of limits to all authority – all of these principles appear to the inquirer as applying to the teachings of Islam and its systems and rules regarding forms of government. Therefore, the Muslim Brothers consider the constitutional system of government to the closest of the world's systems of government to Islam, and they do not call for any other system.[35]

It could be argued, then, that when today's Muslim Brothers speak of their commitment to parliamentary politics, they are not so much partaking of a newly moderate discourse as reaching into the Brotherhood's early history and enunciating something they have long been taught. A testament to the importance of electoral participation, even in the Brotherhood's early years, is found in a 1944 essay penned by al-Bannā in which he recounts his attempt to settle a dispute between two Muslim Brothers. Remarkably, the dispute that al-Bannā was asked

[34] Tawfīq Al-Wā'ī, Al fikr al siyāsi al mu'āṣir 'ind al ikhwān al muslimīn (Modern Political Thought of the Muslim Brotherhood), Maktabat al-Manār al-Islāmiyya, 2001, pp. 136–139

[35] Hassan al-Bannā, "Risālat al-Mu'tamar al-Khāmis" [Statement to the Fifth Conference], in Majmū'at rasā'il al-Imām al-Shahīd Ḥasan al-Bannā [The Collected Letters of the Martyred Imam, Hassan al-Bannā], Maktaba al-Tawfiqiya, pp. 202–203.

to settle was over which of the two men would get to be the movement's candidate in a particular district:

> [There was] a nice gathering in which an electoral district came up in discussion, and one of the Brothers said that this district is one in which I have worked to propagate the 'idea', and he began to expand on this when another Brother said, "You are going to crowd me. My chances there are better than your chances, for the sake of our message." And the other said, "I don't know about that. We have the standard that whoever is most useful to the cause should run in the district, so we should compare circumstances and capabilities." I left them to speak. Then I said to them, "Are you both serious?" And they said, "Yes, and we want your opinion." So I said, in terms of faith and service to the cause, you are both at the pinnacle, and I think you should both draw lots. And they said, "Neither lots nor anything else." Then one of them said to the other: "You nominate yourself, and I will pay the election fees." And the other replied, "No, you nominate yourself, and I will pay your fees and costs." This, my brethren, is true brotherhood.[36]

Though the story ends with each of the two electorally ambitious Muslim Brethren ostentatiously demurring in his colleague's favor, it is eloquent of just how early in its history the Muslim Brotherhood took to the electoral game, and how important it was even to the movement's earliest members. Thus, far from being an "anti-system" party that only gradually came around to accepting democracy or running in elections (Wickham 2013), electoral participation is practically encoded in the movement's DNA. It is beyond our ken to know whether this electoral heritage will be enough to keep the movement from giving itself over to violence. More likely, the movement's storied reputation for cohesion will prove insufficient to prevent it from fragmenting along precisely these lines, with some Muslim Brothers suing for inclusion in the political system, and others peeling off to pursue a more "revolutionary" path.

The question we are left with is which of these two heritages – that of violence, or that of democratic participation – the majority of Muslim Brothers will find most compelling. This will depend, I believe, on two factors. The first is whether there are still people who would vote for the Brotherhood in an election. Nothing makes democracy less attractive than the prospect of losing. As we saw in Figure 8.1b, the movement retains at least some support – almost 13 percent of citizens surveyed on the eve of the July 3 coup were willing to declare that they possessed "a great deal of confidence" in the Brotherhood, despite the great deal of negative discourse then directed at the movement. The same survey asked respondents whom they would vote for "if a presidential election were held tomorrow." More than a quarter (the largest bloc by far) said they did not know, followed

36 Ḥasan al-Bannā, "Naẓārāt fī Iṣlāḥ al-Nafs: Talkhīṣ min muḥāḍarāt haḍrat ṣāḥib al-faḍīla al-murshid al-ʿām li al-Ikhwān al-Muslimūn al-ustādh Ḥasan al-Bannā (Ideas on Reform of the Self: Summary of the lectures of his grace, the General Guide of the Muslim Brothers, Ḥasan al-Bannā," *al-Iʿtisām*, Volume 6, Issue 6, December 21, 1944, p. 9

by 24.68 percent who named Aḥmad Shafīq, the man who had lost to Morsi in the 2012 presidential election. But more than 17 percent of respondents said they would vote for Morsi, suggesting that, while the Muslim Brotherhood is down, it certainly is not out, particularly in the south and the countryside (where most of these self-proclaimed Morsi voters were concentrated).[37] Thus, if the Brotherhood chooses to continue playing the electoral game, there is every reason to believe it would manage to secure representation, especially under a proportional electoral system.

The second determinant of the Muslim Brotherhood's eventual path is perhaps the more important one: that is, whether the post-Morsi regime prefers to co-opt the movement, or to crush it. As of this writing, we have seen more evidence of the latter than the former, with more than a thousand Muslim Brothers killed in clashes since July 3, 2013, and most of the movement's top leadership – including its general guide, Muḥammad Badīʿ – in prison.[38] In August 2013, interim prime minister Hazem Al Beblawi floated the idea of banning the Brotherhood entirely, but later backtracked on this threat, declaring that "dissolving the party or the group is not the solution."[39] Whether this will continue to be the position of Egypt's interim rulers is not clear. But what is clear is this: Whether members of the Brotherhood choose ballots over bullets in the coming years may have less to do with their own democratic commitments (as tentative and questionable as they may be) than with those of their opponents.

37 Former Muslim Brotherhood member ʿAbd al-Munʿim Abū al-Futūḥ was mentioned by 4.23 percent of respondents, while Salafist Ḥāzim Salāḥ Abū Ismāʿīl was mentioned by fewer than two tenths of a percent of respondents, suggesting that the Islamist space had constricted considerably since Mubarak's overthrow.

38 Kareem Fahim and Mayy El Sheikh, "Soldiers Storm a Mosque in Cairo, as Egyptian Leaders Struggle for Order," *New York Times*, August 17, 2013

39 Lin Noueihed, "Egypt backs away from plan to dissolve the Muslim Brotherhood," *Reuters*, August 28, 2013

Bibliography

Abdo, Geneive. 2000. *No God But God: Egypt and the Triumph of Islam*. Oxford, UK: Oxford University Press.

Abed-Kotob, Sana. 1995. "The Accommodationists Speak: Goals and Strategies of the Muslim Brotherhood of Egypt." *International Journal of Middle East Studies* 27(3):321.

Abu-Lughod, Lila. 2006. *Local Contexts of Islamism in Popular Media*. Amsterdam: Amsterdam University Press.

Agati, Mohamed. 2007. "Undermining Standards of Good Governance: Egypt's NGO Law and Its Impact on the Transparency and Accountability of CSOs." *International Journal of Not-for-Profit Law* 9(2):56–83.

Ahmed, Mohammed Sid, Judith Tucker, Joe Stork, Penny Johnson, and Selma Botman. 1982. "Mohammed Sid Ahmed: 'The Masses Speak the Language of Religion to Express Themselves Politically.'" *MERIP Reports* 102:18–23.

Ajami, Fouad. 1978. "The End of Pan Arabism." *Foreign Affairs* 57(2):355–73.

Alexander, Anne. 2012. "The Egyptian Workers' Movement and the 25 January Revolution." *International Socialism* 133.

Alexander, Christopher. 2000. "Opportunities, Organizations, and Ideas: Islamists and Workers in Tunisia and Algeria." *International Journal of Middle East Studies* 32(4):465–90.

Almond, Gabriel A., R. Scott Appleby, and Emmanuel Sivan. 2003. *Strong Religion: The Rise of Fundamentalisms Around the World*. Chicago: University of Chicago Press.

Aminzade, Ronald R., and Elizabeth J. Perry. 2001. "The Sacred, Religious, and Secular in Contentious Politics: Blurring Boundaries." In *Silence and Voice in the Study of Contentious Politics*, ed. Doug McAdam, Elizabeth J. Perry, William H. Sewell, Jr., Sidney Tarrow, Charles Tilly, Ronald R. Aminzade, and Jack A. Goldstone. Cambridge, UK: Cambridge University Press, pp. 155–79.

Ansari, Hamied. 1986. *Egypt, the Stalled Society*. Albany, NY: SUNY Press.

Ashour, Omar. 2009. *The De-radicalization of Jihadists: Transforming Armed Islamist Movements*. London: Routledge.

Assaad, Ragui. 1993. "Formal and Informal Institutions in the Labor Market, with Applications to the Construction Sector in Egypt." *World Development* 21(6):925–39.

ʿAwaḍ, Hudā Rāghib and Ḥassanayn Tawfīq. 1996. *Al Ikhwān al Muslimūn wa al Sīyāsa fī Miṣr: Dirāsa fī al-taḥālufāt al intikhābīya wal mumārasāt al barlamānīya lil ikhwān al muslimūn fī dhil al taʿdudīya al sīyāsīya al-muqayadah (The Muslim Brothers and Egyptian Politics: A Study of the Electoral Alliances and Parliamentary Participation of the Muslim Brothers in the Shadow of Limited Political Pluralism).* Cairo, Egypt: Kitāb al-Maḥrūsa.

al ʿAnānī, Khalīl. 2007. *Al-Ikhwān al-Muslimūn fī Miṣr: Shaykhūkha tuṣārʿ al-zaman? The Muslim Brotherhood in Egypt: Gerontocracy Wrestling Time?* Cairo, Egypt: Maktaba al-Shurūq al-Dawliyya

al Awadi, Hesham. 2004. *In Pursuit of Legitimacy: The Muslim Brothers and Mubarak, 1982–2000.* London, UK: Tauris Academic Studies.

Ayubi, Nazih N. M. 1980. "The Political Revival of Islam: The Case of Egypt." *International Journal of Middle East Studies* 12(4):481–99.

al Azm, Sadik J. 1997. Is Islam Secularizable? In *Civil Society, Democracy, and the Muslim World*, ed. Elisabeth Ozdalga and Sune Persson. Swedish Research Institute in Istanbul, Curzon Press.

al Bannā, Gamāl. 1998. *Al-Islām Huwa al-Ḥal: Dirāsa fī al-taghyīr al-ijtimāʿī wa ifsād al-fikr al-Miṣrī wa ṭarīqat al-khulāṣ min al-maʾzaq, fi ḍawʾ intikhābāt Ibrīl 1987 – Shaʾbān 1407 (Islam Is the Solution: A Study in Social Change and the Corruption of Egyptian Thought and the Way Out of the Impasse, in Light of the April 1987 Elections).* Cairo: Dār al-Fikr al-Islāmī.

al Bannā, Ḥasan. n.d. *Majmūʾat Rasāʾil al-Imām al-Shahīd Ḥasan al-Bannā (The Collected Letters of the Martyred Imam, Hassan al-Bannā).* Cairo: al-Maktaba al-Tawfiqiyya.

Barber, Benjamin R. 1995. *Jihad vs. McWorld: How the Planet Is Both Falling Apart and Coming Together – and What This Means for Democracy.* New York: Times Books.

Bartolini, Setafano. 2007. *The Political Mobilization of the European Left, 1860–1980: The Class Cleavage.* Cambridge: Cambridge University Press.

Bayat, Asef. 2002. "Activism and Social Development in the Middle East." *International Journal of Middle East Studies* 34:1–28.

2007. "Radical Religion and the Habitus of the Dispossessed: Does Islamic Militancy Have an Urban Ecology?" *International Journal of Urban and Regional Research* 31(3):579.

Baylouny, Anne Marie. 2010. *Privatizing Welfare in the Middle East: Kin Mutual Aid Associations in Jordan and Lebanon.* Bloomington: Indiana University Press.

Beinin, Joel. 2005. "Popular Social Movements and the Future of Egyptian Politics." *Middle East Report Online.*

2012. "The Rise of Egypt's Workers." *Carnegie Papers.* Washington, DC: Carnegie Endowment for International Peace.

Beinin, Joel, and Hossam el Hamalawy. 2007. "Strikes in Egypt Spread from Center of Gravity." *Middle East Report Online.*

Benford, Robert D., and David A. Snow. 2000. "Framing Processes and Social Movements: An Overview and Assessment." *Annual Review of Sociology* 26:611–39.

Berlin, Isaiah. 1959. *Two Concepts of Liberty: An Inaugural Lecture Delivered before the University of Oxford on 31 October 1958.* London: Clarendon.

Berman, Sheri. 2003. "Islamism, Revolution, and Civil Society." *Perspectives on Politics* 1(2):257–72.

Bianchi, Robert. 1986. "The Corporatization of the Egyptian Labor Movement." *Middle East Journal* 40(3):429–44.

1990. "Interest Groups and Politics in Mubarak's Egypt." *The Political Economy of Contemporary Egypt*. Washington, DC: Center for Contemporary Arab Studies, Georgetown University.

Bin-Nafīsa, Sārah and ʿAlaʾuddīn ʿArafāt. 2005. *al-Intikhābāt wa al-Zabaʾinīyya al-Sīyāssīya fī-Miṣr (Elections and Political Clientelism in Egypt)*. Cairo: Cairo Center for Human Rights Studies.

Blaydes, Lisa. 2006. "Who Votes in Authoritarian Elections and Why? Vote Buying, Turnout, and Spoiled Ballots in Contemporary Egypt." Los Angeles: University of California Press.

2010. *Elections and Distributive Politics in Mubarak's Egypt*. Cambridge, UK: Cambridge University Press.

Boldt, Julius. 1904. *Trachoma*. London: Hodder and Stoughton.

Brinkerhoff, Derick, John S. Holtzman, Adel Mostafa, and Nabil Habashi. 2002. The Impact of the Agricultural Policy Reform Program on the Roles of the Public and Private Sectors in Egyptian Agriculture. Technical Report, Government of Egypt, Ministry of Agriculture and Land Reclamation, United States Agency for Interational Development/Egypt Office of Economic Growth, Compeititveness and Agricultural Development Division.

Brody-Barre, Andrea G. 2013. "The Impact of Political Parties and Coalition Building on Tunisia's Democratic Future." *Journal of North African Studies* 18(2):211–30.

Brooks, Risa A. 2002. "Liberalization and Militancy in the Arab World." *Orbis* 46(4):611–21.

Brown, Nathan J. 1990. *Peasant Politics in Modern Egypt: The Struggle against the State*. New Haren, CT: Yale University Press.

2012. *When Victory Is Not an Option: Islamist Movements in Arab Politics*. Ithaca, NY: Cornell University Press.

Brown, Nathan J., and Michele Dunne. 2007. "Egypt's Controversial Constitutional Amendments: A Textual Analysis." Carnegie Endowment for International Peace.

Brownlee, Jason. 2002. "The Decline of Pluralism in Mubarak's Egypt." *Journal of Democracy* 13(4):6–14.

2007. *Authoritarianism in an Age of Democratization*. Cambridge, UK: Cambridge University Press.

al Buraʿī, Nījād, ed. 1996. *Al Dīmūqrāṭīyya fī khaṭar: Intikhābāt lam yanjaḥ fīhā aḥad (Democracy in Danger: Elections without Winners)*. Cairo: Egyptian Organization for Human Rights.

Bush, Ray. 2011. "Egypt: A Permanent Revolution?" *Review of African Political Economy* 38(128):303–7.

Byman, Daniel L. 2005. "The Implications of Leadership Change in the Arab World." *Political Science Quarterly* 120(1):59–83.

Calmfors, Lars, and John Driffill. 1988. "Bargaining Structure, Corporatism and Macroeconomic Performance." *Economic Policy* 3(6): 14–61.

Cammett, Melani, and Sukriti Issar. 2010. "Bricks and Mortar Clientelism: Sectarianism and the Logics of Welfare Allocation in Lebanon." *World Politics* 62(3):381–421.

Cantori, Louis J. 1966. *The Organizational Basis of an Elite Political Party: The Egyptian Wafd*. Chicago: University of Chicago Press.

Carey, John M., and Matthew Soberg Shugart. 1995. "Incentives to Cultivate a Personal Vote: A Rank Ordering of Electoral Systems." *Electoral Studies* 14(4):417–39.

Carothers, Thomas, and Marina Ottaway. 2004. "Think Again: Middle East Democracy." *Foreign Policy* . November–December:18–29.

Chhibber, Pradeep. 1996. "State Policy, Rent Seeking, and the Electoral Success of a Religious Party in Algeria." *Journal of Politics* 58(1):126–48.

Cho, Wendy K. Tam. 1998. "If the Assumption Fits ...: A Comment on the King Ecological Inference Solution." *Political Analysis* 7(1):143–63.

Cho, Wendy K. Tam, and Brian J. Gaines. 2004. "The Limits of Ecological Inference: The Case of Split-Ticket Voting." *American Journal of Political Science* 48(1):152–71.

Chong, Dennis. 1991. *Collective Action and the Civil Rights Movement*. Chicago: University of Chicago Press.

Chwe, Michael Suk-Young. 2001. *Rational Ritual: Culture, Coordination, and Common Knowledge*. Princeton, NJ: Princeton University Press.

Clark, Janine A. 2004a. *Islam, Charity, and Activism: Middle-Class Networks and Social Welfare in Egypt, Jordan, and Yemen*. Bloomington: Indiana University Press.

2004b. "Social Movement Theory and Patron-Clientelism: Islamic Social Institutions and the Middle Class in Egypt, Jordan, and Yemen." *Comparative Political Studies* 37(8):941–68.

Cleary, Matthew R. 2006. "Explaining the Left's Resurgence." *Journal of Democracy* 17(4):35–49.

Cook, Joseph A., and Silvio Mariotti. 2011. *Water and Sanitation Related Diseases and the Environment: Challenges, Interventions, and Preventive Measures*. New York: Wiley-Blackwell, pp. 175–85.

Cox, Gary. 2007. "Swing Voters, Core Voters, and Distributive Politics." Prepared for delivery at the Conference on Representation and Popular Rule, October 27–28, 2006, Yale University, New Haren, CT.

Darra, Ūsāma. 2011. *Min al-Ikhwān ila Mīdān al-Taḥrīr (From the Brotherhood to Tahrir Square)*. Cairo: Dar al-Misri lil Nashr.

Davis, Eric. 1984. Ideology, Social Class and Islamic Radicalism in Modern Egypt. In *From Nationalism to Revolutionary Islam*, ed. Said Amir Arjomand. Albany, NY: SUNY Press pp. 134–57.

Davis, Nancy J., and Robert V. Robinson. 2007. "Freedom on the March? Bush's Democracy Doctrine for the Muslim World." *Contexts* 6(2):22–7.

Davis, Nancy J., and Robert V. Robinson. 2009. "Overcoming Movement Obstacles by the Religiously Orthodox: The Muslim Brotherhood in Egypt, Shas in Israel, Comunione e Liberazione in Italy, and the Salvation Army in the United States1." *American Journal of Sociology* 114(5):1302–49.

Deeb, Marius. 1979. *Party Politics in Egypt: The Wafd and its rivals, 1919–39*. St. Antony's Middle East Monographs. London: Ithaca Press.

Dekmejian, R. Hrair. 1995. *Islam in Revolution: Fundamentalism in the Arab World*. Syracuse, NY: Syracuse University Press.

Desai, Manali. 2002. "The Relative Autonomy of Party Practices: A Counterfactual Analysis of Left Party Ascendancy in Kerala, India, 1934–1941." *American Journal of Sociology* 108(3):616–57.

Dessouki, A. E. H. 1973. "Arab Intellectuals and Al-Nakba: The Search for Fundamentalism." *Middle Eastern Studies*. 9(2):187–95.

DiMaggio, Paul. 1998. The Relevance of Organization Theory to the Study of Religion. In *Sacred Companies. Organizational Aspects of Religion and Religious Aspects of Organizations*. Oxford, UK: Oxford University Press, pp. 7–23.

Dobson, Andrew. 2009. *An Introduction to the Politics and Philosophy of Jose Ortega y Gasset*. Cambridge, UK: Cambridge University Press.

Dobson, William J. 2012. *The Dictator's Learning Curve: Inside the Global Battle for Democracy*. New York: Vintage Digital.

Downs, Anthony. 1957. *An Economic Theory of Democracy*. New York: Harper & Row.

Durkheim, Emile. 1951. *Suicide: A Study in Sociology*. New York: Free Press.

Ehteshami, Anoushiravan, and Emma C. Murphy. 1996. "Transformation of the Corporatist State in the Middle East." *Third World Quarterly* 17(4):753–72.

Eickelman, Dale, and James Piscatori. 1996. *Muslim Politics*. Princeton, NJ: Princeton University Press.

El Amrani, Issandr, and Ursula Lindsey. 2011. "Tunisia Moves to the Next Stage." Middle East Research and Information Project Online.

Elaguizy, Abd el Aziz F. 1907. *Trachoma in Egypt*. London: John Bale, Sons & Danielsson, Ltd.

El-Fattah, Mohamed A. Abd. 2012. "A Survey-Based Exploration of Statisfaction and Profitability in Egypt's Informal Sector. Working Paper 169, Egyptian Center for Economic Studies, Cairo.

El-Ghobashy, Mona. 2005. "The Metamorphosis of the Egyptian Muslim Brothers." *International Journal of Middle East Studies* 37(3):373–95.

2006. "Egypt's Paradoxical Elections." *Middle East Report* 238.

El-Khawas, Mohamed. 2012a. "Egypt's Unfinished Revolution." *Mediterranean Quarterly* 23(1):52–66.

El-Khawas, Mohamed A. 2012b. "Tunisia's Jasmine Revolution: Causes and Impact." *Mediterranean Quarterly* 23(4):1–23.

El Saadawi, Nawal. 2007. *Woman at Point Zero*. London, UK: Zed Books.

Esposito, John L. 1999. *The Islamic Threat: Myth or Reality?* Oxford, UK: Oxford University Press.

Fahmy, Ninette S. 1998b. "The Performance of the Muslim Brotherhood in the Egyptian Syndicates: An Alternative Formula for reform?" *The Middle East Journal* 52(4):551–62.

Flint, J. Wayne. 1980. *Dixie's Forgotten People: The South's Poor Whites*. Bloomington: Indiana University Press.

Frank, Thomas. 2004. *What's the Matter with Kansas? How Conservatives Won the Heart of America*. New York, NY: Metropolitan Books.

Fuller, Graham E. 2004. *The Future of Political Islam*. London: Palgrave MacMillan.

Gaffney, Patrick D. 1994. *The Prophet's Pulpit: Islamic Preaching in Contemporary Egypt*. Los Angeles: University of California Press.

Gandhi, Jennifer and Ellen Lust-Okar. 2009. "Elections Under Authoritarianism." *Annual Review of Political Science* 12:403–422.

Garay, Candelaria. 2007. "Social Policy and Collective Action: Unemployed Workers, Community Associations, and Protest in Argentina." *Politics & Society* 35(2):301–28.

al Gawwād, Gamāl ʿAbd. 2005. *Dalīl idārat al-ḥamalāt al-intikhābīyya* (*Guide to managing election campaigns*) Cairo: United Group.

Gellner, Ernest. 1991. "Islam and Marxism: Some Comparisons." *International Affairs* 67(1):1–6.

Gelman, Andrew, and Cexun Jeffrey Cai. 2008. "Should the Democrats Move to the Left on Economic Policy?" *Annals of Applied Statistics* 2(2):536–49.

Goldberg, Ellis. 1992. "The Foundations of State-Labor Relations in Contemporary Egypt." *Comparative Politics* 24(2):147–61.

Golden, Miriam. 1993. "The Dynamics of Trade Unionism and National Economic Performance." *American Political Science Review* 87(2):437–54.

Greene, Kenneth F. 2007. *Why Dominant Parties Lose: Mexico's Democratization in Comparative Perspective*. Cambridge, UK: Cambridge University Press.

Halliday, Fred. 1995. *Islam and the Myth of Confrontation: Religion and Politics in the Middle East*. London: I. B. Tauris.

Halliday, Fred. 2007. "The Jihadism of Fools." *Dissent* 54(1):53–6.

Ḥatḥūt, Hasan. 2000. *al-ʿAqd al-farīd: ʿashar sanawāt maʿ al-imām Ḥasan al-Bannā, 1942–1952 (The Singular Contract: Ten Years with Imam Hasan al-Banna)*. Cairo: Dar al-Shuruq.

Hawthorne, Amy. 2001. "At the Bottom of the Bush-Mubarak Agenda: The Slow Pace of Political Reform in Egypt." *Policy Watch: Washington Institute for Near East Policy* 528.

Hechter, Michael C. 2004. "From Class to Culture." *American Journal of Sociology* 110(2):400–45.

Heggammer, Thomas. 2013. "Should I Stay or Should I Go: Explaining Variation in Western Jihadists' Choice between Domestic and Foreign Fighting." *American Political Science Review* 107(1):1–15.

Hendriks, Bertus. 1987. "A Report from the Election Campaign: Egypt's New Political Map." *MERIP Middle East Report* 147:23–30.

Hinnebusch, Raymond A. 1984. "The Reemergence of the Wafd Party: Glimpses of the Liberal Opposition in Egypt." *International Journal of Middle East Studies* 16(1):99–121.

Huntington, Samuel P. 1968. *Political Order in Changing Societies*. New Haven, CT: Yale University Press.

1993. *The Third Wave: Democratization in the Late Twentieth Century*, Vol. 4. Norman, UK: University of Oklahoma Press.

Ibrāhīm, Ḥassanayn Tawfīq. 1998. *Al-Niẓām al-sīyāsī wa al-ikhwān al-muslimūn fī miṣr: min al tasāmuḥ ilā al-muwājaha (The Political Order and the Muslim Brotherhood in Egypt: From Accommodation to Confrontation)*. Beirut, Lebanon: Dār al-Ṭalīʿa lil-Ṭibāʿa wal-Nashr.

Ibrahim, Saad Eddin. 1980. "Anatomy of Egypt's Militant Islamic Groups: Methodological Note and Preliminary Findings." *International Journal of Middle East Studies* 12(4):423–53.

Inhorn Millar, M., and S. D. Lane. 1988. "Ethno-ophthalmology in the Egyptian Delta: An Historical Systems Approach to Ethnomedicine in the Middle East." *Social Science & Medicine* 26(6):651–7.

Ismael, Tareq Yousif, and Rif'at Sa'īd. 1990. *The Communist Movement in Egypt: 1920–1988*. Syracuse, NY: Syracuse University Press.

Ismail, Salwa. 1998. "Confronting the Other: Identity, Culture, Politics, and Conservative Islamism in Egypt." *International Journal of Middle East Studies* 30(2):199.

Jamal, Amaney A. 2012. *Of Empires and Citizens: Pro-American Democracy Or No Democracy at All?* Princeton, NJ: Princeton University Press.

Jankowski, James P. 1975. *Egypt's Young Rebels: Young Egypt, 1933–1952*. Stanford, CA: Hoover Institution Press.

Juergensmeyer, Mark. 1995. "The New Religious State." *Comparative Politics* 27(4):379–91.

Kalyvas, Stathis N. 1996. *Rise of Christian Democracy in Europe*. Ithaca, NY: Cornell University Press.

Kamrava, Mehran. 1998. "Frozen Political Liberalization in Jordan: The Consequences for Democracy." *Democratization* 5(1):138–57.

Kandil, Amani. 2004. "Civic Service in the Arab Region." *Nonprofit and Voluntary Sector Quarterly* 33(4 Suppl):39S–50S.

Kassem, May. 1999. *In the Guise of Democracy: Governance in Contemporary Egypt*. London: Ithaca Press.

2004. *Egyptian Politics: The Dynamics of Authoritarian Rule*. Boulder, CO: Lynne Rienner Publishers.

Keefer, P., Ambar Narayan, and Tara Vishwanath. 2005. "Decentralisation in Pakistan: Are Local Politicians Likely to be More Accountable." Technical Report, Working Paper, Development Research Group, World Bank, Brussels.

Kepel, Gilles. 1985. *The Prophet and Pharaoh: Muslim Extremism in Egypt*. London: Al Saqi Books.

1994. *The Revenge of God: The Resurgence of Islam, Christianity and Judaism in the Modern World*. University Park: Pennsylvania State University Press.

Kerr, Malcolm H. 1962. "The Emergence of a Socialist Ideology in Egypt," *Middle East Journal*, 16(2):127–44.

Khadduri, Majid. 1999. "Interpretations of Islam." *Journal of Palestine Studies* 28(3):98–100.

Khaldun, Ibn, Franz Rosenthal, and N. J. Dawood. 1978. *The Muqaddimah*. Cambridge, UK: Cambridge University Press.

Kienle, Eberhard. 2001. *A Grand Delusion: Democracy and Economic Reform in Egypt*, London: I. B. Tauris.

King, Gary. 1997. *A Solution to the Ecological Inference Problem: Reconstructing Individual Behavior from Aggregate Data*. Princeton, NJ: Princeton University Press.

1999. "The Future of Ecological Inference Research: A Comment on Freedman et al." *Journal of the American Statistical Association* 94(445):352–5.

King, Gary, Michael Tomz, and Jason Wittenberg. 2000. "Making the Most of Statistical Analyses: Improving Interpretation and Presentation." *American Journal of Political Science* 44(2):347–61.

Kirchheimer, Otto. 1966. "The Transformation of the Western European Party Systems." in Joseph LaPalombara and Myron Weiner, eds. *Political Parties and Political Development*. Princeton, NJ: Princeton University Press. pp. 177–200.

Kitschelt, Herbert. 1989. The Logics of Party Formation: Ecological Politics in Belgium and West Germany. Ithaca, NY: Cornell University Press.

Krause, Elliott A. 2001. "Professional Group Power in Developing Societies." *Current Sociology* 49(4):149–75.

Kuran, Timur. 1998. "The Vulnerability of the Arab State: Reflections on the Ayubi Thesis." *Independent Review* 3:111–24.

Kurzman, Charles, and Ijlal Naqvi. 2010. "Do Muslims Vote Islamic?" *Journal of Democracy* 21(2):50–63.

Kurzman, Charles. 1994. "A Dynamic View of Resources: Evidence from the Iranian Revolution." *Research in Social Movements, Conflicts and Change* 17:53–84.

Laitin, David D. 1986. *Hegemony and Culture: Politics and Religious Change among the Yoruba*. Chicago: University of Chicago Press.

Langohr, Vickie. 2001. "Of Islamists and Ballot Boxes: Rethinking the Relationship Between Islamisms and Electoral Politics." *International Journal of Middle East Studies* 33:591–601

Lee, Andrea. 2006. *Russian Journal*. New York: Random House.

Lenin, Vladimir Ilich. 2002. *Revolution at the Gates: A Selection of Writings from February to October 1917*. London: Verso Books.

Lesch, Ann M. 1995. "Domestic Politics and Foreign Policy in Egypt." In *Democracy, War, and Peace in the Middle East*, ed. Mark Tessler and David Garnham. Bloomington: Indiana University Press, Chap. 10, pp. 223–43.

Levitsky, Steven. 2001. "Organization and Labor-Based Party Adaptation: The Transformation of Argentine Peronism in Comparative Perspective." *World Politics* 54(1):27–56.

Levitsky, Steven, and Kenneth M. Roberts, eds. 2011. *The Resurgence of the Latin American Left*. Baltimore: Johns Hopkins University Press.

Lewis, Bernard. 1990. "The Roots of Muslim Rage." *Atlantic Monthly* 266(3):47.

1996. "Islam and Liberal Democracy: A Historical Overview." *Journal of Democracy* 7(2):52–63.

Lia, Brynjar. 1998. *The Society of the Muslim Brothers in Egypt: The Rise of an Islamic Mass Movement, 1928–1942*. London: Ithaca Press.

Liddle, R. William, and Saiful Mujani. 2005. "Indonesia in 2004: The Rise of Susilo Bambang Yudhoyono." *Asian Survey* 45(1):119–26.

Linz, Juan. 1990. "The Perils of Presidentialism." *Journal of Democracy* 1(1):51–69.

Lipset, Seymour Martin, and Stein Rokkan. 1967. "Cleavage Structures, Party Systems, and Voter Alignments: An Introduction." In *Party Systems and Voter Alignments: Cross-National Perspectives*, ed. Seymour Martin Lipset and Stein Rokkan. New York: Free Press, pp. 1–64.

Lughod, Lila Abu. 1995. "Movie Stars and Islamic Moralism in Egypt." *Social Text* 42:53–67.

Lust-Okar, Ellen. 2001. "The Decline of Jordanian Political Parties: Myth or Reality." *International Journal of Middle East Studies* 33(4):545–69.

2005. *Structuring Conflict in the Arab World: Incumbents, Opponents, and Institutions.* Cambridge, UK: Cambridge University Press.

2006. "Elections under Authoritarianism: Preliminary Lessons from Jordan." *Democratization* 13(3):456–71.

Lust-Okar, Ellen, and Amaney Ahmad Jamal. 2002. "Rulers and Rules: Reassessing the Influence of Regime Type on Electoral Law Formation." *Comparative Political Studies* 35(3):337–366.

Lust-Okar, Ellen and Tarek Masoud. 2010. "Cash or Kinship? Voting and social order in the developing world," Unpublished paper.

Lynch, Marc. 2007. "Young Brothers in Cyberspace." *Middle East Report* 245.

MacCallan, Arthur Ferguson. 1913. *Trachoma and Its Complications in Egypt.* Cambridge, UK: Cambridge University Press.

1931. "The Epidemiology of Trachoma." *British Journal of Ophthalmology* 15(7):369.

Magaloni, Beatriz. 2006. *Voting for Autocracy: Hegemonic Party Survival and Its Demise in Mexico.* Cambridge, UK: Cambridge University Press.

Mahmood, Saba. 2005. *Politics of Piety: The Islamic Revival and the Feminist Subject.* Princeton, NJ: Princeton University Press.

Maḥmūd, ʿAlī ʿAbd al-Ḥalīm. 1991. *Manhaj al-tarbīya ʿind al-Ikhwān al-Muslimīn: dirāsa taḥlīlīya wa tārīkhīya (The Educational Curriculum of the Muslim Brotherhood: An Analytical and Historical Study),* Vol. 2. al-Mansūra, Egypt: Dār al-Wafā lil-Ṭibāʿ wa al-Nashr.

al Majīd, Waḥīd ʿAbd and Nivīn ʿAbd al Munʿim Musʿad, eds. 1992. *Intikhābāt Majlis al-Shaʿb 1990: Dirāsa wa Taḥlīl (The 1990 People's Assembly Elections: Study and Analysis).* Cairo: Cairo University Center for Political Research and Studies.

Makram-Ebeid, Mona. 1989. "Political Opposition in Egypt: Democratic Myth or Reality?" *The Middle East Journal* 43(3):423–436.

1989. "The Role of the Official Opposition." In *Egypt Under Mubarak*, edited by Charles Tripp and Roger Owen, 21–52. London: Routledge.

Maldonado-Denis, Manuel. 1961. "Ortega y Gasset and the Theory of the Masses." *Western Political Quarterly* 14(3):676–90.

Marx, Karl, and Friedrich Engels. 2012. *The Communist Manifesto.* New Haven, CT: Yale University Press.

Masoud, Tarek. 2011. "The Road to (and from) Liberation Square." *Journal of Democracy* 22(3):20–34.

2011. "Liberty, Democracy, and Discord in Egypt." *The Washington Quarterly.* 34(4):117–129.

Mehanna, Omnia. 2008. "Internet and the Egyptian Public Sphere." 12th General Assembly of the Council for the Development of Social Science Research in Africa.

Michels, Roberto. 1915. *Political Parties: A Sociological Study of the Oligarchical Tendencies of Modern Democracy.* New York: Heart's International Library Co.

Miller, Judith. 1996. *God Has Ninety-Nine Names: Reporting from a Militant Middle East.* New York: Simon & Schuster.

Mitchell, Richard P. 1993. *The Society of the Muslim Brothers.* New York: Oxford University Press.

al Munūfī, Kamāl. 1980. Al-Thaqāfa al-Sīyāsīya li al-Falāḥīn al-Miṣrīyīn: Taḥlīl Naẓarī wa Dirāsa Midanīyya Fī Qarya Miṣrīyya *(The Political Culture of Egyptian Peasants: A Theoretical Analysis and Field Study in an Egyptian Village).* Beirut: Dār Ibn Khaldūn.

Mohamed Elhachmi Hamdi. 1998. "The Politicization of Islam: A Case Study of Tunisia. Boulder, CO: Westview Press.

Monroe, Kristen Renwick, and Lina Haddad Kreidie. 1997. "The Perspective of Islamic Fundamentalists and the Limits of Rational Choice Theory." *Political Psychology* 18(1):19–43.

Moore, Barrington. 1967. *Social Origins of Dictatorship and Democracy; Lord and Peasant in the Making of the Modern World*. Boston: Beacon Press.

Mozzato-Chamay, Nadia, Olaimatu S. M. Mahdi, Ousman Jallow, David Mabey, Robin L. Bailey, and David J. Conway. 2000. "Polymorphisms in Candidate Genes and Risk of Scarring Trachoma in a *Chlamydia trachomatis*–Endemic Population." *Journal of Infectious Diseases* 182(5):1545–48.

Munson, Ziad. 2001. "Islamic Mobilization: Social Movement Theory and the Egyptian Muslim Brotherhood." *Sociological Quarterly* 42(4):487–510.

Murphy, Caryle. 2002. *Passion for Islam: Shaping the Modern Middle East: The Egyptian Experience*. New York, NY: Scribner.

Naipaul, Vidiadhar Surajprasad. 1998. *Beyond Belief: Islamic Excursions among the Converted Peoples*. New York: Random House.

al Nafīsī, ʿAbd Allah, ed. 1989. *Al-Ḥaraka al-Islāmīyya: Rūʿya Mustaqbalīyya: Awrāq fī al-Naqḍ al-Dhātī (The Islamic Movement: A Futuristic Viewpoint: Papers in Self-Criticism)*. Kuwait: Self-published.

Nasr, Seyyed Vali Reza. 1994. *The Vanguard of the Islamic Revolution: The Jamaʿat-i Islami of Pakistan*, Vol. 19. Los Angles: University of California Press.

Norris, Pippa, and Ronald Inglehart. 2011. *Sacred and Secular: Religion and Politics Worldwide*. Cambridge, UK: Cambridge University Press.

Olcott, Martha Brill, and Marina Ottaway. 1999. "Challenge of Semi-Authoritarianism." *Carnegie Paper No*. 7. Washington, DC: Carnegie Endowment for International Peace.

Olson, Mancur. 1965. *The Logic of Collective Action: Public Goods and the Theory of Groups*. Cambridge, MA: Harvard University Press.

Onians, Charles. 2004. "Supply and Demand Democracy in Egypt." *World Policy Journal* 21(2).

Pappe, Ilan. 2006. "Arab Nationalism." In *The Sage Handbook of Nations and Nationalism*, ed. Gerard Delanty and Krishan Kumar. Chap. 41, pp. 500–12. New York, NY: Sage Publications.

Pepinsky, Thomas B., R. William Liddle, and Saiful Mujani. 2012. "Testing Islam's Political Advantage: Evidence from Indonesia." *American Journal of Political Science*. 56(3):584–600.

Posusney, Marsha Pripstein. 1997. *Labor and the State in Egypt: Workers, Unions, and Economic Restructuring*. New York: Columbia University Press.

2002. "Multi-Party Elections in the Arab World: Institutional Engineering and Oppositional Strategies." *Studies in Comparative International Development* 36(4):34–62.

Przeworski, Adam, and John Sprague. 1986. *Paper Stones: A History of Electoral Socialism*. Chicago: University of Chicago Press.

Quṭb, Sayyid. 1964. *Maʿālim fī al-Ṭarīq (Milestones)*. Ramallah: Dār al-Kutub al-Thaqāfiyya.

Rabīʿ, ʿAmr Hāshim. 1997. "The 1995 Elections in the Context of Egyptian Political Development." In *The 1995 Parliamentary Elections in Egypt*, ed. Hala Mustapha. Cairo: Al-Ahram Center for Political and Strategic Studies.

Rabī', 'Amr Hāshim. 2006. *Dalīl al-Nukhba al-Barlamāniyya al-Miṣriyya 2005* (2005 Egyptian Parliamentary Directory). Cairo, Egypt: al-Ahram Center for Strategic and Political Studies.

Radcliff, Benjamin, and Patricia Davis. 2000. "Labor Organization and Electoral Participation in Industrial Democracies." *American Journal of Political Science* 44(1):132–141.

Raslān, Hānī. 1992. "Hizb al-Wafd al-Jadīd (The New Wafd Party)." In *Intikhābāt Majlis al-Sha'b: Dirāsa wa Taḥlīl (The 1990 People's Assembly Elections: Study and Analysis)*, ed. *Waḥīd 'Abd al-Majīd and Nivīn 'Abd al-Mun'im Mus'ad.* Cairo: Cairo University Center for Political Research and Studies, chap. 7, pp. 171–85.

Razi, G. Hossein. 1990. "Legitimacy, Religion, and Nationalism in the Middle East." *American Political Science Review* 84(1):69–91.

Reid, D. M. 1979. "The Return of the Egyptian Wafd, 1978." *International Journal of African Historical Studies* 12(3):389–415.

Roberts, Kenneth M. 2003. "Social Correlates of Party System Demise and Populist Resurgence in Venezuela." *Latin American Politics and Society* 45(3):35–57.

Rodenbeck, Max. 1998. "Is Islamism Losing its Thunder?" *Washington Quarterly* 21(2):177–93.

Rubin, Barry. 2007. "Comparing Three Muslim Brotherhoods: Syria, Jordan, Egypt." *Middle East Review of International Affairs* 11(2):107–16.

2002. *Islamic Fundamentalism in Egyptian Politics.* London: Palgrave Macmillan.

Rugh, William A. 2004. *Arab Mass Media: Newspapers, Radio, and Television in Arab Politics.* Westport, CT: Greenwood Publishing.

Russell, Bertrand. 1954. *Human Society in Ethics and Politics*, London, UK: George Allen & Unwin Ltd.

Rutherford., Bruce K. 2008. *Egypt after Mubarak: Liberalism, Islam, and Democracy in the Arab World.* Princeton, NJ: Princeton University Press.

Said, Edward. 1978. *Orientalism: Western Conceptions of the Orient.* New York: Pantheon.

Said, Mohamed El-Sayed. 2005. "Global Civil Society: An Arab Perspective." In *Global Civil Society: 2004–2005*, ed. Helmut K. Anheier and Mary Kaldor, chapter 3, pp. 60–72. Thousand Oaks, CA: Sage Publications.

Sanyal, Bishwapriya. 1991. "Organizing the Self-Employed: The Politics of the Urban Informal Sector." *International Laborotary Review* 130:39.

al Ṣāwī, 'Alī. 2001. *Mashrū' lā'iḥa jadīda li Majlis al-Sha'b: Dirāsa sīyāsīyya wa qānūnīyya (The Project for New Parliamentary Procedures: A Political and Legal Study).* Cairo: Dār al-Nahḍa al-'Arabiyya.

al-Sayyīd 'Abd al Wahhāb, 'Ayman. 2011. "Al-Mujtama' al-madanī al-Miṣrī wa al-intikhābāt: Ishkālīyāt al-dūr (Egyptian Civil Society and Elections: The Problems of Role)." *Aḥwāl Miṣriyya (Egyptian Affairs)*, July.

al Sayyid, Mustapha Kamel. 1993. "A Civil Society in Egypt?" *Middle East Journal*, 47(2): 228–42.

Scarrow, Susan E. 1996. *Parties and Their Members: Organizing for Victory in Britain and Germany.* Oxford, UK: Oxford University Press.

Schmitter, Philippe C. 1986. "An Introduction to Southern European Transitions from Authoritarian Rule: Italy, Greece, Portugal, Spain, and Turkey." In *Transitions from Authoritarian Rule: Southern Europe*, eds. Guillermo O'Donnell, Philippe C. Schmitter, and Laurence Whitehead. Baltimore, MD: Johns Hopkins University Press, pp. 3–10.

Schraeder, Peter J., and Hamadi Redissi. 2011. "Ben Ali's Fall." *Journal of Democracy* 22(3):5–19.

Schwedler, Jillian. 2006. *Faith in Moderation: Islamist Parties in Jordan and Yemen*. Cambridge, UK: Cambridge University Press.

Sen, Amartya. 1985. "Well-Being, Agency and Freedom: The Dewey Lectures 1984." *Journal of Philosophy* 82(4):169–221.

Sfakianakis, John. 2004. "The Whales of the Nile: Networks, Businessmen, and Bureaucrats during the Era of Privatization in Egypt." In *Networks of Privilege in the Middle East: The Politics of Economic Reform Revisited*, ed. Steven Heydemann. London: Palgrave Macmillan, pp. 77–100.

Shapiro, Ian. 2002. "Problems, Methods, and Theories in the Study of Politics, or What's Wrong with Political Science and What to Do about It." *Political Theory* 30:596–619.

Shehata, Samer, and Joshua Stacher. 2006. "The Brotherhood Goes to Parliament." *Middle East Report* 240.

Shipley, Peter. 1977. "Trotskyism: Entryism and Permanent Revolution." *Conflict Studies* 81:1–20.

Sid-Ahmed, Mohamed. 1987. "Egypt: The Islamic Issue." *Foreign Policy* 69:22–39.

Singerman, Diane. 1995. *Avenues of Participation: Family, Politics, and Networks in Urban Quarters of Cairo*. Princeton University Press.

2004. "The Networked World of Islamist Social Movements." In *Islamic Activism: A Social Movment Theory Approach*, ed. Quintan Wiktorowicz. Bloomington: Indiana University Press.

Snee, Ronald D., and Donald W. Marquardt. 1984. "Comment: Collinearity Diagnostics Depend on the Domain of Prediction, the Model, and the Data." *American Statistician* 38(2):83–7.

Snow, David A. and Robert D. Benford. 1988. "Ideology, Frame Resonance, and Participant Mobilization." *International Social Movement Research* 1:197–218.

Springborg, Robert. 1989. *Mubarak's Egypt: Fragmentation of the Political Order*. Boulder, CO.: Westview Press.

Stacher, Joshua. 2002. "Post-Islamist Rumblings in Egypt: The Emergence of the Wasat Party." *Middle East Journal* 56(3):415–32.

Stark, Rodney. 2003. *For the Glory of God: How Monotheism Led to Reformations, Science, Witch-Hunts, and the End of Slavery*. Princeton, NJ: Princeton University Press.

Starrett, Gregory Steven. 1991. "Our Children and Our Youth: Religious Education and Political Authority in Mubarak's Egypt" Ph.D. thesis, Stanford University.

Sullivan, Denis J. 1994. *Private Voluntary Organizations in Egypt: Islamic Development, Private Initiative, and State Control*. Gainesville: University of Florida Press.

Sullivan, Denis J., and Sana Abed-Kotob. 1999. *Islam in Contemporary Egypt: Civil Society vs. the State*. Boulder, CO: Lynne Rienner Publishers.

Tadros, Mariz. 2005. "Egypt's Election All About Image, Almost." *Middle East Report Online*, September 6.

Tahi, Mohand Salah. 1992. "The Arduous Democratisation Process in Algeria." *Journal of Modern African Studies* 30(3):397–419.

Ṭālib, Hassan ʾAbū. 2006. "Al-ʿUnf fī al-Intikhābāt: Tafāqum al-Balṭaga wa al-Tadakhullāt al-ʾAmniyya (Violence in Elections: Explosion of Thuggery and Security Interference)." In *Intikhābāt Majlis al-Shaʿb 2005 (2005 Parliamentary Elections)*, ed. ʿAmr Hāshim Rabīʿ. Cairo: Al-Ahram Center for Political and Strategic Studies, chap. 4, pp. 325–76.

Tamām, Ḥusām. 2006. Taḥawulāt al-Ikhwān al-Muslimīn: Tafakuk al-ʾaīdīūlūjiyā wa nihāyat al-tanẓīm (Transformations of the Muslim Brotherhood: Disintegration of ideology and the end of the organization), Cairo: Maktabat Madbūlī

Tanuwidjaja, Sunny. 2010. "Political Islam and Islamic Parties in Indonesia: Critically Assessing the Evidence of Islam's Political Decline." *Contemporary Southeast Asia: A Journal of International and Strategic Affairs* 32(1):29–49.

Tanwir, Farooq. 2002. "Religious Parties and Politics in Pakistan." *International Journal of Comparative Sociology* 43(3–5):250–68.

Taraki, Lisa. 1995. "Islam Is the Solution: Jordanian Islamists and the Dilemma of the 'Modern Woman.'" *British Journal of Sociology* 46(4):643–61.

Tarrow, Sidney G. 1998. *Power in Movement: Social Movements and Contentious Politics.* Cambridge, UK: Cambridge University Press.

Tessler, Mark, and Jodi Nachtwey. 1998. "Islam and Attitudes toward International Conflict: Evidence from Survey Research in the Arab World." *Journal of Conflict Resolution* 42(5):619–36.

Thachil, Tariq. 2011. "Embedded Mobilization: Nonstate Service Provision as Electoral Strategy in India." *World Politics*. 66(3):434–69

Tibi, Bassam. 2009. "Islam and Modern European Ideologies." *International Journal of Middle East Studies* 18(1):15–29.

al-Tilmissānī, ʿUmar. 1985. *Dhikrayāt La Mudhakkirāt (Memories, Not Memoirs).* Cairo: Dār al-Ṭibāʿ wa al-Nashr al-Islāmiyya.

Tingay, Caroline Laetitia. 2006. "Agrarian Transformation in Egypt: Conflict Dynamics and the Politics of Power from a Micro Perspective" Ph.D. thesis, Free University of Berlin.

Tomsa, Dirk. 2008. *Party Politics and Democratization in Indonesia: Golkar in the Post-Suharto Era.* London: Routledge.

Tomsa, Dirk et al. 2009. "Uneven Party Institutionalization, Protracted Transition and the Remarkable Resilience of Golkar." In *Democratization in Post-Suharto Indonesia.* London: Routledge, 176–98.

Trager, Eric. 2011. "Unbreakable Muslim Brotherhood: Grim Prospects for a Liberal Egypt." *Foreign Affairs* 90:114.

2013. "Egypt's Looming Competitive Theocracy." *Current Trends in Islamist Ideology* 14:27–38.

Tsai, Lily L. 2007. "Solidary Groups, Informal Accountability, and Local Public Goods Provision in Rural China." *American Political Science Review* 101(2):355.

Varshney, Ashutosh. 2002. *Ethnic Conflict and Civic Life: Hindus and Muslims in India.* Yale University Press.

Waltz, Susan. 1986. "Islamist Appeal in Tunisia." *Middle East Journal* 40(4):651–70.

Warburg, Gabriel R. 1982. "Islam and Politics in Egypt: 1952–80." *Middle Eastern Studies* 18(2):131–57.

Watts, Susan. 1993. "Local Level Political and Social Structure: The Literature in English." United States Agency for International Development, Washington, DC.

Webber, Patrick. 2009. "Entryism in Theory, in Practice, and in Crisis: The Trotskyist Experience in New Brunswick, 1969–1973." *Left History* 14(1):33–57.

Weber, Max. 1946. "Science as a Vocation." In *From Max Weber: Essays in Sociology*, ed. H. H. Gerth and C. Wright Mills. Oxford, UK: Oxford University Press, pp. 129–56.

Wedeen, Lisa. 1998. "Acting 'As If': Symbolic Politics and Social Control in Syria." *Comparative Studies in Society & History* 40(3):503.

1999. *Ambiguities of Domination: Politics, Rhetoric, and Symbols in Contemporary Syria.* Chicago: University of Chicago Press.

2002. "Conceptualizing Culture: Possibilities for Political Science." *American Political Science Review* 96(4):713.

2003. "Beyond the Crusades: Why Huntington, and Bin Laden, Are Wrong." *Middle East Policy* 10(2):56–61.

Weinbaum, Marvin G. 1996. "Civic Culture and Democracy in Pakistan." *Asian Survey* 36(7):639–54.

Welner, Michael. 2007. "Psychopathy, Media and the Psychology at the Root of Terrorism and Mass Disasters." In *Forensic Investigation and Management of Mass Disasters*, p. 189. Tuscon, AZ: Lawyers and Judges Publishing Company.

Wickham, Carrie Rosefsky. 2003. *Mobilizing Islam: Religion, Activism, and Political Change in Egypt.* New York: Columbia University Press.

2004. "The Path to Moderation: Strategy and Learning in the Formation of Egypt's Wasat Party." *Comparative Politics* 36(2):205–28.

2013. *The Muslim Brotherhood: Evolution of an Islamist Movement.* Princeton, NJ: Princeton University Press.

Wiktorowicz, Quintan. 2000. "Civil Society as Social Control: State Power in Jordan." *Comparative Politics* 33(1):43–61.

2001. *The Management of Islamic Activism : Salafis, the Muslim Brotherhood, and state power in Jordan.* Albany, NY: SUNY Press.

ed. 2004. *Islamic Activism: A Social Movement Theory Approach.* Bloomington: Indiana University Press.

Woodward, Mark. 2008. "Indonesia's Religious Political Parties: Democratic Consolidation and Security in Post-New Order Indonesia." *Asian Security* 4(1):41–60.

Ẓahrān, Jamāl ʿAlī. 1992. "*Al-Mustaqillūn* (The Independents)." In *Intikhābāt Majlis al-Shaʿb: Dirāsa wa Taḥlīl (The 1990 People's Assembly Elections: Study and Analysis)*, ed. Waḥīd ʿAbd al-Majīd and Nivīn ʿAbd al-Munʿim Musʿad. Cairo: Cairo University Center for Political Research and Studies, chap. 9, pp. 198–208.

Zakarīyya, Hūda. 1990. "Ḥālāt Muḥāfāẓa al-Sharqīyya (The case of the governorate of al-Sharqīyya)." In *Al-Intikhābāt al-Barlamānīyya fī Miṣr: Dars intikhābāt 1987 (Parliamentary Elections in Egypt: The Lesson of the 1987 Elections)*, ed. Fuʾād Mursī. Dār Sīnā lil-Nashr. pp. 157–190.

Zaki, Moheb. 1995. *Civil Society and Democratization in Egypt: 1981–1994.* Konrad Adenauer Stiftung.

Zakī, Muḥammad Shawqī. 1980 (1952). *Al-Ikhwān al-Muslimūn wal Mujtamaʿ al Miṣrī*, (The Muslim Brotherhood and Eyption, Society) 2nd ed. Cairo: Dār al-Anṣār.

Zartman, Ira William. 1990. "Opposition as Support of the State." In *The Arab State*, ed. Giacomo Luciani. Berkeley: University of California Press, chap. 9, pp. 220–46.

Zeghal, Malika. 2013. "Competing Ways of Life: Islamism, Secularism, and Public Order in the Tunisian Transition." *Constellations* 20(2):254–274.

Zeidan, David. 1999. "Radical Islam in Egypt: A Comparison of Two Groups." *Middle East* 3(3):2.

Zeldin, Mary-Barbara. 1969. "The religious nature of Russian Marxism." *Journal for the Scientific Study of Religion* 8(1):100–111.

Zollner, Barbara. 2008. *The Muslim Brotherhood: Hasan al-Hudaybi and Ideology.* London: Routledge.

Index

Note: Page numbers followed by f indicate a figure; those with t indicate a table.

Jamaat-e-Islami (Pakistan), 202
al-Jamʿiyya al-Khayriyya al-Islāmiyya (Islamic Charitable Association), 35
al-Jamʿiyya al-Sharʿiyya li-Taʿāwun al-ʿĀmilīn bil-Kitāb wa al-Sunna al-Muḥammadiyya (JS), 35, 79–83, 168; on constitutional amendments, 134, 170; rejection of Muslim Brotherhood candidates by, 205–6
jihadist ideology, 217–21
Jordan, 19, 33n20
Jribi, Maya, 197
judiciary: anti-Morsi actions of, 216–17; election oversight by, 60n27, 96–98, 125–26, 133
Juergensmeyer, Mark, 219
Justice and Construction Party, 2
Justice Party, 132f

Kamrava, Mehran, 56
al-Karāma Party, 127, 140, 186, 188
Kassem, May, 68
Kepel, Gilles, 25
Kerr, Malcolm H., 30
Khamīs, Maḥmūd, 83–84
al-Kharbāwī, Tharwat, 213
Kifāya (Egyptian Movement for Change) (al-Ḥarakaal-Miṣriyya min ajl al-Taghyīr), 51
King, Gary, 108, 178
kinship. *See* family/kinship networks
Kirchheimer, Otto, 26
Kissinger, Henry, 41–42
Kreidie, Lina Haddad, 21
Kuran, Timur, 23, 139
Kurzman, Chalres, 208
Kuwait, 2–3

labor movement. *See* trade unions
Labor Party, 74
Laitin, David, 19
landholding patterns, 203, 204t
Lane, Edward William, 33
Law 40 of 1977, 74
Law 73 of 1956, 60n27
Law 114 of 1984, 62–63, 67
Law 188 of 1986, 67, 70
Lee, Andrea, 29–30
leftist parties, xiii; in the authoritarian era, 45–73; clientelistic disadvantages of, 39–40; cohesion and discipline in, 29–30; connectedness disadvantages of, 5–13, 166–69, 179–82, 204–6; illiteracy rates and, 65–66, 104–5; in Latin America, 56; legislative victories of, 45; local successes in post-revolutionary elections of, 183–84, 188–94; losses in post-revolutionary elections of, 9–10, 11, 156–58, 165–66; niche appeal of, 26; organizational challenges of, 34, 156–58, 165–66; potential for success of, 208–9; redistributionist economic policies of, 147–55, 178–80, 208–9; revolution of 2011 and, 8–9, 126–27, 131; rigged electoral losses of, 48–50, 59–60; socialist associations with, 48, 56–59, 72–73; state co-optation of, 48, 50–55; targeted repression of, 50, 55, 176
Lewis, Bernard, 16, 21
Liberal Constitutionalist Party, 114
Liberal Party (Ḥizb al-Aḥrār), 46f, 47, 74, 95t
Liberty and Justice Party (Ḥizb al-Ḥurriya wa al-ʿAdāla), 164t
Libya, 2
Liddle, R. William, 152
linkages. *See* connectedness
Lippmann, Walter, 12
Lipset, Seymour Martin, 17, 208
literacy rates. *See* illiteracy rates
Lust-Okar, Ellen, 51, 56, 60, 61

Maʿālim fī al-Ṭarīq (Quṭb), 219
MacCallan, Arthur F., 115–17
Magaloni, Beatriz, 120
al-Maghāwrī, ʿĀtif, 94, 95t
al-Maghrabi Eye Hospitals, 90–91
Mahfūẓ, Nagīb, 63
Mahmood, Saba, 25
majoritarian elections, 67–71, 72t, 94–95, 111, 130–31, 202
Makram-Ebeid, Mona, 19n
al-Malṭ, Aḥmad, 77
Marx, Karl, 20, 38
Marzouki, Moncef, 197, 200–201
Masjid al-Madīna al-Munawwara, 28
Masjid ʿUmar Makram, 24
master narratives. *See* social cleavages
material explanations, 16, 22–30; party cohesion and discipline as, 26–30; social services and benefits as, 30–40, 166; suppression of dissent as, 22–24, 32
Michels, Roberto, 26
middle classes, xiv; blindness and, 115–19; clientelist appeals to, 99; education levels of, 98–100; electoral mobilization of, 104–20; Internet use by, 94, 100–101; Muslim

86547106R00165

Made in the USA
Middletown, DE
30 August 2018